The Revolutionary Era

Recent Titles in
Debating Historical Issues in the Media of the Time

The Antebellum Era: Primary Documents on Events from 1820 to 1860
David A. Copeland

The Reconstruction Era: Primary Documents on Events from 1865 to
1877
Donna L. Dickerson

THE REVOLUTIONARY ERA

*Primary Documents on Events
from 1776 to 1800*

Carol Sue Humphrey

Debating Historical Issues in the Media of the Time
David A. Copeland, Series Editor

GREENWOOD PRESS
Westport, Connecticut • London

Library of Congress Cataloging-in-Publication Data

Humphrey, Carol Sue.
The Revolutionary era : primary documents on events from 1776 to 1800 / Carol Sue Humphrey.
p. cm.—(Debating historical issues in the media of the time, ISSN 1542–8079)
Includes bibliographical references and index.
ISBN 0–313–32083–7 (alk. paper)
1. United States—History—Revolution, 1775–1783—Sources. 2. United States—History—Revolution, 1775–1783—Press coverage. 3. American newspapers—History—18th century. I. Title. II. Series.
E203.H88   2003
973.3–dc21   2002041597

British Library Cataloguing in Publication Data is available.

Library of Congress Catalog Card Number: 2002041597
ISBN: 0–313–32083–7
ISSN: 1542–8079

First published in 2003

Greenwood Press, 88 Post Road West, Westport, CT 06881
An imprint of Greenwood Publishing Group, Inc.
www.greenwood.com

Printed in the United States of America

The paper used in this book complies with the
Permanent Paper Standard issued by the National
Information Standards Organization (Z39.48–1984).

10 9 8 7 6 5 4 3 2 1

Contents

Series Foreword   vii
Introduction   ix
Chronology of Events   xix

Chapter 1:   The Reality of Independence, 1776–1781   1
Chapter 2:   Wartime Morale, 1776–1781   33
Chapter 3:   The Battles of the Revolutionary War, 1776–1781   49
Chapter 4:   General George Washington, 1776–1783   67
Chapter 5:   Benedict Arnold, 1780–1781   81
Chapter 6:   The Articles of Confederation, 1777–1781   93
Chapter 7:   The Union in Crisis? 1782–1787   105
Chapter 8:   Shays's Rebellion, 1786–1787   119
Chapter 9:   Constitutional Convention, 1787   127
Chapter 10: Ratification Struggle, 1787–1789   137
Chapter 11: The Bill of Rights, 1787–1791   161
Chapter 12: The Issue of the Native Americans, 1791–1797   181
Chapter 13: The Role of Women, 1780–1798   189
Chapter 14: Slave Revolt in Santo Domingue (Haiti), 1791–1793   201
Chapter 15: President George Washington, 1789–1799   211
Chapter 16: The Early Years of the French Revolution,
                1789–1793   223
Chapter 17: The Whiskey Rebellion, 1794   233
Chapter 18: Jay's Treaty, 1795–1796   243
Chapter 19: The Rise of the Party Press, 1797–1800   253
Chapter 20: The French Revolution Gone Crazy, 1793–1798   263

Contents

Chapter 21: American Neutrality, 1793   277
Chapter 22: The Election of 1796, September–November 1796   295
Chapter 23: The Quasi-War with France, 1797–1798   303
Chapter 24: The XYZ Affair, 1798   313
Chapter 25: The Sedition Act, 1798–1800   323
Chapter 26: The Election of 1800, February 1800–March 1801   337

  Selected Bibliography   349
  Index   353

Series Foreword

As the eighteenth century was giving way to the nineteenth, the *Columbian Centinel* of Boston, quoting a wise judge on January 1, 1799, said, "Give to any set of men the command of the press, and you give them the command of the country, for you give them the command of public opinion, which commands everything." One month later, Thomas Jefferson wrote to James Madison with a similar insight. "We are sensible," Jefferson said of the efforts it would take to put their party—the Republicans—in power, "The engine is the press."

Both writers were correct in their assessment of the role the press would play in American life in the years ahead. The press was already helping to shape the opinions and direction of America. It had been doing so for decades, but its influence would explode following the Revolutionary War and continue into the 1920s and farther. From fewer than 40 newspapers in 1783—each with circulations of around 500—the number of papers erupted in the United States. By 1860, newspaper circulation exceeded 1 million, and in 1898, Joseph Pulitzer's *World* alone had a daily circulation of 1.3 million. By the beginning of World War I, about 16,600 daily and weekly newspapers were published, and circulation figures passed 22.5 million copies per day with no slowdown in circulation in sight. Magazines grew even more impressively. From around 5 at the end of the Revolution, journalism historian Frank Luther Mott counted 600 in 1860 and a phenomenal 3,300 by 1885. Some circulations surpassed 1 million, and the number of magazines continued to grow into the twentieth century.

The amazing growth of the press happened because the printed page of periodicals assumed a critical role in the United States. Newspapers and magazines became the place where Americans discussed and debated the issues that affected them. Newspapers, editors, and citizens took sides, and they used the press as the conduit for discussion. The *Debating Historical Issues in the Media of the Time* series offers a glimpse into how the press was used by Americans to shape and influence the major events and issues facing the nation during different periods of its development. Each volume is based on the documents–that is, the writings that appeared in the press of the time. Each volume presents articles, essays, and editorials that support opposing interests on the events and issues; and each provides readers with background and explanation of the events, issues, and, if possible, the people who wrote the articles that have been selected. Each volume also includes a chronology of events and a selected bibliography. Books in the *Debating Historical Issues in the Media of the Time* series cover the following periods: the Revolution and the young republic, the Federalist era, the antebellum period, the Civil War, Reconstruction, the Progressive era, and World War I.

This volume focuses upon the issues that affected America as it fought the Revolution through the pivotal first years of the new republic, from 1776 to 1800, or from the Declaration of Independence through the election of Thomas Jefferson. The papers of this period grew to be highly partisan in their content, especially in the period following the ratification of the Constitution and the Bill of Rights. As the United States moved forward away from the war for independence, its citizens turned to the press as never before to discuss the issues surrounding the development of the new nation and to debate the issues that shaped America's political direction for the nineteenth century.

Introduction

The last quarter of the eighteenth century was a time of great change for the United States. Symbolically, the period stretched from Thomas Jefferson's Declaration of Independence, adopted on July 4, 1776, to his first inaugural address, delivered on March 4, 1801. Jefferson's words framed the era both in reality and in his reflection of the issues and debates of the era. His Declaration of Independence discussed tyranny and liberty, issues that Americans debated as they fought for their freedom from Great Britain in the 1770s and 1780s. And his inaugural address discussed what it meant to live in a republic, the issue that had riveted many people's attention through the 1780s and 1790s. In a nutshell, from 1776 to 1800, the United States went from being a fantastic dream to a stable reality. The process of national growth and maturation proved difficult in many ways, but most Americans of any influence seemed basically satisfied with the nation they saw as Thomas Jefferson became the third president in March 1801.

Newspapers reflected all of these issues in the materials they printed. Increasingly, newspapers became a major source of information about people and events outside the local community. Even before the Revolution, people took an avid interest in happenings in the other colonies and across the Atlantic in Europe. The war with Great Britain accelerated this interest as people sought to determine which side was winning and what impact that might have on their own future. Strong interest in national and international events continued and increased as the United States took shape in the 1780s and sought its place in the world in the 1790s.

This interest was reflected in the growth of the number of newspapers published in the United States. At the time of the adoption of the Declaration of Independence, 37 newspapers, all weeklies, appeared throughout the British colonies. Most were published in seaports along the Atlantic coast. Twenty-five years later, when Jefferson was inaugurated as president, more than 200 newspapers were published throughout the states from Maine to Georgia and from the Atlantic Ocean to the Mississippi River. One fourth of these publications appeared more than once a week, with 18 appearing daily.[1]

Visually, the newspapers looked and read much as they had during the colonial era. There were no set spelling or grammar rules, which sometimes made the newspapers difficult to read. However, Noah Webster had begun his work to standardize American English with his publication in 1783 of *A Grammatical Institute of the English Language* (the famed "Blue-Backed Speller"), and so the language was becoming somewhat more predictable. Most news sheets were four pages in length, with two or three columns of type per page. Beyond the masthead of the newspaper, which contained the title and the date, the front page differed little from the other pages. News, essays, and advertisements were scattered throughout the paper, although printers increasingly tried to group together materials from one city. Printers continued to label news generally according to the story's city of origin rather than the place where the event actually occurred. Foreign items about the activities of European governments continued to appear frequently, but domestic news from the states became increasingly common as readers became more interested in events elsewhere around the country. Local pieces remained of lesser importance, although they began to occupy a larger percentage of the available space. The biggest change in the newspapers came as printers became more willing to comment on the news and essays they published. Although not clearly labeled as editorials during the Revolutionary era, such opinion statements laid the groundwork for the frequent use of editorials during the party press conflicts of the 1790s.

The primary source of news and information remained the same as it had during the colonial era: private letters, official messages, and other newspapers. Each paper printed some local information that others picked up, but even those materials were sometimes paltry; and reports of major events sometimes consisted of no more than a paragraph. The postal service, originally developed during the 1750s, had continued to grow slowly. However, it was still a slow process and newspapers were occasionally dumped or left behind in order to make room for letters. As a result, news of major events was sometimes delayed a month or more. The situation improved in the 1790s with the development of political ties between various papers scattered across the country, but the modern idea of timely news remained nonexistent.

Throughout the entire era, the primary role of the newspapers was to provide information to the reading public. The details of this role, however, changed somewhat from decade to decade. During the 1770s, the focus was on the war and how the fight for independence was progressing. During the 1780s, the focus shifted to concerns about the government and in what direction the United States was headed. By the 1790s, the focus moved to politics, as the newspapers became ever more partisan in their efforts to support one of the two major political parties. But, even with these differences in focus, Americans turned to the newspapers to find out what was going on in their country and elsewhere around the world.

During the American Revolution, the newspapers played a vital role in providing information about the war. The role of the press as a source of news proved so essential that Congress provided for a printer for the army so the troops could maintain access to a newspaper. George Washington also arranged to keep abreast of events throughout the colonies and Britain by exchanging, through enemy lines, local sheets for the papers of New York. In attempting to keep their readers informed about the war, printers included accounts of battles and the actions of Congress and state legislatures in each week's production. Because many battle reports proved unreliable, John Adams urged General Nathaniel Greene to arrange for publication of accurate descriptions of the actions he fought in order to prevent the spread of false information. Along with battle tales, printers also published troop movements, a practice that concerned American leaders because they feared what the British would do if they acquired the information. Pleas for men and supplies became common in the newspapers. Important public documents, such as the Declaration of Independence and the Articles of Confederation, were published in full, while important essays like "The Crisis" appeared everywhere.

While not always accurate in their reports, printers did the best with what they had. No reporters traveled with the army at this time; that practice did not become common until the Civil War in the 1860s. As a result, much of the material printed consisted of rumor and secondhand information. Delays in receiving news often made stories several weeks out of date. Most newspapermen, however, felt that any information was better than none at all. People turned to the public prints for news of the war from other parts of the country. Inclusion of such items made readers more aware of a national war effort. More than any other institution, the press encouraged the people to support the war effort. Thus, newspapers became the primary morale boosters throughout the Revolutionary era. Printers such as Benjamin Edes and Isaiah Thomas from Massachusetts used a variety of means to lift public confidence in the drive for independence. Throughout the war, essays and news stories emphasized the tyranny and corruption of the British and the glory and justness of the American cause. Patriot newspapers sought to destroy any remaining colonial ties to Great Britain by attacking George III, his army, and the American Tories who supported the British cause. While castigating the British and their allies, these newspapers also praised American success and urged everyone to keep fighting because victory was within reach. Patriot printers rejoiced with everyone when victory was finally won.

The road to victory, however, had been paved with many difficulties and losses for everyone, and the press had joined in the suffering. War was not good for the press. While readership and circulation may have increased because of interest in military events, war's damages were generally greater than its benefits. Military operations disrupted publishing, fervor created by the dangers and passions of war restricted freedom of expression, news coverage was made difficult, printing materials were in short supply, and newspaper survival was endangered. Although not telling the whole story, the figures on newspaper mortality reveal something of the effect of the Revolution on newspapers. At one time or another, 70 different papers were being published during the Revolution; only half survived. Such a high death rate during a period of seven years illustrates the hazards war posed for publishing.

Those printers who managed to overcome the difficulties of the Revolution, through luck or hard work, or both, faced the uncertain future with hope and optimism. For them, the war had served as a testing ground to toughen not only the press, but also all Americans, to face the future together. Newspaper printers came out of the Revolution believing that their weekly sheets had played an essential role in the conflict, and they planned to continue that role in the future. The possibilities were almost endless, since newspapers would provide information and encouragement for the new nation as it developed and grew.

In many ways, these hopes for the future proved to be true. The decade of the 1780s marked the beginning of a new era in American journalism. Fresh faces appeared among the printers and publishers throughout the country. Having come of age and learned their trade during the Revolution, these younger newspaper producers, such as Benjamin Russell of Boston, exuded optimism and believed strongly in the important role of the press in the political arena of the new republic. With the arrival of peace in 1783, these new printers began to make their presence felt in the young nation. Trained by older artisans during the years of fighting with Great Britain, they assumed that the press had played a central role in the move for independence and would continue to be essential for the maintenance of republicanism in the new nation that emerged from the Revolution. These politically oriented printers would dominate the trade by the 1790s as their predecessors retired or died. While all did not succeed in their newspaper enterprises, they brought new blood into the trade.

In conjunction with the appearance of new printers, the 1780s witnessed considerable growth in the newspaper industry in the United States. When the Revolution ended in 1783, printers produced 35 news sheets throughout the young nation, one of them the first attempt at publishing a daily newspaper. By the time of the first national census in 1790, 92 publications had appeared throughout the country, including 8 dailies. The years of peace had been good for the press, allowing it to increase to almost three times its size only seven years after the war ended.

By the 1780s, the public view of newspapers had changed. No longer were they just purveyors of news and information to the "better sort"; now they belonged to everyone. Much of this change resulted from the part the press had played in bringing about a successful separation from Great Britain. Also, increasingly, newspapers came to be seen as a means for the people to keep tabs on their government and its officials. The 1780s witnessed the occasional publication of legislative debates in the newspapers. Peter Edes, editor of the *Newport Herald,* published a series of reports on the actions of the Rhode Island General Assembly from the spring of 1787 to January 1790. This type of detailed coverage, however, was unusual. Most newspaper coverage of state legislatures consisted of the publication of speeches from time to time. Detailed reports of state and federal legislative debates and actions became common after the adoption of the Constitution. Following the inauguration of the new federal legislature in March 1789, most newspapers carried congressional debates regularly.

Throughout these years of growth, newspaper printers discussed the successes and failures of the new government. Most believed that the structure created by the Articles of Confederation could not succeed and, thus, they actively supported the move toward a new government, which grew throughout the decade. American newspapers of the 1780s reflected the growing anxieties of the printers for the security and efficacy of the national government, and the continual discussion of such issues encouraged readers to be concerned as well. Such worries, whether based on actual fact or not, helped set the stage for the adoption of the new form of government in 1787–1788.

The establishment of the new government under the Constitution in 1789 opened a new era in American history, and newspapers of the 1790s reflected the changes that occurred. Many people agreed that the United States would be a republic, but they disagreed over how to put republican ideals into practice. As American leaders moved from discussion of political theories to attempts to implement these theories, discord arose. Arguments and disagreements over how to run the government increased throughout the 1790s, differences that influenced the growth of the press. The French Revolution also influenced the appearance of divisions. Americans had trouble deciding what to do about the changes in France because that revolt took a much bloodier turn than the American Revolution. Once the Reign of Terror began in 1793, many people simply could not believe that the revolution in France had anything in common with the revolt that had produced the United States.

The contentions over these issues between government officials eventually coalesced into two political parties: the Federalists, led by Alexander Hamilton and John Adams, and the Republicans, led by Thomas Jefferson and James Madison. Leaders on each side quickly sought out journalists to support their position because these men had learned the potential effect of newspapers during the revolutionary conflict with Great Britain. Thus developed the first party press in American history. The 1790s were a time of great conflict and distrust because the United States had not yet developed a concept of "loyal opposition." For most Americans, political dissent and faction were dangerous and led to tyranny. People on both sides of an argument quickly accused their opponents of treason and sought to silence them. The newspapers became the major arena for such accusations. It would take a major confrontation over the First Amendment, in the guise of the Sedition Act, before Americans would generally accept the idea that a person could publicly disagree with the national government without advocating treason and revolution.

Political leaders emerged from the Revolutionary War with a growing respect for the possible impact newspapers could produce and, as a result, quickly sought out friendly printers willing to support a particular viewpoint in the columns of their publications. The rise of political parties, however, produced changes in how newspapers were run and resulted in the development of the distinct position of editor. The director of the newspaper was now a writer and commentator rather than simply a printer. Newspaper printers prior to the 1790s had often written the news that had appeared in their productions, but they seldom commented about the news. That job had been carried out primarily by anonymous essayists who wrote for the newspaper. But, by the 1790s, if a newspaper intended to support a particular cause, the producer had to write not only news, but also opinion to back up the political stand in question. Along with the development of the position of editor came the regular appearance of a recognizable editorial. Again, the need for political commentary led to the appearance of brief, but clearly labeled, editorial comments by the newspaper managers of the

1790s. Both editors and editorials became an accepted part of journalistic practice from that point on.

Both political parties sought to use the press to influence public opinion because both realized the increasing influence of public opinion in the political arena. The Federalists and Alexander Hamilton struck first, with the publication of John Fenno's *Gazette of the United States* on April 15, 1789. The first official organ of the Republicans, Philip Freneau's *National Gazette*, appeared in 1791. Numerous politicians gave active support to various newspapers in an effort to get their ideas out to the public. Republicans who promoted the circulation of various news sheets included Thomas Jefferson, James Madison, Albert Gallatin, John Hancock, and Samuel Adams. At the instigation of Hugh Henry Breckinridge, Printer John Israel moved to Pittsburgh to start a Republican paper. By 1800, one report stated that the Republicans had established newspapers throughout the country in order to push Jefferson's election as president. Among the Federalists, Alexander Hamilton led the way in providing financial support for newspapers, but John Jay, Rufus King, and others joined him on several occasions to establish Federalist newspapers in major cities throughout the country.

Editors agreed with political leaders and always emphasized the power of their publications in influencing public opinion and political action. If for no other reason, the role of the newspapers as the primary source of political information made the press an essential cog in the operation of the government. However, editors also believed that the publication of editorial opinion had great influence and played just as important a role in the political arena as did the publication of news and information. Because of this belief, newspaper producers increasingly filled the pages of their publications with more and more political information and opinion in hopes of convincing the people to support the "right" side of the growing political debate on the national government. For more and more editors, supporting a partisan cause became the primary reason for a newspaper's existence. Throughout the 1790s and beyond, newspaper editors increasingly used both their news reports and their opinion columns to take strong political stands and to encourage their readers to do the same. To do less was to fail as an editor. Clearly, the view of the role of a newspaper had changed from the colonial era when printers were to be impartial and publish what came to hand with no comments at all.

Stylistically, Federalist and Republican editors differed very little. As political disagreements increased, both used invective and personal attacks to further their cause. Both accused the other side of accepting bribes and spreading lies as the primary means of political advancement. The leading party journals did not hesitate to attack the enemy in any way possible, and thus used much rumor, innuendo, and personal denunciations in their attempts to win the political loyalty and support of the American people. The press of the first party era was full of vituperation and scurrility. Both Thomas Jefferson and Alexander Hamilton complained about their treatment in the press, but they also both encouraged their supporters to strongly attack the opposition in the newspapers. With no concept of loyal party opposition, only one side was right, while the opposition was lying. Therefore, strong attacks were felt to be justified and necessary in order to prevent tyranny or anarchy. Both sides in the growing political debate believed in the influence of the press and sought to use the newspapers to espouse their cause and influence public opinion. For almost everyone concerned, the primary purpose of the press in the 1790s was not to be non-partisan and present "the news," but to support a political cause and strongly to advocate one side of an issue while attacking the other side. If political partisanship constituted the standard by which to measure the press, the newspapers of the 1790s did a good job.

Most of the growing political conflict of the 1790s centered on the role the United States should play in the conflict between Great Britain and France. Although some disagreements over implementing the Constitution surfaced in 1789 and 1790, true discord appeared because of the French Revolution and the European war that resulted. Although President Washington urged neutrality as essential for the survival of the young nation, others stated that the United States should at least support one side or the other ideologically, if not in any other manner. Hamilton and the Federalists affirmed that the United States, with a population primarily of English-speaking descent, had more interests in common with Great Britain than France, and urged support for the British. Jefferson and the Republicans, remembering French aid during America's own revolution and seeing the French Revolution as following the model set by the United States, invoked the names of Lafayette and Rochambeau and urged Americans to side with France. American support for the French cooled somewhat as the French Revolution took a more violent turn with the Reign of Terror in 1793–1794. It became more difficult for many people to understand how the relatively bloodless American revolt against Great Britain could have much in common with the increasingly violent conflict in France. The attempts of the French ambassador, Edmond Genet, to raise American financial support helped worsen the situation and provided the context for the first major conflict in the press between the Federalists and the Republicans.

Conflict over what the United States should do concerning the European conflict continued to fuel the arguments between the Republicans and the Federalists. Jay's Treaty of 1795 provided the basis for the next round of arguments. Continuing disagreements between Great Britain and the United States over the Ohio Valley and the issue of neutral rights at sea caused President Washington to send John Jay to London as negotiator in order to try to settle the differences between the two countries peacefully. The resulting agreement, Jay's Treaty, produced a cacophony of criticism from the Republicans and support from the Federalists, most of which appeared in the partisan newspapers of both sides.

Ratification of Jay's Treaty offended the French, and relations deteriorated between France and the United States. By 1797, French naval ships began seizing American vessels carrying British goods. President John Adams (elected in 1796) hoped to avoid war through negotiation. French Foreign Minister Maurice Talleyrand sought a bribe of $250,000 and a loan of $12 million before he would begin negotiations. In response to this action, two of the three American representatives, John Marshall and Charles Cotesworthy Pinckney, sailed home. This event became known as the XYZ Affair because President Adams identified the French representatives as X, Y, and Z in reporting the incident to Congress. The newspapers discussed and debated these issues in great detail.

Jay's Treaty and the XYZ Affair helped produce the undeclared naval war between France and the United States and provided the premise for the Alien and Sedition Acts, an attack on First Amendment freedoms designed by the Federalists to stifle the Republicans. The Sedition Act specifically attacked the press and produced the first serious discussion of the meaning of freedom of the press as protected by the First Amendment. The challenge of the Sedition Act was important because it forced editors and politicians to discuss seriously just what it meant to have a free press. All agreed that there should be no prior restraint of publication, but here agreement ceased. Division over whether one could openly criticize or disagree with the government abounded, with the Federalists denying that one could do so, while the Republicans declared that a representative government could not exist if ideas could not be discussed and debated. Ultimately, the Federalists and Republicans did not settle this argument because the Federalists were voted out of office in the midst of the debate. However, the discussions over the Sedition Act provided the basis for a definition of a free press that allowed wide latitude in discussing and criticizing the actions of government. They helped to establish the idea that disagreements and differences of opinion were part of the political system that existed in the United States.

This book presents debates over the issues that dominated the newspapers from the adoption of the Declaration of Independence in July 1776 to Thomas Jefferson's inauguration as president in March 1801. Each chapter presents writings on both sides of the debates as Americans discussed what to do about the issues under consideration. A variety of newspapers—from large and small cities, from north to south and east to west—are included. Basically, the book is organized chronologically. Twenty-six topics are included, with a variety of opinions expressed on each subject. The majority of the issues included are political in nature, because politics and political concerns proved of primary importance to Americans as they successfully revolted from the control of Great Britain and established their own independent nation.

NOTE

1. Throughout this introduction, the numbers of newspapers published at any given time are counts based on materials in Clarence S. Brigham, *History and Bibliography of American Newspapers, 1690–1820,* 2 volumes (Worcester, Massachusetts: American Antiquarian Society, 1947).

Chronology of Events

1776   July—Declaration of Independence adopted.

July—The Articles of Confederation, written by John Dickinson, proposed to the Continental Congress.

August—The British army, having departed Boston in March, takes control of New York following its victory at the Battle of Long Island.

December—"Crisis #1," written by Thomas Paine, published in the *Pennsylvania Journal.*

December—George Washington leads the Continental army to victory over the Hessians at Trenton, New Jersey.

1777   October—The British under Sir Henry Clinton defeat the Americans under General George Washington at Germantown, Pennsylvania.

October—The Americans under General William Howe defeat the British under the command of General John Burgoyne at Saratoga, New York.

October—The Articles of Confederation approved by the Continental Congress.

December—Washington takes the Continental army into winter quarters at Valley Forge, Pennsylvania.

1778   February—The United States signs a treaty of alliance with France that was negotiated following the victory at Saratoga, which convinced the French that the revolt against Great Britain could be successful.

1780   June—Esther DeBerdt Reed calls on American women to help
              fight the Revolution by raising money for a bounty to give
              the soldiers.

              August—The British under Lord Cornwallis defeat the
              Americans under General Horatio Gates at Camden, South
              Carolina.

              October—Benedict Arnold seeks to betray the fortress at West
              Point, New York, to the British, thus becoming the most
              infamous traitor in American history.

1781   January—The Americans under General Nathaniel Greene
              defeat the British under Lord Cornwallis at Cowpens,
              South Carolina.

              March—Maryland finally adopts the Articles of Confederation
              when Virginia surrenders her claims to territory in the
              Ohio Valley.

              October—A combined American and French army under
              General George Washington defeats the British army under
              Lord Cornwallis at Yorktown, Virginia. This was the final
              battle of the American Revolution.

1783   May—The first daily newspaper, the *Pennsylvania Evening Post*,
              is published in Philadelphia.

              September—The Treaty of Paris is accepted by the British and
              the Americans, thus ending the American Revolution.

              November—The British army leaves New York City, ending
              176 years of British colonial rule.

1785   January—New York becomes the capital of the United States.

              March—A meeting takes place at Mount Vernon between
              Maryland and Virginia to discuss issues of trade on the
              Potomac River. It ends with a call for another meeting of all
              the states to discuss the problems facing the United States.

              May—The Articles Congress adopts the Land Ordinance of
              1785, which provided for an organized surveying and
              purchasing plan for western lands that was used for almost
              all lands west of the Appalachian Mountains.

1786   September—The Annapolis Convention takes place. Delegates
              from five states met to discuss the problems facing the
              United States. They issued a call for another convention to
              take place the next year in Philadelphia to discuss the
              weakness of the Articles government.

              Fall, and into 1787—In western Massachusetts, Shays's
              Rebellion breaks out. Farmers protested state policies,
              which they blamed for the loss of their farms through
              foreclosure because of failure to pay their taxes.

1787 May–September–The Constitutional Convention meets in
      Philadelphia. They approved the new proposed govern-
      ment contained in the Constitution on September 17.

      July–The Articles Congress approves the Northwest
      Ordinance, which provided a government structure for new
      territories as American settlement moved westward.

1788 June–The Constitution is ratified by the required number of
      states, when New Hampshire becomes the ninth to do so.

      Late Summer–Maryland and Virginia offer to give land on the
      Potomac River to Congress as the site for a national capital.

      Fall–First elections are held under the new Constitution.

1789 February–The first electoral college unanimously elects
      George Washington to be president.

      March–April–The new government created by the
      Constitution begins operation when Congress meets in
      March and George Washington is inaugurated as the first
      president in April.

      April–John Fenno founds the *Gazette of the United States* in
      New York.

      July–With the fall of the Bastille, the French Revolution
      begins.

      August–Congress passes the Judiciary Act, creating the
      Supreme Court, 13 district courts, and 3 circuit courts.
      John Jay becomes the first chief justice of the Supreme
      Court.

      July–September–Congress creates the first Cabinet depart-
      ments: State, War, Treasury, and the Attorney General.

      September–Twelve amendments are approved by Congress
      and sent to the states for consideration. Ten of these will
      become the Bill of Rights.

      November–North Carolina ratifies the Constitution,
      becoming the twelfth state.

1790 January–Alexander Hamilton, first secretary of the Treasury,
      proposes a plan to stabilize the American economy, pay the
      national debt, and firm up the credit of the United States
      government.

      May–Rhode Island finally ratifies the Constitution, becoming
      the thirteenth state.

      December–The national capital moves from New York to
      Philadelphia.

      December–Samuel Slater builds the first American steam-
      powered cotton-processing machines, thus beginning the
      Industrial Revolution in the United States; The first

national census places the national population at 4
    million people.

1791   March—Vermont becomes the fourteenth state.

October—Philip Freneau founds the *National Gazette*.

December—The Bill of Rights is approved, with the ratification
    of Virginia.

1792   May—The New York Stock Exchange is organized.

June—Kentucky becomes the fifteenth state.

Fall—The second presidential election takes place.

December—The electoral college reelects George Washington
    as president of the United States.

1793   February—Congress passes the Fugitive Slave Act, making it
    illegal to help runaway slaves.

April—Washington declares the United States neutral in the
    war between Great Britain and France.

June—Eli Whitney invents the cotton gin, which will revive the
    slave economy in the South.

1794   Summer—Western farmers protest the excise tax, part of
    Hamilton's financial program, in what came to be called the
    Whiskey Rebellion. President Washington called out the
    militia to face the rebels, but no real conflict occurred.

August—At the Battle of Fallen Timbers, the Indians of the
    Ohio Valley are defeated by an American force under
    General Anthony Wayne.

1795   June—Although not perfect, Jay's Treaty with Great Britain is
    approved by the Senate, thus avoiding a war.

Late Summer—General Anthony Wayne signs the Treaty of
    Greenville with the Indians of the Ohio Valley, who cede
    large portions of the Northwest Territory to the United
    States.

October—Pinckney's Treaty (or the Treaty of San Lorenzo)
    settles the northern boundary of Florida and gives the
    United States the right to navigate the Mississippi River to
    the Gulf of Mexico.

1796   June—Tennessee becomes the sixteenth state.

September—George Washington issues his Farewell Address,
    stating that he would not run for reelection as president.
    He urged Americans to avoid partisan strife and to stay out
    of entangling alliances that could get them involved in an
    unwanted war.

Fall—The third presidential election takes place.

	December—John Adams defeats Thomas Jefferson in the electoral college vote for president.
1797	Spring—The Quasi-War with France breaks out.
	Fall—The XYZ Affair takes place, as agents of French Foreign Minister Talleyrand attempt to extort money from the United States.
1798	Spring—The XYZ Affair becomes known in the United States.
	June–July—Congress passes the Alien and Sedition Acts to deal with the perceived French threat and to silence their political opposition.
	November–December—The state legislatures of Virginia and Kentucky adopt resolutions (written by James Madison and Thomas Jefferson) declaring the Alien and Sedition Acts to be unconstitutional.
1799	December—George Washington dies at Mount Vernon.
1800	April—The Library of Congress is founded.
	November—The national capital moves to its new permanent home, Washington, D.C.
	Spring–Summer—John Chapman ("Johnny Appleseed") travels through the Ohio Valley.
	Fall—The fourth presidential election takes place; second national census shows a population of 5.3 million.
1801	February—Thomas Jefferson is finally elected president by the House of Representatives.

CHAPTER I

The Reality of Independence, 1776–1781

When the Second Continental Congress adopted the Declaration of Independence on July 4, 1776, and then had it published in the *Pennsylvania Evening Post* on July 6, 1776, no one really knew what it all meant. The delegates who later signed the Declaration believed that Great Britain sought to control their lives in ways that were unacceptable. They had accepted the political philosophy of Englishman John Locke, who stated that a government should pay attention to the needs and desires of its subjects. A government's failure to listen and respond provided a reason for rebellion; and John Adams, Thomas Jefferson, John Hancock, and the rest of the Continental Congress believed that Britain's "tyranny" justified their revolution. These men had embraced the ideas of the Enlightenment, an eighteenth-century philosophical outlook which emphasized man's rationality and his ability to use his mind to solve all problems. If a person gathered information and studied it carefully, the answer to any question would be obvious. The delegates to the Continental Congress believed that their revolution fit this description—anyone looking at the actions of Great Britain would agree that the colonies could do nothing else but revolt in order to guarantee their political rights.

But believing that their actions were justified did not mean that these men knew the consequences of those actions. They could declare the colonies independent, but what exactly did that action mean? Besides the obvious fact of the need to win the war against Great Britain, the colonies would have to define what it meant to be "free and independent states" by developing a government structure and fleshing out how the previously distinct and separate colonies would relate to each other and how they would face the future together as one nation. It would take decades to answer many of these questions, but many of them were discussed immediately. As

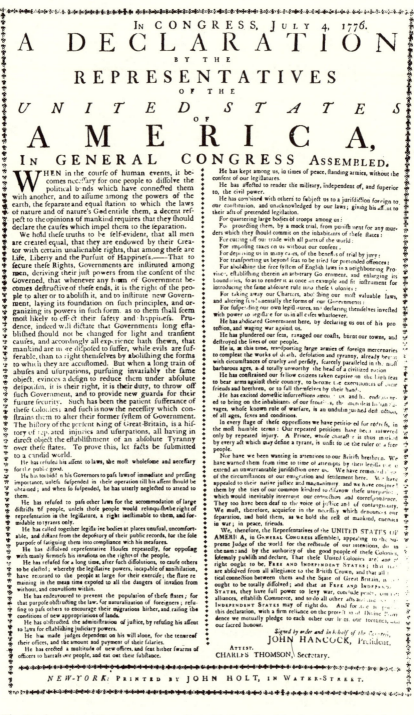

The Declaration of Independence. *One of the benefits of the shortness of the Declaration was that it could be easily printed in a newspaper or as a broadside. Here is a broadside version printed by John Holt, a printer in New York, in July 1776.*

the colonies fought to win the war in order to make independence a reality, they used the pages of the newspapers to discuss independence and what it all meant.

The documents that question the wisdom of independence all appeared in Loyalist newspapers throughout the course of the war. The printers of these news sheets decided that independence was folly, and their publications reflected that attitude. The first two essays accuse the members of the Continental Congress of showing an unwillingness to negotiate a peaceful solution to the conflict because they were greedy and power-hungry. The third piece is a letter from Jacob Duché, former chaplain of the Continental Congress, who had written a letter urging George Washington to use his considerable influence to work for peace while there was still time to negotiate a settlement. The next two documents emphasize the insanity of independence and urge the colonials to turn back before it is too late. The final document opposing independence is an attempt to turn the logic of independence upside down. In this piece published in 1781, an anonymous author, in a perfect mimic of the Declaration of Independence, accuses the Continental Congress of tyranny and despotism in the same manner that they had accused George III five years earlier.

The documents in favor of independence all appeared fairly early in the conflict, when people had more time for thought and celebration. The first is an anonymous poem praising the independent states and calling on God to bless the people's fight for liberty. Following the poem is a news report which reports that the Governor of Halifax feared that the publishing of the Declaration would encourage his subjects to revolt. The next five documents in favor of independence are a series of reports of public celebrations of independence from places all over the country. Each one describes the various forms of celebration, but they also emphasize the joy and satisfaction of the people that they are finally free from British tyranny. The last document supporting independence is actually an attack on Jacob Duché for his letter to George Washington urging him to work to end the war. This letter reflects the horror of Americans at what seemed a major betrayal and presages the later reactions to the treason of Benedict Arnold.

OPPOSITION TO INDEPENDENCE

Anonymous: "The Avarice of Some Indigent Men"

Loyalists believed that independence was insanity and that the colonies would be much better off if they remained a part of the British empire. This

*essayist attacks the Continental Congress for misleading the people because
of its own personal greed, arguing that peace commissioners sent from
Great Britain could have resulted in a reconciliation if only the Congress
had been willing to listen.*

New York Gazette and Weekly Mercury, 21 October 1776

To the PRINTER. It is an Observation of the celebrated Montesquieu,
"That Individuals rarely incline to part with Power; great Bodies never." The
Conduct of the Congress furnishes another Instance of the Truth of this Remark. "Though it is the grand Interest of America to be reconciled to Great
Britain, and though it has been the constant and repeated Profession of the
several Assemblies, that Reconciliation was their Object, yet, when Reconciliation was held out by Government, and Commissioners were appointed
to confer with the Colonies upon their own Ground for that Purpose; these
ambitious Incendiaries, seeing that, upon such an Event, all their affirmed
Consequence must be lost, had Art enough to hasten a Declaration of Absolute Independence, before the desired Commission could possibly arrive.
The Delegates had perfect Information of what was intended; and fearing
that this Act of Benevolence and Conciliation might operate upon many Persons in the Colonies, whose Properties made it their Interest to solicit Peace,
resolved to put it out of the Power of the several Assemblies to listen to the
Overtures, by previously drawing them into Acquiescence with the Avowal
of Independence. Thus the Avarice of some indigent Men, Bankrupts both
in Fortune and Character, and the Ambitions of others who lusted after
Power, has plunged this once happy Country into a Flood of Miseries, for
which the Lives and Fortunes of these Parricides, would in the issue make
but a poor Atonement. "Tis easy to foresee, that, so long as these Demagogues have the Directions of Affairs, no Peace of Settlement can be hoped
for. And it is not to be believed, that the Colonies can have had Reconciliation sincerely in View, because they have hitherto employed Means which
they must have known were exceptionable and offensive, nor can it be supposed that they will ever be really desirous of it, till they have applied themselves, not through the Medium of a Congress, but of their own respective
Assemblies, to the promoting of this salutary Measure.

Anonymous: "A Phantom Called Independency"

*This essayist expresses dismay that the Congress continues to pursue the
unwise course of independence. According to this essayist, Great Britain
has offered to return the colonies to the status they held in 1763, but the*

*Congress has refused to accept this proposal (which is what they had orig-
inally said they wanted).*

Royal Pennsylvania Gazette (Philadelphia), 5 May 1778

The principle claims of the majority of the people of America are–To be
relieved from parliamentary taxation, and to be placed as they stood in the
year 1763. The King and Parliament of Great-Britain have manifested a disposition to accede to their claims; and, that every point in dispute may be
freely discussed and amicably compromised, a cessation of hostilities may
be proposed. Here then is a good foundation, and now is the favourable
opportunity of opening a treaty of re-union and peace. But the Congress
have thought fit to declare that America shall have no peace; that she shall
not accept the very conditions originally proposed by herself; that she shall
submit to a burthen of taxes more grievous than she ever even apprehended
that Great-Britain would have attempted to impose upon her; that the hopes
of every family shall be dragged into the field, there to perish by war, pestilence, or insupportable distresses–And all this for what?–to pursue a phantom called Independency; or, in other words to support, at the expence of
her own blood and treasure, the power and consequence of a set of men
who oppose peace merely because such an event would sink them into obscurity.

America then, it seems, may on the one hand be blessed with immediate
peace; may be freed forever from British taxation; and may be put precisely
in the situation of 1763. On the other hand, she must provoke the farther
ravages of an unnatural war; must yield to endless oppression, and lay down
even life and property, in support of such individuals as compose the Congress government. But will America be thus duped, thus trampled upon,
thus driven to slaughter? No–she will rather exert her reason and her
strength, to prevent the farther prosecution of a now groundless contest.
She will resist the arbitrary demands of recruits and supplies, and compel, if
she cannot persuade her self-interested rulers to exchange their own power
for the peace and happiness of their country.

Jacob Duché: "The Idea of Independency"

*In this letter, Jacob Duché, former chaplain to the Continental Congress,
urges George Washington to use his considerable influence to end the war
before it is too late. Duché is very critical of Congress and the Continental
army, reflecting the ideas of the Loyalists in America who sincerely believed that the United States could not win the fight against Great Britain.*

Pennsylvania Evening Post (Philadelphia), 13 December 1777

SIR, If this letter should find you in council, or in the field, before you read another sentence, I beg you to take the first opportunity of retiring, and weighing well its important contents.

You are perfectly acquainted with the part I formerly took in the present unhappy contest. I was, indeed, among the first to bear my public testimony against having any recourse to threats, or indulging a thought of an armed opposition. But the torrent soon became too strong for my feeble efforts to resist. I wished to follow my countrymen as far only as virtue, and the right-eousness of their cause, would permit me. I was, however, prevailed on among the rest of my clerical brethren of this city, to gratify the pressing de-sires of my fellow-citizens, by preaching a sermon to one of the city battal-ions. I was pressed to publish this sermon, and reluctantly consented. From a personal attachment, of near twenty years' standing, and a high respect for your character in private as well as public life, I took the liberty of dedicat-ing it to you. I had your affectionate thanks for my performance in a letter, wherein was expressed in the most delicate and obliging terms, your regard for me, and your wishes for a continuance of my friendship and approbation of your conduct.

Farther than this I intended not to proceed. My sermon speaks for itself, and utterly disclaims the idea of independency. My sentiments were well known to my friends. I communicated them without reserve to many re-spectable members of Congress, who expressed their warm approbation of them. I persisted in using the public prayers for my sovereign and the royal family to the very last moment, though threatened with insult from the vio-lence of a party.

On the declaration of independency, I called my vestry, and solemnly put the question to them, whether they thought it best for the peace and welfare of the congregation to shut up the churches, or to continue the ser-vice, without using the petitions for the Royal Family. This was the sad al-ternative. I concluded to abide by their decisions, as I could not have time to consult my spiritual superiors in England. They deemed it most expedient, under such critical circumstances, to keep open the churches, that the con-gregations might not be dispersed, which we had great reason to appre-hend.

A very few days after the fatal declaration of independency, I received a letter from Mr. Hancock, sent by express to Germantown, where my family were for the summer season, acquainting me, that I was appointed chaplain to the congress, and desired to attend at nine o'clock the next morning. Sur-prised and distressed by an event I was not prepared to expect, obliged to give an immediate answer without the opportunity of consulting my friends, I rashly accepted the appointment. I could have but one motive for taking this step. I thought the churches in danger, and hoped by these means to be instrumental in preventing those evils, I had so much cause to apprehend. I can, however, with truth declare, that I then looked upon independency rather as an expedient, and an hazardous one indeed, thrown out in terrorem,[1] in order to procure some favorable terms, than as a measure that was seriously to be persisted in at all events. My sudden change of conduct will clearly evince this to have been my idea of the matter.

Upon the return of the committee of congress appointed to confer with Lord Howe, I soon discerned their real intentions.—The different accounts, which each member gave of this conference, the time they took to make up the matter for public view, and the amazing disagreements between the newspaper accounts and the relation I myself had from the mouth of one of the Committee, convinced me there must have been some unfair and ungenerous procedure. This determination to treat on no other strain than that of independency, which put it out of his Lordship's power to mention any terms at all, was sufficient proof to me that independency was the idol they had long wished to set up, and that, rather than sacrifice this, they would deluge their country with blood.

From this moment I determined upon my resignation, and, in the beginning of October, 1776, sent it in form to Mr. Hancock, after having officiated only two months and three weeks; and from that time, as far as my safety would permit, I have been opposed to all their measures. This circumstantial account of my conduct, I think due to the friendship you were so obliging as to express for me, and, I hope, will be sufficient to justify my seeming inconsistencies in the part I have acted.

And now, my dear Sir, suffer me, in the language of truth and real affection, to address myself to you. All the world must be convinced, that you engaged in the service of your country from motives perfectly disinterested. You risked every thing that was dear to you. You abandoned all those sweets of domestic life, of which your affluent fortune gave you an uninterrupted enjoyment. But had you? Could you have had the least idea of matters being carried to such a dangerous extremity, as they are now? Your most intimate friends, at that time, shuddered at the thought of a separation from the mother country; and I took it for granted that your sentiments coincided with theirs. What have been the consequences of this rash and violent measure? And degeneracy of representation, confusion of councils, blunders without number. The most respectable characters have withdrawn themselves, and are succeeded by a great majority of illiberal and violent men.

Take an impartial view of the present congress. What can you expect from them? Your feelings must be greatly hurt by the representation from your native province. You have no longer a Randolph, a Bland, or a Braxton, men whose names will ever be revered, whose demands never rose above the first ground on which they set out, and whose truly generous and virtuous sentiments I have frequently heard with rapture from their own lips. Oh my dear Sir! What a sad contrast! Characters now present themselves, whose minds can never mingle with your own. Your Harrison alone remains, and he disgusted with his unworthy associates.

As to those of my own Province, some of them are so obscure, that their very names were never in my ears before, and others have only been distinguished for the weakness of their understandings, and the violence of their tempers. One alone I except from the general charge; a man of virtue, dragged reluctantly into their measures, and restrained, by some false ideas of honor, from retreating, after having gone too far. You cannot be at a loss to discover whose name answers to this character.

From the New England provinces can you find one that, as a gentleman, you could wish to associate with, unless the soft and mild address of Mr. Hancock can atone for his want of every other qualification necessary for the seat which he fills? Bankrupts, attorneys, and men of desperate fortunes, are his colleagues.

Maryland no longer sends a Tilghman and a protestant Carroll. Carolina has lost her Lynch; and the elder Middleton has retired.

Are the dregs of Congress, then, still to influence a mind like yours! These are not the men, whom you engaged to serve; these are not the men that America has chosen to represent her. Most of them elected by a little low faction, and the few gentlemen, that are among them now well known to be upon the balance, and looking up to your hand alone to move the beam. It is you, sir; and you alone, that support the present congress. Of this you must be fully sensible. Long before they left Philadelphia, their dignity and consequence was gone. What must they be now, since their precipitate retreat? I write with freedom, but without invective. I know these things to be true: And I write to one whose own observation must have convinced him, that they are so.

After this view of congress, turn to your army. All the whole world knows, that its very existence depends upon you; that your death or captivity disperses it in a moment, and that there is not a man on that side of the question in America capable of succeeding you. As to the army itself, what have you to expect from them? Have they not frequently abandoned even yourself in the hour of extremity? Have you, can you have the least confidence in a set of undisciplined men, and officers, many of whom have been taken from the lowest of the people, without principle, without courage. Take away those that surround your person, and how very few are there, that you can ask to sit at your table!

Turn to your little navy. Of that little, what is left? Of the Delaware fleet, part are taken, the rest must soon surrender. Of those in the other provinces, some are taken, one or two at sea, and others lying unmanned and unrigged in your harbours.

And now, where are your resources? Oh my dear sir! How sadly have you been abused by a faction void of truth, and void of tenderness to you and your country? They have amused you with hopes of a declaration of war on the part of France. Believe me, from the best authority, it was a fiction from the first. Early in the year 1776, a French Gentleman was introduced to me, with whom I became intimately acquainted. His business, to all appearance, was to speculate in the mercantile way. But I believe, it will be known that in his own country, he moved in a higher sphere. He saw your camp. He became acquainted with all your military preparations. He was introduced to congress, and engaged with them in a commercial contract. In the course of our intimacy, he has frequently told me, that he hoped the Americans would never think of independency. He gave me his reasons. "Independency, said he, can never be supported, unless France should declare war against England. I well know the state of her finances. Years to come will not put them in a situation to venture upon a breach with England. At this moment, there are two parties at the Court of Versailles; one enlisted under the Duke de Choiseul, the other under the count Maurepas. Choiseul has no chance of succeeding. He is violent for war. Maurepas must get the better. He is for economy and peace." This was his information, which I mentioned to several members of congress. They treated it as a fable, depending intirely on the intelligence from Dr. Franklin. The truth of the matter is this, Dr. Franklin built upon the success of Choisuel. Upon his arrival in France, he found him out of place, his counsels reprobated, and his party dwindled into an insignificant faction. This you may depend upon to be the true state of the court of France. And farther by vast numbers of letters, found on board prizes taken by the king's ships, it appears, that all commerce with the merchants of France, through whom alone the supplies have been conveyed, will be at an end, the letters being full of complaints of no remittances from America, and many individuals having greatly suffered on that account.

From your friends in England you have nothing to expect, their numbers are diminished to a cipher; the spirit of the whole nation is in full activity against you. A few sounding names among the nobility, though perpetually rung in your ears, are said to be without character, without influence. Disappointed ambition, I am told, has made them desperate; and that they only wish to make the deluded Americans instruments of revenge. All orders and ranks of men in Great-Britain are now unanimous, and determined to risk their all in the contest. Trade and manufactures are found to flourish, and new channels are continually opening, that will perhaps more than supply the loss of the old.

In a word, your harbours are blocked up, your cities fall one after another; fortress after fortress, battle after battle is lost. A British army, after having passed almost unmolested through a vast extent of country, have possessed themselves with ease of the capital of America. How unequal the contest now! How fruitless the expense of blood!

Under so many discouraging circumstances, can virtue, can honour, can the love of your country, prompt you to persevere? Humanity itself, (and sure I am, humanity is no stranger to your breast) calls upon you to desist. Your army must perish for want of common necessaries, or thousands of innocent families must perish to support them. Wherever they encamp, the country must be impoverished. Wherever they march, the troops of Britain will pursue, and must complete the devastation which America herself had begun.

Perhaps it may be said, that it is "better to die than to be slaves." This indeed is a splendid maxim in theory, and perhaps in some instances may be found experimentally true. But where there is the least probability of an happy accommodation, surely wisdom and humanity call for some sacrifices to be made, to prevent inevitable destruction. You well know, there is but one invincible bar to such an accommodation. Could this be removed, other obstacles might readily be overcome. 'Tis to you, and you alone, your bleeding country looks and calls aloud for this sacrifice. Your arm alone has strength sufficient to remove this bar. May heaven inspire you with the glorious resolution of exerting this strength, at so interesting a crisis, and thus immortalizing yourself as the friend and guardian to your country.

Your penetrating eye needs not more explicit language to discern my meaning. With that prudence and delicacy, therefore, of which I know you to be possessed, represent to congress the indispensable necessity of rescinding the hasty and ill-advised declaration of independency. Recommend (and you have an undoubted right to recommend) an immediate cessation of hostilities. Let the controversy be taken up where that declaration left it, and where lord Howe certainly expected to have found it. Let men of clear and impartial characters, in or out of congress, liberal in their sentiments, heretofore independent in their fortunes (and some such are surely to be found in America) be appointed to confer with his majesty's commissioners. Let them, if they please, prepare some well-digested constitutional plan, to lay before them at the commencement of a negociation. When they have gone thus far, I am confident that the most happy consequences will ensue. Unanimity will immediately take place thro' the different provinces. Thousands, that are now ardently wishing and praying for such a measure, will step forth and declare themselves the zealous advocates of constitutional liberty, and millions will bless the hero, that left the field of war to decide this most important contest with the weapons of wisdom and humanity.

Oh sir! let no false ideas of worldly honor deter you from engaging in so glorious a task. Whatever censures may be thrown out by mean and illiberal minds, your character will rise in the estimation of the virtuous and noble. It will appear with lustre in the annals of history, and form a glorious contrast to that of those, who have fought to obtain conquest and gratify their own ambition, by the destruction of their species, and the ruin of their country.

Be assured that I write not this under the eye of any British officer, or any person connected with the British army, or ministry. The sentiments I have expressed are the real sentiments of my heart, such as I have long held, and which I should have made known to you by letter before, had I not fully expected an opportunity of a private conference. When you passed thro' Philadelphia on your way to Wilmington, I was confined by a severe fit of the gravel to my chamber. I have since continued so much indisposed, and times have been so very distressing, that I had neither spirits to write a letter, nor opportunity to convey it, when written. Nor do I yet know by what means I shall get these sheets to your hands.

I would fain hope, that I have said nothing, by which your delicacy can be in the least hurt. If I have, it has, I assure you, been without the least intention, and therefore your candour will lead you to forgive me. I have spoken freely of congress and of the army. But what I have said is partly from my own knowledge, and partly from the information of some respectable members of the former, and some of the best officers of the latter. I would not offend the meanest person upon earth. What I say to you, I say in confidence, to answer what I cannot but deem a most valuable purpose. I love my country. I love you. But to the love of truth, the love of peace, and the love of my God, I hope I shall be enabled, if called to the trial, to sacrifice every other inferior love.

If the arguments made use of in this letter should have so much influence, as to engage you in the glorious work I have so warmly recommended, I shall ever deem my success as the highest temporal favour, that providence could grant me. Your interposition and advice, I am confident, will meet with a favourable reception from the authority under which you act.

If it should not, you have one infallible recourse still left—negociate for your country at the head of your army.

After all, it may appear presumption in an individual to address himself to you upon a subject of such magnitude, or to say what measures would best secure the interest and welfare of a whole continent. The favourable and friendly opinion you have always expressed of me, emboldened me to undertake it; and (which has greatly added to the weight of this motive) I have been strongly impressed with a sense of duty upon this occasion, which left my conscience uneasy, and my heart afflicted, 'till I had fully discharged it. I am no enthusiast. The case is new and singular to me. I could not enjoy a moment's peace, till the letter was written.

With the most ardent prayers for your spiritual as well as temporal welfare, I am, sir, Your most sincere friend and obedient servant, Jacob Duché.

Pacificus: "The Phantom of Independency"

This essayist clearly perceived independence to be an insane idea and calls on the American people to change their minds before it is too late. He emphasizes that George III would forgive them and welcome them back into the British Empire, the place where their allegiance clearly belonged.

Royal Pennsylvania Gazette **(Philadelphia), 24 March 1778**

Sure it behooves the deluded people of this country to consider these things maturely, and to fly from this prospect of inevitable ruin, back to the constitutional ground of peace and safety from which they have been seduced by the phantom of Independency! Let them in time renounce this folly, and return to their allegiance. The King, with paternal goodness, will rejoice to see them rescued from destruction; the mother country is ready with open arms to receive them, on generous terms of reconciliation, to her wonted affectionate protection, and to that mutual reciprocation of kind offices, by which the two countries have heretofore been, and may be again, for ages to come, able to bid defiance to the envy or ambition of all the world!

An American Loyalist: "Standing on a Precipice"

This essayist urges Americans to back out of independence before it is too late. Great Britain is the greatest protector of freedom in the world, and to leave that protection would be foolhardy, dangerous, and result in the ruin of the colonies. His use of the term felo de se, *which means the act of deliberate self-destruction, clearly shows his opinion of the idea of independence.*

Royal Gazette **(New York), 21 October 1780**

You ought to consider yourselves as standing on a precipice;—on one side certain ruin attends you—from the other, a safe retreat may yet be made. The improbability of your finally succeeding in this arduous enterprize, ought at least, to suggest to you lessons of prudence. But when you see it clear, as you certainly must, that victory will be the heaviest curse that angry heaven could inflict upon you while in this world, still to persist in the pursuit, would make you guilty FELO DE SE, you would become proscribers of your own liberties. I know this war has been called a cruel one on the part of Great Britain by her numerous libellants: the measures that have been taken by his Majesty to recall you from the despotism of democratical phrenzy, to the enjoyment of the blessings of rational government, you have wrongly ascribed, or rather you have been taught to ascribe, to the result of sanguinary councils, and a desire of treating you as conquered subjects. You have been told, and it will probably be repeated, because it is consistent with their wicked plans to assert it, that the conciliatory overture made by the Crown was delusive, and ought to be considered only as a mask to cover the real views of the Court.—There is no guarding against the malignant suggestions of a corrupt heart; you have no better way of judging of the sincerity of the British nation now, than to take a short retrospect of her former conduct on different occasions: you have seen her all along the uniform defender of the Protestant Faith, both at home and abroad. She has been always employed as lowering the crest of dangerous ambition, and rescuing her oppressed neighbours; how many millions has she expended, and how much blood has she spilt in contests, where she could gain nothing but the satisfaction of having done good.—She has been long looked upon by the jealous eye of despotism, as the scourge of guilty ambition, a rod to chastise the violations of public faith, and the faithful guardian of injured freedom; and this scourge you are aiming to destroy, that the crimson triumph of ambition may be complete.

Anonymous: "When in the Course of Human Events"

In what has to be the ultimate attack on the idea of independence, an anonymous essayist uses the form of the Declaration of Independence to attack the Continental Congress. He accuses its delegates of being tyrants in the same way that they had accused George III five years earlier. Since the battle of Yorktown had occurred in October of 1781, the Revolution was basically over. However, the appearance of this piece clearly shows that some people still hesitated to believe that independence was the answer and that the United States really should sever forever the bonds that tied them to Great Britain.

South Carolina Royal Gazette (Charleston), 22 December 1781

When in the course of human events it becomes necessary for men, in order to preserve their lives, liberties and properties, and to secure to themselves, and to their posterity, that peace, liberty and safety, to which by the laws of nature and nature's God they are entitled, to throw off and renounce all allegiance to a government, which under the insidious pretences of securing those inestimable blessings to them, has wholly deprived them of any security of either life, liberty, prosperity, peace or safety; a decent respect to the opinions of mankind, requires that they should declare, the injuries and oppressions, the arbitrary and dangerous proceedings, which impel them to transfer their allegiance from such their oppressors, to those who have offered to become their protectors.

We hold these truths to be self evident, that all men are created equal; that they are endowed by their Creator with certain rights, that among those, are life, liberty, and the pursuit of happiness; that to secure those rights, governments are instituted; that whenever any form of government becomes destructive of these ends, it is the right of the people to alter or abolish it, or to renounce all allegiance to it, and to put themselves under such other government, as to them shall appear best calculated and most likely to effect their safety and happiness; it is not indeed prudent to change for light and transient causes and experience hath ever shown, that men are disposed to suffer much before they can bring themselves to make a change of government; but when a long train of the most licentious and despotic abuses, pursuing invariably the same objects, evinces a design to reduce them under anarchy, and the distractions of democracy, and finally to force them to submit to absolute despotism, it is their right, it becomes their duty, to disclaim and renounce all the allegiance to such government, and to provide new guards for their future security.

Such has been our patient sufferings, and such is now the necessity which constrains us to renounce all allegiance to Congress, or to the governments lately established by their direction.

The history of Congress, is a history of continued weakness, inconsistency, violation of the most sacred obligations of all public faith and honor, and of usurpation, all having in direct object the producing of anarchy, civil feuds, and violent injustice, which have rendered us miserable, and must soon establish tyranny over us and our country.

To prove this let facts be submitted to the candid world.

They have recommended and caused laws to be passed, the most destructive of the public good, and ruinous to individuals.

Availing themselves of our zeal and unanimity to oppose the claims of the British Parliament, and of our unsuspecting confidence in their solemn professions and declarations, they have forbidden us to listen to, or to accept any terms of peace, until their assent should be obtained.

They have refused to accept of, or even to receive proposals and terms of accommodation and peace, though they knew the terms offered exceeded what the Colonies in America had unanimously declared would be satisfactory, unless the Crown would relinquish a right inestimable to it and the whole empire, and formidable to Congress only.

They have excited and directed the people to alter or annul their ancient constitutions, under which, they and their ancestors, had been happy from many ages, for the sole purpose of promoting their measures.

They have by mobs and riots awed Representative Houses, repeatedly into a compliance with their revolutions, though destructive of the peace, liberty and safety of the people.

They have by their misconduct, reduced us to all the dangers and distress of actual invasion from without, and to all the horrors of a cruel war within.

They have not only prevented the increase of the population of these states, but by fines, imprisoning and banishments, with the losses by war, they have caused a rapid depopulation.

They have corrupted all the sources of justice and equity by their Tender Law, by which they destroyed the legal force of all civil contracts, wronged the honest creditor, and deserving salary man of his just dues, stripped the helpless orphan of his patrimony, and the disconsolate widow of her dower.

They have enacted a multitude of new offices, and have filled them with men from their own body, or with their creatures and dependents, to eat out the substance of the people; they have made their officers dependent on their will for the tenure of their offices, and the payment of their salaries.

They have raised a standing army and sent it into the field, without any act of legislature, and have actually rendered it independent of the civil power, by making it solely dependent on them.

They have combined with France, the natural and hereditary enemy of our civil constitution, and religious faith, to render us dependent on and subservient to the views, of that foreign, ambitious and despotic monarchy.

They have suffered their troops to live repeatedly on free quarters on the inhabitants, and to strip them by force of the necessaries of life, and have protected them from either trial or punishment under the plea of necessity, which necessity if real, was caused by their treacherous views, or unpardonable negligence.

They have ruined our trade, and destroyed our credit with all parts of the world.

They have forced us to receive their paper, for goods, merchandize, and for money due to us, equal to silver and gold, and then by a breach of public faith in not redeeming the same, and by a most infamous bankruptcy, have left it in our hands, to the total ruin of multitudes, and to the injury of all.

They have driven many of our people beyond sea, into exile, and have confiscated their estates, and the estates of others who were beyond sea before the war, or the existence of Congress, on the pretence of offences, and under the sanction of a mock trial, to which the person condemned was neither cited nor present.

They have abolished the true system of the English constitution and laws, in thirteen of the American Provinces, and established therein a weak and factious democracy, and have attempted to use them as introducing the same misrule and disorder into all the Colonies on the continent.

They have recommended the annihilating of our charters, abolishing many of our most valuable laws, and the altering fundamentally the form of our government.

They have destroyed all good order and government, by plunging us into the factions of democracy, and the ravages of civil war.

They have left our seas unprotected, suffered our coasts to be ravaged, our towns to be burnt, some of them by their own troops and the lives of our people destroyed.

They have without the consent or knowledge of the legislatures, invited over an army of foreign mercenaries to support them and their faction, and to prevent the dreadful scenes of death and desolation from being closed by an honorable peace and accommodation with our ancient friend and parent.

They have fined, imprisoned, banished and put to death some of our fellow citizens, for no other cause but their attachment to the English laws and constitution.

They have countenanced domestic tumults and disorders in our capital cities, and have suffered the murder of a number of our fellow citizens perpetrated under their eyes in Philadelphia to pass unnoticed.

They first attempted to gain the savage and merciless Indians to their side, but failing in making them the presents promised and expected, have occasioned an undistinguished destruction to ages, sexes and conditions on our frontiers.

They have involved us in an immense debt, foreign as well as internal, and did put the best port and inland on our continent into the hands of the foreigners, who are their creditors.

They have wantonly violated our public faith and honor, and destroyed all grounds for private confidence, or the security of private property, have not blushed to act in direct contradiction to their most solemn declaration, and to render the people under their government, a reproach and bye word among the nations.

In every stage of these proceedings, they have not been wanting to throw out before us, specious excuses for their conduct, as being the result of necessity, and tending to the public good.—In every stage since their public conduct began to contradict their public declarations, our minds have been overwhelmed with apprehensions; and as our sufferings have increased, our tears have flowed in secret. It has been dangerous and even criminal to lament our situation in public. The unsuspecting confidence which we with our fellow citizens reposed in the Congress of 1774, the unanimous applause with which their patriotism and firmness were crowned, for having stood forth, as the champions of our rights, founded on the English constitution; at the same time that it gave to Congress the unanimous support of the whole continent, inspired their successors with very different ideas, and emboldened them by degrees to pursue measures, directly and the reverse of those before adopted, and were recommended, as the only just, constitutional and safe.—Congress in 1774, reprobated every idea of a separation from Great Britain, and declared that they looked on such an event as the greatest of evils.—They declared that a repeal of certain acts, complained of, would restore our ancient peace and harmony—That they *asked but for peace, liberty and safety— That they wished not for a dimunition of the royal prerogative, nor did they solicit the grant of any new right.* And they pledged themselves in the presence of Almighty God, that they *will ever carefully and zealously endeavor to support and maintain the royal authority of Great Britain over us, and our connection with Great Britain; and our councils had been influenced only by the dread of impending destruction.*

The acts complained of have been repealed, yet how have Congress given the lie, to these their most solemn professions! In 1774, they declared themselves concerned for the honor of Almighty God, whose pure and holy religion, our enemies were undermining—They pointed out those enemies, and the danger in which our holy religion was by their complaints of the establishment of the Roman Catholic religion in Canada; they say, "It is a religion which has deluged the Island of Great Britain with blood, and dispersed impiety, persecution, murder, and rebellion through every part of the world." We find the present Congress not only claiming a new right, and hazarding every thing valuable in life, to the present and future generations in support of it; but we also find them, leagued with the eldest son of these bloody, impious, biggotted and persecuting church, to ruin the nation from whose loins we sprung, and which has ever been the principal bulwark in Europe, against the encroachments and tyranny of that Church, and of the kingdoms devoted to her: we think it not too severe to say, that we find them as intoxicated with ambition of independent sovereignty, as that execrable Roman daughter, who drove the wheels of her chariot over the mangled body of her murdered father, in her way to the capitol.

We find that all their fears and apprehensions from the Roman Catholic religion in Canada, have vanished, or sunk to nothing, when put in competition with their political views, and that they have attempted to seduce the Canadians to their side, by promises of still greater religious establishments;

and to show that they were in earnest, have countenanced this impious religion by attending its ceremonies and worship in a body—We find them at one time boasting of their patriotic and religious ancestors, who braved every danger of unknown seas, and coasts, to preserve civil and religious freedom, and who chose rather to become exiles, and suffer every misery that must await them, on a savage and unexplored coast, than submit to civil, but above all religious innovations—at another time we find them destroying the British Constitution, the pride of their ancestors, and encouraging a religion which they held in abhorrence, as idolatrous and tyrannical.—we find them contending for liberty of speech and at the same time controlling the press, by means of a mob, and persecuting every one who ventures to hint his disapprobation of their proceedings.

We find them declaring in September 1779, that to pay off their paper money, at less than its nominal value, would be an unpardonable sin, and execrable deed. "That a faithless bankrupt republic would be a novelty in the political world, and appear like a common prostitute among chaste and reputable matrons," would be, "a reproach and a bye word among the nations, &c."

We find the same Congress in March following, liquidating their paper debt at 2 1/2 per cent. or 6d. in the pound.

We should fill volumes, were we to recite at large their inconsistency, usurpations, weaknesses and violations of the most sacred obligations—We content ourselves with the above brief recital of facts known to the world and attested by their own records.

We have sufficiently shown that a government thus marked and distinguished from every other, either despotic or democratic, by the enormity of its excesses, injustice and infamy, is unfit to rule a free people.

We therefore, Natives and Citizens of America, appealing to the impartial world to judge of the justice of our cause, but above all to the supreme Judge of the World for the rectitude of our intentions, do renounce and disclaim all allegiance, duty, or submission to the Congress, or to any government under them and declare that the United Colonies or States, so called, neither are, nor of right ought to be independent of the crown of Great Britain, or unconnected with that empire; but that we do firmly believe and maintain "*That the Royal Authority of the Crown of Great Britain over us and our connection with that kingdom ought to be preserved and maintained,* and that we will *zealously endeavor to support and maintain the same;*" and in the support of this Declaration, with a firm reliance on the protection of Divine Providence, we mutually pledge to each other, and to the crown and empire of Great Britain, our lives, our fortunes, and our sacred honor.

SUPPORT FOR INDEPENDENCE

An Anonymous Poet: "An Ode"

*Poetry often appeared in the newspapers of the eighteenth century. It enter-
tained by poking fun at various things or by praising successes. This poem,
written shortly after independence was declared, praises the future possibilities for the colonies now that they have become free states. The poet urges
the people to pray that God bless their endeavors and give them ultimate
victory in the fight against Great Britain. The poet imitates the style of
Alexander Martin, a graduate of the College of New Jersey (now Princeton
University), who had written a poem entitled "America" in 1769. Martin
served in the Revolutionary War and the Constitutional Convention and
went on to serve as governor and United States Senator for North Carolina. In several places, the poet uses* it's *where modern writers would use*
its. *This reflects the lack of standardization in English during the eighteenth century.*

Virginia Gazette **(Dixon and Hunter—Williamsburg),
24 August 1776**

An ODE, In imitation of one written in the year 1769, by Alexander Martin, Esq; of North Carolina.

I.
FREE STATES, attend the song,
Now independent on
    The British throne:
To earth's remotest bound
Echoing skies resound
The sweet melodious sound—
    LIBERTY's our own.

II.
Virginia's fields unfold,
Where our great fathers bold
    Intrepid stood:
On what embattled plain
The ever glorious train
Pil'd hills of Indians stain—
    Pour'd seas of blood.

III.

Such our free State now shines,
Worthy the wreath that binds
      It's awful brows:
It each true Whig now warms
With those resplendent charms,
It's inward greatness forms—
      Confound it's foes.

IV.

Let haughty Britons feel
It's dread victorious steel
      Make them to fall:
Crush all the tyrant's crew,
Dogs that our lives pursue;
Washington them subdue—
      Conquer them all.

V.

GOD bless the COMMONWEALTH,
May it increase in strength,
      It's foes annoy.
That George is now no more
King of this fertile shore,
From whence he drew his store,
      Completes our joy.

VI.

GOD save great WASHINGTON,
Virginia's warlike son,
      And make him brave.
Defend him from the blows
Of Howe, and all his foes,
Guard him where'er he goes—
      WASHINGTON save.

VII.

Let now the sounding prayer
Re-pierce the yielding ear,
      Through the Heav'ns ring:
O Lord! who councils sway,
In this momentous day,
Direct our Gen'ral's way—
      Convert the King.

VIII.

Arise, O GOD! arise,
Scatter our enemies,

And let them fall.
May impious battles cease;
Grant us eternal peace,
And make thy cause increase—
    GOD SAVE US ALL.

Anonymous: "His Majesty's Loyal and Faithful Subjects"

When the Continental Congress met in Philadelphia, only thirteen of Great Britain's mainland colonies attended. For various reasons, two chose not to get involved. The colony of Quebec, conquered from France in 1763, consisted primarily of Frenchmen who had little in common with the colonists along the Atlantic seaboard. The colony of Nova Scotia, however, had been settled by large numbers of people moving from New England. This news report from Halifax reflects the potential impact of the Declaration of Independence on the people of Nova Scotia.

Pennsylvania Gazette (Philadelphia), 25 September 1776

The Governor of Halifax received the Declaration of Independency, about four weeks since, but would not permit the poor dupe of a printer (had he ever so good a mind) to publish any more of it than barely the last clause, where it says; 'We therefore, the Representatives of the United States of America in General Congress assembled, Do, &c. &c.' And his reason (as we are credibly informed) was 'because it may gain over to them (the rebels) many converts; and inflame the minds of his Majesty's *loyal* and *faithful* subjects of the province of Nova-Scotia.'

Isaiah Thomas: "We Hope It Is True"

Isaiah Thomas published the Massachusetts Spy *in Worcester, Massachusetts. One of the first to report on the battles of Lexington and Concord, Thomas strongly believed that the colonies needed to break away from the political control of Great Britain. Hence, he rejoiced when word reached him that the Continental Congress had declared independence.*

Massachusetts Spy (Worcester), 10 July 1776

It is reported that the Honorable Continental Congress have declared the American colonies INDEPENDENT of that Monster of imperious domination and cruelty—Great Britain! Which we hope is true.

Anonymous: "True Friends to Liberty"

Once the Declaration of Independence was adopted, public celebrations took place throughout the colonies. The one described here took place in New York, where people rejoiced over their independence and destroyed the symbols of the British tyrant.

Virginia Gazette (Dixon and Hunter—Williamsburg), 10 August 1776

Thursday the Declaration of the Independency of the United States of America was published at the courthouse, where a number of people, true friends to the rights and liberties of this country, attended, and signified their approbation to it by loud acclamations. After which the coat of arms of his Majesty George III was torn to pieces and burnt in the presence of the spectators.

John Dixon and William Hunter: "That Grand Occasion"

In Williamsburg, Virginia, the first public celebration of independence was held as part of the regularly scheduled court day, when large numbers of people would be in town taking care of legal business. The co-printers of the Virginia Gazette *described the celebration. The great emphasis placed on the "decorum" of the celebration was intended to show that a revolution was not automatically an event of horror and bloodshed.*

Virginia Gazette (Williamsburg), 10 August 1776

On Monday last, being court day, the Declaration of Independence was publicly proclaimed in the town of Richmond, before a large concourse of respectable freeholders of Henrico county, and upwards of 100 of the militia, who assembled on that grand occasion. It was received with universal shouts of joy, and re-echoed by three vollies of small arms. The same evening the town was illuminated, and the members of the committee held a club, when many patriotic toasts were drank. Although there were near 1000 people present, the whole was conducted with the utmost decorum, and the satisfaction visible in every countenance sufficiently evinces their determination to support it with their lives and fortunes.

Anonymous: "We Are a People"

Public celebrations of independence also took place among the troops. The stories written about these events generally emphasized the joy of the troops and their readiness to win the war. This piece also indicates the importance of the official vote for independence because many people saw it as the means of gaining a national identity—"Now we are a people!"

Pennsylvania Evening Post (Philadelphia), 15 August 1776

We hear from Ticonderoga, that on the 28th of July, immediately after divine worship, the Declaration of Independence was read by Col. St. Clair, and having said, 'God save the Free Independent States of America!' the army manifested their joy with three cheers. It was remarkably pleasing to see the spirits of the soldiers so raised after all their calamities; the language of every man's countenance was, Now we are a people! we have a name among the states of this world.

William and David Hall and William Sellers: "Anniversary of Independence"

The Fourth of July quickly became an important holiday in the United States. Public celebrations first started in 1776 and have continued since then. This celebration in Philadelphia described by these two printers marked the first full year of independence and once more emphasized the solemnity and decorum of the festivities. A feux de joie *(correctly spelled* feu de joie*) was a salute fired by rifles in rapid succession along a line of troops in order to celebrate a victory. It was a common part of public celebrations during the eighteenth century.*

Pennsylvania Gazette (Philadelphia), 9 July 1777

Friday, the 4th of July inst. being the Anniversary of the Independence of the United States of America, was celebrated in this city with demonstrations of joy and festivity. About noon all the armed ships and gallies in the river were drawn up before the city, dressed in the gayest manner, with the colours of the United States and streamers displayed. At one o'clock, the yards being properly manned, they began the celebration of the day by a discharge of thirteen cannon from each of the ships, and one from each of the thirteen gallies, in honour of the thirteen United States. In the afternoon an elegant dinner was prepared for Congress, to which were invited the President and Supreme Executive Council, and Speaker of the Assembly of this State, the General Officers and Colonels of the army, and strangers of eminence, and the Members of the several Continental Boards in town. The Hessian band of music, taken in Trenton the 26th of December last, attended, and heightened the festivity with some fine performances suited to the joyous occasion, while a corps of British deserters, taken into the service of the continent by the state of Georgia, being drawn up before the door, filled up the intervals with feux de joie. After dinner a number of toasts were drank, all breathing independence, and a generous love of liberty, and commemorating the memories of those brave and worthy patriots who gallantly exposed their lives, and fell gloriously in defence of freedom and the righteous cause of their country.

Each toast was followed by a discharge of artillery and small arms, and a suitable piece of music by the Hessian band.

The glorious fourth of July was reiterated three times, accompanied with triple discharges of cannon and small arms, and loud huzzas that resounded from street to street through the city. Towards evening several troops of horse, a corps of artillery, and a brigade of North Carolina forces, which was in town on its way to join the grand army were drawn in Second-street, and received by Congress and the General Officers. The evening was closed with the ringing of bells, and at night there was a grand exhibition of fireworks (which began and concluded with thirteen rockets) on the commons, and the city was beautifully illuminated. Everything was conducted with the greatest order and decorum, and the face of joy and gladness was universal.

John Parke: "The Poison of Your Precepts"

In 1778, the former chaplain of the Continental Congress, Jacob Duché, wrote to George Washington to try and convince him that American independence could not be won militarily. When word of this letter leaked out, people reacted in horror at such an idea. John Parke, a colonel in the Continental army, publicly responded to Duché's suggestion in this letter.

Maryland Journal and Baltimore Advertiser, 24 February 1778

Sir,

Lest the poison of your precepts should mislead the ignorant and credulous, or corrupt the honest, I have ventured, with much deference to abler pens, to make a few observations on some of the most remarkable passages in your celebrated letter to his Excellency our Commander in Chief.

Great pain and many words have been used to palliate your former conduct, and reconcile it with the part you now act;—you have found it an Herculean labor, and it still rests in the same place where you began. That the grass is green, is self-evident; that the sun shines, needs no demonstration; and that you have acted the most base and treacherous part, is a truth that wants no proof. As well might you attempt to reconcile jarring elements, as to dupe us into a belief of the integrity of your heart. "You wished to follow your countrymen as far *only as virtue* and *the righteousness* of their cause would permit you;" that is to say, as far as your interest and safety were concerned, then you was their man: But by forsaking us at this time, it would lead us to infer, that with you, every principle of virtue and humanity have likewise abandoned us. You shudder at the idea of an independency, and yet suffered Mr. Hancock "who has nothing but a soft middle address to atone for his want of every other qualification necessary for the station he fills."—*Redemptum nulla virtute a vittiis*[2]—I say you suffered this *cypher* of a man to attack you by surprize with a commission and dub you a chaplain. 'Tis true, you say you was much distressed, but *quarenda pecunia primum est, virtus post nummos*[3]—your conscience afterwards became easy, and your pockets were lined: At the *same* time you insinuate that you utterly depre-cated *such* service; being inconsistent with your new-adopted faith of ab-solute submission and non-resistance. This danger of the episcopal church, lest it should fall into anarchy, by absurdity praying for the tyrant we op-pose, is one specious reason for your lapses; and to prevent that misfortune, you adopted a conduct which you *now* confess your sentiments reprobated at *that* very time. But perhaps you may be one of those who believe, "that it is lawful to do *evil,* that *good* may come of it."

How often, with pleasure, have I heard you declaim on the blessings of liberty, the horrors of a despotic government, and exhorting us to firmness and unanimity! But, alas! little did I then think you "spoke a language for-eign to your heart," and that your soul was all deceit and treachery. Your good sense and sound judgment were not proof against the popular torrent and the violence of party, so as a lamb to the slaughter you were borne down by the general voice.

Like all young sinners, you soon became familiar with vice, and *reluc-tantly* preached a sermon to one of the city battalions, encouraging them to stand fast in their opposition. You afterwards became well acquainted with that *monster* independency, and seem never to have discovered its Gorgon head till we had been defeated on Long-Island, lost the city of New-York, and our affairs in that State wore a melancholy aspect. These circumstances, I say, (truly terrifying to little minds) determined you at once to get out of the *supposed* scrape as well as you could; you were conscious at the same time, how fatal such an inconsistent step would be to your character as a man of virtue, as a man of honour, and therefore cautiously concealed the reasons of your resignation from the candid public, till, like a true pol-troon,[4] you sheltered yourself under the arm of that very power which from the sacred pulpit, you exhorted us to oppose. It is needless to prove the ne-cessity of that *definitive* measure, which you hold forth as the chief cause of your defection, it having been often and wisely demonstrated, but only to mention it as far as it interferes with your apology. You considered it as a bugbear,[5] "held up in terrorem to frighten our oppressors into *some* terms, but not as a measure to be persisted in at all events;" that is to say, if military parade and threats were not sufficient to intimidate this foe, to concede those privileges which you have *often acknowledged* to be our *just* and *natural* rights, and which no powers ought to divest us of—then to sit down patiently, bow the neck to the yoke, and bare the shoulders to the lash. "This, indeed, is a splendid maxim in theory," but the experiment applies so strongly to the senses, that even you, Sir, have not Stoicism[6] to reduce it to practice.

I pass by your remarks on the result of the conference between Lord Howe, his Britannick Majesty's Commissioner, and the Committee of Congress, not being conclusive arguments against the necessity of independency.

"All the world," you say, "are convinced that the illustrious personage to whom you write, is engaged in the Service of his country from motives perfectly disinterested." It is a catholic faith, that no action can be praiseworthy, whose principles are unjust and cruel, and which is not only *malum in se,*[7] but practiced to obtain the most villainous and pernicious ends. On the other hand, it is acknowledged by you, for yourself and the whole world, that *he* is engaged to *serve* his country, and that from the most laudable motives; how then can you be so inconsistent, after such declaration, to dissuade from that honourable service? To bring ruin and destruction on our country, or to suffer others to do it, cannot certainly be called *saving it;* but an opposite conduct implies benefits, favours, and every good gift that can be conferred, and which at this very time you amply confess, are the motives of action in the Personage to whom you write.

"But," you again say, "could you have had the least idea of matters being carried to such a dangerous extremity as they are now?" Or in words tantamount, Had you any prospect of the hardships of war, of marching and counter-marching, cold and heat, wet and dry, hunger and thirst; but above all, of coming to battle? I myself, one of your *most* intimate acquaintances, who have known you near twenty years, could not believe you would have persisted. And now to prove, that from the measure of independency has flowed a degeneracy of representation, confusion of councils, and numberless blunders; that the most worthy characters have withdrawn, and are succeeded by fools and madmen, we have your ample testimony: And who had a better opportunity of knowing the characters of those Gentlemen, than their own Chaplain, after preaching up Liberty for two months and three weeks to them?

No candid person can believe, from the general tenor of your letter, you ever meant it should have the effect proposed, otherwise you would not have begun with such illiberal, false, ungentleman-like aspersions on the greatest body politick in America, the *only* power which could bring about that important change for which you solicit. The first who met the fire of your pen, are the Delegates from Virginia.—You recapitulate the virtues of the *deceased* and superannuated, or persons who, after long and faithful services, had retired to manage their private affairs, which had suffered by their absence, or to be more immediately aiding the public business of their own States: I say, some of these aforesaid causes affect every Gentleman whom you have thought proper to discriminate from the rest, and daub with fulsome adulation.–Even the members of your own State or the catholic Carroll, do not hold you in a more contemptible view than those very men who have been the subjects of your flattery. In the New-England States it is well known, even by our enemies, that the general voice is for supporting our independency at all events; those people being unanimous, their elections cannot be called the result of a low faction. Certainly then, under such circumstances, men of virtue and property, men of wisdom and experience, would be chosen to represent them—men, who having the real interest of their country at heart, would be the properest guardians of their rights and privileges. That the Congress have lost their influence the following circumstances will prove to be false–The paper currency circulates freely under their credit, the camp is stored with every necessary; their troops have taken one powerful army, and strongly blockaded the other—These are facts among thousands, that give the lye to your assertions.

Notwithstanding our illustrious General is the idol of his army, and though by his death or captivity we should experience a most heavy and sensible loss; yet the principles upon which we have taken up arms, are such as indissolubly cement, our interests and consequently our powers. The merits of our cause are the same now as at first, only our opposition is more confirmed by accumulated injuries and aggravated insults. Be assured, we never mean to quit the field, to expose our country to the ravages of a foe, whose tender mercies are death and cruelty. Happy for America we have officers amongst us, who, by imitating the conduct of our great General, (if under the circumstances you mention) would arrive at such a military perfection, as might in a great measure supply so capital a loss.

To your bitter sarcasms on our army, I reply–That some of our men are, and all have been undisciplined, is a truth that needs no controverting, only that our opposition thereby becomes more glorious. True it also is, that we have sometimes given way before superior numbers and advantageous attacks; but our misfortunes, therefore, are not to be imputed to cowardice. No, Sir, every gentleman of candor in the British army must acknowledge that we are not cowards: Mr. Duché himself, was he not under the influence of fear, must acknowledge it. And though many of our officers are men who heretofore never shone in private life, more than in the character of honest citizens, or farmers; yet we have numbers who have held the most considerable posts in government, and highly respected as private Gentlemen, such whose names have often reached *your* ears, and whom you have not been ashamed to profess a friendship for, exclusive of those Gentlemen who surround his Excellency's person.

As to our little fleet, which you have already annihilated in idea; believe me, that does not form the nerves of our opposition. Your arguments against the probability of a French war, and the fine-spun anecdote of a certain speculative French trader, I purposely omit, leaving the event in the hands of all-revealing time, which doubtless we shall have no cause to be dissatisfied with. We do not court the friendship of England, its inhabitants have never done us any material services; on the contrary, they have voted ample supplies to hire foreigners to spill our blood unjustly: they never exerted themselves to effect; it was once in their power to have spared the lives of our butchered countrymen,—to have prevented the tears of many widows and orphans, now deprived of their dearest connections by a band of hireling Scotch and German ruffians. We know that the spirit of the whole nation is in full activity against us, and we have already experienced the effects of that *humane* spirit, which you say is united and determined. Some few noble patriotic souls are yet left in both Houses of Parliament, though you have the consummate assurance to say, they are without *character* and without *influence,* whose steady opposition has no other motive than despair, vengeance, and disappointment.—But America will ever have a grateful sense of their merits, in spite of the calumny of their and our enemies.

Since the Declaration of Independency, the ground of our contest is materially changed; and it is not rights and priviledges for which we now fight, but dominion and empire are the objects of both parties. Britain is endeavouring to reduce us to conquered provinces, and again to monopolize our trade. Why then this immense expence of blood and treasure? when you tell us that "new channels are continually opening, that will perhaps *more* than supply the loss of the old."—It is only changing the navigation from America to Europe, and the loss of our trade and manufactures will never be felt by England.

The whole navy of Great-Britain is not sufficient to block up all our harbours; and though fortresses are taken and battles lost, the victors have every reason to lament the conquest. Every day their army moulders away, whilst ours, like the Hydra, encreases two-fold; and notwithstanding they now possess our unfortunate capitol, I may justly cry out with you, "How unequal the contest! how fruitless the expence of blood!"

After recapitulating every discouragement calculated to terrify weak minds, like an able logician, you draw an inference as foreign from the premises, as probably you and I will be, before this letter reaches you. Ergo, "Under so many discouraging circumstances, can *virtue,* can *honour,* or the *love* of your *country,* prompt you to persevere? Humanity itself (and then a stroke of flattery) calls upon you to desist." The very idea of virtue implies difficulties and disappointments; was it not so, patriotism would degenerate into licentiousness, and liberty be of no real value.

True it is, that where-ever our army encamps, it becomes somewhat burthensome to the inhabitants of the vicinage: But observe the progress of the British spoilers—murder, rape, robbery, and burning, mark their footsteps—And though sometimes they may pursue, they as often shamefully retreat, and continue the devastation which they (not we) have begun.

Wisdom dictates a glorious and happy peace, and humanity wishes for it, but accommodation seems to imply dependence: A sacrifice which I am confident America will never make. You call upon his Excellency, in the name of the whole Continent, to make this destructive sacrifice, and to become "the *friend* and *guardian* of his country"—by *withdrawing* his protection.

As a full and conclusive answer to the two following paragraphs, I refer you to a serious perusal of Lord Chatham's speech in the House of Lords, June third, 1777.

That you did not write this letter under the eye, or immediate inspection of any British officer, or any person connected with the British army or ministry, is the only assertion in your whole performance which is believed; but that you wrote it at the instigation of some, and for the perusal and eclat[8] of all *such* persons, appears very evident. This is a master piece of casuistry,[9] and would do honour to the eldest son of St. Ignatius[10] himself.

After casting the foulest aspersions on Congress, scandalizing the officers and the army, and affronting His Excellency with the most villainous propositions, you say, "I would fain hope that I have said nothing by which your delicacy can in the least be hurt, if so, 'twas without intention, and your candour will lead you to forgive me." O most consummate assurance! You would not offend the meanest person on earth; I believe you, Sir—you *cannot* offend, your obscurity hides you, and your insignificance renders harmless the shafts of your malice.

I never before saw a discrimination between the love of truth, of peace, of our God, and the love of our country. The end of war is peace—'tis for that we are now contending. Peace promotes truth and Religion; your principles would annihilate both. 'Tis for our country we fight, for her we dare bleed——Religion and justice approve the conflict.

In fine, your whole performance is a rhapsody, without pathos to soften, or arguments to convince, and your last proposition is of such horrid, villainous nature, that I blush to think of it.

Indeed, Sir, I sincerely lament your departure from virtue, from honour, from your country which, alas! you have for-ever sold. This, perhaps, may be said in your excuse.——

Incenditque Animum Famae venientis Amore.[11]

But can riches, can fame, or *clerical* preferment repay you for a *lost* character & *prostituted* conscience? These shores, as well as your own reflections, will be forever hostile to you. You are now going to a country where you must flatter for a subsistance, and exist upon the smiles of the great. A miserable state of dependance and servility is the only prospect before you; and this is the eligible exchange you have made—O Tempora![12] O Mores![13]—Your talents will perhaps be exercised thereto as little purpose as here: You will ever be the contempt of honest men, and the tool of the high-priests and knaves in power.

I leave you in the hands of Heaven and a guilty conscience; and am your humble servant, JOHN PARKE, Lieut. Colonel.

Questions

1. Why would some people such as Pacificus and An American Loyalist consider independence to be a crazy idea?
2. Why did the anonymous writer from South Carolina use the form of the Declaration of Independence to protest the idea of independence? This piece is relatively unknown and has not been widely republished (unlike a later copying of the form of the Declaration by the Seneca Falls Women's Rights Convention in 1848). Why do you think this is so?
3. Why did the Governor of Halifax believe that the Declaration of Independence could have a big impact?
4. What characteristics did the various public celebrations of independence have in common? Why would these events be so similar in nature?
5. Why was there such a strong reaction against Jacob Duché's letter? What difference could one letter make? Why do you think Duché decided that independence was a bad idea?

Notes

1. "In terror," as a warning.
2. "Whose vices are not allayed with a single virtue." Juvenal *Satire* 4.
3. "Money is to be sought for first of all; virtue after wealth." Horace *Epistle* 1. 1, 53.
4. A mean-spirited wretch, a coward.
5. An object or source of dread or fear.

6. The principle or practice of showing indifference to pleasure or pain—impassiveness or repression of feeling.

7. An offense which is such from its very nature—part of the natural law rather than part of statutory law.

8. A public exposure.

9. False application of principles, especially in regard to law or morals.

10. Ignatius of Loyola, the founder of the Jesuits, an order of monks that tried to turn back the Reformation in Europe.

11. "Inspiring a love for future fame." Virgil *Aeneid* 6. 889.

12. Time.

13. Ethical customs and folkways that have the force of law.

CHAPTER 2

Wartime Morale, 1776–1781

The fighting in the American Revolution began on April 19, 1775, at the battles of Lexington and Concord in Massachusetts. The adoption of the Declaration of Independence in July 1776 may have justified the fighting, but it did not guarantee a military victory in the war. The colonies seemed to be facing an impossible situation. Great Britain had a population four times the size of the United States. It had one of the best armies in the world, and it was supplemented by hundreds of Hessians, hired mercenaries from central Europe. And Britain had the best navy in the world, which should have enabled it to blockade American ports and shut the United States off from contact with the rest of the world. In the eyes of many people, the chances for the colonials to win their independence seemed very slim.

But the colonials were optimistic and believed they could, and would, win. And, ultimately, they were right. Great Britain seemed to have the necessary pieces to win but could not put them all together for victory. Conducting a war across a 3,000-mile ocean was almost impossible. Coordinating supplies and battle plans was a nightmare when it took six to eight weeks for ships to travel from Europe to America. Also, the colonies had no center to conquer. One major city after another fell to the British, and the war continued.

Because of all these problems, the war dragged on and on. The fighting lasted more than six years, and it finally ended when the British grew too weary to continue. Because of the length of the war, one of the major concerns for both sides was keeping up morale, both of the military men and the general civilian population. Hence, newspapers carried numerous pieces that sought to boost the morale of one side while assuring their readers that the "enemy" was ready to give up.

VOL. VI. — NUMB. 268.

DUNLAP'S

Pennsylvania Packet

OR THE GENERAL ADVERTISER

FRIDAY, DECEMBER 27, 1776.

THE AMERICAN CRISIS. No. I.

THESE are the times that try mens souls: The summer soldier and the sunshine patriot will, in this crisis, shrink from the service of his country; but he that stands it NOW, deserves the love and thanks of man and woman. Tyranny, like hell, is not easily conquered; yet we have this consolation with us, that the harder the conflict, the more glorious the triumph. What we obtain too cheap, we esteem too lightly:—'Tis dearness only that gives every thing its value. Heaven knows how to set a proper price upon its goods; and it would be strange indeed, if so celestial an article as FREEDOM should not be highly rated. Britain, with an army to enforce her tyranny, has declared that she has a right (*not only to* TAX *but*) "*to* BIND *us in all cases whatsoever*," and if being *bound in that manner* is not slavery, then is there not such a thing as slavery upon earth. Even the expression is impious, for so unlimited a power can belong only to GOD.

Whether the Independence of the Continent was declared too soon, or delayed too long, I will not now enter into as an argument; my own simple opinion is that had it been eight months earlier it would have been much better. We did not make a proper use of last winter, neither could we, while we were in a dependent state.—However, the fault, if it were one, was all our own; we have none to blame but ourselves*. But no great deal is lost yet; all that Howe has been doing for this month past is rather a ravage than a conquest, which the spirit of the Jerseys a year ago would have quickly repulsed, and which time and a little resolution will soon recover.

I have as little superstition in me as any man living, but my secret opinion has ever been, and still is, that GOD Almighty will not give up a people to military destruction, or leave them unsupportedly to perish, who had so repeatedly and earnestly sought to avoid the calamities of war by every decent method which wisdom could invent. Neither have I so much of the infidel in me as to suppose, that he has relinquished the government of the world, and given us up to the care of Devils; and as I do not, I cannot see on what grounds the King of Britain can look up to Heaven for help against us: A common murderer, a highwayman, or a housebreaker, has as good a pretence as he.

'Tis surprising to see how rapidly a panic will sometimes run through a country. All nations and ages have been subject to them: Britain has trembled like an ague at the report of a French fleet of flat bottomed boats; and in the fourteenth century the whole English army, after ravaging the kingdom of France, was driven back like men petrified with fear; and this brave exploit was performed by a few broken forces collected and headed by a woman, Joan of Arc. Would that Heaven might inspire some Jersey Maid to spirit up her countrymen, and save her fair fellow sufferers from ravage and ravishment! Yet panics, in some cases, have their uses; they produce as much good as hurt. Their duration is always short; the mind soon grows thro' them, and acquires a firmer habit than before. But their peculiar advantage is, that they are the touchstones of sincerity and hypocrisy, and bring things and men to light, which might otherwise have lain for ever undiscovered. In fact, they have the same effect on secret traitors, which an imaginary apparition would upon a private murderer. They sift out the hidden thoughts of man, and hold them up in public to the world. Many a disguised Tory has lately shewn his head, that shall penitentially solemnize with curses the day on which Howe arrived upon the Delaware.

As I was with the troops at Fort Lee, and marched with them to the edge of Pennsylvania, I am well acquainted with many circumstances, which those, who lived at a distance, know but little or nothing of. Our situation there was exceedingly cramped, the place being on a narrow neck of land between the North river and the Hackensack. Our force was inconsiderable, being not one fourth so great as Howe could bring against us. We had no army at hand to have relieved the garrison, had we shut ourselves up and stood on the defensive. Our ammunition, light artillery, and the best part of our stores, had been removed upon the apprehension that Howe would endeavor to penetrate the Jerseys, in which case Fort Lee could be of no use to us; for it must occur to every thinking man, whether in the army or not, that these kind of field forts are only for temporary purposes, and last in use no longer than the enemy directs his force against the particular object, which such forts are raised to defend. Such was our situation and condition at Fort Lee on the morning of the 20th of November, when an officer arrived with information, that the enemy with 200 boats had landed about seven or eight miles above: Major General Green, who commanded the garrison, immediately ordered them under arms, and sent express to his Excellency General Washington at the town of Hackensack, distant by the way of the ferry six miles. Our first object was to secure the bridge over the Hackensack, which laid up the river between the enemy and us, about six miles from us and three from them. General Washington arrived in about three quarters of an hour, and marched at the head of the troops towards the bridge, which place I expected we should have a brush for; however they did not chuse to dispute it with us, and the greatest part of our troops went over the bridge, the rest over the ferry, except some which passed at a mill on a small creek, between the bridge and the ferry, and made their way through some marshy grounds up to the town of Hackensack, and there passed the river. We brought off as much baggage as the waggons could contain, the rest was lost. The simple object was to bring off the garrison, and to march them on till they could be strengthened by the Jersey or Pennsylvania militia, so as to be enabled to make a stand. We staid four days at Newark, collected in our out-posts with some of the Jersey militia, and marched out twice to meet the enemy on information of their being advancing, though our numbers were greatly inferior to theirs. Howe, in my little opinion, committed a great error in generalship, in not throwing a body of forces off from Staten-Island through Amboy, by which means he might have seized all our stores at Brunswick, and intercepted our march into Pennsylvania: But, if we believe the power of hell to be limited, we must likewise believe that their agents are under some providential controul.

I shall not now attempt to give all the particulars of our retreat to the Delaware; suffice it for the present to say, that both officers and men, though greatly harrassed and fatigued, frequently without rest, covering, or provision, the inevitable consequences of a long retreat, bore it with a manly and a martial spirit. All their wishes were one, which was, that the country would turn out and help them to drive the enemy back. Voltaire has remarked, that king William never appeared to full advantage but in difficulties and in action; the same remark may be made on General Washington, for the character fits him. There is a natural firmness in some minds which cannot be unlocked by trifles, but which, when unlocked, discovers a cabinet of fortitude; and I reckon it among those kind of public blessings, which we do not immediately see, that God hath blest him with uninterrupted health, and given him a mind that can even flourish upon care.

I shall conclude this paper with some miscellaneous remarks on the state of our affairs; and shall begin with asking the following question, why is it that the enemy hath left the New-England provinces, and made these middle ones the seat of war? The answer is easy: New-England is not infested with Tories, and we are. I have been tender in raising the cry against these men, and used numberless arguments to shew them their danger, but it will not do to sacrifice a world to either their folly or their baseness. The period is now arrived, in which either they or we must change our sentiments, or one or both must fall. And what is a Tory? Good GOD! what is he? I should not be afraid to go with an hundred Whigs against a thousand Tories, were they to attempt to get into arms. Every Tory is a coward, for a servile, slavish, self-interested fear is the foundation of Toryism; and a man under such influence, though he may be cruel, never can be brave.

But before the line of irrecoverable separation be drawn between us, let us reason the matter together: Your conduct is an invitation to the enemy, yet not one in a thousand of you has heart enough to join him. Howe is as much deceived by you as the American cause is injured by you. He expects you will all take up arms, and flock to his standard with muskets on your shoulders. Your opinions are of no use to him, unless you support him personally, for 'tis soldiers, and not Tories, that he wants.

I once felt all that kind of anger, which a man ought to feel, against the mean principles that are held by the Tories: A noted one, who kept a tavern at Amboy, was standing at his door with as pretty a child in his hand, about eight or nine years old, as most I ever saw, and after speaking his mind as freely as he thought was prudent, finished with this unfatherly expression, "*Well! give me peace in my day.*" Not a man lives on the continent but fully believes that a separation must some time or other finally take place, and a generous parent would have said "*If there must be trouble, let it be in my day, that my child may have peace*;" and this single reflection, well applied, is sufficient to awaken every man to duty. Not a place upon earth might be so happy as America. Her situation is remote from all the wrangling world, and she has nothing to do but to trade with them. A man may easily distinguish in himself between temper and principle, and I am as confident, as I am that GOD governs the world, that America will never be happy till she gets clear of foreign dominion. Wars, without ceasing, will break out till that period arrives, and the Continent must in the end be conqueror; for, though the flame of liberty may sometimes cease to shine, the coal can never expire.

[*To be continued.*]

* "*The present winter*" (*meaning the last*) "*is worth an age, if rightly employed, but if lost, or neglected, the whole Continent will partake of the evil; and there is no punishment that man does not deserve, be he who, or what, or where he will, that may be the means of sacrificing a season so precious and useful.*" COMMON SENSE.

TO BE SOLD,

THE TIME of a Dutch servant boy, who has nine years to serve.—Enquire of the Printer.

PHILADELPHIA, *December* 27.

Extract of a letter from an officer of distinction in the American Army.

"*Since I wrote you this morning, I have had an opportunity of hearing a number of the particulars of the horrid depredations committed by that part of the British army, which was stationed at and near Pennytown, under the command of Lord Cornwallis. Besides the sixteen young women who had fled to the woods to avoid their brutality, and were there seized and carried off, one man had the cruel mortification to have his wife and only daughter (a child of ten years of age) ravished; this he himself, almost choaked with grief, uttered in lamentations to his friend, who told me of it, and also informed me of another girl of thirteen years of age was taken from her father's house, carried to a barn about a mile, there ravished, and afterwards made use of by five more of these brutes. Numbers of instances of the same kind of behaviour I am assured of have happened: here their brutish lusts were their stimulus; but wanton mischief was seen in every part of the country; every thing portable they plunder and carry off, neither age nor sex, Whig or Tory, is spared; an indiscriminate ruin attends every person they meet with, infants, children, old men and women, are left in their shirts without a blanket to cover them in this inclement season; furniture of every kind destroyed or burnt, windows and doors broke to pieces; in short, the houses left unhabitable, and the people left without provisions, for every horse, cow, ox, hogs and poultry, carried off; a blind old gentleman near Pennytown plundered of every thing, and on his door wrote, 'Capt. Wills of the Royal Irish did this.' As a notable proof of their regard and favour to their friends and well wishers, they yesterday burnt the elegant house of Daniel Cox, Esq; at Trenton ferry, who has been their constant advocate, and supporter of toryism in that part of the country: this behaviour of theirs has so exasperated the people of the country, that they are flying to arms, and forming themselves into parties to way lay them and cut them off wherever they can meet with them: this, and other efforts which are making, I hope will so streighten them that they will soon find their situation very disagreeable in New-Jersey. Another instance of their brutality happened near Woodbridge: One of the most respectable gentlemen in that part of the country was alarmed by the cries and shrieks of a most lovely daughter; he found an officer, a British officer, in the act of ravishing her, he instantly put him to death; two other officers rushed in with fusees, and fired two balls into the father, who is now languishing under his wounds. I am tired of this horrid scene; Almighty Justice cannot suffer it to go unpunished: he will inspirit his people (who only claim that liberty which he has entitled them to) to do themselves justice, to rise universally in arms, and drive these invading tyrants out of our country.*"

Published by order of the Council of Safety.
GEO. BICKHAM, Secretary, pro. tem.

THIS *day is published, (price two coppers each, or one shilling and threepence per dozen)* THE AMERICAN CRISIS, No. I. *By the author of* Common Sense.
Printed and sold by STYNER and CIST, *in Second street, six doors above Arch street, Philadelphia.*

Princeton, N. Jersey, Dec. 5, 1776.

STOP THE ROBBERS!

One Hundred DOLLARS Reward.

LAST Tuesday three villains came to the house of Mr. Howel Furman, near Princeton, and, after abusing the family in a barbarous manner, took with them goods to the amount of between one and two hundred pounds, consisting of fifty of Germantown worsted stockings milled, of several colours, large pocket handkerchiefs of several kinds of red and blue stripes, bunting ditto, pins of the small kind, four dozen razors, one pair of four thread fine black worsted hose, black leather pocket books, pocket almanacks, a few pieces of childrens garters, and many other goods unknown.

One of the above rogues is an Irishman, a middle sized man, well set, has bushy sandy hair, and supposed to be marked with the small pox; had on a blue coat, his name is said to be WATSON, *and have been informed he belongs to Capt. Brown's company of Pennsylvania Riflemen, under Col. Brodhead. The second person I cannot describe. The third is a tall slim man, with light colored clothes. It is said they have already changed their clothes. They put the goods into bags or knapsacks. They were seen near the Baptist meeting house at Hopewell on Wednesday evening, but could not be taken for want of men of resolution, and 'tis supposed they are bound for Delaware, and so on to Shamokin. Whoever secures said goods and the men, so that they be convicted, shall have the above reward, or Fifty Dollars for the men, or in proportion for any of the men or part of the goods, by applying to Mr.* STACY POTTS, *at Trenton, or Mr.* WILLIAM WOODHOUSE, *in Philadelphia, or the subscriber in Princeton.* † JOHN DENTON.

"American Crisis #1." *Here is the first of a series of essays which Thomas Paine wrote to encourage Patriot morale. Note that it does not really stand out in any way from the rest of the materials printed on that page of the newspaper.*

The pieces boosting Patriot morale begin with a comment about the British withdrawal from Boston in March 1776. Following that is probably the most famous morale-booster of the war, Thomas Paine's first "Crisis" essay. The third piece calls on people to be firm in the face of loss because the causes of independence and freedom remain unchanged. The final piece praises the expanding abilities of the Continental army and its successes on the battlefield.

The pieces boosting Tory morale reflected similar ideas. Loyalist printers particularly liked to emphasize the number of desertions from the Continental army. The first four pieces reflect on this idea, using it to encourage Loyalist morale by pointing out how hopeless the Patriot cause truly was. The last essay, written by James Rivington, declared that the Patriot cause was not one worthy of fighting for and that more and more Americans were coming over to the Loyalist side as they realized the degradation and hopelessness of the American effort.

PATRIOT MORALE

Solomon Southwick: "A Terrible Panick"

The British army left Boston in March 1776 and went to New York. In this piece, Solomon Southwick, printer of the Newport Mercury, *stresses that the British left in a hurry for fear of further attacks from the Continental army surrounding the city.*

Newport Mercury (Rhode Island), 25 March 1776

We are assured that General Howe fled from Boston in such a terrible panick, that he left behind cannon and other military stores to the amount of sixty thousand pounds sterling; and that the whole gang of mandamus counsellors[1] and commissioners, with a number of other infamous Tory Traitors to their country, pushed off so horribly affrighted, that some left their wives and some their children, to the mercy of that people, the Yankies, whose destruction they had for many years been seeking!!

Common Sense (Thomas Paine): "The Crisis," #1

By the end of December 1776, the situation did not look good for the Continental army. Pushed out of New York and New Jersey, the Americans seemed to be facing utter defeat at the hands of the British. In writing the first of the "Crisis" essays, Thomas Paine (the author of Common Sense*)*

*sought to urge the army regulars, and American citizens in general, to keep
fighting because their cause was worthy and just. In some ways, his call for
dedication in "the times that try men's souls" worked. A week after this
essay first appeared in the newspapers, the Continental army won the Battle of Trenton, its first real military success since the adoption of the Declaration of Independence.*

Pennsylvania Journal (Philadelphia), 19 December 1776

These are the times that try men's souls. The summer soldier and the
sunshine Patriot will, in this crisis, shrink from the service of his country; but
he that stands it NOW deserves the love and thanks of man and woman.
Tyranny, like hell, is not easily conquered; yet we have this consolation with
us, that the harder the conflict, the more glorious the triumph. What we obtain too cheap, we esteem too lightly:—'Tis dearness only that gives every
thing its value. Heaven knows how to put a proper price upon its goods; and
it would be strange indeed, if so celestial an article as FREEDOM should
not be highly rated. Britain, with an army to enforce her tyranny, has declared that she has a right (not only to TAX) but "to BIND us in ALL CASES
WHATSOEVER," and if being bound in that manner, is not slavery, then is
there not such a thing as slavery upon earth. Even the expression is impious,
for so unlimited a power can belong only to God.

Whether the independence of the continent was declared too soon or
delayed too long I will not now enter into as an argument; my own simple
opinion is that, had it been eight months earlier, it would have been much
better. We did not make a proper use of last winter, neither could we while
we were in a dependent state. However, the fault, if it were one, was all our
own; we have none to blame but ourselves. But no great deal is lost yet. All
that Howe has been doing for this month past is rather a ravage than a conquest, which the spirit of the Jerseys, a year ago, would have quickly repulsed, and which time and a little resolution will soon recover.

I have as little superstition in me as any man living, but my secret opinion has ever been, and still is, that God Almighty will not give up a people to
military destruction, or leave them unsupportedly to perish, who have so
earnestly and so repeatedly sought to avoid the calamities of war, by every
decent method which wisdom could invent. Neither have I so much of the
infidel in me, as to suppose that He has relinquished the government of the
world, and given us up to the care of the devils; and as I do not, I cannot see
on what grounds the king of Britain can look up to heaven for help against
us: a common murderer, highwayman, or a housebreaker, has as good a pretense as he.

'Tis surprising how rapidly a panic will sometimes run through a country. All nations and ages have been subject to them. Britain has trembled

like an ague at the report of a French fleet of flat-bottomed boats, and in the fourteenth century the whole English army, after ravaging the kingdom of France, was driven back like men petrified with fear; and this brave exploit was performed by a few broken forces collected and headed by a woman, Joan of Arc. Would that heaven might inspire some Jersey maid to spirit up her countrymen and save her fair fellow sufferers from ravage and ravishment! Yet panics, in some cases, have their uses; they produce as much good as hurt. Their duration is always short; the mind soon grows through them and acquires a firmer habit than before. But their peculiar advantage is that they are the touchstones of sincerity and hypocrisy, and bring things and men to light which might otherwise have lain forever undiscovered. In fact, they have the same effect on secret traitors which an imaginary apparition would have upon a private murderer. They sift out the hidden thoughts of man and hold them up in public to the world. Many a disguised Tory has lately shown his head that shall penitentially solemnize with curses the day on which Howe arrived upon the Delaware.

As I was with the troops at Fort Lee, and marched with them to the edge of Pennsylvania, I am well acquainted with many circumstances, which those who live at a distance know but little or nothing of. Our situation there was exceedingly cramped, the place being a narrow neck of land between the North River and the Hackensack. Our force was inconsiderable, being not one fourth so great as Howe could bring against us. We had no army at hand to have relieved the garrison, had we shut ourselves up and stood on our defense. Our ammunition, light artillery, and the best part of our stores, had been removed, on the apprehension that Howe would endeavor to penetrate the Jerseys, in which case Fort Lee could be of no use to us; for it must occur to every thinking man, whether in the army or not, that these kind of field forts are only for temporary purposes, and last in use no longer than the enemy directs his force against the particular object, which such forts are raised to defend. Such was our situation and condition at Fort Lee on the morning of the 20th of November, when an officer arrived with information that the enemy with 200 boats had landed about seven miles above; Major General Greene, who commanded the garrison, immediately ordered them under arms, and sent express to General Washington at the town of Hackensack, distant by way of the ferry six miles. Our first object was to secure the bridge over the Hackensack, which laid up the river between the enemy and us, about six miles from us, and three from them. General Washington arrived in about three quarters of an hour, and marched at the head of the troops towards the bridge, which place I expected we should have a brush for; however they did not choose to dispute it with us, the greatest part of our troops went over the bridge, the rest over the ferry, except some which passed at a mill on a small creek, between the bridge and the ferry, and made their way through some marshy grounds up to the town of Hackensack, and there passed the river. We brought off as much baggage as the wagons could contain, the rest was lost. The simple object was to bring off the garrison, and march them on till they could be strengthened by the Jersey or Pennsylvania militia, so as to be enabled to make a stand. We stayed four days at Newark, collected our outposts with some of the Jersey militia, and marched out twice to meet the enemy, on being informed that they were advancing, though our numbers were greatly inferior to theirs. Howe, in my little opinion, committed a great error in generalship in not throwing a body of forces off the Staten Island through Amboy, by which means he might have seized all our stores at Brunswick, and intercepted our march into Pennsylvania: but if we believe the power of hell to be limited, we must likewise believe that their agents are under some providential control.

I shall not now attempt to give all the particulars of our retreat to the Delaware; suffice it for the present to say, that both officers and men, though greatly harassed and fatigued, frequently without rest, covering, or provision, the inevitable consequences of a long retreat, bore it with a manly and martial spirit. All their wishes centered in one, which was, that the country would turn out and help them to drive the enemy back. Voltaire has remarked that King William never appeared to full advantage but in difficulties and in action; the same remark may be made on General Washington, for the character fits him. There is a natural firmness in some minds which cannot be unlocked by trifles, but which, when unlocked, discovers a cabinet of fortitude; and I reckon it among those kind of public blessings, which we do not immediately see, that God hath blest him with uninterrupted health, and given him a mind that can even flourish upon care.

I shall conclude this paper with some miscellaneous remarks on the state of our affairs; and shall begin with asking the following question, Why is it that the enemy have left the New England provinces, and made these middle ones the seat of war? The answer is easy: New England is not infested with Tories, and we are. I have been tender in raising the cry against these men and used numberless arguments to show them their danger, but it will not do to sacrifice a world either to their folly or the baseness. The period is now arrived, in which either they or we must change our sentiments, or one or both must fall. And what is a Tory? Good God! what is he? I should not be afraid to go with an hundred Whigs against a thousand Tories, were they to attempt to get into arms. Every Tory is a coward; for servile, slavish, self-interested fear is the foundation of Toryism; and a man under such influence, though he may be cruel, never can be brave.

But, before the line of irrecoverable separation be drawn between us, let us reason the matter together: your conduct is an invitation to the enemy, yet not one in a thousand of you has heart enough to join him. Howe is as much deceived by you as the American cause is injured by you. He expects you will all take up arms, and flock to his standard with muskets on your shoulders. Your opinions are of no use to him, unless you support him personally, for 'tis soldiers, and not Tories, that he wants.

I once felt all that kind of anger, which a man ought to feel, against the mean principles that are held by the Tories: a noted one, who kept a tavern at Amboy, was standing at his door, with as pretty a child in his hand, about eight or nine years old, as I ever saw, and after speaking his mind as freely as he thought was prudent, finished with this fatherly expression, "Well! give me peace in my day." Not a man lives on the continent but fully believes that a separation must some time or other finally take place, and a generous parent should have said, "If there must be trouble, let it be in my day, that my child may have peace;" and this single reflection, well applied, is sufficient to awaken every man to duty. Not a place upon earth might be so happy as America. Her situation is remote from all the wrangling world, and she has nothing to do but to trade with them. A man can distinguish in himself between temper and principle, and I am as confident as I am that God governs the world that America will never be happy till she gets clear of foreign dominion. Wars, without ceasing, will break out till that period arrives, and the Continent must in the end be conqueror; for though the flame of liberty may sometimes cease to shine, the coal can never expire.

America did not nor does not want force, but she wanted a proper application of that force. Wisdom is not the purchase of a day, and it is no wonder that we should err at the first setting off. From an excess of tenderness, we were unwilling to raise an army and trusted our cause to the temporary defense of a well-meaning militia. A summer's experience has now taught us better; yet with those troops, while they were collected, we were able to set bounds to the progress of the enemy, and, thank God! they are again assembling. I always considered militia as the best troops in the world for a sudden exertion, but they will not do for a long campaign. Howe, it is probable, will make an attempt on this city; should he fail on this side of the Delaware, he is ruined. If he succeeds, our cause is not ruined. He stakes all on his side against a part on ours; admitting he succeeds, the consequence will be that armies from both ends of the continent will march to assist their suffering friends in the middle states; for he cannot go everywhere, it is impossible. I consider Howe as the greatest enemy the Tories have; he is bringing a war into their country, which, had it not been for him and partly for themselves, they had been clear of. Should he now be expelled, I wish with all the devotion of a Christian that the names of Whig and Tory may never more be mentioned; but should the Tories give him encouragement to come or assistance if he come, I as sincerely wish that our next year's arms may expel them from the continent, and the Congress appropriate their possessions to the relief of those who have suffered in well-doing. A single successful battle next year will settle the whole. America could carry on a two years' war by the confiscation of the property of disaffected persons and be made happy by their expulsion. Say not that this is revenge; call it rather the soft resentment of a suffering people who, having no object in view but the *good* of *all,* have staked their *own all* upon a seemingly doubtful event. Yet it is folly to argue against determined hardness; eloquence may strike the ear and the language of sorrow draw forth the tear of compassion, but nothing can reach the heart that is steeled with prejudice.

Quitting this class of men, I turn with the warm ardor of a friend to those who have nobly stood and are yet determined to stand the matter out; I call not upon a few but upon all—not on *this* state or *that* state, but on *every* state—up and help us, lay your shoulders to the wheel, better have too much force than too little when so great an object is at stake. Let it be told to the future world that in the depth of winter, when nothing but hope and virtue could survive, that the city and country, alarmed at one common danger, came forth to meet and to repulse it. Say not that thousands are gone, turn out your tens of thousands; throw not the burden of the day upon Providence, but "show your faith by your works," that God may bless you. It matters not where you live or what rank of life you hold, the evil or the blessing will reach you all. The far and the near, the home counties and the back, the rich and the poor will suffer or rejoice alike. The heart that feels not now is dead; the blood of his children will curse his cowardice who shrinks back at a time when a little might have saved the whole and made *them* happy. I love the man that can smile in trouble, that can gather strength from distress and grow brave by reflection. 'Tis the business of little minds to shrink, but he whose heart is firm and whose conscience approves his conduct will pursue his principles unto death. My own line of reasoning is to myself as straight and clear as a ray of light. Not all the treasures of the world, so far as I believe, could have induced me to support an offensive war, for I think it murder; but if a thief breaks into my house, burns and destroys my property, and kills or threatens to kill me or those that are in it and to "bind me in all cases whatsoever" to his absolute will, am I to suffer it? What signifies it to me whether he who does it is a king or a common man, my countryman or not my countryman; whether it be done by an individual villain or an army of them? If we reason to the root of things, we shall find no difference; neither can any just cause be assigned why we should punish in the one case and pardon in the other. Let them call me rebel and welcome, I feel no concern from it; but I should suffer the misery of devils were I to make a whore of my soul by swearing allegiance to one whose character is that of a sottish, stupid, stubborn, worthless, brutish man. I conceive likewise a horrid idea in receiving mercy from a being who, at the last day, shall be shrieking to the rocks and mountains to cover him and fleeing with terror from the orphan, the widow, and the slain of America.

There are cases which cannot be overdone by language, and this is one. There are persons, too, who see not the full extent of the evil which threatens them; they solace themselves with hopes that the enemy, if he succeed, will be merciful. It is the madness of folly to expect mercy from those who have refused to do justice; and even mercy, where conquest is the object, is only a trick of war; the cunning of the fox is as murderous as the violence of the wolf, and we ought to guard equally against both. Howe's first object is, partly by threats and partly by promises, to terrify or seduce the people to deliver up their arms and receive mercy. The ministry recommended the same plan to Gate, and this is what the Tories call making their peace, "a peace which passeth all understanding" *indeed.* A peace which would be the immediate forerunner of a worse ruin than any we have yet thought of. Ye men of Pennsylvania, do reason upon these things! Were the back counties to give up their arms, they would fall an easy prey to the Indians, who are all armed: this perhaps is what some Tories would not be sorry for. Were the home counties to deliver up their arms, they would be exposed to the resentment of the back counties, who would then have it in their power to chastise their defection at pleasure. And were any one state to give up its arms, *that* state must be garrisoned by all Howe's army of Britons and Hessians to preserve it from the anger of the rest. Mutual fear is the principal link in the chain of mutual love, and woe be to that state that breaks the compact. Howe is mercifully inviting you to barbarous destruction, and men must be either rogues or fools that will not see it. I dwell not upon the vapors of imagination; I bring reason to your ears and, in language as plain as A, B, C, hold up truth to your eyes.

I thank God that I fear not. I see no real cause for fear. I know our situation well and can see the way out of it. While our army was collected Howe dared not risk a battle, and it is no credit to him that he decamped from the White Plains and waited a mean opportunity to ravage the defenseless Jerseys; but it is a great credit to us that, with a handful of men, we sustained an orderly retreat for near a hundred miles, brought off our ammunition, all our field pieces, the greatest part of our stores, and had four rivers to pass. None can say that our retreat was precipitate, for we were near three weeks in performing it, that the country might have time to come in. Twice we marched back to meet the enemy and remained out till dark. The sign of fear was not seen in our camp; and had not some of the cowardly and disaffected inhabitants spread false alarms through the country, the Jerseys had never been ravaged. Once more we are again collected and collecting; our new army at both ends of the continent is recruiting fast, and we shall be able to open the next campaign with sixty thousand men, well armed and clothed. This is our situation, and who will may know it. By perseverance and fortitude we have the prospect of a glorious issue; by cowardice and submission, the sad choice of a variety of evils—a ravaged country, a depopulated city, habitations without safety and slavery without hope, our homes turned into barracks and bawdyhouses for Hessians, and a future race to provide for whose fathers we shall doubt of. Look on this picture and weep over it! and if there yet remains one thoughtless wretch who believes it not, let him suffer it unlamented.

A Countryman: "The Cause Is Still the Same"

By the summer of 1777, the military situation had not improved for the Americans. Boston had been evacuated, but New York had been occupied and it seemed that the British were poised to gain control of the middle colonies and split the United States in half. A Countryman reminds Americans that the cause they are fighting for is one worth dying for and that everyone should keep up the struggle until victory is achieved.

Providence Gazette (Rhode Island), 17 May 1777

Remember, my brethren, that the cause in which we are engaged is still the same—that the prize for which we contend has not diminished, but increased its value, in proportion to the losses we have sustained. Let us therefore unitedly resolve, with firm reliance on the goodness of Almighty God, that tyranny and oppression shall not enter and possess our land, till the body of the last freeman hath filled the breach.

Bennett Wheeler: "The Exemplary American Army"

One of the big problems facing the Americans was the fact that they had an untrained and unorganized army facing one of the best in the world. Almost from the beginning of the war, George Washington sought to train his men to become an acceptable fighting force by European standards. He was aided in this effort by Frederick William Augustus, Baron von Steuben, who began training the Continentals at Valley Forge in 1778. By 1779, as printer Bennett Wheeler notes, the Continental army could hold its own on the battlefield with the redcoats of Great Britain.

American Journal (Providence, Rhode Island), 16 December 1779

It is allowed on all hands that the American Army is now equal at least to any in the world for discipline, activity and bravery. There are no soldiers in Europe more exemplary for subordination, regularity of conduct, patience in fatigues and hardships, perseverance in service, and intrepidity in danger. To whatever quarter of the continent they belong, they are all animated with one spirit to honour and defend their country; are all equally and invincibly attached to their General, ready to follow him through every hazard and toil, and determined not to relinquish the glorious service in which he is engaged till it shall be happily compleated. This great man was born to give a consistency and cement to the military efforts of these states, in one of the most important and honorable causes that any nation was engaged in.

LOYALIST MORALE

Hugh Gaine: "His Majesty's Free Pardon"

One of the major ways in which Loyalist printers tried to boost the morale of their readers was through reports of numerous desertions from the Patriot forces, both civilian and military. Here, Hugh Gaine, a Loyalist printer in New York, reports about the large numbers of Americans who fled to the British lines in order to seek the King's pardon.

New York Gazette and Weekly Mercury, 30 December 1776

We hear, that many Thousands from the Provinces of New-York, New-Jersey, Connecticut, and Pennsylvania, have already come in and claimed the Benefit of the late Proclamation for His Majesty's free Pardon; and they bring Intelligence of great Numbers from various Parts of the above Colonies, who have expressed their Intentions of following them.

By a Gentleman just arrived from Philadelphia we learn, that but thirteen Members of the whole Congress, which originally consisted of above fifty, were to be found to carry on Business; that they had removed their Minutes and other Papers relative to their Proceedings, in four large Chests, towards the Back Country; and that the Quakers begin to speak openly of their Attachment to the British Constitution, in which they are joined by other loyal Subjects of the Province in great Numbers.

It is observable, that the Congress, in their last Declaration, have put a public Affront upon their once famous Leader Mr. *Washington*, by stating their whole Dependence upon Mr. *Lee,* who, we hear, they intended to have made their Commander in Chief.

One of the Delegates to the Congress from New-Jersey, we hear, has come in and claimed the Benefit of the last Proclamation.

Several other Persons, who have been principal Agitators in the present Troubles, have also obtained their free Pardon, upon signing the Declaration required by the Proclamation, and are restored to their Estates and Properties.

James Robertson: "Deserters"

As a Loyalist printer, James Robertson followed the British army from place to place, publishing newspapers in Philadelphia, Savannah, and Charleston. In this piece, he continues the emphasis on frequent desertions from the Patriot forces. He also points out that men were refusing to serve in the local militia if called up to fight the British. Such comments were designed to convince Loyalists that the Patriots would soon run out of fighting men.

Royal Pennsylvania Gazette (Philadelphia), 14 April 1778

Several deserters have come in during the last week; who agree in the same story, that a general uneasiness prevails in the rebel camp to the service, and that the new levies come in very slow. We learn also from Virginia and Maryland, that the people are very far from being disposed to turn out when drafted; many of the militia there have absolutely refused to go when so drawn.

James Robertson: "The Real Patriots"

James Robertson, in emphasizing the number of desertions from the Continental army, states there was a growing dissension because of concerns over whether the war could be won. The alliance with France would not really help change the outcome of the war, he argues, and so Loyalists should not be concerned.

Royal Pennsylvania Gazette (Philadelphia), 15 May 1778

Fifty deserters came in yesterday from Wilmington, who had address enough to deceive the rebels, and arrived in this city with safety.

Notwithstanding the expected confederacy with France, the utmost uneasiness prevails in the rebel camp, and the adjacent country. The real patriots despair now of an end of the war, from an apprehension that the same spirit that has hitherto animated and influenced the leaders, will prevent the endeavours of the real friends of their country from taking effect, as they perceive the same propagation of falsehood, and dissemination of error is still industriously kept up, to further delude their misguided adherents, and to involve them in inextricable distress. Upon the news of the supposed alliance arriving in the rebel camp, they celebrated it with as much pomp and magnificence as rebel opulence and taste could exhibit. The General gave a public entertainment to the choice spirits of sedition, and the whole was concluded with a preposterous parade of military arrangement.

James Robertson: "Anxious to Pay Their Respects to the Ragged Army"

Besides the continual discussions of desertions, Loyalist newspapers also often described the situation of the Continental army as dire because of a lack of supplies. Their situation was so bad that it should not be difficult at all for the British army to defeat them easily and bring an end to the war.

Royal Pennsylvania Gazette (Philadelphia), 20 March 1778

The troops never were in better health, nor more anxious to pay their respects to the ragged army, who now hover about Peek's Kill and Cortland's Mannor—The loyal inhabitants are not less desirous to assist in bringing those sons of rapine to justice; but, were you to see the numbers who daily come in with their arms, and hear their different accounts, humanity would blunt the sword of justice, and make you pity the deluded wretches attached to the interest of that Congress, whose poisonous breath hath, like pestilence, dealt death and destruction to those who have sucked it in, and filled the country with widows and orphans, whose curses will ascend to heaven, and recoil with a ponderous weight on the heads of the authors of their misfortunes.

James Rivington: "The Tory View of the Patriots"

James Rivington, a printer in New York who had opposed the arguments with Great Britain even before the fighting started, became one of the most famous Loyalists in America. He often attacked the Patriots as greedy men who had lost their sense of direction in believing that they could successfully revolt against Great Britain. In this piece, he points out the hopelessness of the American cause because of the lack of financial stability. The rebels could not possibly hope to win a war when they had no money and supplies with which to fight it.

Royal Gazette (New York), 26 August 1780

Without money and without credit, the rebel interest is now supported by depredation and spoil.

No man will now part with any thing for paper money, old or new.—The rebel Commissaries have not credit for a farthing, in any part of the Continent; in every place they take what they want from the farmers, a horse, a cow, grain, hay, straw, and leave a certificate to be paid at Doom's Day, and in spite of all this licentiousness, Washington's army between Pompton and Tapan are at three quarters of a pound allowance of flour and fresh meat.

At the last irruption of their light horse (about 60) to Bergen, on Sunday the 13th inst. they found the inhabitants going to the church; some they insulted, others they robbed, and condescended to such pitiful exploits, as changing hats and cloaths, taking the buckles from their shoes, and in one instance of stripping off a man's breeches, and leaving an old pair of trowsers to cover his nakedness.

The most horrible oppressions are at the same time, used to force the militia to join them in their career to destruction. All their bands are made up of men and boys drafted from an unwilling militia, except the continentals who had been early beguiled to inlist in the continental army, and whose times are not yet out, or who, if they are, cannot get their dismissions.—Who at the opening of the present campaign were about 3 or 4000 in Jersey, and another 1000 in the Highlands, and Fort Stanwix.—They rely for augmentations entirely upon a militia, every where a majority abhorring the French, &c. against the protraction of the rebellion. They have departed from the old practice of classing them, forcing a number to produce a man, by extorted contributions, and now class them according to their property, and not their number of polls.—A man of between five and six thousand pounds estate, is obliged to find a substitute in the Delaware counties, or turn out himself, yet a certain county there, that was to have furnished long since 88 men, had not collected but 24 on the 10th instant.

The loyalists increase hourly, scarce a day passes without fugitives to this place, from the barbarities perpetrated by the usurpers in the upper parts of this, as well as from the neighbouring provinces.

QUESTIONS

1. Why is the encouraging of morale so important in wartime? What common traits do you see in the morale-boosting efforts of the Patriots and Loyalists?

2. Solomon Southwick indicates that the British left Boston quickly. Why would it help the American cause for the British to have fled in a hurry?
3. What approach does Paine use to boost the morale of the Patriot forces? How effective do you think this type of approach would be?
4. Why do the Loyalist printers Hugh Gaine and James Robertson place so much emphasis on desertions from the Continental army?
5. Why does James Rivington believe that the revolt against Great Britain will ultimately fail?

Note

1. *Mandamus counsellors* refers to advisers who force subjects to perform some act or duty.

CHAPTER 3

The Battles of the Revolutionary War, 1776–1781

The fighting in the American Revolution lasted from April 19, 1775, to October 19, 1781. During these six-plus years, both sides won some battles and lost some battles.

The British concentrated their efforts on conquering population centers because that was how wars were won in Europe—you took control of the major city or cities and the country surrendered. But that did not work in the American colonies. At one time or another, the British occupied every major American city (including New York from September 15, 1776, to November 25, 1783), and still the war went on.

The colonials, under the leadership of George Washington, just tried to survive. While trying to win military engagements, Washington realized that the most important goal was for the Continental army to continue to function. As long as the army existed the war would go on. Washington tried to reduce major losses in men and supplies by avoiding major battles. Only when the circumstances were almost perfect at Yorktown, with Cornwallis holed up on a peninsula and the French fleet threatening to defeat the British navy, did Washington commit the bulk of his forces to a single battle.

Throughout the conflict, the newspapers worked to keep their readers informed and to put the best face on the results of various military engagements. Thus, the paper's side—be it Patriot or Loyalist—always came out on top, no matter what the actual outcome had been.

The documents below are divided into five sections by the battles that are discussed: Trenton, Germantown, Saratoga, Camden, and Yorktown. In each section, both Patriot and Loyalist views of what happened at the battle are included. And, in each case, the winners emphasize the glories of victory while the losers downplay or almost ignore the losses of defeat.

Trenton

The battle that occurred at Trenton on December 25, 1776, was really more of a skirmish than a battle. It involved 2,400 Continentals under the command of Washington. He crossed the Delaware River from Pennsylvania on Christmas Eve and attacked a force of 1,400 Hessians encamped at Trenton, New Jersey. It was a great victory for the Americans. The Hessians suffered casualties of 30 and approximately 918 taken prisoner, while the Americans had no deaths and only 3 wounded. Although a small battle in comparison to later engagements, the victory at Trenton was one of Washington's greatest successes.

PATRIOT VIEW

George Washington: "Official Report to Congress"

George Washington attacked Trenton primarily because he felt something needed to be done in the wake of the precipitous retreat from New York. But, as he indicates in this official report, the sortie succeeded beyond his wildest dreams. Not only did his troops successfully capture the garrison at Trenton, but they did so under severe weather conditions and while suffering almost no casualties.

Virginia Gazette (Dixon and Hunter—Williamsburg), 10 January 1777

Sir, I have the pleasure of congratulating you upon the success of an enterprise, which I had formed against a detachment of the enemy lying in Trenton, and which was executed yesterday morning.

The evening of the 25th, I ordered the troops intended for this service to parade back of McKenky's ferry, that they might begin to pass as soon as grew dark, imagining we should be able to throw them all over, with the necessary artillery, by 12 o'clock, and that we might easily arrive at Trenton by five in the morning, the distance being about nine miles. But the quantity of ice, made that night, impeded the passage of the boats so much, that it was three o'clock before the artillery could all be got over, and near four before the troops took up their line of march.

I formed my detachment into two divisions, one to march up the lower or river road, the other by the upper or Pennington road. As the divisions had nearly the same distance to march, I ordered each of them immediately upon forcing the out guards, to push directly into the town, that they might charge the enemy before they had time to form. The upper division arrived at the enemy's advanced post exactly at 8 o'clock, and in three minutes after, I found, from the fire on the lower road, that that division had also got up: The out guards made but a small opposition, though, for their numbers, they behaved very well, keeping up a constant retreating fire from behind bodies.

We presently saw their main body formed, but, from their motions, they seemed undetermined how to act. Being hard pressed by our troops, who had already got possession of part of their artillery, they attempted to file off by a road, on their right, leading to Princeton; but perceiving their intention, I threw a body of troops in their way, which immediately checked them: Finding, from our disposition, that they were surrounded, and they must inevitably be cut to pieces, if they made any further resistance, they agreed to lay down their arms. The number that submitted, in this manner, was 23 officers, and 886 men. Col. Rohl, the commanding officer, and seven others, were found wounded in the town. I do not exactly know how many they had killed; but I fancy not above twenty or thirty, as they never made any regular stand. Our loss is very trifling indeed; only two officers and one or two privates wounded.

I find that the detachment of the enemy consisted of the three Hessian regiments of Landspatch, Kniphausen, and Rohl, amounting to about 1500 men, and a troop of British light-horse; but immediately upon the beginning of the attack, all those who were not killed or taken, pushed directly down the road toward Burden-Town. These would likewise have fallen into our hands, could my plan have been completely carried into execution. General Ewing was to have crossed before day at Trenton ferry, and taken possession of the bridge leading out of town; but the quantity of ice was so great, that though he did every thing in his power to effect it, he could not get over. This difficulty also hindered General Cadwallader from crossing, with the Pennsylvania militia, from Bristol; he got part of his foot over, but finding it impossible to embark his artillery, he was obliged to desist. I am fully confident, that could the troops under Generals Ewing and Cadwallader have passed the river, I should have been able, with the assistance, to have driven the enemy from all their posts below Trenton; but the numbers I had with me being inferior to theirs below me, and a strong battalion of light infantry being at Princeton, above me, I thought it most prudent to return the same evening with the prisoners, and the artillery we had taken. We found no stores of any consequence in the town.

In justice to the officers and men I must add, that their behaviour upon this occasion reflects the highest honour upon them. The difficulty of passing the river, in a very severe night, and their march through a violent storm of snow and hail, did not in the least abate their ardour; but when they came to the charge, each seemed to vie with the other in pressing forward, and were I to give a preference to any particular corps, I should do great injustice to the others.

LOYALIST VIEW

Hugh Gaine: "Trenton"

The British and their Loyalist allies such as printer Hugh Gaine downplayed the American victory at Trenton. The length of his report indicates that this engagement was seen by the British as an unimportant skirmish.

New York Gazette and Weekly Mercury, 30 December 1776

Wednesday Morning last one of the Hessian Brigades stationed at Trenton, was surprised by a large Body of Rebels, and after an Engagement which lasted for a little Time, between 3 and 400 made good their Retreat, and the whole Loss is about 900 Men.

Germantown

On October 4, 1777, George Washington attacked the British forces outside Philadelphia. Miscommunication between parts of the army, as well as a heavy fog, created problems for the Continental army. The result was an American panic when two units mistook each other for the enemy and fired at their own army's men.

PATRIOT VIEW

An Officer in Camp: "The Late Unhappy Circumstance"

In this piece, one of the officers of the Continental army expresses regrets over the failure of the army to win at the battle of Germantown. He believed that a victory here could have potentially changed the course of the war. He is discouraged because of the loss, but he has not given up hope.

Virginia Gazette (Dixon and Hunter—Williamsburg), 24 October 1777

I sit down to give you an account of one of the most important actions that ever happened in America. I call it important, for it was, I think, very near putting an end to the campaign, and perhaps the war. It was as follows: On Friday evening the lighthorse were all sent down towards Philadelphia, to secure the different roads, and see that no person advanced towards the city. About sun-set the infantry began their march, and arrived in the neighbourhood of Germantown about day-break. Between day-break and sunrise General Conway began the battle on the right with fixed bayonets, and drove the enemy from their picket, and advanced on with rapidity. And at the same time in good order; in about 15 minutes the battle became more general, as General Wayne reinforced our left wing and General Sullivan the right; we then drove the enemy about three quarters of a mile, where they made another stand, at this time the action became general almost from right to left. Our army rushed up as if determined to overset the whole of the British army, till they came about the middle of Germantown, where the enemy made a stand at a church, and a large stand building: It was now about half after 8 o'clock, and the enemy had retreated about 2 miles, where the firing continued some time. Upon hearing the fire so warm for a considerable time at one place, General McDougall advanced to the support of our left wing; the morning being very foggy, and so much smoke in the valley, our people took them for the enemy, and some unlucky dog cried out the enemy are surrounding us, the cry went through the whole line, and in less than 15 minutes our army were retreating from victory: I say victory, because in many parts our army was pursuing the enemy with fixed bayonets; and we are told that the stand at the church was only to secure a retreat, General Howe having given orders to that purpose. Thus you see, what a trifling thing has spun out the campaign, and perhaps the war; though I trust in God we shall give them a severe drubbing before the end of this month. Our army never were in better spirits; the officers and soldiers desire another opportunity of drubbing our enemies, and I believe will improve from the late unhappy circumstance, and not imagine they are surrounded, when they intended to be support.

LOYALIST VIEW

Anonymous: "The Total Rout of the Rebel Army"

This author reports the victory at Germantown and describes the confusion which the loss had produced in the Continental army. Although not explicit in his hope, this author clearly wishes that this battle would bring an end to the war.

Royal Gazette (New York), 18 October 1777

Since my last, we have got a confirmation of the TOTAL ROUTE and DISPERSION of the REBEL ARMY on the 4th instant, and that their scattered remains had been collected, as far as was practicable, at Perkiomy creek, which they had passed, and taken refuge on the mountains in its vicinity; establishing a post also at the Trap, on the Schuylkill.—A waggoner from their camp, which he left on Monday evening, says, they were then in the utmost confusion, their camp being alarmed with an account of the approach of the King's troops, and the next day he was informed a body of British had attacked their post at the Trap, killed thirty, and made about seventy prisoners. He says, that on his way hither from Sherrod's ferry (where he crossed the Delaware) on Thursday morning, he heard a very heavy firing from sun-rise till past 8 o'clock, in a direction towards the camp, which gives room for conjectures.

By a person who arrived here last evening, from the rebel army, which he left on Tuesday the 7th instant, we have the following account.—That on Friday the 3d the rebel army received orders to draw one day's provision, and to march; which they did, within a small distance of the ROYAL ARMY, in the night, and lay upon their arms until day-break: That they attacked the Royal army, and a General engagement commenced; that both armies fought (as he says) very obstinately; that part of the British gave way, but rallied; at the same time the left wing of the rebel army gave way, and in an instant the whole was in the greatest confusion, put to flight, and ran (in his own words) as if the devil was after them, when they were pursued by the light-horse, who made great havock among them; that there was a great number missing, and that the report in the camp, after their return, was THREE THOUSAND; but he verily believed there were double that number. He does not know whether they lost any cannon. He also says they begin to be much tired of the war and are determined to make an end of it this campaign. He further says, that the rebels had lost a great number of their best officers, who had the day before received orders not to run until the word retreat was given, which they most courageous of them observed, and were left standing without men till they were either taken or shot. He further add, that the Delaware frigate was taken, and was sitting out; that Lord Howe had ordered several floating batteries to be made; that the fort on the Jersey shore, near the cheveaux de frize, was taken, but he heard nothing of the shipping. He also says, that there were upwards of a hundred waggons employed to carry the wounded to East Town; and when he left the rebel army they were thirty miles distant from Philadelphia. This person has been a eye witness of the last engagement, and when he came away he heard considerable firing, which he supposed to be from the shipping.

Saratoga

The battle of Saratoga took place in October 1777 in upstate New York. A British force of 6,000 men under General "Gentleman Johnny" Burgoyne invaded from Canada, hoping to split the colonies in half down the Hudson River. The British force was attacked by an American army under the command of General Horatio Gates. After several engagements, Burgoyne surrendered his army on October 17, 1777. This American victory set the stage for the alliance with France in 1778.

PATRIOT VIEW

Alexander Purdie: "The Surrender of General Burgoyne"

News of the victory at Saratoga excited everyone because it was the first big victory for the Americans. There were public celebrations everywhere, as shown by this description of the joy in Williamsburg, Virginia, written by Alexander Purdie, one of several printers in the city.

Virginia Gazette (Williamsburg), 31 October 1777

By the Northern post yesterday are received a solid confirmation of the success of arms to the North, in the surrender of General Burgoyne, with his whole army, to the victorious and immortal GATES. Upon receiving this great and glorious news a general joy diffused itself amongst all ranks, the regular troops and militia of the city were instantly paraded, and both from artillery and small arms resounded the glad tidings, the inhabitants illuminated their houses, and, with the gentlemen of the General Assembly, spent a cheerful and agreeable evening, wherein the names of WASHINGTON, GATES, ARNOLD, LINCOLN &c. &c. &c. were often bumpered, with huzzas to the independence of America.

Patrick Henry: "A Proclamation"

Because of the importance of the victory at Saratoga, most state leaders called on the people to thank God for the success of the army. In this proclamation, Patrick Henry, the governor of Virginia, calls for a day of public thanksgiving and prayer to be celebrated on November 13, 1777.

Virginia Gazette (Purdie—Williamsburg), 31 October 1777

A PROCLAMATION. Whereas I have received certain intelligence, that General Gates, after repeated advantages gained over General Burgoyne, compelled him on the 14th day of this month to surrender himself and the whole army prisoners of war: NOW to the end that we may not, through a vain and presumptuous confidence in our own strength, be led away to forget the hand of Heaven, whose assistance we have so often in times of distress implored, and which, as frequently before, so more especially now, we have experienced in this signal success of the arms of the United States, whereby the divine sanction of the righteousness of our cause is most illustriously displayed, I have thought proper, by and with the advice of the Council of State, to appoint *Thursday* the thirteenth day of the next month to be observed, in all churches and congregations of Christians throughout this state, as a day of general and solemn thanksgiving; and it is most earnestly recommended to the several ministers and teachers of the Gospel, and they are hereby enjoined, to embrace this opportunity of impressing on the minds of their hearers those sentiments of pious joy which the glorious occasion so aptly calls for. . . . P HENRY. GOD save the UNITED STATES.

LOYALIST VIEW

James Rivington: "The Situation of General Burgoyne's Army"

The Loyalists in New York originally refused to believe that Burgoyne's army had been defeated. Printer James Rivington reflected the ideas of many when he stated that some of the reports were "too ridiculous to justify a repetition." It seemed almost incredible to the British and their supporters that the ragtag army of Americans could defeat the organized redcoats of Great Britain.

Royal Gazette (New York), 25 October 1777

Various reports have been propagated in this city since our last, relative to the situation of General Burgoyne's army; some of them too ridiculous to justify a repetition.

It seems this news originated with, and came from the rebels, who fabricated the story with a view to inlist men; and, to give an air of truth to it, at Elizabeth Town they caused guns to be fired, bonfires to be made, and every other demonstration of joy and triumph, at the same time dealing out rum to the rabble, without measure.

James Humphreys, Jr.: "Curious Particulars"

In discussing rebel reports concerning the battle at Saratoga, Loyalist printer James Humphreys, Jr., emphasizes the exaggerations of the Americans concerning the size of the victory. Again, as was true with Rivington in the piece above, the Loyalists had trouble believing that Burgoyne had lost to the Continental army.

Pennsylvania Ledger (Philadelphia), 26 November 1777

Was LOST, on Thursday last, by the Printer hereof, a Rebel News-PAPER printed at Baltimore, containing, among other curious particulars— A pompous Congress account of the number of prisoners taken by Gen. Gates, which they have swelled to the amount of 6013–but they have very cautiously avoided giving one word of the Convention obtained by General Burgoyne. A *mighty big* letter from General Gates to General Vaughan, forbidding him burn the houses, &c. on the North river and acquainting him with his *greatness*–that he has much abler Generals than ever he was, or ever will be, in his possession. Also, a Congress proclamation for a *Fast day*, sometime in December next. It is imagined their army, having enough of them, would be much better pleased with a *Feast day*, and with some warm shoes and stockings.

As the Printer borrowed the above Paper, with a promise of returning it, he will gratefully thank whoever has it, if they will send it to him.

Camden

The battle of Camden, South Carolina, took place on August 16, 1780. The British forces under the command of Lord Charles Cornwallis soundly defeated the Americans under the leadership of the hero of Saratoga, General Horatio Gates. Many people thought this loss would be too much for the Americans to overcome.

PATRIOT VIEW

Samuel Loudon: "A Bloody Battle"

New Yorker Samuel Loudon blamed the loss on the undependability of the militia, who fled the battle just when it looked as if the Americans could win. Here, he concludes that Gates would regroup his forces, gain reinforcements, and defeat Cornwallis at a later date.

New York Packet (Fishkill), 14 September 1780

We are assured, by good authority, that on the 16th Inst. at 2 o'clock, A.M. a bloody battle was fought within 8 miles of Camden, South Carolina, between his Excellency General Gates at the head of about 3000 men, 900 of whom were regulars, and the British forces, under the command of Earl Cornwallis, consisting of 1800 regulars and 2400 refugees, &c. The contending armies engaged each other with the greatest fury, and the prospect, for some time, was extremely favourable to the American troops, who charged bayonets on the enemy, which obliged them to give ground, and leave some of their artillery in the possession of our advancing troops—but, unfortunately, at this critical moment the premature flight of militia terminated the conflict in favour of the enemy—an event which hath proved fatal to many of our brave countrymen of the regular troops, 4 or 500 of whom have been killed and taken.—Among them are several valuable officers, whose names we think it prudent to omit for the present. The enemy's loss hath been much more considerable. Lord Cornwallis, or some other British Gen. it is conjectured, is among the slain. Notwithstanding this misfortune, Gen. Gates, whose Head Quarters are at Hillsborough, is collecting a force much superior to the late army, and appears resolved to try the fortune of another day.

Nathaniel Willis: "Battle between General Gates and Lord Cornwallis"

Nathaniel Willis announces that he has gained further information about the battle of Camden, which indicates that American losses were not as severe as feared at first. In fact, the British lost more men than the Americans did, although they maintained control of the battlefield. Hence, Willis, printer of the Independent Chronicle *throughout the Revolution, downplays the loss by emphasizing the losses of the enemy.*

Independent Chronicle (Boston), 21 September 1780

By a gentleman of veracity, just arrived from Philadelphia, we are informed that a letter had been received there from Governor Nash, of North-Carolina, giving an account of the late battle between General Gates and Lord Cornwallis, near Camden, much more favorable on the side of our forces than was at first represented. According to this account, General Gates's army received the attack of the enemy with great firmness, many of whom fell; and even the militia, were not broken till some time after the fight had been carried on by the push of the bayonet: After our line was broken, a body of Continental troops, amounting to about 900, and the South-Carolina militia, continued in good order, and fought bravely, but finding themselves overpowered, retreated, though still keeping in a body. The enemy's horse pursued our broken militia some miles, and upon their return, falling in with the body of Continental troops, the fight was renewed, and the greater part of the horse was slain. This account adds, that General Smallwood remained with the Continentals and was safe; that Baron Kalb was missing, and said to be wounded; that of all the American forces on the field, not more than 300 were missing; and that the number of killed in this action was greatest on the side of the enemy.

LOYALIST VIEW

Hugh Gaine: "The Rout"

Hugh Gaine also credits the victory to the training of the British regulars and the lack of bravery and training on the part of the American militia. The implication is that the Americans can never win as long as they continue to depend on the militia for any of the important fighting.

New York Gazette and Weekly Mercury, 11 September 1780

Last Wednesday a Report was brought to Town from the Country, that an Action had happened about the Middle of August between the Royal Army, in South Carolina, near Camden, under the Command of the Earl of Cornwallis, and the Rebels under General Gates, in which the latter was defeated: The like Accounts were received the two succeeding Days but was confirmed last Saturday Morning by the Receipt of Mr. Kollock's *New-Jersey Journal* of the 6th Instant, from which the following Paragraph was extracted, and printed in a Hand-Bill, by H. Gaine, on Saturday last, viz.

By Intelligence from the Southward, we learn, that our Army in South Carolina, under the Command of General Gates, has lately been repulsed, with the Loss of upwards of ONE THOUSAND MEN killed and taken Prisoners; and that General Gates with Difficulty escaped sharing the fate of the latter; That Baron De Kalb, who commanded the Maryland Line of Continental Troops, was wounded and taken; That the two Armies met one another in the Night, both endeavouring to gain a certain Piece of Ground; That to the pusillanimous Behaviour of the Militia the Disaster may be attributed.

By a Philadelphia Paper of the 29th Ult. it appears, Gates's Army consisted of the Maryland Division of Continental Troops, with a Park of Artillery; Col. Arnold's Corps, a Regiment of Virginia State Troops, and a Party of South Carolina Refugees, under Col. Marian, besides the North Carolina Militia, under Generals Caswell and Rutherford, supposed to amount in the whole to about three Thousand Men.

Besides the above we have learnt, That the Action happened about two o'Clock in the Morning of the 16th ult. when both Armies were manoeuvering, in order to obtain an Eminence, they unexpectedly fell in with each other; that the Royal Army discharged a very heavy Fire upon the Rebel Militia, who were in Front, which soon put them to the Rout; they then fell back on the Continental Troops, which threw them into Confusion, and they being immediately charged by the Royalists, were soon dispersed, and the whole Body, (General Gates, and his Suite, with about 50 of their Cavalry excepted) killed, wounded or taken Prisoners. Those who escaped were pursued many Miles from the Field of Action.

Hugh Gaine: "The Perfect Victory"

Hugh Gaine describes the battle of Camden as "the perfect victory." Camden encourages the Loyalists to continue to believe that the British could win the war, primarily because their army is better trained for battle.

New York Gazette and Weekly Mercury, 18 September 1780

The ship Lyon, bound from Charlestown to Jamaica, having been taken by the enemy, was happily recovered and brought to Sandy-Hook by Admiral Sir George Rodney's fleet; the perfect victory gained on the 16th of August by Earl Cornwallis over the rebel army under Mr. Gates, is confirmed by this ship, with the addition, that TWO THOUSAND FIVE HUNDRED MEN were killed or taken.

Yorktown

In the summer of 1781, Cornwallis took his army to Yorktown, Virginia, hoping to be resupplied by the British fleet. Washington, believing that he could box in Cornwallis with the help of the French fleet, moved his army to lay siege to Yorktown in September. This strategy worked. On October 19, 1781, Cornwallis surrendered his army. This American victory marked the end of the fighting in the Revolution.

PATRIOT VIEW

George Washington: "Official Report"

George Washington rejoiced greatly in his victory over Cornwallis because he knew that it might be the last battle. Here, he praises both his own men and his French allies for their efforts in bringing about this very important victory.

Freeman's Journal (Philadelphia), 31 October 1781

Head Quarters, Near York, 19 October 1781. I have the honor to inform congress that a reduction of the British Army under the command of Lord Cornwallis is most happily effected. The unremitted ardour which actuated every officer and soldier in the combined army on this occasion has principally led to this important event, at an earlier period than my most sanguine hopes had induced me to expect.

The singular spirit of emulation which animated the whole army from the first commencement of our operations has filled my mind with the highest pleasure and satisfaction and has given me the happiest presage of success.

On the 17th a letter was received from Lord Cornwallis, proposing a meeting of commissioners to consult on terms for the surrender of the posts of York and Gloucester.

This letter (the first which had passed between us) opened a correspondence—a copy of which I do myself the honor to inclose—that correspondence was followed by the definite capitulation, which was agreed to and signed on the 19th, a copy of which is also herewith transmitted, and which, I hope, will meet with the approbation of congress.

I should be wanting in the feelings of gratitude, did I not mention on this occasion, with the warmest sense of acknowledgments, the very cheerful and able assistance which I have received in the course of our operations, from his excellency, the Count Rochambeau, and all officers of every rank, in their respective capacities. Nothing could equal this zeal of our allies, but the emulating spirit of the American officers, whose ardour would not suffer their exertions to be exceeded.

The very uncommon degree of duty and fatigue which the nature of the service required from the officers of the engineers and artillery of both armies, obliges me particularly to mention the obligations I am under to the commanding and other officers of these corps.

I wish it was in my power to express to congress how much I feel myself indebted to the Count de Grasse and the officers of the fleet under his command, for the distinguished aid and support which had been afforded me by them; between whom and the army the most happy concurrence of sentiments and views have subsisted and from whom every possible co-operation has been experienced which the most harmonious intercourse could afford.

The return of the prisoners, military stores, ordnances, shipping and other matters I shall do myself the honor of transmitting to congress as soon as they can be collected by the heads of the departments to which they belong.

Col. Laurens and the Viscount de Noailles, on the part of the combined army, were the gentlemen who acted as commissioners for forming and settling the terms of capitulation and surrender herewith transmitted—to whom I am particularly obliged for their readiness and attention exhibited on the occasion.

Col. Tighlman, one of my aids de camp, will have the honour to deliver these dispatches to your excellency. He will be able to inform you of every minute circumstance which is not particularly mentioned in my letter. His merits, which are too well known to need any observations at this time, have gained my particular attention; and I could wish that they may be honoured by the notice of your excellency and congress.

Your excellency and congress will be pleased to accept my congratulations on this happy event, and believe me to be, with the highest esteem and respect, Sir,

Your excellency's

Most obedient, humble servant,

G. Washington

His Excellency, the President of Congress.

P.S. Though I am not possessed of the particular returns, I have reason to suppose that the number of prisoners will be between 5 and 6000 men, exclusive of seamen and others.

Samuel Hall: "The Capture of Lord Cornwallis and His Army"

Samuel Hall had just begun the publication of his newspaper a few weeks before the battle of Yorktown. He celebrates the victory and urges his readers to rejoice in the good news.

Salem Gazette (Massachusetts), 1 November 1781

It is with the most singular satisfaction, that the Publisher of this Paper can, so soon after the commencement of its publication, congratulate his Readers on so great an event as the capture of Lord Cornwallis and his army.—He has inserted every particular yet come to hand.—The greatest joy and satisfaction were shown, in this and the neighbouring towns, on the receipt of this most interesting intelligence.

Barzillai Hudson and George Goodwin, "The Surrender of Lord Cornwallis"

Hudson and Goodwin, printers in Hartford for many years, poke fun at the New York printers for their unwillingness to admit that Cornwallis had lost. They imply that the Tories were in a panic because they knew this victory marked the beginning of the end of the war.

Connecticut Courant (Hartford), 20 November 1781

All the late New-York papers have at length confessed the surrender of Lord Cornwallis to be real. They have even condescended to insert the articles of capitulation verbatim from the Philadelphia gazettes. The women are in tears, the soldiery in a panic, the merchants selling off their goods for much less than the first cost in Europe, the tories are in the utmost consternation, and Benedict Arnold himself, it is said trembles like an aspen leaf—in the midst of this scene of distress and wretchedness, with a superior French fleet on the coast ready to swallow them, the demagogues of that city are publishing in their gazettes contents of rebel mails and criticisms upon poems written by the King of Prussia; which is full as ridiculous and stupid as if a criminal on his way to the gallows, and sitting on his coffin, should at the same time be amusing himself with Ben Johnson's jests, or writing strictures on the stile and language of the sheriff's warrant which condemns him to be hanged.

LOYALIST VIEW

James Rivington: "Paid with French Money"

Loyalist printers found it very difficult to put a positive spin on the loss at Yorktown. Generally, they did not even try. Instead, they poked fun at the Americans or criticized them for their actions or the actions of their allies. Here, James Rivington asserts that the Americans are not really revolting. Rather, they were fighting for Louis XVI and that the United States will soon become a part of France.

Royal Gazette (New York), 7 November 1781

We can assure the public from recent information, that the whole Continental army is at this time in the actual *service* of his Most Christian Majesty Louis the Sixteenth, and are paid with French money, which has been for that purpose remitted to Mr. Washington, Lieutenant-General and Commander in Chief of all the French and Rebel forces in this country, so that every American soldier of this alliance is now become in ever sense a *Frenchman*. The Congress have no sort of interference with his power, and they lately felt the humiliating mortification of perceiving General Washington *alone* entrusted with the cash received from France to pay the army. The people of America since their revolt from Great Britain, will have no other choice to make of a Ruler, as their Congress's command and influence now exists in the *Frenchified* Mr. Washington alone.

James Rivington: "A Shadow of Liberty Left"

James Rivington once more attacks the French, asserting that Americans were beginning to regret the alliance because of how they had been mistreated by the French. He thought that this mistreatment might convince the rebels that the Revolution had been a mistake and that maybe they would end the war before it was too late. By late 1781, this was clearly wishful thinking on the part of many Loyalists.

Royal Gazette (New York), 19 December 1781

I have now to inform you that the unjust and haughty treatment the inhabitants of York Town in Virginia, and other parts of the country, have met with from the French army, since the event of the 19th of October, has occasioned a strong debate in Congress upon the propriety of seeking an immediate truce with Great-Britain for three years, leaving their garrisons in status quo; and 'tis believed that secret orders will be immediately forwarded to our Envoys in Europe to propose and effect it, if possible, this winter. The wisest men amongst us are at last convinced, that no other step can be fallen upon to save this country from being reduced to the lowest degree of slavery. We now feel most sensibly that we have only a shadow of Liberty left, served out by our own military with a sparing hand, and nothing but a peace or truce with England can preserve us from being not only subjects but slaves to a nation aspiring to universal empire. The late success in Virginia has opened our eyes, and shewn the cloven foot of our great and good allies. Subjects we cannot be again to Great-Britain; the injuries done to both parties are too many, and too recent, for justice to be obtained from either. A truce may afford every advantage to both countries that a peace can do. It will leave Great Britain at liberty to take her full satisfaction out of the Family Compact, her natural enemies, rid our country of them, save our honour, and secure our trade.

QUESTIONS

1. Newspaper printers always tried to put the best face on any military engagement, no matter what the results had truly been. What were the major ways in which Patriot and Loyalist printers tried to portray the wins and losses of their respective armies?
2. In looking at the pieces by George Washington and the Continental army officer, what do their comments indicate that these various battles have in common?
3. Why, apparently, did the British lose at Trenton, Saratoga, and Yorktown? Why, apparently, did the Americans lose at Germantown and Camden?
4. All the Patriot reports about the battle of Yorktown express great joy over the victory. Why do you think this was so?

CHAPTER 4

General George Washington, 1776–1783

George Washington was appointed commander in chief of the Continental army on June 15, 1775. He had previously gained some military renown during the French and Indian War, particularly for his service with the British under the command of General Edward Braddock. Washington was one of the few colonials with active duty military experience with the British army, which was one of the main reasons Congress turned to him to command the Continental army.

Washington was idolized by many colonial Americans almost from the moment he was appointed. Wherever he went, he was toasted and dined and applauded for his wisdom and leadership in the Revolutionary War effort. His birthday quickly became a time for public celebrations all over the country.

Washington took his role as commander in chief seriously. He fretted about whether he was up to the challenge or not. He worried when his men suffered because of lack of supplies, and he continually urged the Continental Congress to make the army more capable of success by properly supplying them.

But Washington's worries did not translate into threats of a military takeover. Most Americans perceived George Washington to be an honorable man, and this proved to be true. He always followed the orders of the civilian government, even when they ordered him to defend Philadelphia in a battle he knew he could not win. Washington became revered during his service as commander in chief because he worked so hard to make American independence a reality. To many people, he seemed to be almost perfect.

The good opinions of George Washington are expressed in several selections here. First is an essay that praises his bravery and urges Americans to follow his good leadership. The essay is followed by an acrostic poem that praises his wise leadership and declares that it was God's blessing and prov-

UNITED STATES in CONGRESS assembled,
(Princeton) Aug. 26, 1783.

According to order, General Washington attended, and being introduced by two Members, the President addressed him as follows:

S I R,

CONGRESS feel particular pleasure in seeing your Excellency, and in congratulating you on the success of a war in which you have acted so conspicuous a part.

It has been the singular happiness of the United States, that during a war so long, so dangerous, and so important, Providence has been graciously pleased to preserve the life of a General, who has merited and possessed the uninterrupted confidence and affection of his fellow-citizens. In other nations many have performed services for which they have deserved and received the thanks of the public; but to you, Sir, peculiar praise is due. Your services have been essential in acquiring and establishing the freedom and independence of your country; they deserve the grateful acknowledgments of a free and independent nation; these acknowledgments Congress have the satisfaction of expressing to your Excellency.

Hostilities have now ceased, but your country still needs your services; the wishes to avail herself of your talents in forming the arrangements which will be necessary for her in the time of peace; for this reason your attendance at Congress has been requested. A committee is appointed to confer with your Excellency, and to receive assistance in preparing and digesting plans relative to those important objects.

To which his EXCELLENCY made the following Reply:

Mr. PRESIDENT,

I AM too sensible of the honorable reception I have now experienced, not to be penetrated with the deepest feelings of gratitude.

Notwithstanding Congress seem to estimate the value of my life beyond any services I have been able to render the United States, yet I must be permitted to consider the wisdom and unanimity of our national councils, the firmness of our citizens, and the patience and bravery of our troops, which have produced so happy a termination of the war, as the most conspicuous effects of the divine interposition, and the surest presage of our future happiness.

Highly gratified by the favourable sentiments which Congress are pleased to express of my past conduct, and amply rewarded by the confidence and affection of my fellow-citizens, I cannot hesitate to contribute my best endeavours towards the establishment of the national security, in whatever manner the sovereign power may think proper to direct, until the ratification of the definitive treaty of peace, or the final evacuation of our country by the British forces; after either of which events, I shall ask permission to retire to the peaceful shade of private life.

Perhaps, Sir, no occasion may offer, more suitable than the present, to express my humble thanks to God, and my grateful acknowledgments to my country, for the great and uniform support I have received, in every vicissitude of fortune, and for the many distinguished honors which Congress have been pleased to confer upon me in the course of the war. Published by Order of Congress,

CHARLES THOMSON, Sec'ry.

SEPTEMBER 3.
By the UNITED STATES in CONGRESS assembled, August 7, 1783.

Resolved unanimously, ten States being present, That an Equestrian Statue of General Washington be erected, at the place where the residence of Congress shall be established.

Resolved, That the statue be of bronze, the General to be represented in a Roman dress, holding a truncheon in his right hand, and his head encircled with a laurel wreath: The statue to be supported by a marble pedestal, on which are to be represented, in basso relievo, the following principal events of the war, in which General Washington commanded in person, viz. the evacuation of Boston—The capture of the Hessians at Trenton—The battle of Princeton—The action of Monmouth—and the surrender of York. On the upper part of the front of the pedestal to be engraved as follows: " The United States in Congress assembled ordered this statue to be erected, in the year our Lord 1783, in honor of George Washington, the illustrious Commander in Chief of the armies of the United States of America, during the war which vindicated and secured their liberty, sovereignty and independence."

Resolved, That a statue conformable to the above plan be executed by the best artist in Europe, under the superintendance of the Minister of the United States at the Court of Versailles, and that money to defray the expence of the same be furnished from the treasury of the United States.

Resolved, That the Secretary of Congress transmit to the Minister of the United States at the Court of Versailles, the best resemblance of General Washington that can be procured, for the purpose of having the above statue erected, together with the fittest description of the events which are to be the subject of the basso relievo.

STATE of PENNSYLVANIA.
In GENERAL ASSEMBLY.
FRIDAY, August 29, 1783, A. M.

THE report of the Committee, appointed to consider of the most eligible means for the accommodation of Congress, should that honorable body determine to reside within this State, read August 27th inst. was read the second time; whereupon,

Resolved unanimously, That, until Congress shall determine upon the place of their permanent residence, it would be highly agreeable to this House, if that honorable body should deem it expedient to return to and continue in the city of Philadelphia; in which case they offer to Congress the different apartments in the State-House, and adjacent buildings which they formerly occupied, for the purpose of transacting the national business therein.

Resolved unanimously, That this House will take effectual measures to enable the Executive of the State to afford speedy and adequate support and protection to the honor and dignity of the United States in Congress, and the persons of those composing the Supreme Council of the nation, assembled in this city.

Resolved unanimously, That, as this House is sincerely disposed to render the permanent residence of Congress, in this State, commodious and agreeable to that honorable body, the Delegates of this State be instructed to request Congress will be pleased to define what jurisdiction they deem necessary to be vested in them, in the place wherein they shall permanently reside.

Ordered, That the remainder of the report be postponed. Extract from the Minutes,

PETER Z. LLOYD, Clerk of the General Assembly.

Last Thursday a small party of whigs in Bucks county, having intelligence that Moses Doane, Levy Doane, his brother, and Abraham Doane, cousin german of the two first, all three outlawed for robbery, were in a ruined house near the mouth of Tohiccton creek, they went there armed to take those leaders of a gang of robbers. On approaching them they were called on to surrender, instead of which they took up their fire arms and discharged them against the party, by which means an officer of militia was shot through the body. A gun was pointed at another by Moses Doane, but the closing in, seized upon the villain, who still resisting, was shot dead by another of the party. Mean while Levy and Abraham Doane escaped by the back door. A person posted behind the house fired as they ran off, and one of them fell, but rising again, got into the thicket which surrounded the house, and escaped.

The most authentic accounts agree, that there are yet between 12 and 15,000 refugees, men, women and children, to be embarked at New-York, Long-Island, and Staten-Island, for Nova-Scotia, St. John's, and Abacco; among these are many persons of fortune and landed estates, who leave nothing but their terra firma behind them. Many of them pretend, that it is no fear or ill treatment, after the departure of the army, that urges them to leave the country, so much as a conviction that the new republic must sink in a short time under their immense national debt, and the exorbitant taxes with which they will be loaded.

A very large fleet is expected hourly at New-York, consisting chiefly of empty transports. New-York from all appearances will be left very bare, the refugees shewing a disposition to carry off not only their own effects, but the very buildings of the city, to their new settlements in the north.

Upwards of seven thousand of the mercenary troops (say some) remain to be accounted for by Great Britain, to their respective princes; these must either be replaced, or the loss compensated by 30 l. sterl. a head, which amounts to 210,000 l. sterling.

SEPTEMBER 10.
Yesterday arrived here the ship General Washington, Capt. Barney, from Havre de Grace, which place he left on the first of August, and touched at Poole, in England, where he landed the Honorable Henry Laurens, Esq; on his way to London. We learn that the definitive treaty was not signed when Capt. Barney sailed: That treaties of commerce with America were signed with the Courts of Holland and Denmark; and that a treaty of alliance was concluded between the Courts of France and England, to support the Turks against the Empress of Russia and the Emperor of Germany.

Last Saturday, being the 6th of September, compleated two years since an army of British troops, under the command of that infamous traitor to his country Benedict Arnold, plundered and burnt the towns of New-London and Groton, and massacred the garrison of Fort-Griswold:—On this occasion a well-adapted discourse was delivered in said fort, to a large and affected auditory, by the Reverend Mr. Hart, of Preston, from the following words,—" Then Abner called to Joab, and said, Shall the sword devour forever? Knowest thou not that it will be bitterness in the latter end?" 2 Sam. ii. 26.

PROVIDENCE, Sept. 20.
The Continental Frigate Alliance, Capt. Barry, is arrived in the Delaware to refit. She was bound to Europe, but sprung a Leak soon after leaving the Chesapeake.

Late Accounts from New-York mention, that it was generally believed the British Troops would leave that Place by the Middle of October.

A R R I V A L S since our last.
Brig Independence, De Ville, from Port-Dauphin.
Sloop Polly, Godfrey, New-York.
Brig Prudence, Macey, Antigua.
Sloop Humbird, Whitney, New-York.

S A I L E D.
Sloop Dove, Lee, for New-York.
Sloop Polly, Godfrey, New-York.

The Retirement of George Washington from the Continental Army. *Because of troubles in the United States, some officers had urged George Washington to use the army to take control of the nation. Washington, who believed in republican government, refused. Here the printer includes the minutes from the Continental Congress that show Washington's retirement from command of the Continental army and the expression of gratitude from the Congress for his efforts. Washington returned to his home in Virginia.*

idence that brought Washington to the American people. The final selection discusses Washington's letter of farewell when he resigned his commission in 1783.

Bad opinions of George Washington were almost never expressed by Patriot printers. The only criticism of any size was Charles Lee's attack on Washington's leadership, contained in the first selection. The other two bad opinions are pieces by James Rivington that accused Washington of having a series of affairs with available women in the vicinity of the Continental army.

GOOD OPINIONS

Anonymous: "Blessed with a Washington for a Leader"

This author praises Washington for his bravery in battle. On several occasions, both in the French and Indian War and the Revolutionary War, Washington rushed into the thick of battle in order to rally the troops. He had several horses shot out from under him and received several bullet holes in his clothes, but was never shot. This author saw such events as the providence of God and calls on the American people to support the "blessed" Washington in the fight for freedom.

Virginia Gazette (Dixon and Hunter—Williamsburg), 24 January 1777

HONOUR, I obey thee! At a crisis when America is invaded by one of the most powerful fleets and armies that ever the world beheld arrayed in order of battle; when the hand of tyranny is uplifted to fell the GLORIOUS PLANT OF LIBERTY, which our ancestors have cherished from the earliest ages, as the tree of life; when war, with all its horrours, is invading this once happy land; when every sacred right is at stake; when every filial and affectionate sentiment should engage us to step forth in support of those who have been the guardians of our tender years, or the sweet companions of our halcyon days; must not that soul be frozen, even to apathy, that is not roused by such important and irresistible impulses! Our COUNTRY, our LIVES, our FORTUNES, our LIBERTIES, our PARENTS, our CHILDREN, and our WIVES, are the SACRED PLEDGES for which we are now contending. We stand on the brink of a precipice, from which we cannot advance without the noblest exertions of VIRTUE, UNANIMITY, and FORTITUDE. A single false step may precipitate us from the enjoyment of the blessings of LIBERTY, PEACE, and INDEPENDENCE, to the abyss of

slavery and woe. But, on the contrary, whilst we are animated by the GLO-
RIOUS CAUSE we are engaged in, whilst we with cheerfulness embark in
the defence of the most valuable of sublunary blessings, whilst we are
united in our sentiment, vigilant in our duty, and active in our operations,
we need not dread the thunder of cannon, nor tremble at the names of heroes arrayed in all the splendour of a corrupt court, or crowned with the
faded laurels which have been plucked by the hand of tyranny.

Such, my countrymen, is the present state of America; such the consequence of slumbering in the arms of peace, whilst your enemy is at your
gates, and such the glorious reward of those who nobly stand forth and oppose the progress of a mercenary army, more venal than a court favourite,
more savage than a band of Tartars, and more spiritless than the sooty sons
of Africa, when opposed by men animated by liberty and the sacred love of
our country.

Should any one among you require the force of example to animate you
on this glorious occasion, let him turn his eyes to that bright luminary of war
in whose character the conduct of Emilius, the coolness of a Fabius, the intrepidity of an Hannibal, and the indefatigable ardour and military skill of a
Caesar, are united. Let not the name of Brutus or Camillus be remembered
whilst that of WASHINGTON is to be found in the annals of America. Great
in the cabinet as in war, he shines with unrivaled splendour in every department of life; and, whilst his abilities as a Statesman and a General excite our
wonder, his disinterested patriotism and domestic virtues command universal veneration. When sent out by Governor Dinwiddie to order the French
to desist from their encroachments on Virginia, view him, in the early period
of life, traversing in the service of his country the dreadful wilds of America,
through nations of savages, with no other attendant but an interpreter. Behold him at the head of a handful of his gallant countrymen, engaged for
many hours with more than treble the number of French at the Meadows,
where the fire first ceased on the side of the enemy, who previously proposed a parley; and, though surrounded by numbers, yet, a stranger to the
impulses of fear, he capitulated only on the terms of retiring with the hon-
ours of war. Follow him to that tremendous scene which struck an universal
panic in the bravest of the British troops, when, as aid de camp to the intrepid Braddock, amidst the dreadful carnage of that day, he was engaged in
giving out the orders of that unfortunate General with a coolness that
marked the hero, and at length brought him off the field of battle after he
had received his mortal wound. Again, behold him exchanging the din of
arms for the calmer scenes of life, still active in the service of his country in
the senate, until the impending storm, which is now bursting on America,
called him forth as the guardian and protector of his country. Behold him
abandoning the delights of peace, the enjoyment of affluence, and the plea-

sures of domestic felicity, and entering with ardour upon a military life again. Let imagination paint him at the head of a few raw undisciplined troops, destitute of arms and ammunition, besieging an army of veterans supported by a powerful navy. Consider with what unparalleled fortitude he withstood the difficulties that surrounded him on every side. Behold him embracing the earliest opportunity of driving the enemy from their advantageous post, and obliging them to abandon the long persecuted town of Boston. Again survey the plains of Long Island, whither he flew like a guardian angel to protect and bring off his brave troops, surrounded on every side by an host of foes, and with a conduct unparalleled in history secured their retreat across a river of which the enemy's ships were in full possession. Surely Heaven interposed in behalf of America on that day, by permitting such numbers to escape with glory from such a superior force! Behold his struggles on the heights of Harlem, and at the White Plains, counteracting the best concerted plans of the ablest Generals of the age. In thought attend him (if thought does not lag behind) when, as it were, he bounded from the White Plains to the Jersey shore, covering the retreat of his men from fort Lee, and throwing himself with them before the enemy, and with the scattered remains of his disbanded army, now amounting only to three thousand men, checking, at every step, the progress of the British army, and often halting to offer battle to numbers vastly superior to his own. Gracious Heaven! can any Virginian his countryman, or can any American who regards him as the saviour of their states, reflect on his situation at that juncture without horrour?—Would he not rather share his fortunes for the rest of the war than hazard the salvation of his country by a short enlistment, at the end of which his General might be left without any army to support him? Yet, even in such a situation his calmness and intrepidity never forsook him, but he appeared still greater in proportion to the dangers that surrounded him. At length, when the enemy flattered themselves with the pleasing expectations of a speedy accomplishment of their darling wish, we behold him by *coup de main* dissipating the fears of his country, and striking a terror into troops who the day before conceived themselves on the eve of a triumph. Whilst each effeminate son of peace was reveling in luxury, his active mind was employed in preparing for scenes equally glorious to himself and terrible to his enemies. Success attended this matchless enterprise, and Philadelphia, with the rest of America, hailed him her deliverer and guardian genius.

Such, my countrymen, is the General who directs the military operations of America; such the glorious leader of her armies; such the HERO whose bright example should fire every generous heart to enlist in the service of his country. Let it not be said you are callous to the impressions of such noble considerations, but, by following his glorious example, shew yourselves worthy of possessing that inestimable jewel LIBERTY, and reflect that you have nothing to dread whilst you are engaged in so glorious a cause, and blessed with a WASHINGTON for a leader.

Anonymous: "Genuine Production of the God's Above"

Poems were popular in eighteenth-century newspapers. Here the poet uses Washington's name to create a poetic tribute in the form of an acrostic. The man described by this poet seems incapable of doing anything wrong or making any kind of mistake.

Independent Chronicle (Boston), 10 July 1777

G enuine production of the God's above,
E merg'd from Heav'n on Wings of sovereign love,
O ver Columbia's host to take command,
R egain her freedom, and defend her land;
G reatness of language can't his praise express,
E clipses but his fame and makes it shine the less.
W isdom and knowledge all his deeds inspire,
A nd his vast soul warm'd with angelic fire;
S tatesman accomplished, hero Brave and Bold,
H is matchless virtue like the Stars untold;
I n utmost perils calm and most serene,
N or over flush'd when he's victorious been;
G odlike his mind's from common changes free,
T urns o'er the fate of nations and their end does see,
O f all the heroes, history doth record,
N one ever were so great, so free from vice, and so well serv'd the Lord.

Barzillai Hudson and George Goodwin: "The Salvation of America"

In this piece, two Connecticut printers discuss Washington's letter of farewell to the American people when he resigned his commission as commander in chief. Again, the providence of God is described as what was behind Washington's success. Not only is he a great military leader, but he is also a great statesman who urged the American people to live together peacefully now that they have won their independence from Great Britain.

Connecticut Courant (Hartford), 9 September 1783

A correspondent says, that he thinks it would become every citizen of America, to pay the greatest attention to General Washington's circular letter; that we should study it as the laws of our country; and that we should make our children understand it next to the principles of religion. He says that he conceives the illustrious commander in chief to be as great a statesman as he is a general; and that the most satisfactory tribute of gratitude that we could pay to him for eight years faithful and disinterested services, and for having redeemed us from the unrelenting hand of oppression, would be to follow the principles which are inculcated in this *immortal letter.* He conceives, in short, General Washington to have been supported by the peculiar superintendance of heaven, to be the scourge of tyrants, and the salvation of America—and that this circular letter *was dictated by the immediate spirit of God.*

BAD OPINIONS

Charles Lee: "Some Queries, Political and Military"

Charles Lee, retired from service in the British army, joined the Patriot cause in 1773. He helped organize the Continental army and was quickly promoted to the rank of major general. Many people, including Lee himself, believed that he should have been the commander in chief of the Continental army. When that did not happen, Lee became increasingly angry. When accused of cowardice and refusal to obey orders following the Battle of Monmouth in 1778, Lee demanded a court-martial. He was convicted and suspended from military service. He then wrote the following attack on Washington and the American military effort in an attempt to defend his honor.

Maryland Journal (Baltimore), 6 July 1779

Some queries, political and military, humbly offered to the consideration of the public.

1st. Whether George the First did not, on his accession to the throne of Great Britain, by making himself king of a party, instead of the whole nation, sow the seeds not only of the subversion of the liberties of the people, but of the ruin of the whole empire?

2nd. Whether, by proscribing the class of men, to which his ministry were pleased to give the appellation of Tories, he did not, in the end, make them not only real Tories, but even Jacobites?

3rd. Whether the consequence of this distinction, now become real, was not two rebellions; and whether the fruit of those rebellions, although defeated, were not septennial parliaments, a large standing army, an enormous additional weight and pecuniary influence thrown into the scale of the crown, which in a few years have borne down, not only the substance, but almost the form of liberty, all sense of patriotism, the morals of the people, and, in the end, overturned the mighty fabric of the British empire?

4th. Whether the present men in power, in this state, do not tread exactly in the steps of this pernicious ministry, by proscribing and disfranchising so large a proportion of citizens as those men whom they find it their interest to brand with the denomination of Tories?

5th. Whether liberty to be durable, should not be construed on as broad a basis as possible; and whether the same causes, in all ages, and in all countries, do not produce the same effects?

6th. Whether it is not natural, and even justifiable for that class of people (let the pretext be ever so plausible) who have been stripped of their rights as men, by the hard hand of power, to wish for, and endeavor to bring about, by any means whatever, a revolution in that state, which they cannot but consider as an usurpation and tyranny?

7th. Whether a subject of Morocco is not, when we consider human nature, a happier mortal, than a disfranchised citizen of Pennsylvania, as the former has the comfort of seeing all about him in the same predicament with himself; the latter, the misery of being a slave in the spacious bosom of liberty? The former drinks the cup, but the latter alone can taste the bitterness of it.

8th. Whether an enlightened member of a French parliament is not a thousand times more wretched than a Russian serf or peasant? As to the former, the chains, from his sensibility, must be extremely galling; and on the latter, they fit as easy as the skin of his back.

9th. Whether it is salutary or dangerous, consistent with, or abhorrent from, the principles and spirit of liberty and republicanism, to inculcate and encourage in the people, an idea, that their welfare, safety, and glory, depend on one man? Whether they really do depend on one man?

10th. Whether, among the late warm, or rather loyal addresses in this city, to his Excellency General Washington, there was a single mortal, one gentleman excepted, who could possibly be acquainted with his merits?

11th. Whether this gentleman excepted, does really think his Excellency a great man; or whether evidences could not be produced of his sentiments being quite the reverse?

12th. Whether the armies under Gates and Arnold, and the detachment under Starke, to the Northward, or that immediately under his Excellency, in Pennsylvania, gave the decisive turn to the fortune of war?

13th. Whether, therefore, when Monsieur Gerard and Don Juan de Miralles, sent over to their respective courts the pictures of his Excellency General Washington at full length, by Mr. Peal, there would have been any impropriety in sending over, at the same time, at least a couple of little heads of Gates and Arnold, by M. de Simitiere.

14th. On what principle was it that Congress, in the year 1776, sent for General Lee quite from Georgia with injunctions to join the army under General Washington, then in York-Island, without lots of time.

15th. Whether Congress had reason to be satisfied or dissatisfied with this their recall of General Lee, from what subsequently happened on York-Island, and at the White-Plains?

16th. Whether Fort Washington, was or was not tenable? Whether there were barracks, café-mates, fuel or water, within the body of the place? Whether in this out-works, the defenses were in any decent order? And whether there were even platforms for the guns?

17th. Whether, if it had been tenable, it could have answered any one single purpose? Did it cover, did it protect a valuable country? Did it prevent the enemy's ships from passing or repassing with impunity?

18th. Whether, when General Howe manifestly gave over all thoughts of attacking General Washington, in the last strong position in the rear of White-Plains, and fell back towards York-Island, orders should not have been immediately dispatched for the evacuation of Fort Washington, and for the removal of all the stores of value from Fort Lee to some secure spot, more removed from the river? Whether this was not proposed and the proposal slighted?

19th. Whether the loss of the garrison of Fort Washington, and its consequent loss of Fort Lee, with the tents, stores, &c. had not such an effect on the spirits of the people, as to make the difference of twenty thousand men to America?

20th. Whether, in the defeat of Brandewine, General Sullivan was really the person who ought to have been censured?

21st. Whether, if Duke Ferdinand had commanded at German Town, after having gained, by the valor of his troops, and the negligence of his enemy, a partial victory, he could have contrived, by a single stroke of the Bathos, to have corrupted this partial victory into a defeat.

22nd. Whether our position at Valley Forge was not such, that if General Howe, or afterwards General Clinton, had been well informed of its circumstances, defects, and vices, they might not at the head of ten, or even of eight thousand men, have reduced the American army to the same fatal necessity as the Americans did General Burgoyne?

23rd. Whether the trials of General St. Clair, of which Court-Martial General Lincoln was president, and that on General Lee, were conducted in the same forms, and on the same principles? Whether in the former, all hearsay evidences were not absolutely rejected; and in the latter hearsay evidence did not constitute a very considerable part?

24th. Whether if the Generals Schuyler and St. Clair, had been tried by the same Court-Martial as General Lee was, and instead of Congress, General Washington had been the prosecutor, those gentlemen (unexceptionable as their conduct was) would not have stood a very ugly chance of being condemned? And whether, if instead of General Washington, Congress had been the prosecutor, General Lee would not probably have been acquitted with the highest honor?

25th. Whether it must not appear to every man who has read General Washington's letter to Congress, on the affair at Monmouth, and the proceedings of the Court-Martial, by which General Lee was tried, that if the contents of the former are facts, not only General Lee's defense must be a tissue of the most abominable, audacious lies, but that the whole string of evidences, both on the part of the prosecution and prosecuted, must be guilty of rank perjury, as the testimonies of those gentlemen, near forty in number, delivered on oath, scarcely in one article coincide with the detail given in his Excellency's letter?

James Rivington: "An Extraordinary and Beautiful Soldier's Girl"

Loyalists also attacked Washington, but they tended to center their comments on his character rather than his military abilities. Washington's position as a slaveholder provided fodder for such attacks because many people assumed that every slaveholder had a sexual relationship with one or more of his slaves, and that slaveholders were just naturally more licentious and likely to have affairs. This attitude is clearly expressed in this piece by Loyalist printer James Rivington. Rivington was one of the best printers in the colonies in the eighteenth century, and he produced an excellent newspaper. But even he could make mistakes, as shown by the use of two auxiliary verbs in a sentence near the end of the first paragraph.

Royal Gazette (New York), 11 November 1780

The following anecdote will give you an idea of the condescending and peculiar way of his lady's sentiments. It is known that the General keeps at head-quarters an extraordinary and beautiful soldier's girl, I have seen her, but to describe her, is my pen not able; enough the nature has formed her lot, that she must be loved of every one that sees her, and nature has not told it in vain to the old General. A long while ago this charming creature was big with child, and the impregnation by express order of the General was kept very secret, but who can keep any thing secret from women? Lady Washington discovered soon the whole affair, and in lieu of being enraged, she did prepare with her own hand, the swaddling cloaths, shirts, and other little furniture for the young hero, which the soldier's girl in December last brought into the world, which was brought to be the font from a provincial French officer as godfather, and by order of the General got the name Habaccue. One says Lady Washington has congratulated her husband, as she saw him again the first time, and expressed to him her joy together over it, that he had could bring forth that, which, she in vain had expected more than ten years from him. Dear friend, where are such like Lady's? Truly not here, when you have such ones in your country inform me of it.—I'll let to put in the Pennsylvania Ledger, in the Philadelphia Packet, and other newspapers, to that end that Lady Washington only sees, that yet a country in the world, in which are some of the same sentiments.

EXTRACT of the POSTCRIPT. If nature provides young Habaccue so abundantly with high and great spirits, as she has been prodigal in respect to his body, so he will not let flow away his life in dark, but you will certainly much hear from a Habaccue Washington in the time of 20 years. This young boy has besides the more as strong limbs, also a great tuft of hairs upon his head brought with him into the world. The Chaplain of the General has accounted these hairs as a great Physiologer, and has found the number to be 2098 in all; in reporting this to the General, it occasioned a noble and generous action, whilst the old General did send still and the same day 2098 dollars ready money to our Police-Committee with the following insinuation: This sum is designed for the poor, and did wish that the money in general would be employed to refresh indigents, and helpless women in the straw. The merited praise this noble deed of the General did not retard as soon as it was known; in every companies was spoken of it with the greatest respect, and the old matrons, which still a few days past had pronounced the name Habaccue with astonishment in their Coffee Clubs, came now again together, drank coffee and agreed to name General Washington their deliberator, the benefactor of the human gender, and the foundation of the independency of the thirteen United States.

James Rivington: "Washington's Dulcinea"

James Rivington continues his attack on Washington's personal character by accusing him of abandoning the child of his first affair because he was involved in a second affair. The implication was that a person with such a character was not worthy of the service and loyalty of Americans. Furthermore, Rivington was trying to imply that the revolt against Great Britain was not worthy either because the leadership of people like Washington was so questionable.

Royal Gazette (New York), 15 November 1780

A correspondent from the country, who knows Washington's Dulcinea as well as he does himself, informs us that the German Wine Merchant, whose letter was published in our last Gazette, is not strickly accurate. Her father was not a soldier, but a tap-house keeper, of the name of Sidman, at the Mouth of Smith's Clove,[1] fourteen miles above Paramus, and has been dead for some time. On the birth of the boy last fall, the mother pronounced his name to be George Washington, and as soon as she was able, proceeded with him to the rebel camp and tendered him to his father for support. To her astonishment the young Hero was denied, tho' his mother named the AMOROUS MOMENT of her conception with the Chieftain, at her uncle Slutt's, another tap-house a mile off, at which Washington then quartered. The lovers maintained their points pro. and con. till poor Betsey Sidman was drummed from the camp, with the young George in her arms, pursuant to orders, which Lord Stirling saw punctually executed.—The General's present *convenience,* is the wife of a corporal, taken in service as his house-keeper, upon Madam Thompson's (alias Mrs. Scotch Johnny's) falling ill at Tappan, where she was left after the murder of Major Andre, and now continues. The cuckold corporal, but his wife's interest, has lately been made a serjeant.

It is to be hoped that these adventures will be recollected at the ensuing Congressional *Thanksgiving Day* of the 7th December, and that the fervor of devotion will have some respect to the true state of the times, especially in the prayers for INVIGORATING the Rebel Generalissimo.

QUESTIONS

1. Why was Washington so revered by the American people during the Revolution?
2. What are the primary characteristics for which the various authors praise Washington? Which ones do you think are the most important? Why?
3. What were the major criticisms leveled at Washington by Charles Lee? Are they direct attacks or does Lee imply them? Why did Lee choose this method of attacking Washington and defending his own personal honor?
4. Why do you think Rivington chose to attack Washington's personal character? What did he hope to gain?
5. Which type of criticism would be more successful—the type levied by Charles Lee or the type delivered by James Rivington? Why? Do you see similar types of criticisms aimed at American leaders today? If so, how are they similar and how are they different from these attacks against Washington?

NOTE

1. *Clove* means "valley." This place was near West Point, New York.

CHAPTER 5

Benedict Arnold, 1780–1781

If George Washington was the ultimate hero, then Benedict Arnold was the ultimate traitor. Even today, his name is synonymous with the worst kind of treachery. What made Arnold's treason so dastardly and horrible was the fact that it was so unexpected.

Early in the war, Benedict Arnold was an up-and-coming military leader with seemingly endless potential. He participated in the invasion of Canada and helped lead the attack on Quebec. Although the attack ultimately failed, Arnold came home a hero and was promoted to brigadier general. His fame continued to increase as the war progressed. The June 20, 1780, *Maryland Journal* described Arnold as "the celebrated Major General Arnold, (styled in Great Britain the American Hannibal)," indicating how much of a public hero he had become.

But, somewhere, somehow, something went wrong. It is still not clear why Benedict Arnold sought to betray the American cause. George Washington placed him in command of Philadelphia in June 1778. While in Philadelphia, Arnold was accused of violating state laws and military regulations to his own personal benefit. He also married Margaret (Peggy) Shippen, the daughter of a Loyalist, on April 8, 1779.

Sometime in May 1779, Arnold first made overtures to the British (apparently after being encouraged to do so by Peggy and her family). Nothing came of these contacts until Arnold was court-martialed for violating regulations. Although only receiving an official reprimand for his conviction, Arnold was highly offended. He once more contacted the British and offered to surrender control of the fort at West Point, New York. His treachery was discovered only when his British contact, Major John André, was stopped while trying to return to the British lines in New York. Because he was in civilian clothes, André was hanged as a spy. Arnold managed to escape to New York, but the taint of his treason followed him for the rest of his life. In 1781, Arnold and his family went to England. He tried to get a military command, but without success. Once the war ended in 1783, Arnold became increasingly unpopular in Great Britain. Over the next two decades, he tried various economic ventures in Great Britain, Canada, and the Caribbean in an attempt to gain financial success. None worked, and Arnold died in London in 1801 from gout and dropsy.

The Patriot discussions of Benedict Arnold's treason all recoiled in horror and shock at what he had done. The first piece is General Nathaniel Greene's official report of Arnold's treachery. Next is a letter from an American officer who described in detail the discovery of the plot. This is followed by an acrostic poem that attacks Arnold and condemns him for his actions and a story about an encounter between Arnold and a captured American captain. The next two selections discuss a "funeral" held for Arnold in Philadelphia. Two short pieces emphasize the depravity of Arnold by first stating that Arnold is not fully accepted among the British and then comparing him to Judas Iscariot. The ninth piece reprimands Arnold for his destructive raid on New London, Connecticut, in 1781. The tenth selection points out that the British attempt at bribery indicates their desperation. Finally, a writer urges Americans to learn a lesson from Arnold's treachery— the lesson that public virtue was essential if the United States was to survive.

The Loyalist discussions of Arnold were somewhat limited because they were not sure how to treat him. The first piece reports his defection to the British. The second selection discusses the wisdom of Arnold's action and why he had changed sides in the war. The final selection praises Arnold for his military activities in Virginia.

PATRIOT VIEWS

General Nathaniel Greene: "Treason of the Blackest Die"

General Greene, in the first official announcement of Arnold's treachery, describes it as "treason of the blackest die." While he emphasizes the horror of the event, Greene also congratulates the army on the fact that the plot was discovered before it was completed. He concludes by praising the army that this was the first event of this type because of the virtue and character of the soldiers.

New York Packet (Fishkill), 12 October 1780

Treason, of the blackest die, was yesterday discovered. General Arnold, who commanded at West-Point, lost to every sentiment of honour, of private and public obligation, was about to deliver up that important post into the hands of the enemy. Such an event must have given the American cause a deadly wound, if not a fatal stab; happily the treason has been timely discovered to prevent the fatal misfortune. The providential train of circumstances which leads to it, affords the most convincing proof that the liberties of America is the object of divine protection. At the same time the treason is to be regretted, the General cannot help congratulating the army on the happy discovery.—

Our enemies, despairing of carrying their point by force, they are practicing every base act to effect by bribery and corruption, what they cannot accomplish in a manly way.

Great honor is due to the American army that this is the first instance of treason of this kind, where many were to be expected from the nature of the dispute, and nothing is so bright an ornament as the character of the American soldiers, as they having been proof against all the arts and seductions of an insidious enemy.

Mr. Andre, Adjutant General to the British army, who came out as a spy to negociate business, is our prisoner.—His Excellency the Commander in Chief is arrived at West Point from Hartford, and is, no doubt, taking the proper measures to fully unravel so hellish a plot.

Anonymous: "A Scene of Villainy"

In this letter, an officer in the Continental army provides a detailed description of how Arnold's treachery was discovered. Because of the horror experienced by many through the betrayal of such a popular hero as Benedict Arnold, newspaper readers would have been eager to read all the details about how the plot was uncovered. Letters such as this one provided that type of detailed information.

Pennsylvania Packet (Philadelphia), 3 October 1780

I make use of the present express to acquaint you with a scene of villainy, which happened in this quarter. A very singular combination of circumstances has preserved to us West-Point and its dependencies. General Arnold, who was the commanding officer, has been bought over to the interest of the enemy, and the place in a few days must have become theirs. They had a part of their army in readiness to act on this occasion, and they could not have failed of success from the concert of Arnold within. Such was the situation of this important post, when a providential event discovered the traitor. Major Andrie, the British Adjutant-General, a person of great talents, appears to have been the principal actor with Arnold. In his return to New-York, after an interview with Arnold, he was stopped near Tarry-town by a few militia, (who, notwithstanding a pass written and signed by General Arnold, by which Andrie was permitted to proceed as a John Anderson) and detained as a spy. As they were conducting him to a party of Continental troops, he offered them a large sum of money, for his release, which they rejected with as much virtue as Arnold received his with baseness.

The state of the garrison, arrangements for its defence in case of attack, a council of war, &c. were found on Andrie, in Arnold's own hand writing.

Col. Jamison, of the light-dragoons, to whom he was conveyed in the first instance, and before a detection of these papers, dispatched an account to Arnold that he had a spy in his care, and described him in such a manner, that Arnold knew it to be Andrie. His Excellency General Washington, the Marquis de LaFayette, General Knox, and their aids were within a few miles of his quarters at this juncture. I had preceeded them with a Major Shaw, to give notice of their coming. Arnold, I think, must have received the advice while we were present, as I observed an embarrassment which I could not at that time account for. The approach of his Excellency, left him but an instant to take measures for his own safety, or it is likely he would have attempted that of Andrie's and, the matter might have remained in obscurity. He ordered his barge, and passing King's ferry as a flag boat, fell down to the Vulture ship of war, which lay below at a short distance. In the meantime an officer arrived with the papers which were discovered, and a letter from Andrie to this Excellency, in which he endeavours to shew that he did not come under the character of a spy. Upon this Col. Hamilton and myself rode to King's ferry, but he had before this gained the enemy's vessel.

We expect Andrie here every minute. I lament at Arnold's escape, that we might have punished such a high piece of perfidiousness, and prevented the enemy from profiting by his informations. Andrie has adventured daringly for the accomplishment of a great end; fortunate for us his abilities failed him, as it was on the point of being finished; and he must in all human probability submit to the fate of a common spy.

Anonymous: "An Unparallelled Traitor"

In the same way that an acrostic was used to praise Washington (see Chapter 4), another poet used that format to castigate Arnold. By the end of this poem, Arnold had been cursed in a variety of ways and condemned to suffer forever in hell for his betrayal of the just cause of the American revolt.

Boston Gazette, 13 November 1780

Mess'rs Printers, Your inserting the subsequent lines in your paper, will oblige one at least of your readers; who has no other way of execrating the memory of an unparallelled TRAITOR, to the Liberties of his Country!

B ORN for a curse to virtue and mankind!
E arth's broadest realms can't show so black a mind.
N ight's sable Veil, your crimes can never hide.
E ach is so great—they'st glut th' historic tide.
D efunct—your memory will ever live.
I n all the glare that Infamy can give!
C urses of ages will attend your name;
T RAITORS alone will glory in your shame.
A lmighty justice sternly waits to roll,
R ivers of Sulphur, on your trait'rous soul—
N ature looks back in conscious error, sad,
O n such a tarnish'd blot, that she has made!
L et HELL receive you rivetted in chains!
D amn'd to the hottest focus of its FLAMES.

Anonymous: "Benedict Arnold's Military Speculations"

This brief story reflects Americans' struggle with explaining how such a hero as Benedict Arnold could have turned into such a traitor. The suggestion of dividing his body in order to praise the wound suffered on behalf of the Revolutionary effort reflected the confusion over how to both praise the hero of the early part of the war and condemn the traitor of the end of the war.

Providence Gazette (Rhode Island), 11 August 1781

During Benedict Arnold's military speculations in Virginia, he took an American Captain prisoner. After some general conversation with the Captain, he asked him "what the Americans would do with him if they caught him.": The Captain at first declined giving him an answer; but upon being repeatedly urged to it, he said, "Why, Sir, if I must answer your question, you must excuse my telling you the plain truth: If my countrymen should catch you, I believe they would first cut off that lame leg, which was wounded in the cause of freedom and virtue, and bury it with the honors of war, and afterwards hang the remainder of your body in gibbets.

John Dunlap: "An Effigy of General Arnold"

Public ceremony played an important role in expressing public opinion during the American Revolution. Here, printer John Dunlap describes a "funeral" for Benedict Arnold which helped the people release some of their frustration and anger over the former hero's treason. The parade reflected the widespread belief that Arnold must be in league with the Devil because nothing else could explain his treachery.

Pennsylvania Packet (Philadelphia), 3 October 1780

A Concise DESCRIPTION of the FIGURES exhibited and paraded through the streets of this city on Saturday last. A STAGE raised on the body of a cart, on which was an effigy of General ARNOLD sitting; this was dressed in regimentals, had two faces emblematical of his traitorous conduct, a mask in his left hand, and a letter in his right from Beelzebub, telling him that he had done all the mischief he could do, and now he must hang himself.

At the back of the General was a figure of the Devil, dressed in black robes, shaking a purse of money at the General's left ear, and in his right hand a pitch fork, ready to drive him into hell as the reward due for the many crimes which his thirst of gold had made him commit.

In the front of the stage and before General Arnold was placed a large lanthorn of transparent paper, with the consequences of his crimes thus delineated, i. e. on one part General Arnold on his knees before the Devil, who is pulling him into the flames—a label from the General's mouth with these words, "My dear Sir, I have served you faithfully;" to which the Devil replies, "And I'll reward you". On another side, two figures hanging, inscribed "The Traitors reward," and wrote underneath "The Adjutant General of the British army, and John Smith; the first hanged as a spy and the other as a traitor to his country." And on the front of the lanthorn was wrote the following:—

"MAJOR GENERAL BENEDICT ARNOLD, late COMMANDER of the FORT WEST-POINT. THE CRIME OF THIS MAN IS HIGH TREASON. "He has deserted the important post WEST-POINT, on Hudson's River, committed to his charge by His Excellency the Commander in Chief, and is gone off to the enemy at New-York.

His design to have given up this fortress to our enemies, has been discovered by the goodness of the Omniscient Creator, who has not only prevented him carrying it into execution, but has thrown into our hands, ANDRÉ, the Adjutant General of their army, who was detected in the famous character of a spy.

The treachery of this ungrateful General is held up to public view, for the exposition of infamy; and to proclaim with joyful acclamation, another instance of the interposition of bounteous Providence.

The effigy of this ingrate is therefore hanged (for want of his body) as a Traitor to his native country, and a Betrayer of the laws of honor."

The procession began about four o'clock, in the following order:

Several Gentleman mounted on horse-back.
A line of Continental Officers.
Sundry Gentlemen in a line.
A guard of the City Infantry.
Just before the cart, drums and fifes playing the Rogues March.
Guards on each side.

The procession was attended with a numerous concourse of people, who after expressing their abhorrence of the treason and the traitor, committed him to the flames, and left both the effigy and the original to sink into ashes and oblivion.

Anonymous: "The Funeral of Benedict Arnold"

Another writer used the "funeral" of Benedict Arnold to call on Americans to continue the struggle against British tyranny. Through the mechanism of a letter from the Devil to Arnold, this writer emphasizes the success of the American effort because of Americans' bravery and hard work. Arnold's job was to undermine this success and help in the utter destruction of the United States as desired by the Devil and his ally, Great Britain.

Pennsylvania Packet (Philadelphia), 7 October 1780

To the Printer of the Pennsylvania Packet: SIR, I was sorry to see that in your last paper, giving an account of the funeral of Benedict Arnold, you took but little notice of the letter written to him by his master. As I am very curious of these original pieces, I took a copy of it, and I beg you to publish it in your next. A Letter from His INFERNAL MAJESTY BURLATATARRA BELZEBUB, to ALAN BUZRAEL, commonly known as BENEDICT ARNOLD, a true copy of the original which he had in his hand before he was burnt, in Philadelphia, September 30, 1780. Faithful Buzrael, YOU remember that before we sent you in the world to prepare the ruin of America (the worthy object of our indignation being by its situation capable of more virtue than any country in the world) we ordered you to begin by great exertions of bravery, to gain the affection of its inhabitants, and bestow on yourself their confidence and their friendship. You succeeded very well in this business, and you was even skilled enough to seduce and associate to your operations some powerful citizens of their country, whom we shall reward in time for their great achievements. We assure you of our royal satisfaction in this particular, and we are glad to see that you obtained the title of a General, in which dignity you may be able to do more mischief than in any other. But we cannot approve of the choice you made of your face, which has something roguish in it, and does not quite inspire all that confidence we expected. We understand by some Savages, both English and Americans, lately arrived in our dominions, that what they call the virtuous citizens of America, suspect you very much of being an enemy to their country. We see with great abhorrence, that, notwithstanding all your secret intrigues to ruin the country, the independence of America acquires every day more strength and solidity; their commerce is flourishing more than ever, their country affords them every kind of provisions, their patriotism grows more and more invincible. We deplore with our friends in England the good condition of their army, and the bravery of their soldiers. Our kingdom trembles at the very name of Washington, and we detest him as much as he is adored by his countrymen. We expect that you will find some effectual means to deliver us from this powerful enemy, but particularly to put an end, by a capital stroke, to all the pretensions of that people, and we flatter ourselves that after their subjection they will be in a few years as corrupted, as wicked, as cruel as their mother country. We rely entirely upon your abilities, but in the same time we require a prompt execution of our orders. Your affectionate King, BELZEBUB.

Anonymous: "Lord Cornwallis Refuses to See Him"

This author states that the British have not accepted Arnold. Americans could not understand Arnold's treachery and they hoped that no good would come of it. This would be true if Arnold did not succeed among the British.

Vermont Gazette (Bennington), 9 July 1781

We hear General Arnold is safely arrived in New-York, from Portsmouth in Virginia, with a cargo of horses and slaves. It is said Lord Cornwallis refuses to see him, and that the officers in his Lordship's army (who are chiefly gentlemen) refused to serve with him. In consequence of these public marks of contempt, poor Benedict is driven to the old trade of 'horse-jockeying' and 'soul driving', which he followed for several years as a skipper in the West-Indies.

Anonymous: "Judas Iscariot"

This author compares Benedict Arnold to Judas Iscariot. He states that Arnold was worse because Judas at least had the nerve to kill himself for his actions.

New Hampshire Gazette (Portsmouth), 20 August 1781

Judas Iscariot betrayed his Master for thirty Pieces of Silver, but repenting of his Guilt, returned the Money into the Treasury, and went and hanged himself.

Judas Arnold received Five Thousand Pounds Sterling for his Treachery, and we find has lodged the Money in the British Funds, but he has not Spirit enough to pursue the Character in the only part worthy of Imitation.

Anonymous: "A Gigantick Overgrown Monster"

Criticism of Arnold continued long after the discovery of his planned treachery. Following his flight to New York, Arnold took a commission in the British army and worked to rally Loyalists to the British cause. On September 6, 1781, he raided New London, Connecticut. This attack was considered particularly odious because Arnold had lived and worked in New Haven, Connecticut, prior to the Revolution. This author attacks Arnold's efforts on behalf of the British Crown and once more underscores the enormity of his betrayal.

Pennsylvania Packet (Philadelphia), 25 September 1781

Is there not stored in heaven's wrath, some red hot thunder bolts to come hurling down with dreadful vengeance upon the unaccountable miscreant wretch, whose serpentine soul betrays his country, and sets the place of his nativity in flames?

TO THE TRAYTOR GENERAL ARNOLD.

Read and tremble at the above awful question! Light as you may think of it, there is a tremendous Judge.

Your actions are so infamous, that if general Clinton had employed the devil and all his imps to have raked hell for a complete villain, they could not have found your equal.

When I consider you as a man mounting rapidly to the highest pitch of honour, all on a sudden descending from that pinnacle to glory to the mean Lucrative Traitor; I am indeed surprized. But, as if your crimes were not yet sufficient, when I find you slaughtering your countrymen, and carrying on the ravages and devastations of the war, with a degree of inveteracy never before heard of; I stand confounded and shocked at the thoughts of such a viper ever being brought into the world. And as if you were determined to outdo the furies of the infernal regions; you have, contrary to what human nature could be supposed capable of, set New-London, the neighbourhood of your nativity in flames, while you murdered its inhabitants and your most intimate acquaintance.

To make up your measure of iniquity, and to hand your name down to posterity, as the most consummate daemon that ever existed; there is only a few crimes more for you to commit, viz. to rip open the womb which gave such a rancourous serpent birth, to embrue your hands in the blood of your dearest connections, then tear out the heart of your patron and protector general Clinton, and to close the scene lay violent hands on your own life.

I took up my pen with an intent to shew a reflective glass, wherein you might at one view behold your actions; but soon found such a horrid ugly deformity in the outlines of your picture, that I was frightened at the sight, so the mirrour dropped and broke to pieces! each of which discovered you to be a gigantick overgrown monster, of such a variety of shapes, all over ulcerated, that it is in vain to attempt to describe them

Common Sense, "Crisis Extraordinary"

In this brief piece, Common Sense states that the attempt to bribe Arnold is a sign that British power is declining. Only desperate people resort to bribery.

Norwich Packet (Connecticut), 21 November 1780

But there is one reflection results from this black business, that deserves notice, which is, that it shows the declining power of the enemy. An attempt to bribe is a sacrifice of military fame, and a concession of inability to conquer; as a proud people they ought to be above it, and as soldiers to despise it; and however they may feel on the occasion, the world at large will despise them for it, and consider America superior to their arms.

Anonymous: "One Important Lesson"

Many Americans considered Arnold's treachery an example of what could happen if the people did not hold true to their moral virtue in the fight against Great Britain. This author urges his readers to realize what could be learned from Arnold's treason. To be true patriots, Americans must put the good of their country above their own personal desires. Only a person of good character could capably serve their country.

Providence Gazette (Rhode Island), 6 October 1781

America has yet to learn one important lesson from the defection and treachery of General Arnold. To cultivate domestick and moral virtue as the only basis of true patriotism. Publick virtue and private vice are wholly incompatible. A speculator in office, a drunkard, a debauchee, a sharper in business, and a man unfaithful to promises, and treacherous in private friendships, should never be trusted with any share of the power, honor, or treasure, of the United States.

LOYALIST VIEWS

Anonymous: "The American Hannibal"

When news of Arnold's treason first spread into territory occupied by the British, many Loyalists rejoiced that it was a sign that the rebels were losing the war. Arnold's defection was an example of what wise men would do if they wanted to survive the war.

South Carolina and American General Gazette (Charleston), 11 October 1780

The famous BENEDICT ARNOLD, Major General in the service of the Congress, whose courageous March to Canada in 1775, has occasioned his being named the American Hannibal, and to whose Prowess and Intrepidity the Surrender of General Burgoyne's Army was in a great Measure owing, we are well informed, last Week went voluntarily into New York, and enrolled himself among the List of British Subjects.

John Wells: "General Arnold Still Attached to America"

Many Loyalists believed that Arnold had just come to his senses and that his actions reflected a sincere desire to do what was best for America. Here, Loyalist printer John Wells points out that it was clear that the United States could never be independent. Arnold, accepting that fact, wanted to be ruled by Great Britain rather than France and so he changed sides in the conflict.

South Carolina and American General Gazette (Charleston), 14 October 1780

It is said, that when General Arnold went into New York, he declared himself as much attached to America as ever, but being convinced, from every circumstance, that either Great-Britain or France must govern her (and that the latter, though the least improbable, was the choice of those in power, in hopes of retaining their importance) this consideration determined him to throw up his command, and offer his service, in whatever station his Excellency Sir Henry Clinton thought proper to employ him, to assist in frustrating the intentions of France, and bringing back the Colonies to their allegiance to Great-Britain.

The humane polite treatment which the friends of Government experienced from General Arnold, particularly when he was Commandant of Philadelphia, was gratefully remembered by many who were in New-York, when he came in there; and it is said that his Excellency Sir Henry Clinton has been pleased to confer on him the rank of Brigadier General.

James Rivington: "Arnold Vastly Successful"

Loyalists also used Arnold's military successes on behalf of the British to indicate that he had made the right decision in changing sides. Printer James Rivington describes his raids in Virginia that greatly hurt the Americans because of the supplies lost to Arnold's forces.

Royal Gazette (New York), 27 January 1781

From Philadelphia we learn, that Brigadier General Arnold was carrying on his operations with vast success, and (from an admirable stratagem by which he had greatly deceived the enemy) with very little opposition. It is said he had proceeded from Richmond to Petersburg, the depositum of provisions for subsisting the Rebel army in Carolina, where he destroyed all the public properties, buildings, magazines, &c. as perfectly as that business had been effected at Richmond.

QUESTIONS

1. Why did Americans react in horror to Arnold's treason? How do General Greene and the various newspaper writers describe the impact of his treachery?
2. Why did the people of Philadelphia hold a "funeral" for Arnold? What function does it fulfill for the citizens of Philadelphia?
3. Why did several of the anonymous writers try to show that Arnold's position was worse now that he had gone over to the British? Was his failure the only way for Americans to accept his treason?
4. Why did the last Patriot writer urge his readers to learn a lesson from Arnold's treason? Why do several other authors urge Americans to be more virtuous? What do they fear?
5. How do the Loyalist writers such as John Wells and James Rivington react to Arnold's treason? Why do you think their comments are so limited in scope?

CHAPTER 6

The Articles of Confederation, 1777–1781

O nce the fighting started in 1775, the British colonial governments slowly ceased to function. The Continental Congress had to take charge and function as a government. On the same day the Congress appointed the committee to write the Declaration of Independence, it also appointed a committee to write a document laying out a form of government for the new nation.

The chair of the committee, John Dickinson, presented the results on July 12, 1776. Following debate and revisions by the Continental Congress, the final version of the Articles of Confederation was approved in November 1777. The government Congress approved addressed many of the concerns that had sparked the American Revolution in the first place. Fearing the power of a strong central government, the Articles proposed a decentralized system with much of the power remaining at the state level. The United States would be ruled by a one-house legislature, with each state having one vote. There would be no independent executive or president, but there was also no prime minister as existed in the British system. The national Congress would concentrate its work and attention primarily in the area of foreign affairs. Congress could request support from the states, financial or otherwise, but there was no mechanism to force state support of the national government.

By and large, the states were supportive of the Articles of Confederation and many approved them fairly quickly. However, there was one major stumbling block. The issue of western lands threatened to derail the entire process. A number of states, especially Virginia, had claims to large areas west of the Appalachian Mountains because of their original sea-to-sea grants from the king of England. Other states, like Pennsylvania and Maryland, had very clearly defined boundaries in their original charters and thus could claim no additional territory.

Maryland, in particular, thought this was unfair. If the war was won, some states would gain additional territory won through the struggles of all the states. They insisted that, before the state of Maryland would approve the Articles of Confederation, all states must surrender any claims to western lands to the national government.

Maryland's leaders were very adamant about this demand. Because of it, the adoption of the Articles of Confederation took almost six years. Finally, in February 1781, Virginia surrendered its western land claims to the United States government. Following this action, the legislature of Maryland approved the Articles of Confederation on March 1, 1781. In many ways, the Articles of Confederation had been operating unofficially since 1776. With Maryland's approval, the first government of the United States became official.

Because of the war, discussion of the proposed Articles of Confederation was limited in the newspapers. The selections in favor of their adoption begin with Maryland's official call for adoption only after all western land claims had been ceded to the national government. The other pieces are congratulatory pieces on the final adoption of the Articles by Maryland.

Three selections opposing the Articles are included. The first appeared in a Loyalist paper and criticizes the attempt to create a new government. The second piece states that the Articles give too much power to Congress, while the third worries that the Articles have been thrown together too quickly and calls for further discussion of a number of issues, including the western lands problem.

Support for the Articles of Confederation

The State of Maryland: "A Declaration"

By and large, the state of Maryland favored the Articles of Confederation, but could not support fighting for land increases by other states. In this declaration, Maryland supports the Articles in general, but also points out its strong reservations because of the issue of western lands.

Maryland Journal (Baltimore), 30 March 1779

Whereas the General Assembly of Maryland hath heretofore resolved, "That the Delegates of this State should be instructed to remonstrate to the Congress, that this State esteem it essentially necessary for rendering the Union lasting, that the United States in Congress assembled, should have full power to ascertain and fix the western limits of those States that claim to the Mississippi or South Sea.

That this State considered themselves justly entitled to a right in common with the other members of the union, to that extensive tract of country, which lies to the westward of the frontiers of the United States, the property of which was not vested in, or granted to individuals at the commencement of the present war; that the same had been, or might thereafter be gained from the King of Great Britain, or the native Indians, by the blood and treasure of all, and ought therefore to be a common estate, to be granted out on terms beneficial to all the United States, and that they should use their utmost endeavors, that an article to that effect be made part of the confederation.

That this State would contribute their quota of men and money, towards carrying on the present war with Great Britain, for the purpose of establishing the freedom and independence of the United States, according to such rule of proportion as should be determined by the United States, in Congress assembled and would pay their proportions of all money issued or borrowed by Congress, or which might thereafter be issued or borrowed for the purpose aforesaid.

And that this State would accede to and faithfully execute all treaties which had been or should be made by authority of Congress; and would be bound and governed by the determination of the United States, in Congress assembled, relative to peace or war.

That this State hath, upon all occasions, shown her zeal to promote and maintain the general welfare of the United States of America: That upon the same principle, they were of opinion, a confederation of perpetual friendship and union between the United States is highly necessary for the benefit of the whole; and that they are most willing and desirous to enter into a confederation and union; but at the same time, such confederation should, in their opinion, be formed on the principles of justice and equity.

Which resolves, remonstrance and instructions, were, by our Delegates, laid before Congress, and the objections therein made to the confederation, were submitted in writing to their confederation, and the several points fully discussed and debated, and the alterations and amendments proposed by our Delegates to the confederation, in consequence of the aforesaid instructions by us to them given, were rejected, and no satisfactory reasons assigned for the rejection thereof.

We do therefore declare, that we esteem it fundamentally wrong and repugnant to every principle of equity and good policy, on which a confederation between free, sovereign, and independent States, ought to be founded, that this or any other State, entering into such confederation, should be burdened with heavy expenses for the subduing and guarantying immense tracts of country, if they are not to share any part of the monies arising from the sales of the lands within those tracts, or be otherwise benefited thereby. In conformity to this our opinion, the sentiments of our constituents, in justice to them and ourselves, and left such construction should hereafter be put on the undefined expressions contained in the third article of the confederation, and the proviso to the ninth (according to which no State is to be deprived of territory for the benefit of the United States) as may subject all to such guaranty as aforesaid, and deprive some of the said States of their right in common to the lands aforesaid.—We declare, that we mean not to subject ourselves to such guaranty, nor will we be responsible for any part of such expense, unless the third article and proviso aforesaid be explained so as to prevent their being hereafter construed in a manner injurious to this State. Willing, however to remove, as far as we can consistently with the trust conferred upon us, every other objection on our part to the confederation, and anxiously desirous us to cement, by the most indissoluble ties, that union which has hitherto enabled us to resist the artifices and the power of Great Britain, and conceiving ourselves, as we have heretofore declared, justly entitled to a right in common with the other members of the union, to the extensive country lying to the westward of the frontiers of the United States, the property of which was not vested in or granted to individuals at the commencement of the present war.

We declare, that we will accede to the confederation, provided an article or articles be added thereto, giving full power to the United States, in Congress assembled, to ascertain and fix the western limits of the States claiming to extend to the Mississippi or South Sea, and expressly reserving and securing to the United States a right in common in and to all the lands lying to the westward of the frontiers aforesaid, not granted to, surveyed for, or purchased by individuals at the commencement of the present war, in such manner that the fair lands be sold out, or otherwise disposed of, for the common benefit of all the States, and that the money arising from the sale of those lands, or the quitrents reserved thereon, may be deemed and taken as part of the monies belonging to the United States, and as such be appropriated by Congress towards defraying the expenses of the war, and the payment of interest on monies borrowed, or to be borrowed, on the credit of the United States, from France, or any other European power, or for any other joint benefit of the United States.

We do farther declare, that the exclusive claim set up by some States to the whole western country, by extending their limits to the Mississippi or South Sea, is, in our judgment, without any solid foundation; and we religiously believe will, if submitted to, prove ruinous to this State, and to other States similarly circumstanced, and in process of time be the means of subverting the confederation, if it be not explained by the additional article or articles proposed so as to obviate all misconstruction and misinterpretation of those parts thereof that are herein before specified.

We entered into this just and necessary war to defend our rights against the attacks of avarice and ambition: We have made the most strenuous efforts during the prosecution of it, and we are resolved to continue them until our independence is firmly established. Hitherto we have successfully resisted and we hope, with the blessing of Providence, for final Success. If the enemy, encouraged by the appearance of divisions among us, and the hope of our not confederating, should carry on hostilities longer than they otherwise would have done, let those be responsible for the prolongation of the war and all its consequent calamities, who, by refusing to comply with requisition: so just and reasonable, have hitherto prevented the confederation from taking place, and are therefore justly chargeable with every evil which hath flowed, and may flow from procrastination.

David C. Claypoole: "This Great Event"

Printer David C. Claypoole reports on the public reaction of the people of Philadelphia when news reached there that Maryland had finally ratified the Articles of Confederation. For many Americans, the approval of the new government set the stage for future greatness for the United States. Feu-de-joye *is correctly spelled* feu de joie *and refers to a salute fired by rifles in rapid succession along a line of troops, usually to celebrate a victory.*

Pennsylvania Packet (Philadelphia), 3 March 1781

This great event, which will confound our enemies, fortify us against their arts of seduction, and frustrate their plans of division, was announced to the public at twelve o'clock under the discharge of the artillery on the land, and the cannon of the shipping in the Delaware. The bells were rung, and every manifestation of joy shown on the occasion. The *Ariel* frigate, commanded by the gallant Paul Jones, fired a *feu-de-joye*, and was beautifully decorated with a variety of streamers in the day, and ornamented with a brilliant appearance of lights in the night.

At two o'clock in the afternoon his excellency the president of Congress received the congratulations of the legislative and executive bodies of this state, of the civil and military officers and many of the principal citizens, who partook of a collation, provided on this happy occasion. The evening was ushered in by an elegant exhibition of fireworks.

Thus has the union, began by necessity, been indissolubly cemented. Thus America, like a well constructed arch, whose parts, harmonizing and mutually supporting each other, are the more closely united the greater the pressure upon them, is growing up in war into greatness and consequence among the nations.

A Citizen: "Final Ratification"

In this short piece, A Citizen rejoices over the final piece of the puzzle for the new nation. With the government format approved, the United States was now fully independent and in control of its own destiny.

Providence Gazette (Rhode Island), 24 March 1781

Thus will the *first of March*, 1781, be a day memorable in the annals of America, for the final ratification of the Confederation and perpetual Union of the Thirteen States of America.—A Union, begun by necessity, cemented by oppression and common danger, and now finally consolidated into a perpetual confederacy of these new and rising States; And thus the United States of America, having, amidst the calamities of a destructive war, established a solid foundation of greatness, are growing up into consequence among the nations, while their haughty enemy, Britain, with all her boasted wealth and grandeur, instead of bringing them to *her feet*, and inducing them to unconditional submission, finds her hopes blasted, her power crumbling to pieces, and the empire which, with overbearing insolence and brutality, she exercised on the ocean, divided among her insulted neighbours.

Anonymous: "This Confederation Is Now Completed"

This author laughs over British attempts to show the weakness of the United States. The British have commented that the Articles are not finished. This author points out that the confederation is complete so the hopes of the British are destroyed.

Providence Gazette (Rhode Island), 7 July 1781

Lord North had the impudence to declare, with an air of triumph, to the parliament of G. Britain, that the confederation of America was not accomplished, and that Maryland had refused to accede to it. The traitor Arnold, or those whom he employed to write for him, foolishly boasted of the same thing. This confederation is now completed, and, by the confession of our enemies, themselves, it is an immense advantage we have gained against them. But the noble motive which actuated Maryland in this accession was, to content Congress, and to satisfy his Most Christian Majesty, who appeared earnestly to wish that the union of the States might be consummated.

OPPOSITION TO THE ARTICLES OF CONFEDERATION

James Robertson: "Curious Production"

Since the Loyalists did not want to break from Great Britain, they downplayed the importance of the proposed Articles of Confederation. In this selection, Loyalist printer James Robertson attacks the proposed government as a further chapter in America's downfall and destruction.

Royal Pennsylvania Gazette (Philadelphia), 10 March 1778

The following curious Production [the Articles of Confederation], calculated to amuse the giddy multitude of apostate subjects, is extracted from a Connecticut Rebel Paper——It is not a little astonishing to see men, endowed with common sense, sucking poison from the pens of those who have neatly accomplished the destruction of them and their country, by the lowest and most shallow artifices ever offered to human understanding.

Independens: "From All Such, May the Lord Deliver Us"

This author urges Americans to seriously consider the Articles of Confederation. He does not think they provide a good government for the United States because they give too much power to the national Congress. Americans were very fearful that they would replace the strong government of Great Britain with another one of their own making.

Freeman's Journal, or New Hampshire Gazette (Portsmouth), 13 January 1778

There never was an Aera recorded in the Annals of the American History, so important and interesting as the present: We are all call'd upon, as well individually as collectively, to act our Parts in the solemn Scene; It is therefore incumbent upon every Member of the Community to appear for himself and his Posterity, and determine whether they shall in future enjoy the Blessings of Peace, Liberty and Safety, or become Hewers of Wood and Drawers of Water to our British Taskmaster.

The climacterick Period is arrived, and we are now about to join in solemn Covenant, for the Preservation of our inestimable Rights & Priviledges, with all the other American States; And for this purpose Thirteen Articles of Confederation are drawn up and destributed throughout America, for the candid and impartial Disquisition of every Friend to this Country: To be silent at this Time may be justly thought a Want of Attention, or rather indifference, to our public Concern, it is therefore earnestly hoped that every able Pen will be imployed at so critical a Juncture, that in the midst of Council we may be safe.

I have carefully perused and candidly examined these Articles of Confederation, and find them to be a Compilation of excellent Wisdom, and the greatest Attention to the general Interest of the United States; they are the Compositions of able and great Politicians, and in the general appear to have a single Eye to the true Interest of the whole, without the sordid Views of private Emoluments; nevertheless I must own, they are not wholly free from Exceptions, which I have candidly undertaken to point out, from a conscientious Attachment to my Country.

In the Eighth Article the Proportion of each State for the supply of the Continental Treasury, is to be estimated by Congress, according to the Value of Lands in each State, as such Lands and the Buildings and improvements thereon shall be estimated, 'in such a Mode as Congress shall direct and appoint;' To this I would observe, the mode of proportioning, ought not to be left to Congress, as they cannot be proper Judges of the Valuation of Lands and the Income of Estates so well as the States themselves, therefore some invariable and fixed Rule ought to be settled by the general Act of Covenancy.

In the Ninth Article Congress claims the Right of appointing & establishing Courts for receiving & determining Appeals in all cases of Capture.— This is rather of too extensive a Nature; for if the Disputes arise between 2 Persons of One & the same State, or between the Subjects of any State, and the subjects of the King of Great Britain, (with whom we are at War) why Need there be Appeals to any other Courts, when the Municipal Laws of each State may as well determine the Dispute; I grant that if the Action or Controversy happens between two Persons of Different States, or between the subjects of Foreign Princes our Allies and the Inhabitants of any of the American States, then such a Court may be proper, but yet with the Addition of a Jury, of which no Mention is made in the said Article :—Furthermore, in the same Article, Congress reserves the Priviledge of appointing all the Officers of the Post Office (which are very many) this I think improper and impolitic, for it invests them with too great a Power of Multiplying their Dependents, and thereby endangering the States in future. I would rather it should be stipulated that such necessary Offices should be appointed in each State, and the Prices of Postage to be affixed by general Rules settled by the Congress, which will have the general Benefit; allowing to all Printers of each State, the free Carriage of their Respective News Papers to each other, as heretofore, for the Preservation of that inestimable Blessing, the Liberty of the Press, whereby Tyrants are made to Tremble, and which, like the Sword of Justice, is a terror to Evil Doers, and a praise to them that do well—In the same 9th Article an essential alteration must be made; far be it from me to suggest that there was a design in the Penman, or that there is any Occasion of Suspicion of that nature, but I observe, that if 9 of the States can determine upon Peace or War, coin Money, emit Bills, borrow Money, &c. that the Number of Nine shall be binding upon the whole, by which the Nine Southern may always determine for the four Northern States, as they are so distinguished; therefore to remove every Doubt or Jealousy, let the Number be Eleven, and then two of the Northern States will certainly be included in all such important Matters.

In the same Ninth Article, Congress reserve the Right of appointing and commissioning all Officers in the Navy, which I think not only impolitic for the same Reasons as appointing Post Officers; but it may be found very detrimental to the public service; for it is more likely ships of War will be mann'd by Officers who are chosen in the States where they are built, than if Officer'd by strangers in those States, for I mean to throw out of sight, every Idea of Impressing Men into the Marine service as being subversive of that Liberty which we have spilt so much Blood to preserve inviolate; if the Officers of the Army are to be appointed by the States, why not of the Navy, excepting Admirals and Generals?

There are some lesser Matters which I rather pass by than recommend any other Alterations to be made in the general Plan; but I am very jealous of investing any one Man, or Body of Men, with too much Power which is a Captivating and bewitching Passion.

The Majesty of the People should ever have Ascendancy, and all Power must be considered by their servants as originating from them and only delegated for a Time; and as we have considered the British Nation undone, by the avaricious Thirst of Placement and Pensioners, from all such, may the Lord deliver us.

Civis: "The Confederacy of the United States"

In this essay, the author states that the Articles of Confederation are a good beginning, but they do not go far enough. They have failed to provide solutions to all the nation's problems, particularly the issue of western land claims. Civis calls for more discussion before the final government structure is established.

Pennsylvania Packet (Lancaster), 18 March 1778

By your Packet I am informed, that the Confederacy of the United States, as proposed by Congress, has been assented to by the State of Virginia; and that the inhabitants of the town of Boston have instructed their Representatives to assent to the ratification of it.

The Confederacy has been drawn up with great judgment, and will be considered by future ages as the strongest efforts of human genius in a political capacity. Indeed it contains *multum in parvo,* being concise, yet copious, and has provided in a great degree, to establish a perpetual union of the thirteen States. Nevertheless, there are some things not noticed, of considerable importance. The hopes that some person of more abilities would attend to them, made me suspend these remarks. But they have not been attended to; and as our Honourable Assembly are now met, and will probably proceed to the consideration of the Confederacy, a regard to the public good induced me to offer them to the consideration of the Members through your paper, lest they should be overlooked, as they have been by the House of Delegates of Virginia, and the inhabitants of the town of Boston.

It is universally known in the States, that there are vast tracts of country on the frontiers of the settlements in some of the States, and quit rents, which were the property of the Crown of Great Britain; but when America secures her independence, a question will arise, whose property those lands, &c. are, whether of the State in which they lay, or of the United States? To me the property appears to be jointly in the United States; for all conquests made at the common expence of blood and treasure, ought to be for a common, and not a partial benefit.

If the benefit should be common, why is it not expressed in the Confederacy? Perhaps it might be thought an improper time, but to me this appears to be the very time when it ought to be determined, as it is most likely to be done consistent with equal justice, and less embarrassment, than at any future time.

It is not my intention to advance any arguments to convince those Gentlemen that it is both just and proper to have the property of those lands and quitrents ascertained, but only to call their attention to these objects, the good sense of the members must suggest many; for at a single glance, the circumstance of this State, New Jersey, Maryland, Rhode-Island, Delaware, &c. when compared with some other States, are too striking to need any remark: Nor can it escape them what prodigious advantages Canada under the new limits would derive, should the Canadians accede to the Confederacy.

Another thing which appears to me to be an omission is, that no provision has been made for the forming of new states, out of the vast unpeopled territory which lay within the undefined limits of the States; and such cases must occur. Perhaps it may be objected to this, that the limits assigned by the Kings of Great-Britain to the several States, will include all such territory that can possibly be annexed to the thirteen States. This requires a very large discussion; but it is to be hoped we are not seized with that phrensy, for having a larger extent of country annexed to any one State than what can be governed with convenience to the people, and the energy of Government be extended through the whole. It is this infatuation and desire for an extensive empire, that has involved, and daily involves, mankind in the miseries of war and slavery throughout the world, and if not guarded against in the infancy of the States, may prompt the stronger, at some future day, to endeavour the conquest of the weaker, which may give rise to feuds that will eventually dissolve the union.

The zeal of some may think a hasty ratification of the articles of Confederacy necessary to cement the union of the States, and be unwilling to discuss these matters; but if we wish a durable, a perpetual union to exist amongst the States, every possible obstacle to it should be removed in the beginning, otherwise it will resemble a house built with untempered mortar that will not cement the parts together of which it is composed, and instead of growing stronger by age, it will moulder to a dissolution.

QUESTIONS

1. Both the Maryland Declaration and the essay by Civis discuss the issue of western lands. Maryland's leaders seemed to think there was a solution, but Civis was not as hopeful without major restructuring. Why were western lands such a major issue?
2. The final ratification of the Articles of Confederation produced comments and public celebrations throughout the country, such as the one

described by David Claypoole. Why did people think this was a major event?

3. How did the Loyalists such as James Robertson respond to the proposed government? Did the final ratification of the Articles of Confederation mean that the Loyalists had finally lost?

CHAPTER 7

The Union in Crisis? 1782–1787

Almost from the time they were finally approved, the Articles of Confederation had critics. Many people worried that the national government was not strong enough to handle the problems facing the young nation. Historians have long debated over how bad the 1780s actually were. John Fiske called the decade the "critical period" in American history and asserted that the United States would have faced certain decline and destruction had the government structure not been changed.[1] Merrill Jensen disagreed, stating that the 1780s were a prosperous time and that there was no real need to change the national government.[2]

It is not clear what the majority of Americans thought about the condition of the United States during the 1780s, but several prominent Americans concluded quite early that the Articles government was not strong enough. By 1783, James Madison believed that something must be done if the United States was going to survive. He and others began to express their concerns in the pages of the newspapers. The result was an ongoing debate throughout the mid-1780s over the strength and success of the Articles government.

Throughout the 1780s, newspaper printers discussed the successes and failures of the Articles government. Most agreed with James Madison, believing that the government structure created by the Articles of Confederation could not succeed. Many newspaper printers actively supported the move toward a new government, which grew throughout the decade. American newspapers of the 1780s reflected the growing anxieties of the printers for the security and efficacy of the national government, and the continual discussion of such issues encouraged readers to be concerned as well. Such worries, whether based on actual fact or not, helped set the stage for the adoption of the new form of government in 1787–1788.

The documents that emphasized the idea of "the union in crisis" stressed the need to strengthen the national government. The first selection, written in 1783, questions very early whether the Articles of Confederation are strong enough to rule the United States. The second piece calls for more power for Congress in order to carry out the powers already granted. The third and fourth selections discuss whether the country could continue to exist without changes to the government. The fifth piece discusses foreign reactions to the problems of the United States. The next selection stresses the international problems the United States faced because its government could not adequately defend itself. The seventh document states that the Articles of Confederation had been written to deal with a wartime situation and that peacetime dictated the need for another form of government. The last piece states that the Confederation is beyond all hope and declares that the states should break into several separate nations.

The documents that downplayed the idea of crisis all stress the presence of tyranny in the calls for more powers for the national government. The first selection states that the future looks bright because the war will soon be over, so Americans should be prepared for better days ahead. The second piece declares that power-hungry leaders were behind the efforts to change the Articles government. The third document states that a stronger national government would result in a standing army, which was very dangerous to the rights of the people. The fourth selection concludes that the proposed methods to raise money for the national government were tyrannical and a threat to the liberty of the people. The final piece states that the problems of the United States stem from a lack of frugality on the part of the Americans rather than a flaw in the government structure.

A CRISIS

Nathaniel Willis: "There Is a Defect Somewhere"

Printer Nathaniel Willis questions whether the Articles of Confederation are strong enough to adequately govern the United States. He was one of the first newspaper printers to question whether the Articles should be changed or not.

Independent Chronicle (Boston), 24 July 1783

It is very extraordinary, says an old correspondent, that so much pains have been taken to form and organize the constitutions of the several individual governments, and so little has been taken, in that which respects the whole nation of America, and which is so superiourly important, that all our greatness, and our greatest concerns rest upon it.

Some bond of confederation was absolutely necessary at the time the present one was formed, and in the then situation of affairs it was a well judged undertaking, because it went no farther than into the first steps of the business. But if the confederation is equal to all the purposes of America, which have arisen since, as well as before that period, why is it that our national honour, character, and abilities have declined, and are declining under it.—Either the defect lies in the confederation itself, or it lies in the several legislatures, or it lies in the bulk of the people.

It is in vain to say that the defect likes in Congress, personally; for the difficulties took place, while those who formed the confederation sat as members, and though they have been charged over and over again, had those who found fault have succeeded to those they found fault with, still those difficulties remain, and the honour of America is daily suffering under them. Bring all the men in Congress now, who were concerned in forming the confederation, and they will not be able to support the character and dignity of the country under it, nor stem the difficulties which it throws in their way.

Without ever enquiring into the personal character and abilities of the members who, at any time, may compose the Congress of the United States, it must ever shock a sensible mind to hear the sovereign authority of all the citizens of America, which is there represented, irreverently spoken of. The individual members may have their various degrees of abilities and accomplishments; but the power and authority which they represent is a sacred thing, and in supporting or debasing that, we support and debase ourselves.

If the defect lies with the several legislatures, that from a desire to aggrandize their personal power, they are undermining the great cause and national dignity of America, let it be known; or if it arises from want of information in the bulk of the people, let it be removed by proper explanations; or if it springs from defect in the confederation, let it be revised, not by Congress, but by a continental convention, elected and authorized for the purpose. One fact however is certain, which is, that there is a defect somewhere, and that it is our duty, interest and happiness to remove it.

John Russell: "Congress Must Be Endowed with More Power"

John Russell printed a newspaper in western Massachusetts. In this piece, he calls on the state legislatures to address the need for more power in Congress. Such a change was absolutely necessary if the United States was

*going to meet her financial obligations resulting from the successful revolt
from British rule.*

Hampshire Herald (Springfield, Massachusetts), 16 November 1784

The contracted limits of Congressional power in this country, is truly lamentable, and a national misfortune that requires the immediate attention of the different legislatures. How absurd, to endow them with power to levy war, to contract loans, and then deprive them of their resources necessary for the discharge of such debts, which the faith of the nation is pledged for.—Congress must be endowed with more power. We are all sensible of the necessity of the measure, and yet all equally supine. Who, with greater confidence, can we entrust our liberties with, than those wise fathers and guardians who have conducted us through a perilous war, and moored us in the haven of independence.

Timothy Green: "To Be, or Not to Be? That Is the Question!"

Timothy Green was a member of a family of printers that worked all over Connecticut. In this piece, he cleverly uses the famous words of Shakespeare's Hamlet *to call for a strengthening of the national government. Failure to do so could only result in the decline of the American nation.*

Connecticut Gazette (New Haven), 24 March 1786

'To be! or not to be? That is the question!' Whether America shall live in the annals of history, as a Wise, Flourishing, Independent Nation! or shall be handed to Posterity, as a specimen of National Pusilanimity, Injustice, and breach of Public Faith?—The time is now arrived, to decide the All Important Question!

Argus: "The Very Existence of the United States"

Reflecting the arguments of many others, Argus declares that the future of the United States depended on changes being made in the Confederation. Failure in this would result in the loss of the liberty so recently earned in the war.

Freeman's Oracle (Philadelphia), 29 August 1786

No arguments are necessary to demonstrate that the very existence of the United States, as a free and happy people, depends, on our establishing the confederation on a broad and firm basis, and scrupulously supporting our public credit. Let these things be done, and we are secure from even the fear of evil: let either of them be neglected, and the loss of our dear-bought liberties follows of course. No exertions that we can make—no assistance that we can procure, will prevent it. These important points, then, claim the serious regard of every patriotic member of the union.

Anonymous: "One Universal Scene of Anarchy"

Here, a piece from Halifax, Nova Scotia, reprinted for an American audience, discusses the problems of the United States and the Pandora's box they have opened by establishing a democratic form of government. In reporting such comments, the Norwich Packet *shows that the situation must be pretty bad if it looks this way from outside the country.*

Norwich Packet (Connecticut), 2 November 1786

By papers and letters from New England, and other parts of the United or rather Disunited States, we find one universal scene of anarchy and confusion prevailing: And it is the opinion of the most intelligent among them, that matters are fast hastening toward another revolution.—Each State at present possesses powers so totally independent of the others, that no general system can be adopted. They begin to find that a government with so many heads is a monster in politics—and that a Democratical government is productive of more real evils than one altogether monarchical.—The happiness which these States formerly enjoyed, under the government of Britain, where the kingly and popular powers are so equally mixed, they will now in vain, lament the want of.—In exchange for this they have obtained Independence!—a charming word indeed! but productive of more ills than Pandora's Box: For the Box of Pandora being suddenly shut, prevented Hope from flying out with its other contents—but the precious box of independence has been so incautiously opened, that even Hope seems to have taken wings.

John Carter: "Invest Congress with Power"

John Carter, printer of the Providence Gazette, *lived in a seaport town and his emphasis was on how Americans involved in foreign commerce were being treated. The American government was so weak that it could do nothing when American subjects were ill-treated overseas. This needed to change and the only way to do so was to increase the powers of the national government.*

Providence Gazette (Rhode Island), 2 December 1786

The little respect that is paid to the American flag, and the repeated insults which subjects of the United States meet with in foreign ports, must convince the good people of this continent, that it is absolutely necessary we should invest Congress with a power to regulate our commerce, and to support our dignity, as free and independent States;—without which, we must very soon become a reproach and bye-word among the nations.

Harrington: "The Present Weak, Imperfect and Distracted Government"

In this piece, Harrington describes the Articles government as totally inadequate to the current situation. It had been drawn up to deal with a wartime situation. It had worked for that time, but it no longer functioned in the way it needed to do. He assumes that the Convention meeting in Philadelphia will produce changes that will solve the nation's problems.

Pennsylvania Gazette (Philadelphia), 30 May 1787

A citizen of Pennsylvania, in a retired situation, who holds and wishes for no share in the power or offices of his country, and who often addressed you in the years 1774 and 1775, upon the interesting subject of the LIBERTIES of America, begs leave to address you again upon the important subject of her GOVERNMENT.

It is impossible to be happy without freedom,—and it is equally impossible to preserve freedom, without such constitutions and laws as are adapted to the circumstances and habits of our country.

The *rights* of mankind are simple. They require no learning to unfold them. They are better *felt,* than explained. Hence, in matters that relate to *liberty,* the mechanic and the philosopher, the farmer and the scholar, are all upon a footing. But the case is widely different with respect to *government.* It is a complicated science, and requires abilities and knowledge of a variety of other subjects, to understand it. Unfortunately, from the general prevalence of despotism, and the monopoly of power in a few hands, mankind have had but few opportunities of profiting by the knowledge they have acquired by experience in this science. The world, for the first time, saw a number of freemen assembled in America, to compose a system of government for themselves. It now beholds a scene equally new and illustrious,—a body of freemen assembled, to correct the mistakes of this government. How different is the situation of the citizens of America from the rest of mankind!—What would be the fate of the millions of our fellow creatures in the kingdoms of Europe, should they assemble by voluntary association for this purpose?—Or, what would not the subjects of Great-Britain, who complain of the defects or corruptions of their government, give for this inestimable privilege?—Let this comparison kindle in our bosoms a due sense of the value of liberty, and let no pains be spared in framing such a form of government, as will preserve it for ever.

The present fœderal constitution was formed amidst the confusions of war, and in the infancy of our political knowledge. It has been found ineffectual to support public credit—to obtain alliances—to preserve treaties—to enforce taxes—to prevent hostilities with our neighbours, and insurrections among our citizens. Hence the name of an American, which was so respectable in the year 1782, in every part of the globe, is now treated every where with obloquy and contempt.

If the evils we have suffered, and the infamy we have incurred, have not been sufficient to induce us to alter our fœderal government, there is one argument that should possess a weight with us, that should be irresistible. Mankind insensibly glide into a stable government. The rich and the poor soon grow tired of anarchy. They prefer the order and tranquility of despotism to popular licentiousness, and the oppression of law. Hence the success of usurpers in every age and country. It becomes us, therefore, to prevent the power which is the offspring of force, by means of a regular constitution, founded in a mutual compact between rulers and the people. There never was a republic of long duration in any country, whose form was not mixed. But the mixture was in most cases, unfortunately, the effect of accidents, or popular commotions. Hence the inequality of liberty in most of them, and hence their corruption or extinction in every part of the world. I see no reason why a republic, composed of a legislature properly compounded and balanced, where representation is equal, and elections annual, have, therefore, my fellow-citizens, no choice left to us. We must either form an efficient government for ourselves, suited in every respect to our exigencies and interests, or we must submit to have one imposed upon by accident or usurpation. A bramble will exercise dominion over us, if we neglect any longer to choose a vine or a fig-tree for that common temptation to ambition. A fœderal Shays may be more successful than the Shays of Massachusetts Bay, or a body of men may arise, who may form themselves into an order of hereditary nobility, and, by surprize or strategem, prostrate our liberties at their feet.

This view of our situation is indeed truly alarming. We are upon the brink of a precipice Heavens! shall the citizens of America—shall the deposers of the power of George the third, and the conquerors of Britain in America—submit to receive law from a bold and successful demagogue, or a confederated body of usurpers?—Shall the United States become a theatre, on which the crimes of the Caesars and Cromwells of past ages are to be acted over again?—Are the freemen of America to be summed up in the ac-compt of universal slavery, and transferred, like cattle at an auction, to the highest bidder?—Are our fields to be scratched (for they will not then be cultivated) by the hands of slaves? And is the product of our industry, whether in arts or agriculture, to be torn from us by arbitrary edicts, issued from a newly established court of American DESPOTS? Was it for this we drew the sword at Lexington, and submitted to, or rather embraced poverty, exile, imprisonment, flames and death, in every stage of the war? Was it for this we triumphed in the recovery of our cities, and in the reduction of the armies of Burgoyne and Cornwallis? Was it for this, we exulted in the peace which we extorted from Great-Britain in the year 1782? If it was,—then virtue has suffered—heroism has bled—and heaven itself has blessed us in vain.

America has it in her power to adopt a government which shall secure to her all the benefits of monarchy, without parting with any of the privileges of a republic. She may divide her legislature into two or three branches. She may unite perfect freedom and wisdom together, and may confer upon a supreme magistrate such a portion of executive power, as will enable him to exhibit a representation of majesty—such as was never seen before—for it will be the majesty of a free people. To preserve a sense of his obligations to every citizen of the republic, he may be elected annually, and made eligible for seven years, or for life.

The more we abridge the states of their sovereignty, and the more supreme power we concenter in AN ASSEMBLY OF THE STATES (for by this new name let us call our fœderal government) the more safety, liberty and prosperity, will be enjoyed by each of the states.

The ambition of the poor, and the avarice of the rich demagogue, can never be restrained upon the narrow scale of a state government. In an assembly of the states they will check each other. In this extensive reservoir of power, it will be impossible for them to excite storms of sedition, or oppression. Should even virtue be wanting in it, ambition will oppose ambition, and wealth will prevent danger from wealth. Besides, while the eyes of the whole empire are directed to one supreme legislature, its duties will be perfectly understood, its conduct will be narrowly watched, and its laws will be obeyed with chearfulness and respect.

Let the states who are jealous of each others competitions and encroachments, whether in commerce or territory, or who have suffered under aristocratic or democratic juntos, come forward, and first throw their sovereignty at the feet of the convention. It is there only that they can doom their disputes—their unjust tender and commutation laws—their paper money—their oppressive taxes upon land—and their partial systems of finance—to destruction.

Let the public creditor, who lent his money to his country, and the soldier and citizen, who yielded her their services, come forward next, and contribute their aid to establish an effective fœderal government. It is from the united power and resources of America, only, that they can expect permanent and substantial justice.

Let the lovers of peace add their efforts to those that have been mentioned, in encreasing the energy of a fœderal government. An assembly of the states alone, by the terror of its power and the fidelity of its engagements, can preserve a perpetual peace with the nations of Europe.

Let the citizens of America who inhabit the western counties of our states fly to a fœderal power for protection. The Indians know too well the dreadful consequences of confederacy in arms, ever to disturb the peaceful husbandman, who is under the cover of the arsenals of thirteen states.

Let the farmer who groans beneath the weight of direct taxation seek relief from a government, whose extensive jurisdiction will enable it to extract the resources of our country by means of imposts and customs.

Let the merchant, who complains of the restrictions and exclusions imposed upon his vessels by foreign nations, unite his influence in establishing a power that shall retaliate these injuries, and insure him success in his honest pursuits, by a general system of commercial regulations.

Let the manufacturer and mechanic, who are every where languishing for want of employment, direct their eyes to an assembly of the states. It will be in their power, only, to encourage such arts and manufactures as are essential to the prosperity of our country.

Anonymous: "How Long Are We to Continue?"

This author believes that the Confederation is beyond all hope. He calls on New England to form a separate nation in order to survive. Such calls became more common in the mid-1780s and fueled the efforts of James Madison and others to make changes in the form of government of the United States.

Independent Chronicle (Boston), 15 February 1787

How long, asks a correspondent, are we to continue in our present inglorious acquiescence in the shameful resistance that some of the states persist in, against federal and national measures? How long is Massachusetts to suffer the paltry politics, weak jealousy, or local interests of New York and Pennsylvania, to distract our own government, and keep us holden to those wretched measures which has so long made America the pity or contempt of

Europe? How long are we to distress our own numerous citizens with the weight of continental taxes, and support our delegation in an assembly, which has no powers to maintain the reputation, or advance the real interest of our commonwealth? This state has made reiterated and strenuous exertions to restore that firmness, confidence, and greatness, which distinguished united America from 1774 to 1782, but to little purpose. It is therefore now time to form a new and stronger union. The five states of New England, closely confederated, can have nothing to fear. Let then our General Assembly immediately recall their delegates from the shadowy meeting which still bears the name of Congress, as being a useless and expensive establishment. Send proposals for instituting a new congress, as the representative of the nation of New England, and leave the rest of the continent to pursue their own imbecile and disjointed plans, until they have experimentally learned the folly, danger and disgrace of them, and acquired magnanimity and wisdom sufficient to join a confederation that may rescue them from destruction.

No Crisis

Plain Dealer: "Our Present Difficulties"

Plain Dealer admits that the nation is having problems, but he perceives them to be a result of the war. He sees a bright future ahead of the United States and urges all Americans to work hard; success will soon be forthcoming.

Providence Gazette (Rhode Island), 23 February 1782

Our present difficulties ought to excite us to industry, and awaken our attention to our free interests, and not to depress our spirits; we are freemen and not slaves, the power is in the hands of the people, we make our own laws, and dispose of our own property; this cordial balsam will revive our spirits under the most pressing load: We should consider the present weight of taxes as the consequence of a late depreciating currency, which cut the sinews of industry, exhausted our magazines, and depraved our morals; that is now dead, and with it let us bury our griefs.—The most prudent arrangements are now taking place in every public department—the violence of war subsiding—government acquiring consistence and energy—and our charges lessening by a financier equal to the task.—In short, nothing now remains but for every one to mind his own business.

Argus: "Grasping At Greater Power"

Argus accuses those desiring more power for the national government of actually wanting more power for themselves. To give Congress more powers would be a decision regretted for generations to come.

Providence Gazette (Rhode Island), 3 August 1782

The confederation has settled the powers of Congress. All are not satisfied, and are grasping at greater. The pleas are specious, and men of ambition may prevail by them upon the minds of the well intentioned, to acquiesce silently in those measures that posterity may repent of to the latest generation. Let us not forget that we have two capital objects in view, while prosecuting the present war, viz.—the establishment of our independency, and the preservation of our liberty for ourselves and posterity, and that though the latter cannot now be secured without the former, yet that the preservation of our liberty is the *main* good, and that the establishment of our independency without it is little worth.

Argus: "An Armed Force"

Again, Argus sees no need to strengthen the powers of Congress. To do so would eventually result in a standing army, which was seen by many as the first step taken by rulers to undermine the rights of the people.

Providence Gazette (Rhode Island), 10 August 1782

A Coercive power in Congress is a softer name for an armed force; and when granted and successfully exercised, may become, if prolific, the embryo of a standing army. . . . The strengthening the main-spring in the political machine, while more works are wanting and the present are no better, will only increase the disorder.

Democritus: "To Supply the Treasury of Congress"

The focus of Democritus was the call to give Congress the ability to levy taxes, which he believed was a dangerous thing to do. The authority to raise money should remain with the state legislatures because that was the only way to protect the liberty of the people.

Providence Gazette (Rhode Island), 3 May 1783

Happily for the American States, it is not yet too late to prevent this fatal mode of raising public aids from taking effect. By the enlightened conduct of Rhode-Island, in refusing to concur in the five per cent impost, and the wise recollection of Virginia, in recalling her grant of it, all is yet safe. The several legislatures are still enabled to assert and secure their sovereign rights, and to supply the treasury of Congress in such way and by such means as shall be consistent with the nature of our government, and the terms of our grand social compact, which remarkably harmonise.

To raise sufficient funds for restoring public credit, and for other general purposes, is a great and important business. But it must be done in such manner as will be consistent with the liberty and safety of the citizens.

Candid: "We Madly Plunge into Extravagance"

In this essay, Candid declares that the problems of the United States are not in the form of government. Rather, they should be blamed on people who are not living frugally. People are not controlling their spending and thus everyone is facing poverty.

Norwich Packet (Connecticut), 11 August 1785

Until more frugality is adopted by all ranks of people in America, from the Senator to the Plebian, there is no reason to expect any mitigation of the calamities of which all classes of people so greatly complain; for instead of regulating our expenditures by our incomes, we madly plunge into extravagance and dissipation; and because we find ourselves involved in debts we cannot discharge, we plaintively cry out, O! the Terrible Times—not willing to think that our superflous expense is the real cause of most of our complaints, or that by retrenching them we should find ourselves in a very different situation from the present one; for I am fully of the opinion that the present embarrassing circumstances of the people at large in this state, are more owing to their unnecessary expence than to the injury derived from the late war.

QUESTIONS

1. What are the main reasons that writers such as printer John Carter and essayist Harrington give for supporting the increase of power in the Confederation Congress?

2. What are the main reasons that essayists such as Democritus and Candid give for opposing the increase of power in the Confederation Congress?
3. Writers in eighteenth-century newspapers often used pseudonymns (fake names). Oftentimes, different people used the same pseudonym. Hence, the piece by Argus in support of the idea of crisis may not be by the same author as the two pieces by Argus that oppose the idea of crisis. However, if all three pieces were written by the same author, how would you explain the different attitudes expressed?

NOTES

1. John Fiske, *The Critical Period of American History, 1783–1789* (Boston: Houghton Mifflin, 1897).

2. Merrill Jensen, *The New Nation: A History of the United States During the Confederation, 1781–1789* (New York: Alfred A. Knopf, 1950).

CHAPTER 8

Shays's Rebellion, 1786–1787

C oncerns over the stability of the national government increased during the 1780s. They crystallized into downright fear in the fall of 1786 because it seemed as if anarchy had taken over in Massachusetts. The growing concern over the future of the nation provided a perfect backdrop for Shays's Rebellion. Fueled by economic problems, the revolt began as a minor conflict in Massachusetts but quickly developed into a national concern. Scarcity of money, intensified by a severe taxation and debt retirement program instituted by the state, created extreme hardships for debtors in rural Massachusetts. Trouble had been brewing throughout rural New England ever since the end of the war. Attempts to force favorable legislation out of state governments occurred in Connecticut and Vermont. In New Hampshire, a mob of disgruntled farmers held the state legislature prisoner for several hours. But the greatest unrest occurred in the frontier counties of western Massachusetts. Trying to stave off property seizures for unpaid taxes, residents met in county conventions in the summer and fall of 1786 to petition the Massachusetts general assembly for help. Failing to get a sympathetic hearing in Boston, the men rebelled. Led by Daniel Shays, an ex-Continental army captain, nearly 2,000 of them joined together in a makeshift army that closed the courts and prevented government officials from foreclosing on anyone's property. Finally, in February 1787, the militia under General Benjamin Lincoln clashed with Shays's men near Petersham, bringing an end to the rebellion.

Shays's Rebellion sent shock waves throughout the country, producing anxiety over the nation's future. People all over the nation saw these actions as signs of lawlessness and anarchy. Although order was eventually restored, many people expressed concern because the national government was unable to do anything to help restore order. As a result, the movement for changes in the national government intensified. The occurrence of Shays's Rebellion captured people's attention and convinced many of them, including George Washington, that something had to be done in order to prevent the downfall of the national government. The Constitutional Convention of 1787 resulted from such growing concern.

Almost no newspapers described Shays's Rebellion as a wonderful and glorious event. Most perceived it as a horrible occurrence that threatened to undermine the entire political system in Massachusetts, if not the whole country. The first group of documents point out these horrors. The first selection blames the insurrection on a bunch of drunks. The second selection declares that a republican government just does not work. The third document worries about the example that the United States was setting for the rest of the world to watch. The fourth selection declares categorically that there was no similarity between Shays's Rebellion and the American Revolution. The final document rejoices that the nation has escaped such a terrible threat.

The second group of documents, while not totally in favor of the rebellion, saw some good possibilities coming out of the insurrection. The first selection urges the Massachusetts state legislature to address the concerns of the rebels and others with complaints in the state. The second document states that the costs of the rebellion will be high. The third piece urges people to support the government in the face of all forms of tyranny. The fourth selection calls on the people of Massachusetts to see the insurrection as a sign of God's wrath for the slave trade. The fifth document reports the founding of a newspaper in the western counties in order to keep the people better informed in the hopes of preventing similar uprisings in the future. The final selection calls for punishment of the true villains, the corrupt lawyers who took advantage of the people.

A Bad Event

Elisha Babcock: "'Public Spirit'"

Printer Elisha Babcock, hearing about the disturbances in Massachusetts, assumed that most of the fault could be blamed on drunkenness. He urges people to recognize that almost everyone has grievances and that protests and neglecting work will not solve them.

American Mercury (Hartford, Connecticut),
4 September 1786

More NEW NEWS!

The virtuous and renowned sons of liberty, in several counties of Massachusetts, have again set us a most laudable example of a liberal use of a liquor, called 'public spirit', as appears by the effects of the annoying quantities they have drank in their various mobs and meetings held the summer past. Too much praise cannot be given to that numerous band of patriots, who for six weeks past by neglecting their crops, farms and manufactures, have expended more in time and money than their whole quota of the national debt; and all to obtain a redress of grievances which are equally felt by most of the United States.

Anonymous: "The Misfortune of Republican Governments"

Noah Webster (of dictionary fame), writing anonymously, declares that he has cooled on the idea of republican governments because of events such as Shays's Rebellion. The people cannot be trusted to do what is best, so a limited monarchy would be a better form of government. His comments reflect the fear aroused by the troubles in Massachusetts.

Connecticut Courant (Hartford), 20 November 1786

This is the misfortune of republican governments. For my own part, I confess, I was once as strong a republican as any man in America. Now, a republican is among the last kinds of government I should choose. I would infinitely prefer a limited monarchy, for I would sooner be subject to the caprice of one man, than to the ignorance and passions of a multitude.

Isaiah Thomas: "The Disorders in This Commonwealth"

Isaiah Thomas, printer in Boston and Worcester, calls on the people of Massachusetts to consider the sort of example they were setting for the rest of the world to see. He did not blame the British for stirring up trouble, as some people had done, but he hated giving them the chance to rejoice and celebrate over American troubles.

Worcester Magazine (Massachusetts), First week of January 1787

The restoration of the publick peace in this county, and those of Hampshire and Berkshire, is an event devoutedly wished for by every good member of society; we flattered ourselves that that period was fast advancing; but the rising of the insurgents last week to prevent the sitting of the Courts of Common Pleas, &c. at Springfield in the county of Hampshire, has damped our hopes, and we are now fearful that the blessing we need, is yet at a distance. The prayer of the wise and good is, "that the inhabitants of these three counties, may know the things that belong to their peace, before they are hid forever from their eyes."—The number of insurgents who prevented the Courts sitting at Springfield, was about three hundred; they were headed by the noted Capt. Shays, and Luke Day and his Brother. A correspondent observes, that for very particular reasons, government did not order any opposition to be made; but that the consequences of another rising to oppose the Courts of Justice, may be justly dreaded.

The disorders in this Commonwealth are now a topick of conversation, not only in the United States, the British Colonies, and West-Indian islands, but also in Europe.—Our character as a State suffers beyond conception; as balls rolled in snow, so do reports concerning us magnify as they encrease their distance. That Great-Britain has sent emissaries amongst us to stir up an insurrection, we do not believe, but that some in this State have vainly thought of, and proposed bringing us again under the subjection of Britain, is not to be denied, and that the British are much pleased with the proceedings of the insurgents, is without doubt.

Anonymous: "Men Have Taken Arms"

This author resents the attempt by the rebels to identify their cause with that of the Patriots who had revolted against Great Britain. In doing so, he reflected the fears of many—that revolution was hard to stop once begun.

Hampshire Gazette (Springfield, Massachusetts), 21 March 1787

Men have taken arms in opposition to public authority, and stopped the administrations of government, pretending that they acted the same part with those who lately opposed the usurped claims of Great-Britain: But the causes are so evidently different, in the view in which they consider them, that it is highly injurious to the one to make it justify the other. To draw a true parellel between that controversy and the present, the conduct of the insurgents must be represented in the opposite view, as succeeding to the place of British usurpation, and not as supporting liberty, which is insepara-bly connected with government.

Camillus: "A Period of Adversity"

Camillus is relieved that the nation has survived the horror and danger of Shays's Rebellion. But the threat is not over. Something must be done to prevent further revolts in the future.

Worcester Magazine (Massachusetts), First week of April 1787

We cannot look back, without terror, upon the dangers we have es-caped—Our country has stood upon the verge of ruin. Divided against itself; the ties of common union dissolved; all parties claiming authority, and re-fusing obedience, every hope of safety except one, has been extinguished; and that has rested solely upon the prudence and firmness of our rulers. Fortunately, they have been uninfected with the frenzy of the times. They have done their duty, and have shewn themselves the faithful guardians of liberty. But much remains to do. Sedition though intimidated, is not dis-armed. It is a period of adversity. We are in debt to foreigners: Large sums are due internally. Our publick debt is formidable: The taxes are in arrear, and are accumulating: Manufactures are destitute of materials, capitals and skill. Agriculture is despondent: Commerce bankrupt. These are themes for factious Clamour, more than sufficient to rekindle the rebellion. The com-bustibles are collected—the mine is prepared—the smallest spark may again produce an explosion.

A GOOD EVENT

Isaiah Thomas: "All Just Complaints of the People"

Although generally opposed to lawless actions, here Isaiah Thomas urges the legislature of Massachusetts to see Shays's Rebellion as a clear sign that there was trouble in the state. If they would only work to correct some of the problems, then peace would easily be restored.

Worcester Magazine (Massachusetts), Fourth week of September 1786

It is earnestly wished that all orders of people in this Commonwealth would use their utmost endeavours to restore the publick tranquility, that peace and harmony may again prevail, and our numerous inhabitants be united and happy. It cannot be doubted but our legislature will immediately attend to all just complaints of the people, and exert themselves for the general good.

Freethinker: "The Late Movements in This County"

Freethinker sees the problems resulting from Shays's Rebellion to be worse than the causes of the revolt in the first place. He states that things would be better if people would just work hard and be frugal. The implication is that, he hopes, the horror of Shays's Rebellion will teach Americans to be wary.

Hampshire Gazette (Northampton, Massachusetts), 11 October 1786

I think that the late movements in this county have cost the people more than all the extraordinary charges they complain of would in several years.

I think that industry, frugality and economy, and not mobbing or breaking up courts, is the way to pay debts and taxes.

A Yeoman: "It Is Time to Rouse"

A Yeoman hates tyranny, but he also sees the need for governments in order to maintain order. He calls on the people to rally to the support of the government in order to improve the situation for everyone.

Worcester Magazine (Massachusetts), Fifth week of November 1786

Mr. Editor, I hate tyranny, and will ever oppose it, be it in the government, or the people. On the one hand, I ever wish to have the government take notice and redress the real grievances of the people; and on the other hand (as every man must know we cannot live without government) I have no notion of having a government that everyone may piss upon and insult with impunity. Friends, Fathers, and Brethren, it is time to rouse, the safety of the Commonwealth demands our help.

Anonymous: "The Origin of Our Present Troubles"

This author states that Shays's Rebellion had occurred as God's punishment on Massachusetts for its participation in the evils of the slave trade. Only when this evil is addressed will the situation of Massachusetts ultimately improve.

Independent Chronicle (Boston), 29 March 1787

A writer in a Philadelphia paper, mentioning the origin of our present troubles having been said to be caused by paper money, says 'I believe this to be the truth, in part, but I think we should look a little higher, and enquire into the cause why God has visited that State and Rhode-Island above all others with such severe afflictions?' The answer to this question will be, their cruelty and hypocrisy in being the authors of the revival of the slave trade in the Southern states. It is a fact, that the greatest part of the Africans that have been imported and sold in South Carolina, since the peace, have been carried there by vessels owned by the merchants in Boston and Rhode-Island. While this is the case, a good man can hardly wish them a deliverance from their present commotions and distresses.

Thomas Adams and John Nourse: "Their Late Irregularities"

Printers Thomas Adams and John Nourse express the belief of many that the problems in the frontier counties of Massachusetts resulted from a lack of dependable information about the doings of the state government. In order to answer this concern, a printing press was established to publish a weekly "news-paper."

Independent Chronicle (Boston), 4 October 1787

Convinced that their late irregularities have proceeded from want of true information respecting the doings of the General Court here, and the danger they are in from the want of a vehicle to convey certain intelligence, they have lately given such encouragement to the establishment of a PRINTING PRESS, as to have one erected in Pittsfield, for the printing a News-Paper; the first number of which made its appearance last Friday.

Honestus: "The Real Grievances"

This author blames crooked lawyers for the insurrection in Massachusetts. He hopes one of the results of the insurrection will be the correction of these problems so that people could once more trust the work of lawyers and the entire legal system of the state.

Independent Chronicle (Boston), 31 July 1788

From the reputed candour of the gentleman who has lately furnished the public with the History of the Insurrections in Massachusetts, I expected to find an impartial delineation of the causes which led to those unhappy difficulties.—But the Historian has waved mentioning any thing on the abuses which prevailed among individuals in the practice of the law, and has placed the writings against those abuses, as one cause which promoted our national difficulties. This representation, I presume, is illiberal; as the abuses must have originated before the writings commenced. The real grievances therefore, which arose in many instances from this mal-conduct, (not the writings on the subject) may very justly be reckoned among the causes which promoted the insurrections.

QUESTIONS

1. Why were people so horrified by Shays's Rebellion? Why, in particular, did the anonymous writer resent the comparison to the American Revolution?
2. Why would printers such as Isaiah Thomas and the essayist Camillus care what the countries of Europe thought about events in the United States? What difference could it possibly make?
3. Why did some writers such as Freethinker and A Yeoman look for good results from the rebellion? Are they being realistic or just hopeful?
4. The first anti-slavery society was founded in the United States by Quakers in Pennsylvania in 1775. Why would one of the anonymous essayists connect Shays's Rebellion and the slave trade together and use the rebellion as a means of attacking slavery?
5. Why would Honestus see lawyers as a target for the rebels? Would they be involved in the issues which caused the insurrection in the first place?

CHAPTER 9

Constitutional Convention, 1787

The perception of instability in the national government worried a number of political leaders and led to efforts to address these concerns. James Madison of Virginia had spearheaded much of the effort to produce a national meeting to review the Articles of Confederation in order to make needed changes. At a meeting in Annapolis, Maryland, in September 1786, Madison convinced the five states represented to issue a call for a meeting of all states in Philadelphia for the following year. This meeting became the Constitutional Convention.

The Convention began its work on May 25, 1787, when delegates from twelve states had finally gathered in Philadelphia. Rhode Island never participated in the Convention. Its leaders believed that such a meeting was totally unnecessary and they refused to send delegates.

Over the course of the summer, 55 men took part in the meeting (not all at the same time). James Madison, who had been worried about the status of the Articles government since at least 1783, came to Philadelphia well prepared. His ideas, presented on May 29 by Edmund Randolph of Virginia, came to shape the debate. Called the Virginia Plan, Madison's ideas favored the large states and called for a legislature with representation based on population. The small states countered on June 15 with the New Jersey Plan, which basically called for the Articles government with Congress having the power to tax. For more than two months, the delegates discussed and debated these ideas. They finally produced a compromise that resulted in the Constitution, adopted on September 17, 1787. The entire document was published in the *Pennsylvania Packet* on September 19, 1787.

Although the Convention delegates discussed and debated for more than three months, most Americans knew very little about the details of their deliberations. On May 29, 1787, the delegates adopted a secrecy agreement, declaring that none of the details of their discussions would leave the

The Pennſylvania Packet, *and Daily Advertiſer*.

[Price Four-Pence.] WEDNESDAY, September 19, 1787. [No. 2690.]

WE, the People of the United States, in order to form a more perfect Union, eſtabliſh Juſtice, inſure domeſtic Tranquility, provide for the common Defence, promote the General Welfare, and ſecure the Bleſſings of Liberty to Ourſelves and our Poſterity, do ordain and eſtabliſh this Conſtitution for the United States of America.

ARTICLE I.

Sect. 1. ALL legiſlative powers herein granted ſhall be veſted in a Congreſs of the United States, which ſhall conſiſt of a Senate and Houſe of Repreſentatives.

Sect. 2. The Houſe of Repreſentatives ſhall be compoſed of members choſen every ſecond year by the people of the ſeveral ſtates, and the electors in each ſtate ſhall have the qualifications requiſite for electors of the moſt numerous branch of the ſtate legiſlature.

No perſon ſhall be a repreſentative who ſhall not have attained to the age of twenty-five years, and been ſeven years a citizen of the United States, and who ſhall not, when elected, be an inhabitant of that ſtate in which he ſhall be choſen.

Repreſentatives and direct taxes ſhall be apportioned among the ſeveral ſtates which may be included within this Union, according to their reſpective numbers, which ſhall be determined by adding to the whole number of free perſons, including thoſe bound to ſervice for a term of years, and excluding Indians not taxed, three-fifths of all other perſons. The actual enumeration ſhall be made within three years after the firſt meeting of the Congreſs of the United States, and within every ſubſequent term of ten years, in ſuch manner as they ſhall by law direct. The number of repreſentatives ſhall not exceed one for every thirty thouſand, but each ſtate ſhall have at leaſt one repreſentative; and until ſuch enumeration ſhall be made, the ſtate of New-Hampſhire ſhall be entitled to chuſe three, Maſſachuſetts eight, Rhode-Iſland and Providence Plantations one, Connecticut five, New-York ſix, New-Jerſey four, Pennſylvania eight, Delaware one, Maryland ſix, Virginia ten, North-Carolina five, South-Carolina five, and Georgia three.

When vacancies happen in the repreſentation from any ſtate, the Executive authority thereof ſhall iſſue writs of election to fill ſuch vacancies.

The Houſe of Repreſentatives ſhall chuſe their Speaker and other officers; and ſhall have the ſole power of impeachment.

Sect. 3. The Senate of the United States ſhall be compoſed of two ſenators from each ſtate, choſen by the legiſlature thereof, for ſix years; and each ſenator ſhall have one vote.

Immediately after they ſhall be aſſembled in conſequence of the firſt election, they ſhall be divided as equally as may be into three claſſes. The ſeats of the ſenators of the firſt claſs ſhall be vacated at the expiration of the ſecond year, of the ſecond claſs at the expiration of the fourth year, and of the third claſs at the expiration of the ſixth year, ſo that one-third may be choſen every ſecond year; and if vacancies happen by reſignation, or otherwiſe, during the receſs of the Legiſlature of any ſtate, the Executive thereof may make temporary appointments until the next meeting of the Legiſlature, which ſhall then fill ſuch vacancies.

No perſon ſhall be a ſenator who ſhall not have attained to the age of thirty years, and been nine years a citizen of the United States, and who ſhall not, when elected, be an inhabitant of that ſtate for which he ſhall be choſen.

The Vice-Preſident of the United States ſhall be Preſident of the ſenate, but ſhall have no vote, unleſs they be equally divided.

The Senate ſhall chuſe their other officers, and alſo a Preſident pro tempore, in the abſence of the Vice-Preſident, or when he ſhall exerciſe the office of Preſident of the United States.

The Senate ſhall have the ſole power to try all impeachments. When ſitting for that purpoſe, they ſhall be on oath or affirmation. When the Preſident of the United States is tried, the Chief Juſtice ſhall preſide: And no perſon ſhall be convicted without the concurrence of two thirds of the members preſent.

Judgment in caſes of impeachment ſhall not extend further than to removal from office, and diſqualification to hold and enjoy any office of honor, truſt or profit under the United States; but the party convicted ſhall neverthelefs be liable and ſubject to indictment, trial, judgment and puniſhment, according to law.

Sect. 4. The times, places and manner of holding elections for ſenators and repreſentatives, ſhall be preſcribed in each ſtate by the legiſlature thereof; but the Congreſs may at any time by law make or alter ſuch regulations, except as to the places of chuſing Senators.

The Congreſs ſhall aſſemble at leaſt once in every year, and ſuch meeting ſhall be on the firſt Monday in December, unleſs they ſhall by law appoint a different day.

Sect. 5. Each houſe ſhall be the judge of the elections, returns and qualifications of its own members, and a majority of each ſhall conſtitute a quorum to do buſineſs; but a ſmaller number may adjourn from day to day, and may be authoriſed to compel the attendance of abſent members, in ſuch manner, and under ſuch penalties as each houſe may provide.

Each houſe may determine the rules of its proceedings, puniſh its members for diſorderly behaviour, and, with the concurrence of two-thirds, expel a member.

Each houſe ſhall keep a journal of its proceedings, and from time to time publiſh the ſame, excepting ſuch parts as may in their judgment require ſecrecy; and the yeas and nays of the members of either houſe on any queſtion ſhall, at the deſire of one-fifth of thoſe preſent, be entered on the journal.

Neither houſe, during the ſeſſion of Congreſs, ſhall, without the conſent of the other, adjourn for more than three days, nor to any other place than that in which the two houſes ſhall be ſitting.

Sect. 6. The ſenators and repreſentatives ſhall receive a compenſation for their ſervices, to be aſcertained by law, and paid out of the treaſury of the United States. They ſhall in all caſes, except treaſon, felony and breach of the peace, be privileged from arreſt during their attendance at the ſeſſion of their reſpective houſes, and in going to and returning from the ſame; and for any ſpeech or debate in either houſe, they ſhall not be queſtioned in any other place.

No ſenator or repreſentative ſhall, during the time for which he was elected, be appointed to any civil office under the authority of the United States, which ſhall have been created, or the emoluments whereof ſhall have been encreaſed during ſuch time; and no perſon holding any office under the United States, ſhall be a member of either houſe during his continuance in office.

Sect. 7. All bills for raiſing revenue ſhall originate in the houſe of repreſentatives; but the ſenate may propoſe or concur with amendments as on other bills.

Every bill which ſhall have paſſed the houſe of repreſentatives and the ſenate, ſhall, before it become a law, be preſented to the preſident of the United States; if he approve he ſhall ſign it, but if not he ſhall return it, with his objections to that houſe in which it ſhall have originated, who ſhall enter the objections at large on their journal, and proceed to reconſider it. If after ſuch reconſideration two-thirds of that houſe ſhall agree to paſs the bill, it ſhall be ſent, together with the objections, to the other houſe, by which it ſhall likewiſe be reconſidered, and if approved by two-thirds of that houſe, it ſhall become a law. But in all ſuch caſes the votes of both houſes ſhall

---

The Constitution. *Like the Declaration of Independence, the Constitution was short enough to be published in one issue of a newspaper. John Dunlap, printer of the* Pennsylvania Packet, *first published the Constitution following its adoption by the Convention.*

convention hall. Over the course of the summer, a few items leaked out, but for the most part, the delegates obeyed the secrecy rule. By and large, the members of the Convention believed that the secrecy agreement would encourage open debate, which would produce a better agreement in the end.

The newspaper printers apparently agreed with the delegates on this issue because they seldom complained about the lack of specific information concerning the meeting. Hence, many of the pieces published about the Convention were very general in content. Instead, the printers concentrated most of their attention on the potential results and whether they would be good or bad.

The documents that praise the Convention as a good event emphasize the wisdom of the membership of the gathering. The first three selections stress the abilities of the delegates and comment that, with George Washington involved, nothing but good could come out of the meeting. The other four documents all emphasize the uniqueness of the Convention because the delegates are trying to peacefully change and improve the government.

The documents that criticize the Convention as a bad event worry about the future if the government is changed. The first selection sees an attempt to create a central government that will be too strong. The second document fears that the Convention will go too far in repairing the government structure and will produce a tyranny like Great Britain.

A Good Event

Anonymous: "The Deliberations of the Sages and Patriots"

This author believes that the results of the Convention will be good ones because of the wisdom of the participants. If for no other reason, the presence of Benjamin Franklin and George Washington would guarantee a successful meeting.

New Hampshire Gazette (Portsmouth), 19 May 1787

Reasonably is it to be expected, says a correspondent, that the deliberations of the sages and patriots, who are to meet in convention at Philadelphia this month, will be attended with much good.—An union of the abilities of so distinguished a body of men, among whom will be a Franklin and a Washington, cannot but produce the most salutary measures.—These names affixed to their recommendations (and it is to be hoped that this will be the case) will stamp a confidence in them, which the narrow-soul'd, anti-federal politicians in the several states, who, by their influence, have hitherto d—'d us as a nation, will not dare to attack, or endeavour to nullify.

Benjamin Russell: "Men in Whom You May Confide"

Benjamin Russell, longtime printer in Boston, also praises the membership of the Convention because all of them were successful men whose patriotism and abilities could not be denied. The people could place complete confidence in these men's efforts.

Massachusetts Centinel (Boston), 13 June 1787

Be assured the men whom you have delegated to work out, if possible, your national salvation, are men in whom you may confide—their extensive knowledge, known abilities, and approved patriotism, warrant it—their determinations must be just, and if you wish well to your country, ye will place such confidence in them, as to sanction with your approbation the measures they may recommend, notwithstanding they may in some small points militate against your ideas of right. Consider, they have at their head a Washington, to describe the amiableness of whose character would be unnecessary.

Harrington: "Wisdom, Patriotism, and Probity"

In this piece, Harrington continues the theme of the wisdom of the members of the Convention. Such great patriots will protect American freedoms and produce a way to preserve the United States.

Providence Gazette (Rhode Island), 30 May 1787

Perhaps no age or country, ever saw more wisdom, patriotism, and probity, united in a single assembly, than we now behold in the Convention of the States.

Who can read or hear, that the immortal Washington has again quitted his beloved retirement, and obeyed the voice of God and his country, by accepting the chair of this illustrious body of patriots and heroes, and doubt of the safety and blessings of the government we are to receive from their hands?

Or who can read or hear of Franklin, Dickinson, Rutledge, R. Morris, Livingston, Randolph, Gerry, Sherman, Mifflin, Clymer, Pinckney, Read, and many others that might be mentioned, whose names are synonimous with liberty and fame, and not long to receive from them the precious ark, that is to preserve and transmit to posterity the freedom of America?

Under the present weak, imperfect and distracted government of Congress, anarchy, poverty, infamy, and SLAVERY, await the United States.

Under such a government as will probably be formed by the present convention, America may yet enjoy peace, safety, liberty and glory.

Barzillai Hudson and George Goodwin: "The Greatest Unanimity"

These Connecticut printers rejoice over the reports of agreement and success coming out of Philadelphia. They believe that nothing but a stronger government can preserve the nation at this point in time.

Connecticut Courant (Hartford), 25 June 1787

We hear that the greatest unanimity subsists in the councils of the Federal Convention. It is to be hoped, says a correspondent, the United States will discover as much wisdom in receiving from them a suitable form of government to preserve the liberties of the people, as they did fortitude in defending them against the arbitrary and wicked attempts of Great Britain. Nothing but union and a vigorous continental government, can save us from destruction.

Benjamin Russell: "A Revolution in Government"

Russell praises the Convention for the unique position it will hold in history. It represents the first attempt on the part of men to sit down and rationally create a form of government designed to fit the needs of the people.

Massachusetts Centinel (Boston), 30 June 1787

Whatever measure may be recommended by the federal convention, whether an addition to the old constitution, or the adoption of a new one, it will, in effect, if agreed to, of which there can be no reasonable doubt, be a Revolution in Government, Accomplished by Reasoning and Deliberation; an event that has never occurred since the formation of society, and which will be strongly characteristic of the philosophers and tolerant spirit of the age.

Barzillai Hudson and George Goodwin: "Novel in the History of Government"

Hudson and Goodwin continue the theme of the exceptionalism of the Convention. Generally, forms of government had been created by a handful of people and forced on everyone else. It seems that the results of the Convention will be different because the delegates represent their states rather than just a handful of influential leaders.

Connecticut Courant (Hartford), 16 July 1787

A correspondent remarks that the Convention now sitting seems quite novel in the history of government, and stands remarkable and alone in political history. After the establishment of governments in various parts of the Continent, some of which have been forced upon the majority of the governed; and after the existence of others which have not only been cheerfully submitted to, but eagerly embraced by the people; it is still singular to see an authority, however great and respectable in itself presiding tacitly over the confederation of states by voluntary election.

May patriotism blow the gale, and virtue be the pilot to the ports of happiness and freedom!

Bennett Wheeler: "A Most Unusual Spectacle"

Bennett Wheeler, a printer in Rhode Island, also emphasizes the uniqueness of the Convention. He is struck by the fact that the proposed change of government is coming in a time of peace rather than as the result of some sort of armed conflict.

United States Chronicle (Providence, Rhode Island), 27 September 1787

The United States of America, says a correspondent, now exhibits to the world a most unusual spectacle—that of a great and numerous people, calmly and deliberately, in time of peace, unawed by arms, and uninfluenced by party faction, appointing their wisest and best men to form a constitution of government, adequate to the great purposes of the general confederacy, and most productive of the prosperity, felicity, safety and welfare of the whole.

A Bad Event

Isaiah Thomas: "One Consolidated Government"

Isaiah Thomas worries that the Convention will undermine the freedom that Americans already enjoy. The creation of one consolidated government, without the divisions of the various states, would make matters worse rather than address the concerns of the nation's citizens.

Worcester Magazine (Massachusetts), Third week of May 1787

Accounts from the southward and westward say, that one *consolidated* government is now fully talked of, to extend from New-Hampshire to Georgia; but it is to be hoped there is yet that virtue in United America, as will enable her to support the free governments her citizens now enjoy.

Z: "The Continental Convention"

Z expands on the concerns of Thomas by stating that the Convention, in seeking a remedy to the many problems the nation faces, will only increase the problems and conflicts between and within states. The Convention should not go too far, and Congress should concentrate its efforts on trade issues and leave everything else alone because it is working fairly well.

Freeman's Journal (Philadelphia), 16 May 1787

It seems to be generally felt and acknowledged, that the affairs of this country are in a ruinous situation. With vast resources in our hands, we are impoverished by the continual drain of money from us in foreign trade; our navigation is destroyed; our people are in debt and unable to pay; industry is at a stand; our public treaties are violated, and national faith, solemnly plighted to foreigners and to our own citizens, is no longer kept. We are discontented at home, and abroad we are insulted and despised.

In this exigency people naturally look up to the continental Convention, in hopes that their wisdom will provide some effectual remedy for this complication of disorders. It is perhaps the last opportunity which may be presented to us of establishing a permanent system of Continental Government; and, if this opportunity be lost, it is much to be feared that we shall fall into irretrievable confusion.

How the great object of their meeting is to be attained is a question which deserves to be seriously considered. Some men, there is reason to believe, have indulged the idea of reforming the United States by means of some refined and complicated schemes of organizing a future Congress in a different form. These schemes, like may others with which we have been amused in times past, will be found to be merely visionary, and produce no lasting benefit. The error is not in the form of Congress, the mode of election, or the duration of the appointment of the members. The source of all our misfortunes is evidently in the want of power in Congress. To be convinced of this, we need only recollect the vigor, the energy, the unanimity of this country a few years past, even in the midst of a bloody war, *when Congress governed the continent.* We have gradually declined into feebleness, anarchy and wretchedness, from that period in which the several States began to exercise the sovereign and absolute right of treating the recommendations of Congress with contempt. From that time to the present, we have seen the great Federal Head of our union clothed with the authority of making treaties without the power of performing them; of contracting debts without being able to discharge them, or to bind others to discharge them; of regulating our trade, and providing for the general welfare of the people, in their concerns with foreign nations, without the power of restraining a single individual from the infraction of their orders, or restricting any trade, however injurious to the public welfare.

To remedy these evils, some have weakly imagined that it is necessary to annihilate the several States, and vest Congress with the absolute direction and government of the continent, as one single republic. This, however, would be impracticable and mischievous. In so extensive a country many local and internal regulations would be required, which Congress could not possibly attend to, and to which the States individually are fully competent; but those things which alike concern all the States, such as our foreign trade and foreign transactions, Congress should be fully authorized to regulate, and should be invested with the power of enforcing their regulations.

The ocean, which joins us to other nations, would seem to be the scene upon which Congress might exert its authority with the greatest benefit to the United States, as no one State can possibly claim any exclusive right in it. It has been long seen that the States individually cannot, with any success, pretend to regulate trade. The duties and restrictions which one State imposes, the neighboring States enable the merchants to elude; and besides, if they could be enforced, it would be highly unjust, that the dues collected in the port of one State should be applied to the sole use of that State in which they are collected, whilst the neighboring States, who have no ports for foreign commerce, consume a part of the goods imported, and thus in effect pay a part of the duties. Even if the recommendation of Congress had been attended to, which proposed the levying for the use of Congress five per centum on goods imported, to be collected by officers to be appointed by the individual States, it is more than probable that the laws would have been feebly executed. Men are not apt to be sufficiently attentive to the business of those who do not appoint, and cannot remove or control them; officers would naturally look up to the State which appointed them, and it is past a doubt that some of the States would esteem it no unpardonable sin to promote their own particular interest, or even that of particular men, to the injury of the United States.

Would it not then be right to vest Congress with the sole and exclusive power of regulating trade, of imposing port duties, of appointing officers to collect these duties, of erecting ports and deciding all questions by their own authority, which concern foreign trade and navigation upon the high seas? Some of those persons, who have conceived a narrow jealousy of Congress, and therefore have unhappily obstructed their exertions of the public welfare, may perhaps be startled at the idea, and make objections. To such I would answer, that our situation appears to be sufficiently desperate to justify the hazarding an experiment of anything which promises immediate relief. Let us try this for a few years; and if we find it attended with mischief, we can refuse to renew the power. But it appears to me to be necessary and useful; and I cannot think that it would in the least degree endanger our liberties. The representatives of the States in Congress are easily changed as often as we please, and they must necessarily be changed often. They would have little inclination and less ability to enterprise against the liberties of their constituents. This, no doubt, would induce the necessity of employing a small number of armed vessels to enforce the regulations of Congress, and would be the beginning of a Continental Navy; but a navy was never esteemed, like a standing army, dangerous to the liberty of the people.

To those who should object that this is too small a power to grant to Congress; that many more are necessary to be added to those which they already possess, I can only say, that perhaps they have not sufficiently reflected upon the great importance of the power proposed. That it would be of immense service to the country I have no doubt, as it is the only means by which our trade can be put on a footing with other nations; that it would in the event greatly strengthen the hands of Congress, I think is highly probable.

QUESTIONS

1. Why do those in support of the Convention such as Benjamin Russell and Harrington stress the wisdom and reputation of the members of the

Convention? What difference could the membership of the Convention make in the reactions of people to the results of the meeting?

2. Why is the presence of George Washington so important? Do you think his presence made a major difference in the results of the Convention?

3. Why is the Convention considered a unique event by writers such as Barzillai Hudson and George Goodwin and Bennett Wheeler? How were governments changed prior to the eighteenth century?

4. Why does Isaiah Thomas fear a consolidated government? What in his previous experience would explain this concern?

5. Why does Z not trust the Convention? What does he believe should be happening to deal with the problems faced by the United States?

CHAPTER 10

Ratification Struggle, 1787–1789

The Constitution contained within itself the mechanism for its ratification and implementation. Since the proposed new structure called for a strengthening of the national government, the Convention delegates feared that the state governments would refuse to consider the Constitution. The ratification process called for each state to call a special convention to discuss the proposed change. When 9 of the 13 states had ratified, the new government would take effect.

Once the Constitution was published on September 19, 1787, many states acted quickly to consider the proposal. Delaware became the first state to ratify the new government on December 7, 1787. Seven other states soon followed suit. By June 1788, eight states had ratified the Constitution, and it was being considered in three others. On June 21, 1788, New Hampshire became the ninth state to adopt the proposed Constitution so the new government would take effect. New York and Virginia also ratified before the end of June. The stage was now set for a change in government in the United States.

During the ratification debates, the newspapers printed many items related to the discussions. Most of the printers favored the Constitution, and so the majority of materials published supported the proposed new government. Still, pieces appeared on both sides of the issue and debated the pros and cons of the Constitution.

The documents in favor of the Constitution tried to present all the positive aspects of the change in government structure. The first selection argues that the new government will be able more capably to control foreign trade, which will improve the American economy. The second piece is the first in probably the most famous set of essays in favor of the Constitution, "The Federalist Papers." The third selection states that Americans should ap-

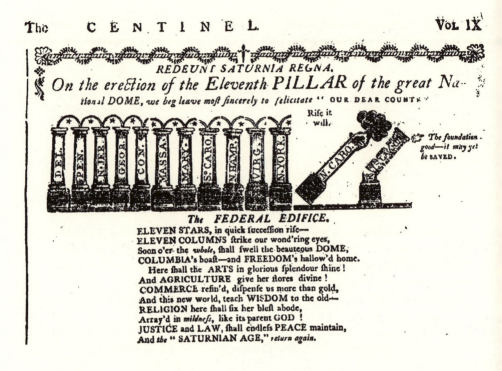

The **CENTINEL.**   Vol. IX

REDEUNT SATURNIA REGNA.

On the erection of the Eleventh PILLAR of the great Na-
tional DOME, we beg leave most sincerely to felicitate " OUR DEAR COUNT "

Rise it will.

The foundation good—it may yet be SAVED.

The **FEDERAL EDIFICE.**

ELEVEN STARS, in quick fucceffion rife—
ELEVEN COLUMNS ftrike our wond'ring eyes,
Soon o'er the *whole,* fhall fwell the beauteous DOME,
COLUMBIA's boaft—and FREEDOM's hallow'd home.
Here fhall the ARTS in glorious fplendour fhine !
And AGRICULTURE give her ftores divine !
COMMERCE refin'd, difpenfe us more than gold,
And this new world, teach WISDOM to the old—
RELIGION here fhall fix her bleft abode,
Array'd in *mildnefs,* like its parent GOD !
JUSTICE and LAW, fhall endlefs PEACE maintain,
And *the* " SATURNIAN AGE," *return again.*

The Columns Cartoon. *A variety of materials were published to support the ratification of the Constitution. Benjamin Russell, printer of the* Columbian Centinel, *created this columns cartoon to visually picture the growing strength of the nation as the Constitution was approved by the various states. Several versions appeared as more and more states ratified. This one appeared in the summer of 1788 following the ratification of the Constitution by 11 of the 13 states.*

prove the Constitution because they will never be able to get such a meeting as the Convention together again. The fourth, fifth, and sixth documents stress the stability that will return to the United States once the Constitution is adopted and operating. The seventh selection pokes fun at the Anti-Federalists, the opponents to the Constitution. The eighth document is a poem praising the future in store for the United States. The next two pieces by John Carter defend the amount of material which he published opposed to the Constitution. The last piece reports the arrival of George Washington in New York for his inauguration, the event generally seen as the beginning of the new government under the Constitution.

The selections opposing the Constitution stress that the changes called for in the government structure go too far and undermine the rights of the people. The first document states that the people are being fooled into accepting the Constitution through the inappropriate use of the names of famous people like George Washington. The second piece expresses concern that the states will be overwhelmed by the new system. The third document accuses the men in support of the Constitution of being power-hungry. The fourth selection states that the people will lose all other personal rights, such as trial by jury and freedom of the press, if the Constitution is approved. The fifth piece, the first of the Centinel essays, points out many problems with the Constitution, and concludes that the final result will be the establishment of an aristocratic government that will weaken the rights of the people. The final two selections declare that the newspaper presses have been shut against the publication of pieces opposed to the Constitution, and so no real debate has occurred.

SUPPORT FOR THE CONSTITUTION

Timothy Green: "The Traces of Wisdom"

Connecticut printer Timothy Green praises the Constitution for its wisdom. It will bring stability to the government, which will result in economic recovery and national happiness.

Connecticut Gazette (New London), 26 October 1787

So evident are the traces of wisdom and sound judgment in the Constitution lately formed by some of the best characters in the United States, that, says a correspondent, I cannot avoid anticipating our future happiness should it be adopted.—It will set all the springs of action in motion. The government will be able to counteract the oppressive acts of other nations respecting our trade, our own ships and seamen will be employed in exporting our own produce. This will revive ship-building; and we may soon expect to see our rivers lined, as heretofore, with new ships; this gives employment to carpenters, joiners, blacksmiths, and even to every species of tradesmen; and not only so, but timber and lumber of every kind, as well as every other produce of the country will find a free vent; to which I may add this happy and agreeable circumstance, that we shall be one people, and governed by the same general laws from New-Hampshire to Georgia.

Publius: "Federalist No. 1"

Publius was either James Madison, Alexander Hamilton, or John Jay, depending on which of the 85 "Federalist" essays is being read. Hamilton wrote this essay, which declares that Publius plans to critique the Constitution in great detail. He concludes that all of the potential criticisms of the Constitution have ready answers and that the United States will be much better off if the Constitution is adopted.

Independent Journal (New York), 27 October 1787

To the People of the State of New York:

AFTER an unequivocal experience of the inefficiency of the subsisting federal government, you are called upon to deliberate on a new Constitution for the United States of America. The subject speaks its own importance; comprehending in its consequences nothing less than the existence of the UNION, the safety and welfare of the parts of which it is composed, the fate of an empire in many respects the most interesting in the world. It has been frequently remarked that it seems to have been reserved to the people of this country, by their conduct and example, to decide the important question, whether societies of men are really capable or not of establishing good government from reflection and choice, or whether they are forever destined to depend for their political constitutions on accident and force. If there be any truth in the remark, the crisis at which we are arrived may with propriety be regarded as the era in which that decision is to be made; and a wrong election of the part we shall act, may, in this view, deserve to be considered as the general misfortune of mankind.

This idea will add the inducements of philanthropy to those of patriotism, to heighten the solicitude which all considerate and good men must feel for the event. Happy will it be if our choice should be directed by a judicious estimate of our true interests, unperplexed and unbiased by considerations not connected with the public good. But this is a thing more ardently to be wished than seriously to be expected. The plan offered to our deliberations affects too many particular interests, innovates upon too many local institutions, not to involve in its discussion a variety of objects foreign to its merits, and of views, passions and prejudices little favorable to the discovery of truth.

Among the most formidable of the obstacles which the new Constitution will have to encounter may readily be distinguished the obvious interest of a certain class of men in every State to resist all changes which may hazard a diminution of the power, emolument, and consequence of the offices they hold under the State establishments; and the perverted ambition of another class of men, who will either hope to aggrandize themselves by the confusions of their country, or will flatter themselves with fairer prospects of elevation from the subdivision of the empire into several partial confederacies than from its union under one government.

It is not, however, my design to dwell upon observations of this nature. I am well aware that it would be disingenuous to resolve indiscriminately the opposition of any set of men (merely because their situations might subject them to suspicion) into interested or ambitious views. Candor will oblige us to admit that even such men may be actuated by upright intentions; and it cannot be doubted that much of the opposition which has made its appearance, or may hereafter make its appearance, will spring from sources, blameless at least, if not respectable, the honest errors of minds led astray by preconceived jealousies and fears. So numerous indeed and so powerful are the causes which serve to give a false bias to the judgment, that we, upon many occasions, see wise and good men on the wrong as well as on the right side of questions of the first magnitude to society. This circumstance, if duly attended to, would furnish a lesson of moderation to those who are ever so much persuaded of their being in the right in any controversy. And a further reason for caution, in this respect, might be drawn from the reflection that we are not always sure that those who advocate the truth are influenced by purer principles than their antagonists. Ambition, avarice, personal animosity, party opposition, and many other motives not more laudable than these, are apt to operate as well upon those who support as those who oppose the right side of a question. Were there not even these inducements to moderation, nothing could be more ill-judged than that intolerant spirit which has, at all times, characterized political parties. For in politics, as in religion, it is equally absurd to aim at making proselytes by fire and sword. Heresies in either can rarely be cured by persecution.

And yet, however just these sentiments will be allowed to be, we have already sufficient indications that it will happen in this as in all former cases of great national discussion. A torrent of angry and malignant passions will be let loose. To judge from the conduct of the opposite parties, we shall be led to conclude that they will mutually hope to evince the justness of their opinions, and to increase the number of their converts by the loudness of their declamations and the bitterness of their invectives. An enlightened zeal for the energy and efficiency of government will be stigmatized as the offspring of a temper fond of despotic power and hostile to the principles of liberty. An over-scrupulous jealousy of danger to the rights of the people, which is more commonly the fault of the head than of the heart, will be represented as mere pretense and artifice, the stale bait for popularity at the expense of the public good. It will be forgotten, on the one hand, that jealousy is the usual concomitant of love, and that the noble enthusiasm of liberty is apt to be infected with a spirit of narrow and illiberal distrust. On the other hand, it will be equally forgotten that the vigor of government is essential to the security of liberty; that, in the contemplation of a sound and well-informed judgment, their interest can never be separated; and that a dangerous ambition more often lurks behind the specious mask of zeal for the rights of the people than under the forbidden appearance of zeal for the firmness and efficiency of government. History will teach us that the former has been found a much more certain road to the introduction of despotism than the latter, and that of those men who have overturned the liberties of republics, the greatest number have begun their career by paying an obsequious court to the people; commencing demagogues, and ending tyrants.

In the course of the preceding observations, I have had an eye, my fellow-citizens, to putting you upon your guard against all attempts, from whatever quarter, to influence your decision in a matter of the utmost moment to your welfare, by any impressions other than those which may result from the evidence of truth. You will, no doubt, at the same time, have collected from the general scope of them, that they proceed from a source not unfriendly to the new Constitution. Yes, my countrymen, I own to you that, after having given it an attentive consideration, I am clearly of opinion it is your interest to adopt it. I am convinced that this is the safest course for your liberty, your dignity, and your happiness. I affect not reserves which I do not feel. I will not amuse you with an appearance of deliberation when I have decided. I frankly acknowledge to you my convictions, and I will freely lay before you the reasons on which they are founded. The consciousness of good intentions disdains ambiguity. I shall not, however, multiply professions on this head. My motives must remain in the depository of my own breast. My arguments will be open to all, and may be judged of by all. They shall at least be offered in a spirit which will not disgrace the cause of truth.

I propose, in a series of papers, to discuss the following interesting particulars— *The utility of the UNION to your political prosperity— The insufficiency of the present Confederation to preserve that Union— The necessity of a government at least equally energetic with the one proposed to the attainment of this object— The conformity of the proposed constitution to the true principles of republican government—Its analogy to your own state constitution—*and lastly, *The additional security, which its adoption will afford to the preservation of that species of government, to liberty and to property.*

In the progress of this discussion I shall endeavor to give a satisfactory answer to all the objections which shall have made their appearance, that may seem to have any claim to your attention. It may perhaps be thought superfluous to offer arguments to prove the utility of the UNION, a point, no doubt, deeply engraved on the hearts of the great body of the people in every State, and one, which it may be imagined, has no adversaries. But the fact is, that we already hear it whispered in the private circles of those who

oppose the new Constitution, that the thirteen States are of too great extent for any general system, and that we must of necessity resort to separate confederacies of distinct portions of the whole.[1] This doctrine will, in all probability, be gradually propagated, till it has votaries enough to countenance an open avowal of it. For nothing can be more evident, to those who are able to take an enlarged view of the subject, than the alternative of an adoption of the new Constitution or a dismemberment of the Union. It will therefore be of use to begin by examining the advantages of that Union, the certain evils, and the probable dangers, to which every State will be exposed from its dissolution. This shall accordingly constitute the subject of my next address.
PUBLIUS.

---

[1] The same idea, tracing the arguments to their consequences, is held out in several of the late publications against the new Constitution.

Federalist: "So Respectable a Body of Citizens"

In this essay, Federalist states that creating such a meeting as the Convention again will be impossible. He urges Americans to approve the work of the Convention in order to avoid anarchy.

Massachusetts Centinel (Boston), 17 November 1787

America can scarcely hope ever to see so respectable a body of her citizens convened on a similar occasion—so great an unanimity we cannot expect again—the spirit of jealousy and discord, which the enemies of our national honour and glory, have excited, leaves no chance of a future coalescence in a Continental Convention—It therefore remains with the people at large to adopt the proposed Constitution, and thereby avail themselves of the last opportunity they will probably enjoy, of establishing in peace, an efficient and permanent government; or by rejecting it, to precipitate themselves into the most abject state of servitude—for that anarchy and confusion which must ensue, upon the last alternative, will most assuredly issue in despotism and slavery.

Robert Gerrish: "An Ark for the Preservation of Justice"

New Hampshire printer Robert Gerrish concludes that the Constitution will receive great praise from Europe. It will show that a republic can work, something that many people doubted in the eighteenth century.

New Hampshire Mercury (Portsmouth), 1 November 1787

We anticipate the praise with which this government will be viewed by the friends of liberty and mankind in Europe. The philosophers will no longer consider a republic as an impracticable form of government; and pious men of all denominations will thank God for having provided in our federal Constitution, an ark for the preservation of the remains of the justice and liberties of the world.

Anonymous: "Be of One Heart and One Mind"

This anonymous writer describes the Constitution as the opportunity for the United States to achieve stability. For this author, it may be the last chance to prevent the fall of the nation from impossible divisions.

Independent Chronicle (Boston), 5 June 1788

Let us then be of one heart, and of one mind. Let us seize the golden opportunity to secure a stable government, and to become a respectable nation. Let us be open, decided and resolute in a good cause. Let us render our situation worthy the ashes of our slaughtered brethren, and our own sufferings. Let us remember our emblem, the twisted serpent, and its emphatical motto, unite or die! This was once written in blood; but it is as emphatical now as then. A house divided against itself cannot stand. Our national existence depends as much as ever upon our union; and its consolidation most assuredly involves our posterity, felicity and safety.

Anonymous: "Adopt or Reject, That Is the Question"

With a play on the words of Shakespeare's Hamlet, *this author states that the Constitution is the last hope of the United States. If it fails to be approved, the nation will decline and fall. This was published as part of the debate in Rhode Island over whether to ratify the Constitution or not.*

Newport Herald (Rhode Island), 27 May 1790

Adopt or Reject, that is the question.

Whether it is better to make one Star in the bright Constellation, and reciprocate light, or like the small meteor, blaze but a moment, and then go to that *Bourn*[1] from which nations, as well as travellers, ne'er return.

By the Adoption, we have nothing to lose, but every thing to gain;—By a Rejection we stab Commerce at its vitals, force the Farmer to hide the fruits of his labour in a napkin, and leave our Government like an isolated column, tottering at the smallest breeze, and exposed to be thrown from its base, by every tempest.

Anonymous: "The Anti-Federal Cause"

This writer attacks the Anti-Federalists as a despicable group of people. He uses the newspaper essayists as the examples for his comments. Actually, relatively few pieces appeared opposing the Constitution.

Massachusetts Gazette (Boston), 29 January 1788

If the anti-federal cause, says a correspondent, is as base and contemptible as the scribblers who advocate it, the federalists have very little to fear, for certainly a more despicable junto than the herd of anti-federal writers were never leagued together.

It is curious to observe, writes a correspondent, with what acrimony the opposers of the new frame of government exclaim against those who pretend to arraign the conduct of their chieftain; and they themselves are exerting their utmost to defame one of the first characters in the university. But inconsistency is a part of the anti-federal creed.

Anonymous: "The Federal Edifice"

This poet rejoices over the great future awaiting the United States under the new Constitution. This poem was generally accompanied in the newspapers with a cartoon (see page 138) showing a group of columns representing the new "Federal Edifice."

Massachusetts Centinel (Boston), 2 August 1788

THE FEDERAL EDIFICE.
ELEVEN STARS, in quick succession rise,
ELEVEN COLUMNS strike our wondering eyes;
Soon, o'er the whole, shall swell the beauteous DOME,
COLUMBIA'S boast, and FREEDOM'S hallowed home.
Here shall the ARTS in glorious splendor shine,
And AGRICULTURE give her stores divine;
COMMERCE refined, dispense us more than gold,
And this new world teach WISDOM to the old;
RELIGION here shall fix her blest abode,
Arrayed in mildness, like its parent, GOD;
JUSTICE and LAW shall endless PEACE maintain,
And the 'SATURNIAN AGE' return again.

John Carter: "An Impartial Printer"

One issue that came up during the debates over the Constitution was the failure of many printers to publish pieces opposed to the proposed new government. In this piece, Rhode Island printer John Carter states that he would be failing in his job as a printer if he did not print materials on both sides of an issue.

Providence Gazette (Rhode Island), 29 December 1787

Whatever may have been my private sentiments respecting public measures, I have never suffered them to interfere with what I conceive to be the indispensible duty of an impartial Printer; nor have I at any time suffered myself to become the 'dupe' or 'tool' of a party. My sentiments are well known in this and most of the other States, particularly on the subject of paper money (to which an allusion seems intended by another writer on this occasion) and the suggestions of my adversaries cannot fix a stain on my reputation. Although a Foederalist, and perhaps zealous as the 'Pamphlet-Monger' himself, yet my conduct as a Printer would certainly merit the severest reprehension, were I impertinently to attempt the preclusion of 'free enquiry'. For this purpose was the Constitution sent to the several States. The cause of truth can never suffer from argument; indeed argument would of course cease, were the papers partially to hold up one side of a question only.—On the broad basis of an *uncontrouled* and *liberal* press, I found a humble claim to public patronage. On these principles I have hitherto had 'spirit' and 'stability' to conduct it, and I trust that the frowns of *disappointed ambition* will not swerve me from the path of rectitude.

John Carter: "As a Printer, Neither Foederal Nor Antifoederal"

John Carter proved the most vocal printer in defending his publication record during the Constitution debates. Here he states that he published everything that came to him, no matter which side of the issue the piece took.

Providence Gazette (Rhode Island), 12 January 1788

As a Citizen, he professes to be a Foederalist; but *as a Printer,* neither foederal nor antifoederal.—On all congressional Measures heretofore proposed—on the Subject of Paper Money—on the Subject of the proposed Constitution and other interesting political questions, he has faithfully and impartially handed to the Public every Performance, pro and con, that has been committed to him, and persevering in this Line of Rectitude, and discharging what he conceives to be the indispensible Duty of an *impartial Printer,* he shall ever with great Chearfulness submit his Conduct to the Judgment of the Public, and by the Decision of that respectable and revered Tribunal stand acquitted or condemned.

Edmund Freeman and Loring Andrews: "Completion of the Government"

For these two printers in Massachusetts, as for many Americans, the initial operation of the new government under the Constitution marked the completion of a struggle to find the right system for the young republic. They rejoice over this success and the glorious future which is to come.

Herald of Freedom (Boston), 28 April 1789

The arrival of the illustrious President and Vice-President of America at the Seat of Federal Government completes the branches of that system which the free born sons of Columbia have formed and assented to, to guard their dearest privileges, and transmit them inviolate to generations yet unborn. Trade and commerce now raise their drooping heads, the Mechanick brandishes the tool of industry in triumph, and the husbandman repairs to the field with fresh vigour; justice, from her sacred seat, views with pleasure the once benighted prospect, now dawning into brightness resplendent as nature's purest light; while publick faith and honour gladden at the thought of our reviving credit. May America never cease to pay the tribute of gratitude she owes to the bountiful Parent of the Universe; may her citizens prove themselves worthy to enjoy the blessings heaped upon them: and may our country increase in splendour and glory 'till the 'course of nature changes, and the sun shall have finished its last diurnal rotation round the skies.'

OPPOSITION TO THE CONSTITUTION

An Officer of the Late Continental Army: "Great Names Taken in Vain"

This author downplays the fact that Benjamin Franklin and George Washington signed the Constitution. Just because their names are on it does not make it a perfect document. The fear expressed by this writer shows the potential impact from the support of Franklin and Washington. Washing-

*ton's support, all by itself, was probably enough to sway a number of peo-
ple to vote for the Constitution.*

Independent Gazetteer (Philadelphia), 6 November 1787

But where argument entirely failed, nothing remained for the supporters of the new Constitution but to endeavor to inflame your passions. The
attempt has been made and I am sorry to find out not entirely without effect. The great names of WASHINGTON and FRANKLIN have been taken
in vain, and shockingly prostituted to effect the most infamous purposes.
What! because our august Chieftain has subscribed his name, in his capacity of President of the Convention, to the plan offered by them to the States;
and because the venerable sage of Pennsylvania has *testified,* by his signature, that *the majority of Delegates of this State* assented to the same plan, will
anyone infer from this, that it has met with their entire approbation, and that
they consider it as a master-piece of human wisdom? I am apt to think the
contrary, and I have good reasons to ground my opinion on.

Cincinnatus: "This New System"

*Cincinnatus expresses concern over the decline in the power and influence
of the states if the Constitution is adopted. For many Americans, the states
were the level of government that protected their rights and freedoms. A
strong national government could easily turn into another tyrannical
Great Britain.*

Providence Gazette (Rhode Island), 8 December 1787

This new system, with one sweeping clause,[2] bears down every Constitution in the Union, and establishes its arbitrary doctrines, supreme and
paramount to all the bills and declarations of rights, in which we vainly put
our trust, and on which we rested the security of our often declared unalienable liberties. But I trust the whole people of this country will unite, in
crying out, as did our sturdy ancestors of old—*Nolumus leges anglicae mu-
tari.*[3]—we will not part with our birth-right.

Edward Eveleth Powars: "The Aristocratic Junto"

*Edward Eveleth Powars, one of the most vocal opponents of the Constitu-
tion, suspects a plot of some sort to gain control over the government. When
the plotters cannot answer the criticisms of the Constitution, they resort to
personal attacks in order to distract the people from their real concerns.*

American Herald (Boston), 7 January 1788

The Aristocratic Junto, and their Tools, being unable to answer the sound reasoning and weighty objections to the New System of Government, which is contained in the pamphlet, entitled, 'Observations, &c.' have been reduced to their usual resort, *personal detraction.*———A Correspondent wishes to knew of what consequence it can possibly be to the public, whether RICHARD HENRY LEE doubted of the military abilities of General Washington in 1775 or not?—If the above mentioned pamphlet contain unanswerable objections, as it undoubtedly does, it is not any thing that the *hireling,* who so malapropos signs himself *New-England,* can possibly say against its respectable author, that will tend, in any manner, to prejudice the minds of the people, or prevent a free circulation of his performance.—We shall pass over, in silence, other parts of this "DAMPER" as a brother Printer is pleased to stile it—His inflammatory threat against a sister State, which undoubtedly originated from the very Demon of Discord, and which appears to be better calculated for the meridian of Connecticut than of our enlightened Commonwealth.

Algernon Sidney: "We Should Oppose the New Constitution"

Again, Algernon Sidney (a pseudonym) worries that the Constitution will destroy the rights of the people and thus the United States will descend into a tyranny like the one that they had so recently escaped. The writer used the pseudonym Algernon Sidney in order to remind Americans of a martyr for republican government. Sidney had been a member of the Long Parliament that had ordered the execution of Charles I in 1649. He was arrested in 1683 for conspiring to kill King Charles II. Following a questionable trial in which Sidney's unpublished "Discourses Concerning Government" were presented as the major evidence against him, Sidney was beheaded on December 7, 1683. Americans such as Samuel Adams and Patrick Henry often referred to Sidney's work as an important influence on American political thought.

Providence Gazette (Rhode Island), 29 March 1788

In short, it is not only the means of taking away the trial by jury in many cases, but the insecurity of the liberty of the press and the rights of conscience, with the abolition of the freedom of election, and other numerous arbitrary principles, which should make us oppose the new Constitution.–If we suffer it to be established, the world will, on account of the gross tyranny which it holds forth, be inclined to suspect, rather than our understandings, our integrity and courage.

Centinel: "Essay I"

Centinel has many criticisms of the Constitution, which he explains here in some detail. In summing them all up, he concludes that the proposed government will be too strong and thus too tyrannical. The result will be that the power in the United States will be in the hands of a small number of men. He declares that those who say the government must be changed in order to solve the nation's problems and prevent European intervention are just wrong. Europe has too many problems of its own at the moment and will not have time or energy to worry about what is happening in the United States.

Independent Gazetteer (Philadelphia), 5 October 1787

Friends, Countrymen and Fellow Citizens: Permit one of yourselves to put you in mind of certain *liberties* and *privileges* secured to you by the constitution of this commonwealth, and to beg your serious attention to his uninterested opinion upon the plan of federal government submitted to your consideration, before you surrender these great and valuable privileges up forever. Your present frame of government secures to you a right to hold yourselves, houses, papers and possessions free from search and seizure, and therefore warrants granted without oaths or affirmations first made, affording sufficient foundation for them, whereby any officer or messenger may be commanded or required to search your houses or seize your persons or property, not particularly described in such warrant, shall not be granted. Your constitution further provides "that in controversies respecting property, and in suits between man and man, the parties have a right *to trial by jury, which ought to be held sacred*." It also provides and declares, "*that the people have a right of FREEDOM OF SPEECH, and of WRITING and PUBLISHING their sentiments, therefore THE FREEDOM OF THE PRESS OUGHT NOT TO BE RESTRAINED*." The constitution of Pennsylvania is *yet* in existence, *as yet* you have the right to *freedom of speech*, and of *publishing your sentiments*. How long those rights will appertain to you, you yourselves are called upon to say, whether your houses shall continue to be your castles; whether your papers, your persons and your property are to be held sacred and free from general warrants, you are now to determine. Whether the trial by jury is to continue as your birthright, the freemen of Pennsylvania, nay, of all America, are now called upon to declare.

Without presuming upon my own judgment, I cannot think it an unwarrantable presumption to offer my private opinion, and call upon others for theirs; and if I use my pen with the boldness of a freeman, it is because I know that the liberty of the press yet remains unviolated, and juries yet are judges.

The late Convention have submitted to your consideration a plan of a new federal government. The subject is highly interesting to your future welfare. Whether it be calculated to promote the great ends of civil society, viz., the happiness and prosperity of the community; it behooves you well to consider, uninfluenced by the authority of names. Instead of that frenzy of enthusiasm, that has actuated the citizens of Philadelphia, in their approbation of the proposed plan, before it was possible that it could be the result of a rational investigation into its principles; it ought to be dispassionately and deliberately examined, and its own intrinsic merit the only criterion of your patronage. If ever free and unbiased discussion was proper or necessary, it is on such an occasion. All the blessings of liberty and the dearest privileges of freemen are now at stake and dependent on your present conduct. Those who are competent to the task of developing the principles of government ought to be encouraged to come forward, and thereby the better enable the people to make a proper judgment; for the science of government is so abstruse, that few are able to judge for themselves; without such assistance the people are too apt to yield an implicit assent to the opinions of those characters, whose abilities are held in the highest esteem, and to those in whose integrity and patriotism they can confide; not considering that the love of domination is generally in proportion to talents, abilities, and superior acquirements; and that the men of the greatest purity of intention may be made instruments of despotism in the hands of the artful and designing. If it were not for the stability and attachment which time and habit gives to forms of government, it would be in the power of the enlightened and aspiring few, if they should combine, at any time to destroy the best establishments, and even make the people the instruments of their own subjugation.

The late Revolution having effaced in a great measure all former habits, and the present institutions are so recent, that there exists not that great reluctance to innovation, so remarkable in old communities, and which accords with reason, for the most comprehensive mind cannot foresee the full operation of material changes on civil polity; it is the genius of the common law to resist innovation.

The wealthy and ambitious, who in every community think they have a right to lord it over their fellow creatures, have availed themselves, very successfully, of this favorable disposition; for the people thus unsettled in their sentiments, have been prepared to accede to any extreme of government; all the distresses and difficulties they experience, proceeding from various causes, have been ascribed to the impotency of the present Confederation, and thence they have been led to expect full relief from the adoption of the proposed system of government; and in the other event, immediate ruin and annihilation as a nation. These characters flatter themselves that they have lulled all distrust and jealousy of their new plan, by gaining the concurrence of the two men in whom America has the highest confidence, and now triumphantly exult in the completion of their long meditated schemes of power and aggrandizement. I would be very far from insinuating that the two illustrious personages alluded to, have not the welfare of their country at heart; but that the unsuspecting goodness and zeal of the one, has been imposed on, in a subject of which he must be necessarily inexperienced, from his other arduous engagements; and that the weakness and indecision attendant on old age, has been practiced on in the other.

I am fearful that the principles of government inculcated in Mr. Adam's treatise,[4] and enforced in the numerous essays and paragraphs in the newspapers, have misled some well-designing members of the late Convention. But it will appear in the sequel, that the construction of the proposed plan of government is infinitely more extravagant.

I have been anxiously expecting that some enlightened patriot would, ere this, have taken up the pen to expose the futility, and counteract the baneful tendency of such principles. Mr. Adams's *sine qua non*[5] of a good government is three balancing powers, whose propelling qualities are to produce an equilibrium of interests, and thereby promote the happiness of the whole community. He asserts that the administrators of every government will ever be actuated by views of private interest and ambition, to the prejudice of the public good; that therefore the only effectual method to secure the rights of the people and promote their welfare, is to create an opposition of interests between the members of two distinct bodies, in the exercise of the powers of government, and balanced by those of a third. This hypothesis supposes human wisdom competent to the task of instituting three coequal orders in government, and corresponding weight in the community to enable them respectively to exercise their several parts, and whose views and interests should be so distinct as to prevent a coalition of any two of them for the destruction of the third. Mr. Adams, although he has traced the constitution of every form of government that ever existed, as far as history affords materials, has not been able to adduce a single instance of such a government; he indeed says that the British constitution is such in theory, but this is rather a confirmation that his principles are chimerical and not to be reduced to practice. If such an organization of power were practicable, how long would it continue? Not a day, for there is so great a disparity in the talents, wisdom and industry of mankind, that the scale would presently preponderate to one or the other body, and with every accession of power the means of further increase would be greatly extended. The state of society in England is much more favorable to such a scheme of government than that of America. There they have a powerful hereditary nobility and real distinctions of rank and interests; but even there, for want of that perfect equality of power and distinction of interests, in the three orders of government, they exist but in name; the only operative and efficient check, upon the conduct of administration is the sense of the people at large.

Suppose a government could be formed and supported on such principles. Would it answer the great purposes of civil society? If the administrators of every government are actuated by views of private interest and ambition, how is the welfare and happiness of the community to be the result of such jarring adverse interests?

Therefore, as different orders in government will not produce the good of the whole, we must recur to other principles. I believe it will be found that the form of government which holds those entrusted with power, in the greatest responsibility to their constituents, the best calculated for freemen. A republican, or free government, can only exist where the body of the people are virtuous, and where property is pretty equally divided. In such a government the people are the sovereign and their sense or opinion is the criterion of every public measure; for when this ceases to be the case, the nature of the government is changed, and an aristocracy, monarchy, or despotism will rise on its ruin. The highest responsibility is to be attained, in a simple struction of government, for the great body of the people never steadily attend to the operations of government, and for want of due information are liable to be imposed on. If you complicate the plan by various orders, the people will be perplexed and divided in their sentiments about the source of abuses or misconduct. Some will impute it to the Senate, others to the House of Representatives, and so on, that the interposition of the people may be rendered imperfect or perhaps wholly abortive. But if, imitating the constitution of Pennsylvania, you vest all the legislative power in one body of men (separating the executive and the judicial) elected for a short period, and necessarily excluded by rotation from permanency, and guarded from precipitancy and surprise by delays imposed on its proceedings, you will create the most perfect responsibility; for then, whenever the people feel a grievance they cannot mistake the authors and will apply the remedy with certainty and effect, discarding them at the next election. This tie of responsibility will obviate all the dangers apprehended from a single legislature, and will the best secure the rights of the people.

Having premised thus much, I shall now proceed to the examination of the proposed plan of government, and I trust, shall make it appear to the meanest capacity, that it has none of the essential requisites of a free government; that it is neither founded on those balancing restraining powers, recommended by Mr. Adams and attempted in the British constitution, or possessed of that responsibility to its constituents, which, in my opinion, is the only effectual security for the liberties and happiness of the people; but on the contrary, that it is a most daring attempt to establish a despotic aristocracy among freemen, that the world has ever witnessed.

I shall previously consider the extent of the powers intended to be vested in Congress, before I examine the construction of the general government.

It will not be controverted that the legislative is the highest delegated power in government, and that all others are subordinate to it. The celebrated Montesquieu establishes it as a maxim, that legislation necessarily follows the power of taxation. By section 8, of the first Article of the proposed plan of government, "the Congress are to have power to lay and collect taxes, duties, imposts and excises, to pay the debts and provide for the common defence and general welfare of the United States; but all duties, imposts and excises, shall be uniform throughout the United States." Now what can be more comprehensive than these words? Not content by other sections of the plan, to grant all the great executive powers of a confederation, and a STANDING ARMY IN TIME OF PEACE, that grand engine of oppression, and moreover the absolute control over the commerce of the United States and all external objects of revenue, such as unlimited imposts upon imports, etc.; they are to be vested with every species of internal taxation. Whatever taxes, duties and excises that they may deem requisite for the general welfare may be imposed on the citizens of these states, levied by the officers of Congress, distributed through every district in America; and the collection would be enforced by the standing army, however grievous or improper they may be. The Congress may construe every purpose for which the state legislatures now lay taxes, to be for the general welfare, and thereby seize upon every object of revenue.

The judicial power by 1st section of Article 3 "shall extend to all cases, in law and equity, arising under this Constitution, the laws of the United States, and treaties made or which shall be made under their authority; to all cases affecting ambassadors, other public ministers and consuls; to all cases of admiralty and maritime jurisdiction, to controversies to which the United States shall be a party, to controversies between two or more states, between a state and citizen of another state, between citizens of different states, between citizens of the same state claiming lands under grants of different states, and between a state, or the citizens thereof, and foreign states, citizens or subjects."

The judicial power to be vested in one Supreme Court, and in such Inferior Courts as the Congress may from time to time ordain and establish.

The objects of jurisdiction recited above are so numerous, and the shades of distinction between civil causes are oftentimes so slight, that it is more than probable that the state judicatories would be wholly superseded; for in contests about jurisdiction, the federal court, as the most powerful, would ever prevail. Every person acquainted with the history of the courts in England knows by what ingenious sophisms they have, at different periods, extended the sphere of their jurisdiction over objects out of the line of their institution, and contrary to their very nature; courts of a criminal jurisdiction obtaining cognizance in civil causes.

To put the omnipotency of Congress over the state government and judicatories out of all doubt, the 6th Article ordains that "this constitution and the laws of the United States which shall be made in pursuance thereof, and all treaties made, or which shall be made under the authority of the United States, shall be the supreme law of the land, and the judges in every state shall be bound thereby, any thing in the constitution or laws of any state to the contrary notwithstanding."

By these sections the all-prevailing power of taxation, and such extensive legislative and judicial powers are vested in the general government, as must in their operation, necessarily absorb the state legislatures and judicatories; and that such was in the contemplation of the framers of it, will appear from the provision made for such event, in another part of it; (but that, fearful of alarming the people by so great an innovation, they have suffered the forms of the separate governments to remain, as a blind). By section 4th of the 1st Article, "the times, places and manner of holding elections for senators and representatives, shall be prescribed in each state by the legislature thereof; but the Congress may at any time, by law, make or alter such regulations, except as to the place of choosing senators." The plain construction of which is, that when the state legislatures drop out of sight, from the necessary operation of this government, then Congress are to provide for the election and appointment of Representatives and Senators.

If the foregoing be a just comment, if the United States are to be melted down into one empire, it becomes you to consider whether such a government, however constructed, would be eligible in so extended a territory; and whether it would be practicable, consistent with freedom? It is the opinion of the greatest writers, that a very extensive country cannot be governed on democratical principles, on any other plan, than a confederation of a number of small republics, possessing all the powers of internal government, but united in the management of their foreign and general concerns.

It would not be difficult to prove, that anything short of despotism could not bind so great a country under one government; and that whatever plan you might, at the first setting out, establish, it would issue in a despotism.

If one general government could be instituted and maintained on principles of freedom, it would not be so competent to attend to the various local concerns and wants, of every particular district; as well as the peculiar governments, who are nearer the scene and possessed of superior means of information. Besides, if the business of the whole Union is to be managed by one government, there would not be time. Do we not already see, that the inhabitants in a number of larger states, who are remote from the seat of government, are loudly complaining of the inconveniences and disadvantages they are subjected to on this account, and that, to enjoy the comforts of local government, they are separating into smaller divisions.

Having taken a review of the powers, I shall now examine the construction of the proposed general government.

Article I, section I. "All legislative powers herein granted shall be vested in a Congress of the United States, which shall consist of a senate and house of representatives." By another section, the President (the principal executive officer) has a conditional control over their proceedings.

Section 2. "The house of representatives shall be composed of members chosen every second year, by the people of the several states. The number of representatives shall not exceed one for every 30, 000 inhabitants."

The Senate, the other constituent branch of the legislature, is formed by the legislature of each state appointing two Senators, for the term of six years.

The executive power by Article 2, section I is to be vested in a President of the United States of America, elected for four years. Section 2 gives him "power, by and with the consent of the senate to make treaties, provided two thirds of the senators present concur; and he shall nominate, and by and with the advice and consent of the senate, shall appoint ambassadors, other public ministers and consuls, judges of the Supreme Court, and all other officers of the United States, whose appointments are not herein otherwise provided for, and which shall be established by law, etc. . . ". And by another section he has the absolute power of granting reprieves and pardons for treason and all other high crimes and misdemeanors, except in the case of impeachment.

The forgoing are the outlines of the plan.

Thus we see, the House of Representatives are on the part of the people to balance the Senate, who I suppose will be composed of the better sort, the wellborn, etc. The number of the Representatives (being only one for every 30,000 inhabitants) appears to be too few, either to communicate the requisite information of the wants, local circumstance and sentiments of so extensive an empire, or to prevent corruption and undue influence, in the exercise of such great powers; the term for which they are to be chosen, too long to preserve a due dependence and accountability to their constituents;

and the mode and place of their election not sufficiently ascertained, for as Congress have the control over both, they may govern the choice, by ordering the Representatives of a whole state, to be elected in one place and that too may be the most inconvenient.

The Senate, the great efficient body in this plan of government, is constituted on the most unequal principles. The smallest state in the Union has equal weight with the great states of Virginia, Massachusetts, or Pennsylvania. The Senate, besides its legislative functions, has a very considerable share in the executive; none of the principal appointments to office can be made without its advise and consent. The term and mode of its appointment will lead to permanency; the members are chosen for six years, the mode is under the control of Congress, and as there is no exclusion by rotation, they may be continued for life, which, from their extensive means of influence, would follow of course. The President, who would be a mere pageant of state, unless he coincides with the views of the Senate, would either become the head of the aristocratic junto in that body, or its minion; besides, their influence being the most predominant, could the best secure his re-election to office. And from his power of granting pardons, he might screen from punishment the most treasonable attempts on the liberties of the people, when instigated by the Senate.

From this investigation into the organization of this government, it appears that it is devoid of all responsibility or accountability to the great body of the people, and that so far from being a regular balanced government, it would be in practice a permanent ARISTOCRACY.

The framers of it, actuated by the true spirit of such a government, which ever abominates and suppresses all free enquiry and discussion, have made no provision for the liberty of the press, that grand palladium of freedom and scourge of tyrants, but observed a total silence on that head. It is the opinion of some great writers, that if the liberty of the press, by an institution of religion, or otherwise, could be rendered sacred, even in Turkey, that despotism would fly before it. And it is worthy of remark, that there is no declaration of personal rights, premised in most free constitutions; and that trial by jury in civil cases is taken away; for what other construction can be put on the following, viz., Article III, section 2d. "in all cases affecting ambassadors, other public ministers and consuls, and those in which a State shall be party, the Supreme Court shall have original jurisdiction. In all other cases above mentioned, the Supreme Court shall have appellate jurisdiction, both as to law and fact." It would be a novelty in jurisprudence, as well as evidently improper to allow an appeal from the verdict of a jury, on the matter of fact; therefore, it implies and allows of a dismission of the jury in civil cases, and especially when it is considered, that jury trial in criminal cases is expressly stipulated for, but not in civil cases.

But our situation is represented to be so critically dreadful, that however reprehensible and exceptionable the proposed plan of government may be, there is no alternative between the adoption of it and absolute ruin. My fellow citizens, things are not at that crisis; it is the argument of tyrants. The present distracted state of Europe secures us from injury on that quarter, and as to domestic dissensions, we have not so much to fear from them, as to precipitate us into this form of government, without it is a safe and a proper one. For remember, of all possible evils, that of despotism is the worst and the most to be dreaded.

Besides, it cannot be supposed, that the first essay on so difficult a subject, is so well digested, as it ought to be. If the proposed plan, after a mature deliberation, should meet the approbation of the respective states, the matter will end; but if it should be found to be fraught with dangers and inconveniences, a future general convention, being in possession of the objections, will be the better enabled to plan a suitable government.

> Who's here so base, that would a bondman be?
> If any, speak; for him have I offended.
> Who's here so vile, that will not love his country?
> If any, speak; for him have I offended.

Eleazer Oswald: "Stopping the Free Circulation of the Newspapers"

In this piece, printer Eleazer Oswald attacks the postmaster general for stopping the free delivery of newspapers. He believes that the act is intended to shut down communication between the states. Many Anti-Federalists accused the Federalists of trying to stop debate over the Constitution through such measures.

Independent Gazetteer (Philadelphia), 16 January 1788

The conduct of Congress or the post-master-general, in stopping the free circulation of the news-papers at this critical juncture is very alarming. From what this extraordinary measure has originated we do not pretend to say, but certainly the freemen of America will never suffer such a bare-faced violation of their liberties to pass with impunity. This is a stretch of arbitrary power that even Britain never attempted before the revolution. By this manoeuvre all communication is cut off between the states; so that the despots may assemble *an army,* and subjugate the freemen in one state, before their friends in another can hear of it.

Shepard Kollock: "A Disgrace to This Enlightened Age"

This New Jersey printer complains that he has received few newspapers from other states lately. He believes that it is an attempt to shut down communication and debate and he urges printers to complain loudly before it is too late.

New Jersey Journal (Elizabeth Town), 30 January 1788

For some weeks past, we have scarcely received a paper from our numerous correspondents in the different states. The motive for this suppression of intelligence is best known to the post-master general! It has an oblique aspect of sinister views.—It is a disgrace to this enlightened age, and an harbinger of slavery, that when the press, under the most arbitrary governments, is daily growing more and more free, that the post-masters, or their jackalls, should essay to stop all communication between the states at this important crisis, by prohibiting that exchange of papers printers have enjoyed since the first establishment of a post-office in this continent. Such a most atrocious attack upon public freedom, demands the attention and resentment of every friend to the rights of his country; for if this mutual exchange cannot be accomplished without being subject to the price of a post-rider, besides satisfying his inordinate and unlimmitted demands, there will be few presses, and they will soon become entirely subservient to the influence of government. Instead of being the guardians of the public rights, they will be made the dangerous engines to gloss and color over the most fatal designs against the common liberty and happiness.—Rouse, Printers! And oppose the hydra in embryo.

QUESTIONS

1. What aspects of the Constitution do supporters such as Timothy Green emphasize to show the wisdom of the document?
2. What does Publius propose to do in his series of essays? Why does he support the Constitution?
3. Robert Gerrish states that the Constitution will be praised in Europe. Why should it matter to Americans what Europeans think about the government of the United States?

4. Why does one of the anonymous essayists in support of the Constitution poke fun at the Anti-Federalists? What does he hope to gain?

5. Why do the critics of the Constitution such as Cincinnatus and Algernon Sydney fear that the new government will be too strong? Where do they believe that the bulk of government power should be?

6. What are Centinel's main criticisms of the Constitution? Does he give any suggestions as to how the problems facing the United States should be addressed?

7. Why is the issue of access to the press so important to people like John Carter and Eleazar Oswald? Do you think the publication of more pieces opposed to the Constitution would have changed the outcome of the debate?

NOTES

1. An old word meaning goal or destination.

2. Supreme law of the land clause.

3. "We do not wish that the laws of England be changed." Statute of Merton, 20 Henry III, 1236. This law was the original basis for English common law until it was repealed in 1948.

4. John Adams, *A Defence of the Constitutions of Government of the United States, 1787–1788,* vol. 1 (London, 1787). This work also appears in *The Works of John Adams,* 10 vols., ed. Charles Francis Adams (Boston: Little, Brown, 1850–1856), 4:269–588.

5. Necessity; an indispensable thing or condition.

CHAPTER II

The Bill of Rights, 1787–1791

The new government created by the Constitution began operation in March 1789 when Congress met for the first time. George Washington took the oath of office as president in April. Over the next several months, American leaders fleshed out the various parts of the government (the Cabinet, the federal courts, etc.) that had not been fully described in the Constitution.

In the midst of all these discussions, Congressman James Madison of Virginia brought up the issue of amendments to the Constitution. One of the major objections to the Constitution during the ratification debates had been the lack of a Bill of Rights. Several states ratified the Constitution with calls for a Bill of Rights to be added as soon as possible, and many people assumed it would be one of the first orders of business for the new government. When running for the House of Representatives, Madison had promised his constituents that he would work for the adoption of a national Bill of Rights. Thus, he introduced a number of amendments on June 8, 1789. Many members of Congress stated that they had more important things to worry about in getting the government up and running. Madison, however, pushed the issue, believing that too many promises had been made to let the issue of a Bill of Rights be overlooked.

Congress slowly agreed and, finally, on September 25, 1789, sent a list of twelve amendments to the states for their consideration. Ten of the twelve proposed amendments were finally ratified by the required number of states late in 1791. Madison's home state of Virginia provided the necessary margin for success when it ratified the ten amendments that became known as the Bill of Rights on December 15, 1791.

During the time that the Bill of Rights was being discussed and ratified, the newspaper printers did not discuss the proposed amendments in any great detail. They apparently assumed, as Madison had, that the adoption of a Bill of Rights was practically a done deal because of all the promises made previously. Thus, most of the newspaper discussion of whether a Bill of Rights was needed had already taken place during the debates over the ratification of the Constitution.

The documents in favor of a Bill of Rights all declare or imply that the national government cannot be trusted to honor the rights of its citizens unless protections are spelled out clearly in some sort of formal statement. Both the first and second selections emphasize that history has shown that people lose their rights if they do not consciously seek to protect them from government infringement. The third document criticizes the idea that the Constitution must be tried out first before amendments can be made to it. The fourth selection urges people to take the state elections seriously in order to choose people who will push for a national Bill of Rights.

The selections that oppose a Bill of Rights all see it as a waste of time for various reasons. The first and second documents state that the national government will not be able to interfere with areas that are not stated in the document and that the issues related to personal rights that have been raised fall into this category. The third piece states that it will not be clear what amendments are needed until the government operates for a while. The final selection sees the issue of amendments as a distraction for Congress, which has more important things to do.

Support for a Bill of Rights

An Old Whig: "To Guard Ourselves against the Invasion of Liberties"

An Old Whig declares that creating a workable form of government is definitely possible, but that it cannot be done without including a Bill of Rights to protect the liberties of the citizens. A Bill of Rights is necessary to prevent the government from becoming too strong and powerful.

Independent Gazetteer (Philadelphia), 27 October 1787

In this country perhaps we are possessed of more than our share of political virtue. If we will exercise a little patience and bestow our best endeavors on the business, I do not think it impossible, that we may yet form a federal constitution, much superior to any form of government, which has ever existed in the world;—but, whenever this important work shall be accomplished, I venture to pronounce that it will not be done without a careful attention to the framing of a bill of rights.

Much has been said and written, on the subject of a bill of rights;—possibly without sufficient attention to the necessity of conveying distinct and precise ideas of the true meaning of a bill of rights. Your readers, I hope, will excuse me, if I conclude this letter with an attempt to throw some light on this subject.

Men when they enter into society, yield up a part of their natural liberty, for the sake of being protected by government. If they yield up less than is necessary, the government is so feeble, that it cannot protect them.—To yield up so much, as is necessary for the purposes of government; and to retain all beyond what is necessary, is the great point, which ought, if possible, to be attained in the formation of a constitution. At the same time that by these means, the liberty of the subject is secured, the government is really strengthened; because wherever the subject is convinced that nothing more is required from him, than what is necessary for the good of the community, he yields a chearful obedience, which is more useful than the constrained service of slaves.—To define what portion of his natural liberty, the subject shall at all times be entitled to retain, is one great end of a bill of rights, firmly securing the privileges of the subject, the government is always in danger of degenerating into tyranny; for it is certainly true, that "in establishing the powers of government, the rulers are invested with every right and authority, which is not in explicit terms reserved."—Hence it is, that we find the rulers so often lording over the people at their will and pleasure. Hence it is that we find the patriots, in all ages of the world, so very solicitous to obtain explicit engagements from their rulers, stipulating, expressly, for the preservation of particular rights and privileges.

In different nations, we find different grants or reservations of privileges appealed to in the struggles between the rulers and the people, many of which in the different nations of Europe, have long since been swallowed up and lost by time, or destroyed by the arbitrary hand of power. In England we find the people, with the Barons at their head, exacting a solemn resignation of their rights from king John, in their celebrated magna charta, which was many times renewed in Parliament during the reigns of his successors. The petition of rights was afterwards consented to by Charles the first, and contained a declaration of the liberties of the people. The habeas corpus act,[1] after the restoration of Charles the Second, the bill of rights, which was obtained from the Prince and Princess of Orange on their accession to the throne, and the act of settlement, at the accession of the Hanover family, are other instances to shew the care and watchfulness of that nation, to improve every opportunity, of the reign of a weak prince, or the revolution in their government, to obtain the most explicit declarations in favor of their liberties. In like manner the people of this country, at the revolution, having all power in their own hands, in forming the constitutions of the several states, took care to secure themselves by bills of rights, so as to prevent, as far as possible, the encroachments of their future rulers upon the rights of the people. Some of these rights are said to be unalienable, such as the rights of conscience: yet even these have been often invaded, where they have not been carefully secured by express and solemn bills and declarations in their favor.

Before we establish a government, whose acts will be THE SUPREME LAW OF THE LAND, and whose power will extend to almost every case without exception, we ought carefully to guard ourselves by A BILL OF RIGHTS, against the invasion of those liberties which it is essential for us to retain, which it is of no real use for government to deprive us of; but which in the course of human events have been too often insulted with all the wantonness of an idle barbarity.

Robert Whitehill: "Speech in Pennsylvania Ratifying Convention"

In the ratifying debates over the Constitution, several people supporting the new government stated that a Bill of Rights was not necessary because the Constitution did not give the national government power over areas of personal rights. In his speech before the Pennsylvania Ratifying Convention, Robert Whitehill states that he does not feel that is enough protection. A Bill of Rights must be included in order to explicitly protect the rights of the people and insure that the government does not even try to infringe on them. Whitehill had been active in the state government of Pennsylvania since its inception and continued to serve his state until his death in 1813. His strong support of the Pennsylvania state constitution provided part of the basis for his opposition to the Constitution.

Pennsylvania Herald and General Advertiser (Philadelphia), 12 and 15 December 1787

I differ, Sir, from the honorable member from the city,[2] as to the impropriety or necessity of a bill of rights . If, indeed, the constitution itself so well defined the powers of the government that no mistake could arise, and, we were well assured that our governors would always act right, then we might be satisfied without an explicit reservation of those rights with which the people ought not, and mean not to part. But, Sir, we know that it is the nature of power to seek its own augmentation, and thus the loss of liberty is the necessary consequence of a loose or extravagant delegation of authority. National freedom has been, and will be the sacrifice of ambition and power, and it is our duty to employ the present opportunity in stipulating such restrictions as are best calculated to protect us from oppression and slavery. Let us then, Mr. President, if other countries cannot supply an adequate example, let us proceed upon our own principles, and with the great end of government in view, the happiness of the people, it will be strange if we err. Government, we have been told, Sir, is yet in its infancy: we ought not therefore to submit to the shackles of foreign schools and opinions. In entering into the social compact, men ought not to leave their rulers at large, but erect a permanent landmark by which they may learn the extent of their authority, and the people be able to discover the first encroachments on their liberties. . . . A bill of rights, Mr. President, it has been said, would not only be unnecessary, but it would be dangerous, and for this special reason, that because it is not practicable to enumerate all the rights of the people, therefore it would be hazardous to secure such of the rights as we can enumerate! Truly, Sir, I will agree that a bill of rights may be a dangerous instrument, but it is to the views and projects of the aspiring ruler, and not the liberties of the citizen. Grant but this explicit criterion, and our governors will not venture to encroach; refuse it, and the people cannot venture to complain. From the formal language of magna charta we are next taught to consider a declaration of rights as superfluous; but, Sir, will the situation and conduct of Great Britain furnish a case parallel to that of America? It surely will not be contended that we are about to receive our liberties as a grant or concession from any power upon earth; so that if we learn anything from the English charter, it is this: that the people having negligently lost or submissively resigned their rights into the hands of the crown, they were glad to recover them upon any terms; their anxiety to secure the grant by the strongest evidence will be an argument to prove, at least, the expediency of the measure, and the result of the whole is a lesson instructing us to do by an easy precaution, what will hereafter be an arduous and perhaps insurmountable task.

Thomas Adams and John Nourse: "The Most Contemptible Idea"

Other supporters of the Constitution suggested that it be tried out and then amended if it was shown that changes were needed. These printers scoff at that idea, stating that no government could be created if one took the attitude that you had to try it first before approving it.

Independent Chronicle (Boston), 5 February 1789

The idea, says a correspondent, that the new constitution must be first tried, before it can be amended, in a single point, is surely the most contemptible that ever entered the head of a politician. It is in fact a reproach to the Federal Convention which formed, as well as to the different assemblies which have since approved this celebrated instrument and who undoubtedly acted merely upon an abstracted view of the subject, without the least experimental knowledge either of its merits or defects. Had this opinion have prevailed previous to its ratification, we should certainly never have had the Government to have tried, for even as yet, we have had no experience respecting it.

Cassius: "To the People of the State of New York"

Cassius sees the issue of a Bill of Rights as still very important, even though the new government is in operation. The upcoming state election in New York will be important because it will decide whether the state's rulers will be men who will push for amendments to the Constitution or not. He urges all the citizens to get out and vote in order to be sure that they are heard on this very important issue.

Country Journal (Poughkeepsie, New York), 3 March 1789

The next Election will perhaps be as important to the general interests of America, as any that ever have been or will be held in this country; for it may greatly depend on them, whether the new constitution is to continue in its present form, or to receive such amendments as have been proposed by many of the State Conventions, and are anxiously desired by so great a proportion of the citizens of these United States. That the leaders of the federal party, throughout these States are opposed to those amendments, which we consider as the most essential, I believe is now beyond a doubt. Their conduct in all the legislatures whose proceedings we have had any account of, the sentiments held out by their writers in the public papers, and the indefatigable pains taken to get in those who call themselves federalists at the ensuing election of State and Continental Representatives, establish this truth in my opinion beyond all contradiction—for if they are not opposed to the amendments, why are they opposed to our having such persons to represent us, as we may be assured will use their endeavors to obtain them? I defy any one to give a satisfactory answer to this question, (for it is clear that the highest or farthest object which the warmest opponent to the new constitution can now have in view, is to have the amendments take place which are so generally esteemed to be necessary for the security of our State governments, and of the inestimable rights of freemen.) We may easily see from this, if we wish for the amendments, the absolute necessity of exerting ourselves to get into the elective offices, both of our own, and of the general government, persons possessed of the same wishes. We cannot suppose any one to be a sincere friend to amendments who shall advise us to trust those of a contrary character to obtain them; the absurdity of such a supposition would be too glaring not to strike the most common observer. It is a favorite sentiment with the federal writers, to postpone amending, till we experience the defects in the system by its operations; which is as much as to say, bow your unwilling necks to the yoke, till the experiment can be fairly tried, whether the people cannot be goaded into a tame submission to this system without alterations. Is this the language of those who wish for amendments? Surely not. For the sake of every thing which is dear to freemen, let us not suffer ourselves to be deceived upon this occasion by *artful* and insidious professions; but let us be fully impressed with this important truth, established by the invariable experience of ages, that if we wait till the fetters are fairly and completely riveted on, nothing but steel will be able to file them off. The people of these States have it yet in their power, by proper and judicious elections, to retrieve and establish their liberties on a sure and permanent foundation.

Every scheme and artifice which can be devised are now using, and will be used to oust our present Governor at the next election, for no other reason but because he is a Whig, a republican, a friend to the liberties of the common people, and a professed enemy to aristocracy; which he and all writers and thinkers upon the subject, justly esteem to be the most oppressive kind of government on earth. They can justly find no fault with his character, none with his public administration; and I believe that no one who is acquainted with the history of his life, will dare to accuse me of partiality, when I say I believe him to be one of the best public characters on the continent. From his (legal) infancy he has been in our assembly an able and steady asserter of the rights of the people, until the commencement of the late war, through which, amidst innumerable difficulties, he has defended them with equal activity, abilities and firmness in the field. Nor was his merit less conspicuous, in the peace and good order which immediately took place upon our taking possession of the southern district of this State, between the jarring elements which came together upon that occasion. When resentments ran so high as to threaten the destruction of part of the community, the peace was preserved, the dignity of government kept up, and the authority of the laws prevailed.—And what is now peculiar to his character, and distinguishes it from most of the shining ones of the time, is, that he does not ask, he does not wish, as a reward for his services, a surrender of those rights into his own hands, but still remains the same steady and sincere friend to the liberties of his country, and the same determined opposer of tyranny, whether it comes in the shape of a royal Prerogative, an act of Parliament, or in one less alarming, and consequently more dangerous.

Some time ago, at a meeting of near forty of the members of the Legislature, friends to amendments, it was by a unanimous ballot, determined to hold up at the ensuing election his excellency George Clinton, Esquire, for Governor, and the honorable Pierre Van Cortlandt, Esquire, for Lieutenant-Governor. It would be highly imprudent if not dangerous to make any great changes in the officers of government at this time, when the cold water which is thrown upon the amendments to the new constitution, will probably prove as oil to the fire of discontent already kindled throughout this continent, by that system of government, which, in its present form, is justly looked upon to be so very defective and dangerous. It would be unwise to dismiss from the helm of government, a pilot of experienced skill, courage and integrity, at a time when the political horizon lowers so heavily.

The friends of freedom in our sister states, at present overpowered by the arts, deceptions, and influence of their great men, turn their eyes to us from every part of the continent with the most anxious solicitude and concern, depending chiefly upon the active exertions of this state and Virginia, and the still, but powerful influence arising from the determination of North Carolina and Rhode Island, not to adopt the system in its present form, to support the cause of amendments, on which depends the liberties of America.

The Conventions of Massachusetts, New Hampshire, New York, Virginia and South Carolina, and a respectable and virtuous minority in the convention of Pennsylvania, have declared to the world in the most unequivocal manner, by the amendments they have proposed to this system, that they look upon it as dangerous to liberty: and the states of North Carolina and Rhode Island, have still more forcibly, though not more clearly, expressed the same sentiment, by their refusing to adopt it. What then, my fellow citizens, must we think of those, who are endeavoring to persuade us, that the amendments are matters of no consequence, that the government will not abuse its powers; that we ought to sit still, and not seek for any alterations, until, like the rest of the nations of the world, we *feel* ourselves enslaved and oppressed (should they not add) and like them unable to resist or shake off tyranny? What must we think of those who are endeavoring, by insidious and malicious insinuations, and the most low and despicable falsehoods, to destroy our confidence in those whose fidelity we have sufficiently proved, by their having long enjoyed that confidence, and having never abused or betrayed it, who have steadily opposed foreign and open attempts upon the liberties of their country, and as steadily refuted the more artful, sly and concealed encroachments of domestic tyranny? What can we think of those who vilify that excellent mode of trial by jury, and thereby shew an inclination to persuade us to give up that invaluable privilege? Is it possible we can suppose that they are friends to our liberties? May Heaven forbid so fatal an infatuation!—It is high time to open our eyes to our true situation. Is not the declared sense of so many respectable public bodies of the defects and dangers in that constitution sufficient to awaken our attention? Is it not a ground that will justify at least some small degree of jealousy concerning the design of those who are opposed to the amendments; especially when we look round and observe who they are? Are they not generally the rich, the powerful, the great, the wellborn and the upstart, the governors (except our own) the senators and the high officers of government? Is it not sufficient to evince the necessity at least of our being cautious whom we trust with power, until the necessary amendments to the new constitution shall be obtained, whereby the powers of the government may be clearly defined and limited, the rights of the state governments (most of them sufficiently extensive for free ones) properly ascertained and established, every idea of their consolidation erased (an idea I will be so bold to say, never contemplated by Congress, or one of the state legislatures, or by the people of any of these states) and the rights and privileges of freemen permanently secured to us and our late posterity?—Let us upon this occasion convince the world that we have the good sense to guard those rights, which we have so lately had the courage to defend.

OPPOSITION TO A BILL OF RIGHTS

Publius: "Federalist #85"

In one of the last of the "Federalist" essays, Alexander Hamilton, writing as Publius, states that amendments to the Constitution are totally unnecessary. He does not understand why people push for a Bill of Rights on the national level when a number of states (including New York) do not have them on the state level. Protections for the rights of the people are only as good as the strength of the government protecting them, and it does not matter whether they are specifically protected in part of the document or not.

Independent Journal (New York), 16, 26 July, 9 August 1788

In the course of the foregoing review of the constitution I have taken notice of, and endeavoured to answer, most of the objections which have appeared against it. There however remain a few which either did not fall naturally under any particular head, or were forgotten in their proper places. These shall now be discussed; but as the subject has been drawn into great length, I shall so far consult brevity as to comprise all my observations on these miscellaneous points in a single paper.

The most considerable of these remaining objections is, that the plan of the convention contains no bill of rights. Among other answers given to this, it has been upon different occasions remarked, that the constitutions of several of the States are in a similar predicament. I add, that New-York is of this number. And yet the opposers of the new system in this state, who profess an unlimited admiration for its constitution, are among the most intemperate partizans of a bill of rights. To justify their zeal in this matter, they alledge two things; one is, that though the constitution of New-York has no bill of rights prefixed to it, yet it contains in the body of it various provisions in favor of particular privileges and rights, which in substance amount to the same thing; the other is, that the constitution adopts in their full extent, the common and statute law of Great-Britain, by which many other rights not expressed in it are equally secured.

To the first I answer, that the constitution proposed by the convention contains, as well as the constitution of this state, a number of such provisions.

Independent of those, which relate to the structure of the government, we find the following:—Article 1. section 3. clause 7. "Judgment in cases of impeachment shall not extend further than to removal from office, and disqualification to hold and enjoy any office of honour, trust, or profit under the United States; but the party convicted shall nevertheless be liable and subject to indictment, trial, judgment and punishment, according to law."—Section 9. of the same article, clause 2. "The privilege of the writ of habeas corpus shall not be suspended, unless when in cases of rebellion or invasion the public safety may require it."—Clause 3. "No bill of attainder or ex post facto law shall be passed."—Clause 7. "No title of nobility shall be granted by the United States: and no person holding any office of profit or trust under them, shall, without the consent of the congress, accept of any present, emolument, office or title of any kind whatever, from any king, prince, or foreign state."—Article III. section 2. clause 3. "The trial of all crimes, except in cases of impeachment, shall be by jury; and such trial shall be held in the state where the said crimes shall have been committed; but when not committed within any state, the trial shall be at such place or places as the congress may by law have directed."—Section 3, of the same article, "Treason against the United States shall consist only in levying war against them, or in adhering to their enemies, giving them aid and comfort. No person shall be convicted of treason unless on the testimony of two witnesses to the same overt act, or on confession in open court."—And clause 3, of the same section, "The congress shall have the power to declare the punishment of treason, but no attainder of treason shall work corruption of blood, or forfeiture, except during the life of the person attainted."

It may well be a question whether these are not upon the whole, of equal importance with any which are to be found in the constitution of this state. The establishment of the writ of habeas corpus, the prohibition of ex post facto laws, and of TITLES OF NOBILITY, to which we have no corresponding provision in our constitution, are perhaps greater securities to liberty and republicanism than any it contains. The creation of crimes after the commission of the fact, or in other words, the subjecting of men to punishment for things which, when they were done, were breaches of no law, and the practice of arbitrary imprisonments, have been in all ages the favourite and most formidable instruments of tyranny. The observations of the judicious Blackstone, in reference to the latter, are well worthy of recital. "To bereave a man of life (says he) or by violence to confiscate his estate, without accusation or trial, would be so gross and notorious an act of despotism, as must at once convey the alarm of tyranny throughout the whole nation; but confinement of the person by secretly hurrying him to gaol, where his sufferings are unknown or forgotten, is a less public, a less striking, and therefore a more dangerous engine of arbitrary government." And as a remedy for this fatal evil, he is everywhere peculiarly emphatical in his encomiums on the habeas corpus act, which in one place he calls "the BULWARK of the British Constitution."

Nothing need be said to illustrate the importance of the prohibition of titles of nobility. This may truly be denominated the corner stone of republican government; for so long as they are excluded, there can never be serious danger that the government will be any other than that of the people.

To the second, that is, to the pretended establishment of the common and statute law by the constitution, I answer, that they are expressly made subject "to such alterations and provisions as the legislature shall from time to time make concerning the same." They are therefore at any moment liable to repeal by the ordinary legislative power, and of course have no constitutional sanction. The only use of the declaration was to recognize the ancient law, and to remove doubts which might have been occasioned by the revolution. This consequently can be considered as no part of a declaration of rights, which under our constitutions must be intended as limitations of the power of the government itself.

It has been several times truly remarked, that bills of rights are, in their origin, stipulations between kings and their subjects, abridgements of prerogative in favour of privilege, reservations of rights not surrendered to the prince. Such was MAGNA CARTA, obtained by the barons, sword in hand, from king John. Such were the subsequent confirmations of that charter by subsequent princes. Such was the petition of right assented to by Charles the First, in the beginning of his reign. Such also was the declaration of right presented by the lords and commons to the prince of Orange in 1688, and afterwards thrown into the form of an act of parliament called the bill of rights. It is evident, therefore, that, according to their primitive signification, they have no application to constitutions professedly founded upon the power of the people, and executed by their immediate representatives and servants. Here, in strictness, the people surrender nothing, and as they retain every thing, they have no need of particular reservations. "WE THE PEOPLE of the United States, to secure the blessings of liberty to ourselves and our posterity, do ordain and establish this constitution for the United States of America." Here is a better recognition of popular rights than volumes of those aphorisms which make the principal figure in several of our state bills of rights, and which would sound much better in a treatise of ethics than in a constitution of government.

But a minute detail of particular rights is certainly far less applicable to a constitution like that under consideration, which is merely intended to regulate the general political interests of the nation, than to a constitution which has the regulation of every species of personal and private concerns. If therefore the loud clamors against the plan of the convention on this score, are well founded, no epithets of reprobation will be too strong for the constitution of this state. But the truth is, that both of them contain all, which in relation to their objects, is reasonably to be desired.

I go further and affirm that bills of rights, in the sense and in the extent in which they are contended for, are not only unnecessary in the proposed constitution, but would even be dangerous. They would contain various exceptions to powers which are not granted; and on this very account, would afford a colourable pretext to claim more than were granted. For why declare that things shall not be done which there is no power to do? Why for instance, should it be said, that the liberty of the press shall not be restrained, when no power is given by which restrictions may be imposed? I will not contend that such a provision would confer a regulating power; but it is evident that it would furnish, to men disposed to usurp, a plausible pretense for claiming that power. They might urge with a semblance of reason, that the Constitution ought not to be charged with the absurdity of providing against the abuse of an authority, which was not given, and that the provision against restraining the liberty of the press afforded a clear implication, that a power to prescribe proper regulations concerning it, was intended to be vested in the national government. This may serve as a specimen of the numerous handles which would be given to the doctrine of constructive powers, by the indulgence of an injudicious zeal for bills of rights.

On the subject of the liberty of the press, as much as has been said, I cannot forbear adding a remark or two: in the first place, I observe that there is not a syllable concerning it in the constitution of this state, and in the next,

I contend that whatever has been said about it in that of any other state, amounts to nothing. What signifies a declaration that "the liberty of the press shall be inviolably preserved"? What is the liberty of the press? Who can give it any definition which would not leave the utmost latitude for evasion? I hold it to be impracticable; and from this, I infer, that its security, whatever fine declarations may be inserted in any constitution respecting it, must altogether depend on public opinion, and on the general spirit of the people and of the government. And here, after all, as is intimated upon another occasion, must we seek for the only solid basis of all our rights.

There remains but one other view of this matter to conclude the point. The truth is, after all the declamation we have heard, that the constitution is itself in every rational sense, and to every useful purpose, A BILL OF RIGHTS. The several bills of rights, in Great-Britain, form its constitution, and conversely the constitution of each state is its bill of rights. And the proposed constitution, if adopted, will be the bill of rights of the union. Is it one object of a bill of rights to declare and specify the political privileges of the citizens in the structure and administration of the government? This is done in the most ample and precise manner in the plan of the convention, comprehending various precautions for the public security, which are not to be found in any of the state constitutions. Is another object of a bill of rights to define certain immunities and modes of proceeding, which are relative to personal and private concerns? This we have seen has also been attended to, in a variety of cases, in the same plan. Adverting therefore to the substantial meaning of a bill of rights, it is absurd to allege that it is not to be found in the work of the convention. It may be said that it does not go far enough, though it will not be easy to make this appear; but it can with no propriety be contended that there is no such thing. It certainly must be immaterial what mode is observed as to the order of declaring the rights of the citizens, if they are to be found in any part of the instrument which establishes the government. And hence it must be apparent that much of what has been said on this subject, rests merely on verbal and nominal distinctions, which are entirely foreign from the substance of the thing.
PUBLIUS

James Wilson: "Speech at a Public Meeting in Philadelphia"

Several states, in expressing concerns about the Constitution, stated that it provided no protection for freedom of the press. Many people saw this protection as essential to keep a republic working well by giving the people a voice in critiquing the government. In this speech, Federalist James Wilson

addresses this concern. He states that the proposed Constitution has no pro-
visions dealing with the press at all. The new government will not have au-
thority over the press, and so it was not necessary to include a provision
protecting the freedom of the press. This piece was published in an "extra,"
a special unscheduled publication. Printers issued extras whenever they
had important materials that could not wait until the regular publication
date for the newspaper.

Pennsylvania Herald (Philadelphia), 9 October 1787 Extra

Mr. Chairman and Fellow Citizens, Having received the honor of an appointment to represent you in the late convention, it is perhaps, my duty to
comply with the request of many gentlemen whose characters and judg-
ments I sincerely respect, and who have urged, that this would be a proper
occasion to lay before you any information which will serve to explain and
elucidate the principles and arrangements of the constitution, that has been
submitted to the consideration of the United States. I confess that I am un-
prepared for so extensive and so important a disquisition; but the insidious
attempts which are clandestinely and industriously made to pervert and destroy the new plan, induce me the more readily to engage in its defense; and
the impressions of four months constant attention to the subject, have not
been so easily effaced as to leave me without an answer to the objections
which have been raised.

It will be proper, however, before I enter into the refutation of the
charges that are alledged, to mark the leading discrimination between the
state constitutions, and the constitution of the United States. When the people established the powers of legislation under their separate governments,
they invested their representatives with every right and authority which
they did not in explicit terms reserve; and therefore upon every question,
respecting the jurisdiction of the house of assembly, if the frame of government is silent, the jurisdiction is efficient and complete. But in delegating
federal powers, another criterion was necessarily introduced, and the congressional authority is to be collected, not from tacit implication, but from
the positive grant expressed in the instrument of union. Hence it is evident,
that in the former case every thing which is not reserved is given, but in the
latter the reverse of the proposition prevails, and everything which is not
given, is reserved. This distinction being recognized, will furnish an answer
to those who think the omission of a bill of rights, a defect in the proposed
constitution: for it would have been superfluous and absurd to have stipulated with a federal body of our own creation, that we should enjoy those
privileges, of which we are not divested either by the intention or the act,
that has brought that body into existence. For instance, the liberty of the
press, which has been a copious source of declamation and oppression,

what control can proceed from the federal government to shackle or destroy that sacred palladium of national freedom? If indeed, a power similar to that which has been granted for the regulation of commerce, had been granted to regulate literary publications, it would have been as necessary to stipulate that the liberty of the press should be preserved inviolate, as that the impost should be general in its operation. With respect likewise to the particular district of ten miles, which is to be made the seat of federal government, it will undoubtedly be proper to observe this salutary precaution, as there the legislative power will be exclusively lodged in the president, senate, and house of representatives of the United States. But this could not be an object with the convention, for it must naturally depend upon a future compact, to which the citizens immediately interested will, and ought to be parties; and there is no reason to suspect that so popular a privilege will in that case be neglected. In truth then, the proposed system possesses no influence whatever upon the press, and it would have been merely nugatory to have introduced a formal declaration upon the subject—nay, that very declaration might have been construed to imply that some degree of power was given, since we undertook to define its extent.

Roger Sherman: "A Citizen of New Haven"

Writing as A Citizen of New Haven, Roger Sherman asserts that the Constitution needs to be tried first before any amendments are made to it. He states that no one can possibly know what works and what does not until the new government has operated for some time. Once it has been tried for a while, it provides an easy mechanism for making changes as needed. Sherman had been active in Connecticut government since the 1750s. He represented Connecticut in the Continental Congress, the Constitutional Convention, the House of Representatives, and the Senate. As part of this service, he signed the Declaration of Independence, the Articles of Confederation, and the Constitution.

New-York Packet, 24 March 1789

All the difficulties proposed to be remedied by amendments, that have come within my notice, may be provided for by law, without altering the Constitution, except the following, on which I would make a few observations, and submit to the public, whether it is proper or necessary to make those alterations.

1. It has been proposed that the consent of two thirds, or three fourths of the members in each branch of Congress should be made requisite for passing certain acts.

But why should a majority in Congress, joined with the concurrent voice of the President, be controlled by a minority? If the President dissents, the constitution requires the consent of two thirds of the members in each branch to pass any act. It is a general maxim in popular government, that the majority should govern.

2. It is objected that the Senate is not the proper tribunal for the trial of impeachment.

But what good reason can be assigned for this objection? The members being eligible by the Legislatures of the several States, they will doubtless be persons of wisdom and probity, and proper guardians of the rights of the community, who can have no motive from the nature of their office to partiality in judgment.

3. It is objected, that the President ought not to have power to grant pardons in cases of high treason.

But what great mischief can arise from the exercise of this power by the President? He cannot pardon in cases of impeachment, so that offenders may be excluded from office notwithstanding his pardon.

4. It is proposed to make the President and Senators ineligible after certain periods.

But this would abridge the liberty of the people, and remove one great motive to fidelity in office. The danger of having the same persons continued long in office is entirely removed, if they are dependent on the people for their continuance by re-election; and by long experience they will be better qualified for usefulness, and nothing renders government more unstable than a frequent change of the persons that administer it.

5. It has been proposed that members of Congress be rendered ineligible to any other office, during the time for which they are elected members of that body.

This is an objection that will admit of something plausible to be said on both sides. The mischief intended to be avoided is, their instituting offices with large salaries, with a view of filling them themselves; but that difficulty is obviated by the provision in the Constitution, that they shall not be eligible to any office that shall have been instituted or the emoluments increased while they were members. On the other hand a person may be best qualified for some office by means of the knowledge of public affairs acquired by being a member of Congress; and it seems reasonable that the public should be at liberty to employ any of the citizens in offices wherein they can be most useful.

6. It has been proposed that no treaty of commerce should be made without the consent of two thirds of the Senators, nor any cession of territory or right of navigation or fishery without the consent of three fourths of the members present in each branch of Congress.

It is provided that the President with the concurrence of two thirds of the Senators present may make treaties, and as each State has an equal representation and suffrage in the Senate, their rights in this respect will be as secure under the new Constitution as under the old; and it is not probable that they would ever make a cession of any important national right, without the consent of Congress. The King of Great-Britain has power by the Constitution of that nation to make treaties, yet in matters of great importance he consults the Parliament.

7. The amendment proposed by the Convention of South-Carolina, respecting religious tests, is an ingenious one, but not very important, because the Constitution as it now stands, will have the same effect, as it would have with that amendment.

On the whole, will it not be best to make a fair trial of the Constitution, before any attempts are made to alter it? It is now become the only frame of government for the United States, and must be supported and conformed to, or they will have no government at all as confederated States. Experience will best show whether it is deficient or not; on trial it may appear that the alterations proposed are not necessary, or that others not yet thought of may be necessary. Everything that tends to disunion, ought to be carefully avoided. Instability in government and laws, tends to weaken a State, and render the rights of the people precarious. The Constitution which is the foundation of law and government ought not to be changed without the most pressing necessity. When experience has convinced, the people in general that alterations are necessary, they may be easily made, but attempting it at present may be detrimental, if not fatal to the union of the States, and to their credit with foreign nations.

Anonymous: "The Subject of Amendments"

This author castigates Congress for spending time on the issue of amendments. He believes that there are more important issues to be addressed, such as getting the government fully organized and running. Amendments can be dealt with later, after everything else is handled.

Gazette of the United States (New York), 15 August 1789

I perceive by the proceedings of Congress, that the house are about to take up the subject of amendments to the constitution.—This, if true, will be considered by the friends to federal measures, as a stretch of complaisance at the expence of the interest of the United States.—I never yet met with a stickler for amendments who entertained an idea that this business would come upon the carpet, so long as Congress had any thing to do, that was essential to the organization of the government. Many persons are seriously alarmed at this appearance, who have hitherto repressed every repining thought, at the slowness with which public business has progressed— supposing that nothing would drive Congress from the steady pursuit of those objects on which the hopes of every friend to the Union are founded, till every department of government was established and completed, and the system put in full operation.

A correspondent observes, that the fears of those who have been anxious on the score of amendments, may be entirely done away; for though the subject of amendments has lain dormant, yea, quite asleep through the States for many months; and though there is confessedly, very important and necessary business yet pending in the legislature, and though the time of adjournment draweth near; and though the subject of amendments is a difficult business and will take time and cause tedious debates, yet to 'quiet the alarms,' to 'dissipate the apprehensions' 'allay the fears' and 'annihilate the jealousies OF THE PEOPLE'—the amendments are to be *immediately* attended to.

The subject of Amendments is now the general topic of conversation:— The suspension that is occasioned in the organization of the government, by taking up this *most important of all subjects* at this *moment of leisure*—this PAUSE *in the general expectations of the people,* must be considered in a proper point of light—for tho in *two days* a certain assembly have hardly got their hand upon the knocker of the Door, as a certain hon. gentleman phrased it, yet the whole *suite* of apartments, NINETEEN in number, may be surveyed, examined, altered, amended, curtailed, enlarged, and appropriated, in——days, weeks, or months, at farthest.

QUESTIONS

1. What are some of the rights that need to be protected, according to those in favor of a Bill of Rights, such as An Old Whig and Robert Whitehill? Were these concerns finally addressed in the Bill of Rights that was adopted?
2. Why does Cassius believe that state elections will be important in what happens to the issue of a Bill of Rights?
3. What are some of the reasons that Publius and the other writers see amendments as unnecessary? Do you agree or disagree with them?
4. Why did the last writer believe that working on amendments was the

wrong thing to do at that time? What did he believe that Congress should be dealing with instead?

NOTES

1. This act provided for a judicial inquiry into whether a person was lawfully imprisoned. A writ of habeas corpus states that the imprisonment is wrong and the person is to be released.

2. James Wilson.

CHAPTER 12

The Issue of the Native Americans, 1791–1797

Almost from the moment of first contact, Europeans had trouble understanding the Native Americans. On the one hand, they admired and coveted the apparent freedom and flexibility of the American Indian lifestyle. But, on the other hand, they did not understand the Native American culture and society and, as a result, feared them greatly.

During the American Revolution, both the British and the Americans tried to get the Native Americans to side with them. The Iroquois Confederacy in New York sided with the British because of long-term economic ties, but most Native Americans tried to remain neutral until they saw who won the war.

The American victory in the Revolution probably sealed the doom of the Native Americans. The British might have set aside a large section of territory for the sole use of the American Indians. But American desire for land meant a steady push westward of settlers, which slowly drove the Native Americans into smaller and smaller pieces of land.

During the 1790s, conflicts with the Native Americans were centered in the Ohio Valley. On August 20, 1794, an American army under the command of General Anthony Wayne defeated a force of Miamis, Shawnees, Ottawas, Chippewas, Sauk, Fox, and some Iroquois at the Battle of Fallen Timbers in modern-day Ohio. Following this victory, Wayne dictated the Treaty of Greenville, signed on August 3, 1795, which opened the territory from the Ohio River north to present-day Cleveland, Chicago, and Detroit. In exchange, the Native Americans would receive $10,000 a year. This opened up more territory for American settlement, but it also increased the tensions between the two competing cultures. Ultimately, Americans of European descent never did understand the Native Americans.

The first group of documents reflects the attitude that the Native Americans were human beings who could be dealt with fairly. The first selection describes the negotiation of a treaty between the United States and the Iroquois. The second piece reports that an American Indian chief accused of plotting war was in fact working for peace. The third selection reports the murder of a group of American Indians by several white men. The final document in this group briefly describes the idyllic life lived by a group of Native Americans.

The second group of documents reflects the more common view that the Native Americans were savages and barbarians. The first piece reports about an attack on the frontier. The second selection describes an early victory against the American Indians by a force under the command of General Anthony Wayne. The third piece accuses the British of stirring up the Native Americans. The final document accuses the same Iroquois chief mentioned above of plotting war.

SUPPORT FOR THE NATIVE AMERICANS

John Fenno: "They Had Determined to Preserve a Strict Neutrality"

In this document, editor John Fenno reports on a treaty negotiation between the United States and the Iroquois. It was primarily intended to keep the Native Americans of New York out of the conflict going on between the Americans and the American Indians of the Ohio Valley. Fenno describes the Iroquois as reasonable and willing to negotiate.

Gazette of the United States (Philadelphia), 30 July 1791

A correspondent informs, that the treaty, lately held under commission from the President of the United States, by Timothy Pickering, Esq. of Wilkesbarre, with those Indian tribes commonly called the Six Nations, at Newtown-Point, on the north-west branch of the Susquehanna, in the state of New-York, was concluded on the eighteenth inst. to the satisfaction of all parties, by a recapitulatory speech from the Commissioner. The principal object of this treaty was, to confirm the peace that has subsisted between us, ever since the treaty of Fort Stanwix, in 1784, and prevent the Five Nations from joining the Western Indians, now at war. This desirable purpose has been fully answered for the present, though it is impossible to answer for the neutrality of the Five Nations, in case they should still meet with repeated injuries from those unprincipled inhabitants of the frontiers, who have never yet learned to distinguish friends from foes, under the undistingushing appellation of Indians, or Savages. The Five Nations, and some other tribes, came down armed to the number of ten or eleven hundred, men, women, and children, as their manner is; but so slowly that the treaty, appointed for the 15th ult. was not opened until the 2d inst. On the 27th, P.M. the customary present, consisting of a large quantity of substantial cloathing, some of husbandry, and a little powder and shot, was distributed to the different tribes; and the next day the commissioners, and the main body of Indians left the ground. A few days before, letters had been received from the Seneca warriors at Buffaloe Creek, complaining of hostilities committed by the Western Indians, and pressing the Chiefs in Council to join the army of the United States in reducing them to terms; but little credit was given to the accounts, and no answer returned, as they had determined to preserve a strict neutrality.

Anonymous: "Declaration of Cornplanter"

This selection presents a statement by Cornplanter, a chief of the Iroquois, in which he declares that he and his people are the friends of the United States. The writer publishes this piece in order to quiet rumors that undermine the reputation of this friendly Native American.

General Advertiser (Philadelphia), 24 July 1794

The printer of the Philadelphia Gazette is requested to lay before the public the following declaration of Obeal (Corn Planter) to a person of reputation, lately from the Indian country:

I know, said this respectable Indian in a tone of anxiety blended with firmness, that the people of the United States make very free with my name in the newspapers and assert things which are false, but you may inform them that I am a friend to peace—a friend to my nation,—a friend to justice and equity.—Buffalo Creek, 5th July inst.

The frequent publications of late respecting the disposition of the six nations, have a tendency to encrease the jealousy on their account, which perhaps already exists in too high a degree; as well as to involve the United States still more in an unhappy war. There is reason to believe that some of our best friends among the Indians, have been weakened in their attachment to the United States, as well as suffered in their reputations, by unmerited calumnies and gross misrepresentations, which they have no opportunity to refute in a correct statement of facts—The Corn-Planter in particular, has lately been spoken of as inimical to us and his conduct stated in such a way as might incline those unacquainted with the probity of the man and too distant from him to form a right judgment of his sentiments or conduct, to suppose him insincere and unfriendly—The above declaration therefore is published, to do justice to an absent character, who has ever distinguished himself as the friend of the United States—who excited general esteem whilst amongst us, and who in the course of his negociations, displayed the orator, the patriot, and the man of feeling.

Benjamin Franklin Bache: "The Late Murder of Certain Indians"

In this piece, editor Benjamin Franklin Bache (grandson of Benjamin Franklin) castigates two white men for murdering several Native Americans and then plundering their village. Such defenses were rare, and seldom were such people brought to justice for their crimes.

Aurora (Philadelphia), 13 March 1797

In our last, we promised a further account of the late murder of certain Indians. A gentleman, who is a neighbour to one of the murderers, has favored us with the following: On or about the first day of Jan. last, EDWARD MITCHELL and WM. LIVINGSTON, went to an Indian camp, and were informed by lame WILL that the old Indian was gone to a camp of the white people; meeting him on his return they killed him and then returned to the camp, where they left the lame Indian, whom MITCHELL fired at, but missed him; on this lame WILL with a knife in one hand and his crutch in the other rode toward MITCHELL, who ran off. LIVINGSTON then encountered the lame man, and after several times attempting to shoot him, drew his tomahawk and killed him. They plundered the Indians of ALL the property they had, viz. eighteen beaver skins, two little old horses, and one brass kettle.

Philip Freneau: "Essay on Tomo-Cheeki"

In this piece, editor and poet Philip Freneau describes a tribe of Native Americans. He emphasizes their ties to nature and that they lived in harmony with the world around them.

Time Piece (New York), 28 April 1797

They built no towns; they seemed to have no idea of war or contention: the spirit of justice, benevolence, and every amiable virtue was prevalent within them; they walked on the margin of the ocean; they dwelt on the green banks of the rivers, but discovered no propensity to build ships, or seek for other continents; they made or retained no slaves of their own or of the inferior species: a constant summer reigned: nor could I perceive that the harmony of Nature was at all disturbed on the ocean, in the woods, or in the elements above.

OPPOSITION TO THE NATIVE AMERICANS

Anonymous: "Those Ferocious Animals"

This author, in discussing recent attacks on the frontier, describes the Native Americans as barbarians. To this writer, the American Indians are animals in human form, and he implies that they should be destroyed.

General Advertiser (Philadelphia), 31 January 1791

Suppose the late depredations of the Indians the subject before the house, and the majesty of the people out of doors. Then in plain language it would be said—The Indians have murdered eleven of the frontier settlers, &c. instead of—The blood of our countrymen—American blood has been spilt by those ferocious animals, under human form, who stimulated by their natural, insatiable thirst after revenge, have attacked the settlements of our brothers on the frontiers; have surprised, tortured, killed—murdered the peaceable and darling child and friend of his. The beautiful maiden's spotless innocence could not save her blooming charms from the blow of death,—a tomahawk!

Benjamin Franklin Bache: "The Ambush Was So Complete"

In this selection, Benjamin Franklin Bache reprints a report from a Hudson, New York, newspaper on the success of General Anthony Wayne in defending the frontier against the Native Americans. The result was the flight of the American Indians westward.

General Advertiser (Philadelphia), 9 January 1794

A report prevails in this town, from Niagara, that Gen. Wayne, by a manoeuvre (every way worthy of the man) had so effectually ambushed the Indians, on the ground of Gen. St. Clair's defeat, as to make a most dreadful slaughter among those tawny sons of the desert, and take a great number of prisoners. It is mentioned, that the ambush was so complete, that the Indians who escaped, did it by dint of the tomahawk, in a desperate sally on our troops, after having thrown away their muskets.

Benjamin Franklin Bache: "The Tawney Sons of the Tomahawk"

Benjamin Franklin Bache reports that the British and the Native Americans in the Ohio Valley are apparently allied together. From the American Revolution through the War of 1812, Americans believed that the British armed the American Indians and stirred them up to war on the United States. Bache's piece clearly reflects this fear.

General Advertiser (Philadelphia), 16 July 1794

A letter from a Gentleman of the Genesee country to the printers hereof, says, 'whatsoever may be the event of Simcoe's movements, and his instigation of the Indians to go to war with the United States, the inhabitants of this country are determined to defend their possessions'—and from our knowledge of their numbers, courage, and patriotism, we are convinced, they will be able to repel any encroachments that may be made on our territory by the minions of Great Britain—and to teach the tawney sons of the tomahawk that their true interest lies in continuing at peace with the United States....

By a gentleman from Whitetown, we are informed, that Simcoe's influence, added to English gold, has induced the Onandaga Indians to leave their possessions in this state, and to take up their residence in the British lines.—Amen, says a correspondent, let them take all those deceitful rascals from the United States in welcome!

Anonymous: "A Conversation with Cornplanter"

This author reports a conversation with Cornplanter, an Iroquois chief. This writer believes that Cornplanter cannot be trusted and is planning for war against the Americans. This piece is in direct contradiction to the earlier statement (see the second document above) that declared that Cornplanter was peaceful. Such contradictory reports were part of the reason there was so much trouble between the Native Americans and the American settlers. It became very difficult to determine the truth.

General Advertiser (Philadelphia), 22 September 1794

I returned yesterday from the Cornplanter's town, he having sent for me to attend a treaty at Buffaloe creek, but as the treaty does not come on so soon as was expected, I come to this place for a few days. I had a good deal of conversation with Cornplanter, from which, and every other circumstance, war appears to me to be inevitable. Give us what we ask for, or abide the consequences, is the language of the Indians. He desired me to request the commanding officers of the posts, not to carry much provisions to Le Boeuf, as it would soon have to be run away from. There were twenty Indians from the other side of the lake, arrived at Cornplanter's whilst I was there, to be a guard to their frontier, as they informed me, and to make a stroke, I suppose, if their demands are not complied with.

QUESTIONS

1. Two of the documents above state that they are presenting statements from Cornplanter, an Iroquois chief. The two selections totally disagree with each other. Is it possible to tell which is correct? What kind of impact would such conflicting reports have on American attitudes toward Native Americans?
2. What kind of world does Philip Freneau describe? He seems envious of the Native Americans and their lifestyle. Why would that be so?
3. Why would Benjamin Franklin Bache be so worried about the involvement of the British with the Native Americans? What difference could it make?
4. Several authors use strong language to describe the Native Americans—for example, "those ferocious animals." Why do they use such descriptions? What kind of impact do these types of labels have, both then and today?

CHAPTER 13

The Role of Women, 1780–1798

In colonial America, women fulfilled an important function in society. Besides the usual roles of wife and mother, women also played an important economic role. In frontier areas, men and women worked together to produce the food and supplies necessary for survival. Even in towns, women often helped their artisan husbands in the shop to produce the family income. Towards the end of the eighteenth century, however, this reality began to change, at least for well-to-do women in the towns and villages along the East Coast. Increasingly, these women were less involved in the day-to-day economics of making a living. By the nineteenth century, the ideal American society would be divided into the man's sphere, the realm of work and making money, and the woman's sphere, the world of the home—the retreat from the evil world. This division was slowly developing in the last quarter of the eighteenth century.

These changes in the role of women encouraged changes in attitudes and ideas about women. In the seventeenth century, women had been seen as the source of much evil in the world. As the "daughters of Eve," women were particularly susceptible to sin and often led men into wrongdoing, as Eve had led Adam to sin.[1] Women were weak, lacking reason, unable to learn and be educated, and easily led astray, so they had to be guarded and protected by the men in their lives. Slowly, through the course of the eighteenth century, these ideas changed. Increasingly, women were seen as rational beings who could be educated to play a useful role in the young republic. Growing emphasis was placed on the role of women as the wives and mothers of citizens of the United States. Increasingly, the marriage vision came to be the "companionate ideal of marriage"[2]—the idea that men and women were friends and companions in marriage. In order to be good companions and good mothers, women needed to be educated. It slowly became a good idea for women to gain a solid elementary education that went beyond the basics of reading and writing. These changes in ideas set the stage for the dominant outlook of the nineteenth century, which saw women as the preservers of morality in an increasingly corrupt and evil world.

These changes in ideas meant that women in general had a somewhat better reputation. They were no longer just the "daughters of Eve," the root of all evil. Still, people could not decide exactly where women should fit in society. Debates over the role of women took place in the newspapers throughout the era.

The first group of documents basically has a positive view of women and their role in society. The first selection is a well-known call for women to raise money to fight the Revolution. The second selection offers praise to the women participating in this effort. The third and fourth pieces call for improved education of women so that they can be better wives and mothers. The final document emphasizes the important role of women in urging men on to victory in military endeavors.

The second group of documents has a negative view of women. The first selection attacks women for bad habits in public. The second piece states that women are very susceptible to sinful behavior. The third document makes it clear that a women's proper role was as a wife and mother. The fourth selection puts women in the same group as children and fools, implying that they have no mental abilities at all. The fifth and sixth pieces fret over the impact of women who get involved in politics when they should not do so.

A POSITIVE VIEW

Anonymous: "The Sentiments of An American Woman"

This piece, written anonymously by Esther DeBerdt Reed, calls on American women to help win the war against Great Britain. She urges women not to depend on others. Rather, they should use the strength they have and get involved to help make the situation better for the soldiers in the Continental army. This call for the women to get involved resulted in a fundraising campaign in several major cities in the United States. The campaign succeeded, raising $300,000. The organizers hoped to give each soldier a bounty, but George Washington urged them to be more practical. At his request, they bought cloth and made shirts for the troops. Esther Reed

*was the wife of the president of the state of Pennsylvania and the mother of
seven children. She died in the fall of 1780, but the campaign was continued by Sarah Franklin Bache, the daughter of Benjamin Franklin.*

Pennsylvania Gazette (Philadelphia), 21 June 1780

On the commencement of actual war, the women of America manifested
a firm resolution to contribute as much as could depend on them, to the deliverance of their country. Animated by the purest patriotism, they are sensible of sorrow at this day, in not offering more than barren wishes for the
success of so glorious a revolution. They aspire to render themselves more
really useful; and this sentiment is universal from the north to the south of
the Thirteen United States. Our ambition is kindled by the fame of those
heroines of antiquity; who have rendered their sex illustrious, and have
proved to the universe, that, if the weakness of our constitution, if opinion
and manners did not forbid us to march to glory by the same paths as the
men, we should at least equal, and sometimes surpass them in our love for
the public good. I glory in all that which my sex has done great and com-
mendable. I call to mind with enthusiasm and with admiration, all those acts
of courage, of constancy and patriotism, which history has transmitted to us:
The people favoured by Heaven, preserved from destruction by the virtues,
the zeal and resolution of Deborah, of Judith, of Esther! The fortitude of the
mother of the Maccabees, in giving her sons to die before her eyes: Rome
saved from the fury of a victorious enemy by the efforts of Volumnia; and
other Roman Ladies: So many famous sieges where the women have been
seen forgetting the weakness of their sex, building new walls, digging
trenches with their feeble hands, furnishing arms to their defenders, they
themselves darting the missile weapons on the enemy, resigning the ornaments of their apparel, and their fortune, to fill the public treasury, and to
hasten the deliverance of their country; burying themselves under its ruins;
throwing themselves into the flames, rather than submit to the disgrace of
humiliation before a proud enemy.

Born for liberty, disdaining to bear the irons of a tyrannic government,
we associate ourselves to the grandeur of those sovereigns, cherished and
revered, who have held with so much splendor the scepter of the greatest
States; the Batildas, the Elizabeths, the Maries, the Catherines, who have extended the empire of liberty, and, contented to reign by sweetness and justice, have broken the chains of slavery, forged by tyrants in the times of
ignorance and barbarity. The Spanish women, do they not make, at this moment, the most patriotic sacrifices, to encrease the means of victory in the
hands of their Sovereign. He is a friend to the French nation. They are our
allies. We call to mind, doubly interested, that it was a French maid who kindled up amongst her fellow-citizens the flame of patriotism, buried under

long misfortunes: it was the Maid of Orleans who drove from the kingdom of France the ancestors of those same British, whose odious yoke we have just shaken off; and whom it is necessary that we drive from this continent.

But I must limit myself to the recollection of this small number of achievements. Who knows if persons disposed to censure, and sometimes too severely with regard to us, may not disapprove our appearing acquainted even with the actions of which our sex boasts? We are at least certain, that he cannot be a good citizen who will not applaud our efforts for the relief of the armies which defend our lives, our possessions, our liberty? The situation of our soldiery has been represented to me; the evils inseparable from war, and the firm and generous spirit which has enabled them to support these. But it has been said, that they may apprehend, that, in the course of a long war, the view of their distresses may be lost, and their services be forgotten. Forgotten! never; I can answer in the name of all my sex. Brave Americans, your disinterestedness, your courage, and your constancy, will always be dear to America, as long as she shall preserve her virtue.

We know that at a distance from the theatre of war, if we enjoy any tranquility, it is the fruit of your watchings, your labours, your dangers. If I live happy in the midst of my family; if any husband cultivates his field, and reaps his harvest in peace; if, surrounded with my children, I myself nourish the youngest, and press it to my bosom, without being afraid of seeing myself separated from it by a ferocious enemy; if the house in which we dwell; if our barns, our orchards are safe at the present time from the hands of those incendiaries, it is to you that we owe it. And shall we hesitate to evidence to you our gratitude? Shall we hesitate to wear a cloathing more simple, hair-dresses less elegant, while at the price of this small privation we shall deserve your benedictions. Who, amongst us, will not renounce with the highest pleasure, those vain ornaments, when she shall consider that the valiant defenders of America will be able to draw some advantage from the money which she may have laid out in these; that they will be better defended from the rigours of the season, that after their painful tolls, they will receive some extraordinary and unexpected relief; that these presents will perhaps be valued by them at a greater price, when they will have it in their power to say— *This is the offering of the Ladies*. The time is arrived to display the same sentiments which animated us at the beginning of the Revolution, when we renounced the use of teas, however agreeable to our taste, rather than receive them from our persecutors; when we made it appear to them that we placed former necessaries in the rank of superfluities, when our liberty was interested; when our republican and laborious hands spun the flax, prepared the linen intended for the use of our soldiers; when exiles and fugitives we supported with courage all the evils which are the concomitants of war. Let us not lose a moment; let us be engaged to offer the homage of our gratitude at the altar of military valour; and you, our brave deliverers, while mercenary slaves combat to cause you to share with them the irons with which they are loaded, receive with a free hand our offerings, the purest which can be presented to your virtue,

BY AN AMERICAN WOMAN.

Anonymous: "Letter to the Editor"

This writer praises the women of America for their efforts to help the soldiers. To do so strengthens the American military effort and frightens the British because of the unity of purpose facing them.

Pennsylvania Packet (Philadelphia), 27 June 1780

It is the spirit of a people which constitutes the strength and duration of resistance, while that is unsubdued, all danger is practicable, all success is certain. In cases of extreme adversity, unusual efforts will be made, and forgetting the difficulty, will be considered only the necessity of the enterprize.

It must strike the enemy with an apoplexy, to be informed; that the women of America, are attentive to the wants of the soldiery, and from a noble benevolence and patriotism of mind, have determined to contribute to their relief. Panegyrists contemplating this instance of female excellence, will say, in the language of figure, "They fought from heaven, the stars in their courses fought against" the British.

Humanus: "Justice in Behalf of the Fair"

Humanus regrets that local authorities do not provide for the education of women. He states that this problem needs to be fixed in order for justice to be fully achieved.

Massachusetts Centinel (Boston), 19 February 1785

The celebrated Dr. Brown says, '*that a proper and effectual education of the Female Sex is one of the very first steps to be taken for the effectual improvement and civilization of the whole empire, for children fall inevitably into the hands, and under the care of women in their infant state, therefore their first and strongest impressions will be good or bad, salutary or destructive, according to the morals, character and conduct of women under whose early tuition they may fall.*'

It has long been a subject of regret that amidst the many institutions for education, the females of this metropolis have hitherto been unprovided for.—This is not the case of any other town in the state,—and why they should be thus pointedly neglected here is a matter of astonishment. To say nothing of the inequality with which the taxes levied on every freeholder for the support of the schools appropriated for the boys, operates, I would ask, what can be the reason of the invidious distinction? Is the female part of the inhabitants unworthy attention? Does ignorance advance their happiness, or promote their usefulness? Are they deficient in capacity, or would any attempts to enlighten and instruct them prove abortive? The publick schools in which the boys are taught reading, writing and arithmetic have proved a source of publick blessings, and those important branches still cultivated with industry and fidelity are all that those institutions are competent to. One or two similar schools for the education of girls, would perhaps be as much as could be effected by the town at present, and it is ardently wished by many, who feel themselves interested by motives of humanity, that the FATHERS of the TOWN would take the matter into serious consideration, and digest some plan for the advantage of those on whose future conduct depends in so eminent a degree the manners and morals of the rising generation. The above it is hoped may induce some abler hand to take up the subject to second the demands of humanity, charity and justice in behalf of the FAIR.

Humanus: "Would We Have Our Wives Rational and Improving Companions"

In this essay, Humanus continues his call for schools for women. He emphasizes the need to educate women in order to better prepare them for their role in society. He states that they are entitled to an education, just as men are entitled to one. Also, more important, an educated woman will be a better wife and mother and thus the nation will be better off if her women as well as her men are educated.

Massachusetts Centinel (Boston), 2 March 1785

It requires no labour of disquisition to prove the necessity and importance of literary institutions for the benefit of the female sex—it is decidedly clear, that they are *equally with ourselves*, entitled to these advantages. Justice, humanity and sound policy please powerfully in their favour—and it is truly unaccountable how so obvious a duty could have been so long neglected—neglected by a people who have been celebrated by their publick provision for the education of the *other* sex—but it is too much to be feared that less liberal sentiments in respect to the fair, than (thank heaven) their instrinsick merit has taught the present enlightened era of mankind to entertain for them, may have operated to induce that publick neglect they have hitherto experienced in this metropolis. Let us no longer be deaf to the voice of humanity, let the multitudes (by far the majority) of our daughters, no longer be exposed to the misfortune, chagrin and mortification of scarcely knowing how to read, and of a total ignorance of writing and figures. The truest policy unites with the voice of justice and benevolence in this indispensable duty—Would we have our wives rational and improving companions—our daughters the objects of attention to the man of sense and virtue, and screened from the shafts of adversity—our widows and orphans secured from being a prey to the artful and rapacious—let us NOW institute publick schools for their education.

Anonymous: "Ladies of Lancaster"

These two letter excerpts, delivered at a public celebration of the Fourth of July, reflect important ideas of this era. Women were supposed to encourage men to fight harder. A woman's strength lay in her ability to encourage the men in her life to work diligently at whatever they did. Increasingly, women were seen as being the virtuous ones in society and they needed to continue to be so in order to guide the nation to victory in all its endeavors.

Porcupine's Gazette (Philadelphia), 10 July 1798

The Ladies of Lancaster to Captain Mosher's Volunteer Light Infantry Company:

Incapacitated by our sex to bear arms in the defence of our country's rights, we with cheerfulness and confidence submit that sacred charge to you.

The alacrity with which you, gentlemen, have associated for that laudable purpose, affords a pleasing presage of the honour you will acquire in the prosecution of it.

Assured, that you will on all proper occasions, display and defend it in the midst of your enemies, the Ladies of Lancaster request your acceptance of this standard, and pray the God of battles to shield you in the day of danger.

Response of soldiers:

Your assurance, that when engaged in the struggle for our liberties, your good will attend us, is highly grateful to our hearts. We anxiously hope, that our lovely Countrywomen may possess the same spirit, to animate the Warriors breast to deeds of noble worth to the latest period of time! For when female excellence shall cease to exist, and the toils of the Soldier be no longer rewarded with the smiles of beauty; the noblest incentive to manly virtue and heroic deeds will be lost, and the military spirit of our country will languish and die!

A NEGATIVE VIEW

Observer: "Letter to the Editor"

Observer criticizes women for using snuff because it is offensive to those who see them doing it. This essayist implies that women cannot resist temptation, even at church, because women are weak in spirit.

Continental Journal (Boston), 1 June 1786

I am often at meeting, and not a little surprised at seeing ladies, dressed very genteely, making signs to each other, and those signs followed by Snuff-Boxes handed from pew to pew, until the congregation is disturbed by immoderate sneezing, and their noses, young and old, have the appearance of being daubed, to say no worse, with Molasses.—As women in general wish to appear amiable in the eyes of men, if they knew how frequently this odious custom subjects them to ridicule, they might possibly make a resolution to snuff no more, and probably be induced to stop the circulation of the box in meeting.

Anonymous: "Women Easily Perverted"

This author clearly perceives women as sinful creatures, the "daughters of Eve." He attacks the theater as a danger to society, particularly to women. Because women are weak and frivolous, they are more susceptible to temptation and attendance at the theater is much more likely to lead them astray into sinful behavior.

New York Daily Advertiser, 18 June 1787

Women especially, whose education is usually more frivolous, and whose nature perhaps is more tender and therefore more easily perverted than that of the other sex, when they come upon the stage but rarely withstand the allurements of vice. Intoxicated with the splendour of their temporary finery, exposed to the observation, and therefore to the arts of wicked men, softened by the very scenes they are obliged to interpret, and often driven to despair by the indigence of their circumstances, in such situations we should not wonder when they fall, but admire those who do not.

Anonymous: "A Young Married Woman"

Although not explicitly negative in its attitude towards women, this piece makes it clear that a woman's proper and only role was as a mother. Such attitudes were common among many people at this time.

Middlesex Gazette (Middletown, Conn.), 17 March 1788

The three greatest Beauties in Nature.

The first is a field of well manured wheat reaped and bound, ready to go in the barn; the second a stock of sheep in the month of May, well fleeced with a good yield of lambs playing about them; the third a young married woman, tidily dressed in her own manufactory, with a babe in her arms.

Anonymous: "Women Have the Greatest Attachment to Their Native Soil"

Although not directly addressing the role of women, this author clearly does not have a high opinion of women's abilities. In discussing political issues, he lumps women with children and fools as having strong attachments to their native lands. In this case, that is not a compliment.

Aurora (Philadelphia), 1 August 1798

The President boasts of having said in the *royal presence of England* that he had no attachment but to his own native country. Grant this to be truth—give even the greatest latitude to the word attachment, call it love or affection, does it follow that he whose affections are the warmest towards America can always see what is her best interest. If it were so, women, children and fools, who have generally the greatest attachment to their native soil, would be the best judges of the means to render their country prosperous and happy.

Anonymous: "These Fiery Frenchified Dames"

This author attacks women who apparently speak out too much on public issues. He sees this as a growing influence of the French, stemming from their revolution. Such women are bullies and should not be tolerated because they are overstepping the acceptable bounds of the role of women in society.

Porcupine's Gazette (Philadelphia), 27 July 1798

For my part, I would almost as soon have a host of infernals in my house, as a knot of these fiery frenchified dames.—Of all the monsters in human shape, a bully in petticoats is the most completely odious and detestable.

Anonymous: "A War Makes Lovers and Husbands Scarce"

This author, despairing over the possibility of war with France, urges women to stay out of politics because wars make men scarce. The implication is that women should care about nothing but getting married, and that they may be unable to deal adequately with anything else.

Aurora (Philadelphia), 30 July 1798

The ladies should be cautious how they suffer themselves to be introduced as parties in the politics of the day. A war makes lovers and husbands scarce, and our most lovely females will be obliged to *lead apes in hell.*

QUESTIONS

1. What does the American Woman believe that women can accomplish in the war effort? What does she urge them to do?
2. Why does Humanus think women should be better educated? What are the arguments for and against women being educated?
3. What general view of women does one get from the negative selections? What do you think are the sources of this attitude?
4. Why are the last two writers worried about women getting involved in politics? What difference, if any, would it make?

NOTES

1. Women were referred to as the "daughters of Eve" beginning in the early Christian era. However, Cotton Mather of the colony of Massachusetts popularized this phrase in 1724: "Poor Daughters of Eve, Languishing under your Special Maladies, Look back on Your Mother, the Woman, who being Deceived, was first in the

Transgression, that has brought upon us, all our Maladies." *The Angel of Bethesda* (1724; reprinted in ed. Jones, G. W., Barre, Mass.: American Antiquarian Society and Barre Publishers, 1972), p. 233.

2. The "companionate ideal of marriage" is a term used by historians to refer to dominant ideas about marriage in the late eighteenth century in the United States. For a discussion of this idea, see Jan Lewis, "The Republican Wife: Virtue and Seduction in the Early Republic," *William and Mary Quarterly*, 3rd series 44, (1987): 689–721.

CHAPTER 14

Slave Revolt in Santo Domingue (Haiti), 1791–1793

On August 22, 1791, the slaves on the island of Hispaniola (modern-day Haiti and the Dominican Republic) revolted. The revolt was concentrated in Santo Domingue, the French colony on the western end of the island. The rule of the mother country had weakened in the two years since the beginning of the French Revolution. The blacks on the island greatly outnumbered the whites. Over the next decade, turmoil dominated on the island as one group after another tried to gain control. Finally, in 1800, Francois Dominique Toussaint L'Ouverture managed to gain control and bring peace to the island (at least for a while).

Americans were in a quandary because they did not know what to do concerning this revolution in the Caribbean. On the one hand, they saw the uprising against the colonial rule of France growing out of their own successful revolt against Great Britain fifteen years earlier. The revolutionaries on Hispaniola preached the rights of man and called for a government that ensured freedom and liberty for its citizens. Toussaint L'Ouverture was hailed as a revolutionary leader for his people in the same way George Washington had been for the Americans.

But Americans also had concerns about the revolt in Santo Domingue. It was, after all, a *slave* uprising. Most Americans in the 1790s did not have major problems with the institution of slavery (that would come later). Blacks, as a group, were generally seen as uncivilized and unable to successfully control and govern themselves. Hence, the revolution in Hispaniola could not succeed. Furthermore, many Americans, particularly in the South, worried that the Revolution in Santo Domingue would set a bad example for their own slaves and encourage insurrections at home.

The newspapers reflected this division of opinion. Some writers praised the calls for liberty in the Caribbean and urged Americans to support the revolutionaries in their fight for freedom. Others could not bring themselves to accept the similarities between the American Revolution and the uprising in Santo Domingue and called on the French government to bring their slaves back under control.

The documents that praise the slave revolt emphasize the similarities between the political revolutions in the United States and France and the revolt in the Caribbean. The first piece praises the slaves for their bravery in facing tyranny. The second selection describes the horror that the slaves have experienced and declares them justified in their revolution. The third document states that the Declaration of Independence declared "all men are created equal"—not all white men, but all men. The fourth piece states the slaves will die before they are beaten and returned to slavery.

The documents that criticize the slave revolt emphasize the barbarity of the revolt. The first piece stresses the destruction that will result if the uprising is not stopped. The second selection pleads for help from the United States and Europe and fears what will happen if no help arrives. The third, fourth, and fifth pieces discuss the fear among Southerners that the revolt in the Caribbean will create unrest among their slaves. The final selection reports on Gabriel's Rebellion, an abortive slave revolt in Virginia that many believed was modeled after the revolt in Santo Domingue.

SUPPORT FOR REVOLT

Anonymous: "Those Who in a Cause Like Ours Fight with Equal Bravery"

This author stresses that the revolution occurring in the West Indies is no different from the American or French revolutions. He urges Americans to be consistent and to realize that these downtrodden souls are fighting for freedom in the same way that Americans had done fifteen years earlier.

The Argus (Boston), 22 November 1791

Review the history of their past sufferings, be but a moment in their situation, and judge whether in a climate warm as theirs your blood would flow coolly. Let us be consistent Americans, and if we justify our own conduct in the late glorious Revolution, let us justify those, who, in a cause like ours fight with equal bravery.

We may feel in the cause of humanity, and may lament, that the blood of white men is spilling. It would be happy indeed, if the rights of man could in all countries be asserted as coolly and judiciously, as they have been in France; but, in the French West-India Islands this could not have been done.

The efforts of Blacks for a peaceable assertion would have cost them their lives. Arms gave them courage in a common cause. If their Lords had kept them in savage ignorance, shall they be blamed, that they fight like savages. Had they been learnt the art of war, they might have conducted their measures more according to Baron Steuben. Had they been treated with mildness, perhaps their measures had been more mild.

We talked in the late war about the hand of Providence. Since then we have seen the wonders of Providence in various parts of the world, and have gloried that men, long oppressed, had dared to assert their rights. Shall we now cease to glory?—Shall we now sacrifice principle to a paltry partiality for colour? Can we believe that the French people were ever oppressed as the Blacks have been?—Let those differ from me, who will, I have a firm confidence, that we shall now see the hand of Providence more visibly, than ever. *The Universal Father seems now demonstrating that of one blood, he has created all nations of men, that dwell on the face of the earth.*

Anonymous: "The Tragical Scenes"

This author sees the revolt in the Caribbean as growing out of the French Revolution. As liberty spreads to France, it must eventually spread to the rest of the French Empire. The revolution is only a natural result of tyranny and monarchy in Europe, and Americans should not interfere with the progress of freedom.

Freeman's Journal (Philadelphia), 23 November 1791

Whoever has read the ancient history of this Island, and noted the cruel extirpation of the original inhabitants, would suppose, from the tragical scenes that have recently been transacted here, that the era of the revenge of the ancient Caribbs was arrived. Leaving others to account for the present revolt of the Negro barbarians in this Island as they please, I, for my part, see nothing more in it than a natural consequence of European despotism and monarchial vanity. The ambition to extend their possessions and authority into every region of the globe must have been attended with a desire to see those possessions peopled and become objects of wealth and commercial importance. To accomplish these ends it was necessary that men should be procured, suited by nature to the climate; and the fruits of whose labour was to be transferred from themselves to their masters. Hence the origin of the African slave trade. I cannot, however, notwithstanding my abhorrence of every species of tyranny, bring myself to think, with certain enthusiastical characters in Great-Britain that an immediate emancipation of West-India slaves would be a desirable event. The effectual prohibition of any further

European or American intercourse with the African coasts ought to satisfy the fondest friends of humanity for some time to come. Men in the situation of the Blacks, must gradually acquire the habits and education of freemen in any country, before they can become useful or even innoxious members of a community. The establishment of liberty and a free government in France, cannot long, in the nature of things, be confined to that kingdom, but must rapidly extend through Europe; the consequence will be, that the lust of European foreign dominions will of itself cease, and it will even become the interest of the insular planters and their reformed or independent governments, that the descendants of the unfortunate Africans in the West-Indies, should become free; America, in general, will then assert her own rights, and make known to Europe that she is the best judge of pursuing such measures as tend to her own peace, emolument and honourable character among the potentates of the earth.

J.P. Martin (Abraham Bishop): "The Words of Truth and Soberness"

Writing under a false name, Abraham Bishop attacks Americans for supporting tyranny in the Caribbean. He questions how that can be done when the American Declaration of Independence states so clearly that "all men are created equal." He urges Americans to pay heed to the ideas of the revolutionaries and forget the issue of color because it is not the important issue at stake.

The Argus (Boston), 2 December 1791

I speak the words of truth and soberness, in saying that the blacks are now fighting in a just cause—My assertion, that they are entitled to freedom, is founded on the American Declaration of Independence:—Upon the language of our petitions to the English court, at the commencement of the late war:—Upon the spirit of freedom, which animated and conducted to victory, the American army:—Upon Paine's *Common Sense:*—Upon the articles of our liberating societies, and upon the Declaration of Rights, to be seen in the different *statute-law-books* throughout the states.

Have we already forgotten the animating sound, *Liberty or Death:* That sound has gone into the world, and is rapidly extending to the ends of the earth. From various parts of Europe we have already heard the echo, *Liberty or Death:* We have firmly asserted, *that all men are free.* Yet, as soon as the poor blacks, who have been oppressed beyond measure, who suffered, till cruelty itself cried out, *It is enough,*—who bore, till patience had done its perfect work, echoed *Liberty or Death,* we have been the first to assist in riveting their chains!—From us the blacks had a right to expect effectual assistance. They were pursuing the principles, which we had taught them, and are now sealing with their blood, *the rights of men;* yet Americans are sending assistance to their enemies. I do not suggest, that the Federal Legislature has sent them assistance, or that any one of the States has officially afforded assistance; but vessel-loads of military stores and provisions have been sent; the public papers have been cautiously filled with reports of the whites.

Every public transaction, and most private conversations have evinced a great zeal in favor of the whites and one can hardly wish the blacks to be victorious without exposing himself to censure, calumny and opprobious names. That conduct and language which, in 1775, would have cost a man the loss of his liberty, will now, in 1791, be applauded.—But my argument for a contrary conduct and language is made up in the following manner.

The blacks are entitled to freedom, for we did not say, all *white* men are *free,* but *all men* are free. The blacks bore their condition of slavery, till it became too terrible. The blacks took up arms to rid themselves of slavery. Arms were their only resource. They use their arms according to the best of their knowledge. They look to the liberating societies for that aid and support which they were taught to expect. It is cruelty then to withhold such aid and support;—Worse than cruelty to assist their enemies. If, at this time, the liberating societies do not come forward, how ridiculous must appear their orations, their publications, their record; their addresses to the passions, and to the reason, in favor of the poor blacks—How profane must appear their appeals to Heaven, for the sincerity of their zeal, and their resolution to exert themselves to liberate the blacks!!

Francis Bailey: "Men Determined to Die or Carry Their Point"

Although not happy about the slave revolt, editor Francis Bailey indicates that the uprising seems to be succeeding. Ultimately, the revolutionaries are determined to win or die for what they believe.

Freeman's Journal (Philadelphia), 30 November 1791

Intelligence is received from Cape-Francois till the 3d inst. at which time every thing wore the gloomy aspect, with respect to the Negro insurrection, as heretofore. The insurgents had lost no ground, and in every skirmish or engagement with the whites, acted like men determined to die or carry their point—of becoming independent possessors of the Island.

OPPOSITION TO REVOLT

Benjamin Franklin Bache: "Accounts Are Very Alarming"

In this piece, editor Benjamin Franklin Bache stresses the fearlessness of the slaves who have revolted. He believes that the revolt will bring ruin to everyone because so many will die and so much property will be destroyed.

General Advertiser (Philadelphia), 21 September 1791

The accounts from St. Domingo are very alarming. In addition to those, we can mention from good authority, that M. BLANCHELANDE,[1] the commander of the forces in that island, having secured the fortifications in Cape Francois by strong guards, with a considerable corps went out of the city to endeavour to disperse the negro slaves assembled in a prodigious body, upwards of 200,000, within a small distance of the Cape. His troops fired three times, but without the least effect. Each negro had provided a kind of light mattress stuffed with cotton, through which the balls could not penetrate, and thus stood the fire, without shewing any signs of fear. They had no firearms, but had procured daggers, knives, swords and other weapons.

Humanity must shudder by anticipating the probable effects of this dreadful insurrection. In its consequences it will be productive, in the first instance, of ruin to the planters, by the loss of their crops; and in the end, the slaves will feel, more than ever the weight of their chains, when famine has, as it indubitably must, obliged them to surrender.

Anonymous: "These Ravagers"

This author stresses the destruction of the slave revolt as the rebels destroy everything and everyone in their path. He also worries about what will happen if the colony receives no help to fight the insurrection. Calls for aid have gone to the United States and to the British and Spanish colonies in the Caribbean, but no help has arrived.

Freeman's Journal (Philadelphia), 5 October 1791

Since our last of the 22d ult. the face of things is quite changed here by an insurrection of the slaves, which broke out on the 23d, in this quarter, from Port-Margos to Limonade, being an extent of 20 leagues. They set fire to all the houses, and butchered all the white people they found in them. Having rendered themselves masters of all the open country, they separated into bodies of three or four hundred each, posting themselves in different houses which serve them as places of refuge. The small number of troops we have to occupy several advantageous posts, which defend the city, does not allow us to do more than sally out against them from time to time, when they approach too near. If we had a greater number of regular troops, we might invest them in their lurking places. These ravagers are too numerous to be attacked; as they have obliged all the house-slaves, even against their will, to join them, and massacred such as attempted to make their escape. After having ravaged all the level, populous country, they made their way through many exterior settlements, and there the unfortunate few soon fell victims to their rage. They set fire to every thing on their way.

We have sent to the United States, to request the assistance of some troops to assist us in destroying these ravages. But are we to expect them? We have sent also to Jamaica, and to the Spaniards. We wait with impatience for the return of our messengers, and earnestly hope they may bring us satisfactory answers. Our only security is this city, which is fortified, and well guarded. At the commencement of these disturbances, our chief apprehensions were from our domestic slaves, who were in great numbers, and might perhaps be in league with the insurgents, to set fire to our houses. But our vigilance, by day and by night, has preserved us from their suspected designs. Several have, however, been seized and brought to justice. The others, who were not suspected, have nevertheless been put in a place of security. By means of this prudent precaution, we now enjoy greater tranquillity.

Philip Freneau: "They Meant to Follow the Example"

Editor Philip Freneau repeats reports about the revolt in the Caribbean. Of particular concern to Americans was the fear that the slave insurrection would spread beyond Santo Domingue.

National Gazette (Philadelphia), 9 February 1792

A letter from Cape Francois dated Dec. 20, informs that 'the revolted slaves, expecting a large army from France, to put an end of their savages, had, by their deputies, demanded freedom from their leaders, and they would agree to a peace. This, was refused, as unconditional submission will in a short time be required of them.

The negroes in Jamaica having intimated that they meant to follow the example of their brethren, the French negroes in Hispaniola, the government has declared the execution of martial law through the island upon all insurgents; which it is thought will have some effect in keeping them quiet, in addition to their dread of the wild mountain negroes who are in alliance with the English.'

A vessel arrived at New-York from Cape-Francois last Thursday, which place they left the 2d of Jan. The negroes were still pursuing their wonted ravages, in burning and destroying the country. Four hundred troops had arrived from France, and three hundred more were hourly expected, besides four thousand to be looked for the beginning of February. Accounts had been received at the Cape that the remains of Port-au-Prince had been totally destroyed, and the white people and mulattoes as much at variance as ever, the latter having taken possession of St. Marks, and armed several small vessels to intercept shipping bound to Port-au-Prince, in which they had been in some measure successful. Other accounts say, that 20,000 troops were daily expected from France to crush the rebellion, and if possible save the colony from total devastation.

Thomas Greenleaf: "The Negroes Have Become Very Insolent"

New York editor Thomas Greenleaf repeats the concerns of Southern slave-owners that their slaves will get a bad idea from the slaves in Santo Domingue. Fears of revolt became widespread throughout the 1790s.

New York Journal and Patriotic Register, 16 October 1793

They write from Charleston that the NEGROES have become very insolent, in so much that the citizens are alarmed, and the militia keep a constant guard. It is said that the St. Domingo negroes have sown those seeds of revolt, and that a magazine has been attempted to be broken open.

William Cobbett: "You Southern Fools"

Editor William Cobbett, reflecting the fears of revolt, urges Southerners to be vigilant. If they fail to pay attention to their own slaves, the result will be a revolt.

Porcupine's Gazette (Philadelphia), 7 June 1798

Take care, take care, you sleepy southern fools. Your negroes will probably be your masters before this day twelve months.

Caleb P. Wayne: "The Insurrection of the Negroes"

In late August 1800, authorities uncovered a plan for a slave revolt in Virginia. The leader, Gabriel Prosser, and 34 conspirators were executed. In this piece, Caleb P. Wayne, who had taken over the Gazette of the United States *from John Fenno, reflected the widespread belief that Prosser and his followers were copying the example set by the slaves in Santo Domingue nine years earlier. He also expresses fears that plots are being planned in the other Southern states. He praises South Carolina for having Charles C. Pinckney as a local leader (and pushes his nomination for Vice President in the 1800 election as well).*

Gazette of the United States (Philadelphia), 23 September 1800

The Insurrection of the Negroes in the southern states, *which appears to be organized on the true French plan,* must be decisive with every reflecting man in those States of the election of Mr. Adams and Gen. Pinckney.

The military skill and approved bravery of the General, must be peculiarly valuable to his countrymen at this trying moment. *He is not of those who shrinks from danger.*—He has met it, and, when occasion requires, he will meet it with firmness in its most horrid form.

We congratulate our fellow citizens of South Carolina on the possession of this Gallant Soldier at this Important crisis. To him they may look with confidence for every aid which courage and talents can supply.

QUESTIONS

1. What sort of comparisons do the first two writers make between the slave revolt and the American and French revolutions? Do you agree with their comparisons?
2. Many people considered slaves to be less than human. In what ways do J.P. Martin and Francis Bailey point out the slaves are human and deserve to be treated as such?
3. What are the major criticisms of the slave revolt expressed by Benjamin Franklin Bache and Philip Freneau?
4. According to Thomas Greenleaf and William Cobbett, why are Southerners so fearful of the slave revolt in Santo Domingue? Do you think that their fears were justified?

NOTE

1. Blanchelande is Philibert-Francois Rouxel de Blanchelande, the governor of Santo Domingue from 1790 to 1792.

CHAPTER 15

President George Washington, 1789–1799

On April 30, 1789, George Washington took the oath of office as the first president of the United States under the government established by the Constitution. He had been elected unanimously by the electoral college, the only president in history to be so elected. Washington would serve two full terms (eight years) as president. As is true with most American presidents, he was not as popular when he left office as he had been when he was elected.

George Washington's first term in office was fairly calm. Most of his efforts were spent overseeing the organization of the new government. He encouraged his secretary of the Treasury, Alexander Hamilton, to develop an economic plan that would bolster the nation's finances (a problem left over from the Articles government). He also declared the United States to be neutral when France and England went to war in 1793.

Washington's troubles began during his second term in office. Some attacked him for running for reelection, stating it was a sign of his strong personal ambition and desire for power. Then, matters became worse as he sought to avoid war with Great Britain.

In 1795, Washington sent John Jay, chief justice of the Supreme Court, to Great Britain to negotiate a treaty. The resulting Jay's Treaty (see Chapter 18) created a lot of debate and helped produce the first political party system in the United States. George Washington was increasingly criticized in the newspapers. Some, at least, had forgotten the hero of the American Revolution (at least, that is what Washington thought). He left office in March 1797, glad to be out of the line of fire of the partisan newspaper editors (see Chapter 19).

The documents that praise George Washington as president emphasize his leadership ability. The first two pieces actually date from before his inauguration, showing his influence throughout this era. The third selection ex-

George Washington's Inauguration. *The left two columns in this newspaper contain a report of George Washington's first inauguration. It includes a description of the procession and the text of Washington's inaugural address. The remainder of the page is filled with advertisements, a necessary part of a newspaper's content if the publication was going to survive.*

alts the success of the nation now that the new government has been put in place. The fourth document states that Washington deserves any praise which the American people choose to give him. The fifth piece expresses dismay that Washington's character is attacked by anyone. The sixth document defends Washington's actions in the Ohio Valley in 1754. The final piece in this group relates the sorrow of Americans at Washington's death in 1799.

The documents that attack Washington accuse him of being ambitious and power-hungry. The first piece urges him to retire as soon as possible, while the second selection castigates him for acting like a king. The third document states that Washington has betrayed his country by undermining freedom. The fourth piece rejoices that Washington has left office and states that the nation can now recover from all the harm that he had done. The last selection accuses Washington of cowardice during the French and Indian War.

Support for Washington

Anonymous: "Called Upon a Second Time"

George Washington's public reputation had been set during the Revolution, and it did not weaken through the 1780s. Thus, as this author points out, Washington was an automatic choice for leadership as the Convention met in Philadelphia.

Pennsylvania Gazette (Philadelphia), 22 August 1787

How great (adds our correspondent) must be the satisfaction of our late worthy Commander in Chief, to be called upon a second time, by the suffrages of three millions of people, to save his sinking country?—In 1775, we behold him at the head of the armies of America, arresting the progress of British tyranny.—In the year 1787, we behold him at the head of a chosen band of patriots and heroes, arresting the progress of American anarchy, and taking the lead in laying a deep foundation for preserving that liberty by a good government, which he had acquired for his country by his sword. Illustrious and highly favored instrument of the blessings of Heaven to America—live—live for ever!

Josiah Meigs and Eleutheros Dana: "The Office of First Magistrate"

As noted by these printers, Washington was an obvious choice for president. No one doubted that he would be chosen to fill this office once the Constitution was approved.

New Haven Gazette and Connecticut Magazine, 19 June 1788

A correspondent observes, that every friend to his country must rejoice at the present smiling prospect of the speedy adoption of the federal constitution; and also at the uncommon spirit of harmony and candor which begins to prevail. It is to be hoped that the new government will soon be organized and furnished with officers. No man doubts who will be honoured with the office of First Magistrate. The eyes of all ranks of people are fixed upon General Washington, who seems to be designed by Providence for this great undertaking.

Benjamin Franklin Bache: "What Blessings May We Not Hope For?"

No one questioned Washington's leadership in the first few years he was in office. Even editor Benjamin Franklin Bache, who became one of his most vocal attackers following the ratification of Jay's Treaty, perceived that the nation was in great shape and that Washington's leadership was part of the reason for the improvements.

General Advertiser (Philadelphia), 27 November 1790

Successful in war, but foiled in the arts of peace the people of the United States were long the dupes of European policy, and were nearly the victims of their own indiscretion. We were animated by a spirit of false trade. Industry was active, but her activity was ill-directed! LIBERTY was tremblingly alive, and BUT alive. Attacked by illiberality and disunion, we dreaded lest she should expire on the threshold of Government. But licentiousness was evidently her most formidable foe. More than one state was convulsed by the efforts of (now) disappointed faction. Commerce stagnated in all her channels, and credit was most deplorably at the lowest ebb.

But the scene is changed. A new, a happy series of years commences. Justice descends from the skies, where too many had compelled her to take refuge. The hands of the manufacturers are beneficially employed. Our ports abound in our own vessels. Agriculture is encouraged. A WASHINGTON presides over us with as much dignity & wisdom as man is capable of exerting. The sound policy of ADAMS shall again be manifested; & the distinguished talents of JEFFERSON advantageously displayed.

With these prospects, which rest on as much security as humanity can effect, what evils have we to fear?—or rather what blessings may we not hope for?"

Anonymous: "Our Supreme Executive Magistrate"

This author assumes that the nation is in safe hands with George Washington as president. There was some discussion over what title the president should be called. Some wanted to avoid titles like "Excellency" because it brought back memories of monarchy, but this author says it does not really matter because the name of Washington is as honorable as any title could be because of all of his service to his country.

General Advertiser (Philadelphia), 7 June 1791

An advocate for titular distinctions, in the last Gazette of the United States, conceives it necessary to annex certain fixed titles to offices. Does not the name of the office convey an idea of the trust which is reposed in the officer?—and what more dignified title could be bestowed on our supreme executive magistrate than GEORGE WASHINGTON? Would the epithet Honor, or even Excellency, annexed to his name express as much as his Name itself? Does Excellency call to mind the services he has rendered to his Country? and is not GEORGE WASHINGTON synonymous with prudent and brave warrior, profound statesman, defender of liberty, good citizen, great man?

John Fenno: "The Father of His Country"

As stated earlier, Benjamin Franklin Bache did not like Washington and attacked him for being too ambitious and power-hungry. In this piece, John Fenno defends Washington. He assumes that Bache's grandfather, Benjamin Franklin, would be ashamed at the actions of his grandson.

Gazette of the United States (Philadelphia), 7 March 1797

What pain must the shade of the immortal Franklin experience in beholding the apostasy of his grandson. It seems that Mr. Bache would wish to be thought the leader of that party which is unceasingly endeavoring to sap the foundation of our government, and sow discord among us. Dead to every normal sentiment that ought to animate the soul—he seems to take a kind of hellish pleasure in defaming the name of WASHINGTON.

That a man who was born in America and is part of the great family of the United States could thus basely aim his poisoned dagger at the FATHER OF HIS COUNTRY is sorely to be lamented.

Anonymous: "Lies to Wound the Reputation of General Washington"

This author defends Washington's honor in his dealings with the French in the Ohio Valley in 1754. The event described here was the primary preliminary event leading up to the French and Indian War. Benjamin Franklin Bache had dragged up this event to attack Washington as he left office in 1797. This author cannot believe that anyone would stoop so low in an effort to win a political point.

Minerva (New York), 17 March 1797

The Aurora, which had accused Gen. Washington, during his administration, of corruption, peculation and almost every crime, as soon as his administration elapsed, charged him with being guilty of *dishonour*.

This charge is, like many of the lies in that paper, taken from the French.

It seems that in the last French war of 1754, when George Washington was a major, and had the command of a small body of troops near fort du Quesne, now Pittsburgh, the French were trying to get some knowledge of the English camp. For this purpose, with that hypocrisy which characterizes the French, they sent a small detachment to patrol in the woods near the camp and one Jumonville had orders to carry a summons to the English to surrender—after two days lurking about like a spy, he was detected by Major Washington, who fired on his party and killed nine of them. The French called it an *assassination*, and this story, with all its French coloring and virulence, is revived in the Aurora.

To what a desperate ebb must a man be reduced, to ransack the musty French journals of 1755, to find *lies* to wound the reputation of General Washington! One would think he might find an ample supply of lies of a more recent date. There must be a wonderful lack of materials among the party, to force them to go back more than forty years for a supply of slander; and hungry indeed must be the men, who are not satisfied with the *Jacobin lies of the day*.

Anonymous: "This Distinguished Character"

Washington's death in 1799 was a time of great mourning for the United States. His passing marked the end of an era, and it seemed fitting that he did not live to see the new century, although he had hoped to do so. This author praises his memory because of all his efforts on behalf of freedom and liberty in the fight against Great Britain.

DIED at Mount Vernon, on Saturday evening, December the 14th, at 11 o'clock, of an illness of 24 hours

GEORGE WASHINGTON

Commander in chief of the American armies during the Revolution, caused by the tyranny of Great Britain; in this distinguished character his name will live to the latest posterity among the greatest men who have ornamented history, by the support of Liberty and their country against tyranny.—As we can offer no higher Eulogium to the memory of a character elevated by fortune, talents and the voice of his country to so high a station, among the benefactors of mankind—we confine ourselves to that alone, recommending the principles for which he fought with so much honor to himself and his fellow citizens, and to the freedom of his country, to the careful and steadfast conservatism of those who survive him.

OPPOSITION TO WASHINGTON

Benjamin Franklin Bache: "Retire Immediately"

Benjamin Franklin Bache attacks Washington for his inability to lead the country. He urges him to retire and leave the country in better hands. Bache never really liked Washington as president, but his dislike increased greatly following the negotiation of Jay's Treaty in November 1794.

Aurora **(Philadelphia), 20 September 1795**

Retire immediately; let no flatterer persuade you to rest one hour longer at the helm of state. You are utterly incapable to steer the political ship into the harbour of safety. If you have any love for your country, leave its affairs to the wisdom of your fellow citizens; do not flatter yourself with the idea that you know their interests better than other men; there are thousands amongst them who equal you in capacity, and who excel you in knowledge.

Philip Freneau: "The Powers and Prerogatives of a King"

Former Republican editor Philip Freneau attacks Washington for acting like a king. He states that Americans have given Washington all the privi-

leges and powers of a king, and that the nation is in danger unless the situation is remedied, and quickly.

The Argus, or Greenleaf's New Daily Advertiser (New York), 26 December 1795

Tho' we have, in this country, foolishly refused our great man the title he ought to have had, we have given the powers and prerogatives of a king; he holds levees, like a king; receives congratulations on his birth day like a King; receives Ambassadors like a King; makes treaties like a King; answers petitions like a King; employs his old enemies like a King; shuts himself up like a King; shuts up other people like a King; takes advice of his councillors, or follows his own opinion, like a King; rules the forms of the constitution, to put off an old ally, or to make a new one, like a King. He swallows adulation, like a King—and pukes up offensive truths in your face.

Benjamin Franklin Bache: "The American Nation Deceived by Washington"

Following the election of 1796, Benjamin Franklin Bache continued his attacks on Washington. In this piece, he declares that Washington has ruined the nation because he acted like a king, deceived the American people, and led them astray. Bache urges Americans no longer to worship any man in the way that they have idolized Washington.

Aurora (Philadelphia), 23 December 1796

When the federal government first began its career, it became a part of the system to keep the President from all intercourse with the people. He was to be seen only at a distance; he was to receive no information nor advice but thro' the organs he had established, and he was not to mix with any but those immediately under the government. GEORGE the third, it seems, became his example, and like GEORGE, he was only to be approached at a levee or seen dragged in a coach and six. The pomp, ostentation and parade of a British monarch was to be appended to the first magistrate of a free people, and hosannas were to be sung to him as the Providence of our country. This is an epitome of the conduct of GEORGE WASHINGTON, and the circumstances attendant on his progress from General to President. If ever a nation was debauched by a man, the American nation has been debauched by WASHINGTON. If ever a nation has suffered from the improper influence of a man, the American nation has suffered from the influence of WASHINGTON. If ever a nation was deceived by a man, the American nation has been deceived by WASHINGTON. Let his conduct then be an example to future ages. Let it serve to be a warning that no man may be an idol, and that a people may confide in themselves rather than in an individual.—Let the history of the federal government instruct mankind, that the masque of patriotism may be worn to conceal the foulest designs against the liberties of a people.

Anonymous: "A Day of Jubilee in the United States"

Although it is not clear who wrote this piece, it sounds very much like Benjamin Franklin Bache. At least, he would have been in agreement with the sentiment that the nation was saved now that George Washington was out of office. This author accuses Washington of single-handedly undermining the principles of freedom and liberty upon which the United States had been founded. He encourages Americans to rejoice that now they can recover from the eight years of disaster under Washington's leadership.

Aurora (Philadelphia), 6 March 1797

'Lord, now lettest thou thy servant depart in peace, for mine eyes have seen thy salvation,' was the pious ejaculation of a man who beheld a flood of happiness rushing in upon mankind. If ever there was a time that would license the reiteration of the exclamation, that time is now arrived; for the man who is the source of all the misfortunes of our country, is this day reduced to a level with his fellow citizens, and is no longer possessed of power to multiply evils upon the United States. If ever there was a period for rejoicing, this is the moment—every heart in unison with the freedom and happiness of the people ought to beat high, with exultation that the name of Washington from this day ceases to give a currency to political iniquity, and to legalize corruption. A new era is opening upon us, a new era which promises much to the people; for public measures must now stand upon their own merits, and nefarious projects can no longer be supported by a name. When a retrospect is taken of the Washingtonian Administration for eight years, it is a subject of the greatest astonishment, that a single individual should have canceled the principles of republicanism in an enlightened people, and should have carried his designs against the public liberty so far, as to have put in jeopardy its very existence. Such, however, are the facts, and with these staring us in the face, this day ought to be a *jubilee* in the United States.

T.T.L.: "The Accusation in Question"

T.T.L. repeats an accusation from the French and Indian War that Washington had fired under a flag of truce. Washington had left office by this time, but Benjamin Franklin Bache still seeks to punish him for his failures as president, and so he readily published this letter.

Aurora (Philadelphia), 13 March 1797

Mr. Bache,

I see in your last Number a letter signed GEN. WASHINGTON, solemnly denying the authenticity of certain private letters dated in 1776, and ascribed to him. For the honor of my country I sincerely rejoice, that those letters were not genuine; but I must say, that I think MR. WASHINGTON blameable for not having earlier noticed the forgery. I own for one, that his long silence produced on my mind disagreeable doubts. Others have felt them, and I cannot but think, that as a servant of the Public, it was his duty immediately to have removed such doubts since it was in his power to do it so readily. His personal pride should have been overcome for the sake of his public duty. The necessity of public confidence being attached to officers in important stations, especially in a government like ours, should have pointed out early to him the necessity, however disagreeable the task to his personal feelings, of stepping forward with a public denial of the unworthy sentiments attributed to him in those spurious letters.

Since he has prevailed upon himself to break the ice, there is another subject on which the public mind, I think, should receive some light. I have not known it lately to be a matter of public discussion, but it has been frequently brought forward in private conversations, and I never could find any one capable of giving a satisfactory explanation, and probably, from the old date of the transaction (1754) Mr. WASHINGTON may be the only person capable of giving an *eclaireissement.*

The accusation in question is no less than of having, while commanding a party of American troops, fired on a flag of truce; killed the officer in the act of reading a summons under the sanction of such a flag; of having attempted to vindicate the act, and yet of having signed a capitulation, in which the killing of that officer and his men was acknowledged as an act of *assassination.*

The charge is of so serious a nature; firing on a flag of truce so unprecedented an act even in savage warfare; and signing an acknowledgement of having been guilty of *assassination* so degrading to a man, and more especially to a military man, that I feel confident, there must have been some egregious mistatement in the account given of the business. I have imagined this also must be some *forgery,* or that Major G. WASHINGTON who was taken at fort Necessity in 1754, could not be the same person as GEORGE WASHINGTON, late President of the United States.

The transaction alluded to is recorded in a pamphlet published here in the year 1757, purporting to be the translation of "a Memorial containing a summary view of facts, with their authorities, in answer to the observations sent by the English Ministry to the courts of Europe."

Mr. WASHINGTON can settle every doubt upon this subject by declaring whether this Memorial was a forgery; whether the Journal it contains, purporting to be his Journal, and especially the capitulation, *acknowledging* the killing of Mr. Jumonville and his men to have been an act of *assassination,* were papers *forged* to answer the purposes of the French court; or whether he is the Major WASHINGTON there alluded to.

QUESTIONS

1. Americans in the 1790s practically worshipped George Washington. Why was that so? Do you agree that the young nation was in good hands with Washington as president?
2. What difference did it make what happened in 1754? Why did this story get brought up in 1797?
3. Why do you think that Washington's death had such a big impact? Do we still react strongly to the death of well-known figures today?
4. Why do you think Benjamin Franklin Bache disliked Washington so much? What kind of leader would he have liked?
5. How do we view George Washington today? Were Bache's ideas and opinions influential?
6. Washington, like most presidents, was more popular when he entered office than when he left office. Why do you think presidents lose popularity while in office?

CHAPTER 16

The Early Years of the French Revolution, 1789–1793

Some would argue that the world changed forever on July 14, 1789. On that day, more than 300 irate French citizens stormed the Bastille, an old jail that many saw as representative of the repression of the French monarchy. In attacking the fortress, the crowd hoped to free political prisoners and to acquire guns and ammunition. When it was all over, only 1 French soldier was dead and 3 were wounded, but 83 members of the crowd were dead while 73 were wounded. However, the garrison at the Bastille had surrendered. Thus began the French Revolution.

In the first stages of the French Revolution, the leaders called for freedom for the people and sought to create a legal code that treated everyone equally. In seeking these goals, the leaders of the Revolution abolished the French monarchy and adopted a republican form of government that provided for a legislature elected by the middle-class members of society. They also adopted the Declaration of the Rights of Man and Citizen to spell out the rights of the people that should be protected and not infringed upon by the government.

During the early days of the French Revolution, many Americans rejoiced at the efforts to bring freedom and republican government to France. Many people, both in France and the United States, believed that France was following the American example and was only the first of many countries that would move from a tyrannical monarchy to freedom. Some of the leaders in the early stages of the French Revolution had fought with the French army in America during the American Revolution. Leading the list of these veterans was the Marquis de Lafayette. He truly hoped to introduce his country to the new ideas of freedom and liberty coming out of the United States. He saw the Declaration of the Rights of Man and Citizen as the French version of the Declaration of Independence and rejoiced as his country began to reorganize its political system in a manner more equitable to the people.

Although most Americans supported the French Revolution, some did question whether it would succeed or not. People such as Alexander Hamilton did not believe that the French had enough experience with local governmental participation (as the Americans had) to provide the kind of leadership needed to guide such a major change in political structure. Questions of whether it would all work or not existed from the very beginning.

The documents that praise the French Revolution as a good event all point out the increase of freedom and liberty that has happened in France as a result of the revolt. The first two documents emphasize the good changes that have taken place as the revolution has succeeded. The third and fourth selections point out that the French learned about freedom and liberty by watching the Americans revolt against Great Britain. The fifth and sixth pieces comment on how unusual an event the French Revolution is and hope that its success will spread elsewhere in Europe. The last two selections worry about what will happen if France loses in its war against the other nations in Europe.

The documents which criticize the French Revolution as a bad event express concerns over the ultimate outcome. The first piece worries that France will experience a bloodbath before it is all over. The second selection accuses the leadership of the French Revolution of too much idealism and not enough realism when deciding what needs to be changed in France. The third piece insists that there is very little similarity between the American and French revolutions. The final document states that the French Revolution has gone too far and has degenerated into the rule of the mob rather than the government of the people.

SUPPORT FOR THE REVOLUTION

Anonymous: "One of the Most Glorious Objects"

This author rejoices over the coming of freedom to France. He points out that many of the leaders of the French Revolution are veterans of the American Revolution, implying that they learned about liberty while fighting for the United States.

Gazette of the United States (New York), 10 October 1789

The revolution in France is one of the most glorious objects that can arrest the attention of mankind: To see a great people springing into light, freedom, and happiness at once, from the depressions of Despotism and Bigotry, is something so novel, and so surprizing, that the philosopher is astonished, and the whole world contemplates the scene with wonder, with rapture, and applause. Americans in a particular manner, rejoice to see among the most shining patriots of France, the most distinguished names of those veterans who fought by her side the battles of Freedom.

Anonymous: "Success to France, Shall Be the Toast"

On the anniversary of the fall of the Bastille, this poet praises the people of France for taking back the liberty they had lost over the years to kings and priests. He reminds everyone that Americans should rejoice because of the spread of the fight for freedom beyond the United States to Europe.

National Gazette (Philadelphia), 14 July 1792

Bright Day, that did to France restore
What priests and kings had seized away
That bade her generous sons disdain
The fetters that their fathers wore,
The titled slave, a tyrant's sway,
That ne'er shall curve her foil again:

Bright day! a partner in thy joy,
Columbia hails the rising sun,
She feels her toils, her blood repaid,
When fiercely frantic to destroy,
(Proud of the laurels he had won)
The Briton, here, unsheath'd his blade.

By traitors driv'n to ruin's brink
Fair freedom dread united knaves,
The world must fall if she must bleed;
And yet, by heaven! I'm proud to think
The world was ne'er subdued by slaves—
Nor shall the hireling herd succeed.

Boy! fill the generous goblet high;
Success to France, shall be the toast:
The fall of kings, the fates foredoom,
The crown decays, its splendours die;
And they, who were a nation's boast
Sink, and expire in endless gloom.

Thou, stranger, from a distant shore,
Where fetter'd men their rights avow,

Why on this joyous day so sad?
Louis insists with chains no more.–
Then why thus wear a clouded brow,
When every manly heart is glad?

Some passing days and rolling years
May sea the wrath of kings display'd,
Their wars to prop the tarnish'd crown;
But orphans' groans, and widows' tears,
And justice lifts her shining blade
To bring the tottering bauble down.

Anonymous: "The Justice of the French Cause"

This writer insists that the French cause is just in the same way that the American cause had been right in the 1770s. He urges Americans to support the French in their fight against despotism and tyranny.

General Advertiser (Philadelphia), 18 September 1792

Take another view of the picture; examine the justice of the French Cause–that of freedom; the base motives of the invaders–to forge chains for thousands; compare the situation of the French with the situation of this country at the commencement of the war here; the manifesto of the commander in chief of the conspiring forces with the proclamation of General Burgoyne, view the effects of our glorious struggle,–then need we one moment doubt the issue of a contest between Liberty and Despotism. That had which enabled us to surmount every difficulty under every disadvantage, will support the French and bring confusion on the enemies of the RIGHTS OF MAN.

Anonymous: "The Era of Freedom"

This writer also rejoices over the spread of freedom. Liberty first began in the New World in the United States and has now spread to Europe.

Gazette of the United States (New York), 29 July 1789

THE ERA OF FREEDOM–OF UNIVERSAL LIBERTY! In this Western world, she first broke the chains which held mankind in servitude–and having fixed her temple in our favoured country, she is spreading her salutary reign throughout the world. Europe bows to her sway.

Benjamin Russell: "One of the Greatest Revolutions"

Editor Benjamin Russell comments on how remarkable an event the French Revolution is. It has restored freedom and liberty to France while undermining the power of kings and monarchs everywhere. Many hoped that the French Revolution would lead to the destruction of monarchies throughout all of Europe.

Massachusetts Centinel (Boston), 19 September 1789

By Capt. BARNARD, arrived yesterday, from London, we have received papers to the 6th of August, *thirty-five* days later than have before been received. These papers are *filled* with accounts of one of the greatest REVOLUTIONS *recorded in the annals of Time*—a Revolution which has *restored the Nation of France its long lost Liberties*—and taught its Monarch that *the Throne of Kings is never solid, unless founded on the* LOVE *and* FIDELITY *of subjects.*

Anonymous: "An Interesting Spectacle to Mankind"

This author congratulates the French on the progress toward freedom which they made in the first two years of their revolution. Many people were surprised that so much change had taken place in so short a time.

Kentucky Gazette (Lexington), 22 October 1791

The affairs of France have long exhibited an interesting spectacle to mankind. The friends of the human race have rejoiced in the downfall of one of the most stupendous fabrics ever erected by the demon of despotism, and have earnestly wished to see the glorious temple of freedom erected on its ruins. The progress that has been made in this great work is truly astonishing.

Anonymous: "Bless the Arms of Freedom with Success"

This anonymous poet castigates the European nations who have attacked France. He then prays that God will continue to give freedom success by granting France military victory.

Columbian Centinel (Boston), 9 January 1793

By hell inspir'd with brutal rage,
Austria and Prussia both engage,
To crush fair freedom's flame;
But the intrepid sons of France
Have led them such a glorious dance
They've turned their backs for shame.

May Heaven continue still to bless
The arms of freedom with success,
Till tyrants are no more;
And still as Gallia's sons shall fly
From victory to victory,
We'll, shouting, cry Encore!

Benjamin Franklin Bache: "To Extinguish the Fire of Freedom"

In this piece, editor Benjamin Franklin Bache worries that the European nations opposed to the French Revolution really want to destroy freedom everywhere. He believes that they will turn toward the United States if they succeed in defeating the French.

General Advertiser (Philadelphia), 26 July 1793

Upon the establishment or overthrow of liberty in France probably will depend the permanency of the Republic in the new world. It is not very absurd to suppose that if complete success attends the arms of the combined powers, that they will endeavor directly or indirectly totally to extinguish the fire of freedom in every part of the globe; hence this country is much deeper concerned in the politics of the European world than might appear to a superficial observer.

OPPOSITION TO THE REVOLUTION

Anonymous: "The Bastille"

This author questions the outcome of events in France. He believes that France will be a freer nation when the Revolution is finished, but he also thinks that there will be much bloodshed before it is all over. From the very beginning, some Americans had questions about the French Revolution because it seemed to be more violent than the American Revolution had been.

New York Daily Gazette, 17 September 1789

In every province of the kingdom the flame of liberty has burst forth; and when a whole nation, with an enlightened mind, asserts their claim to the privileges of men, experience has told us, that it is not in the power of monarchs to withhold their rights. But before they have accomplished their end, France will be deluged with blood.

Anonymous: "A Very Curious Subject of Political Speculation"

This author criticizes the revolutionary leaders of France for being idealists instead of realists. As a result, they have been unable to maintain real control. Many Americans wondered if France was too old and well-established to really change its form of government enough to establish freedom.

New York Daily Gazette, 24 October 1789

The National Assembly forms at present a very curious subject of political speculation. In the members of which compose it, we are supposed to see the Representative Wisdom of France. And how is this wisdom employed? in forming Utopian plans of reformation which cannot succeed—in laying down Theories of Government which cannot be reduced to practice, in short, in building castles in the air, and neglecting the means not only to preserve good order, but even to quench the spirit of licentiousness, rapine and freebooting which prevails in and threatens to desolate every part of the kingdom.

Anonymous: "No Comparison"

This author denies completely that there is any similarity between the American and French revolutions. In fact, he sees events in France as merely an insurrection that will end in a restoration of the monarchy to all its previous power. In many ways, this author reflects the thinking of many Americans who believed that France, and the rest of Europe, could not overcome the problems created by the various class divisions that had existed for centuries.

Gazette of the United States (New York), 13 January 1790

A Correspondent begs leave to observe, that nothing can be more absurd than to pretend the least resemblance between the American Revolution and the French Revolution, in the present insurrection in France. The one effected by the united efforts of an oppressed people—The other proceeding from the ebullitions of a frantic population, who always clamor against the government in time of scarcity; who so far from being enslaved by Louis XVI, never experienced so mild a reign, nor possessed a Sovereign so truly deserving of the appellation of *Father of his People*. Every American ought to regret, that the gallant Marquis de Lafayette has suffered his disappointment of the Mareschal's staff to induce him to head the popular clamors. A knowledge of French history alone is enough for prophecy. The few respectable characters supporting the popular cause will drop off. When disturbances cease, government will be restored in its original form, unless Louis XVI really wants to resign some power. Former insurrections have increased the king's power, but it is not likely that the pacific Louis will accept such. Those who are called the people of Paris are perhaps the most versatile of the human race—generally actuated by the mere impulse of the moment, and after one great exertion return to ease and imbecility.

The American: "The Struggles of the Nation"

This author believes that the leaders of the French Revolution have gone too far. In creating their new government, they have failed to ensure that there are controls on the powers of the government. The Revolution in France is quickly degenerating into an insurrection of the mob rather than a revolution of the people. The increasing violence and seizure of property scared many Americans and they feared what the future held for the Revolution in France.

Connecticut Courant (Hartford), 7 January 1793

The struggles of the nation against monarchical despotism have been marred by the same want of moderation, and still more disgraced by the violence of the passions. From this source have been derived all the misfortunes, which they have hitherto felt, and which for a considerable time they must necessarily continue to feel. France had it in her power to have been happy, almost by a single effort. At an early period of the contest, the king openly favored a reformation in government. The first exertions gave to the people, an house of representatives, by free election. This is the grand security of liberty, and no nation while it continues, can ever be enslaved. The circumstances of France, totally different from those of America, naturally pointed out for them a constitution similar to that of Great-Britain, but which should extend more equally the rights of suffrage, and be better guarded against the arts of corruption and the influence of the courts. The king readily submitted to a sufficient limitation of his prerogative. A Senate might have been constituted from the chief of the nobility as in England, or perpetuated as in Scotland by free election: And the house of Representatives would have formed a sufficient barrier against all usurpations of monarchical or aristocratical power. This was the plan of the amiable, but unfortunate *Marquis LaFayette*. He fell a victim to his own moderation, and the violence of his enemies.

For the leaders of the French revolution, having succeeded in destroying a tyrannical government, made an immediate attack on government itself. Happily broken loose from the chains of despotism, with all the enthusiasm of newly recovered freedom, and all the madness of revengeful passion, they rushed headlong into perfect anarchy. They inculcated the pure doctrines of levellism. They dethroned the king, degraded the nobility, banished the clergy, confiscated an immense property by a vote, massacred thousands without a trial, and after having been guilty of more wanton acts of tyrannical barbarity, than have in this century disgraced all the annals of despotism, have left their National Assembly, without power, and without assistance, to be governed and insulted by the mob of Paris.

QUESTIONS

1. Why do many newspaper writers, such as Benjamin Russell, praise the French Revolution? What long-term impacts do they hope it will have? Do you think they were right?
2. Why do the first four writers want to see connections between the American and French revolutions? Were they correct to see these connections?
3. Why do some Americans, like The American, fear the French Revolution? Was the French Revolution different from the American Revolution?

CHAPTER 17

The Whiskey Rebellion, 1794

When George Washington became president, he appointed his former aide-de-camp, Alexander Hamilton, to be the secretary of the Treasury. Hamilton saw his primary responsibility to be getting the finances of the United States on a stable footing. In order to raise some money, Congress approved an import tax in 1789. However, getting America's financial status straightened out would take some planning as well as some money.

Hamilton proposed a four-part plan. He stated that the federal debt should be funded at face value in order to show that the United States would pay its bills. He urged that state debts incurred in fighting the Revolution be paid by the national government because they were debts incurred fighting for everyone's freedom. He also proposed the creation of a national bank. These three ideas passed Congress without too much trouble. His fourth proposal, a protective tariff designed to encourage American manufacturing, failed.

As part of his proposals, Hamilton got Congress to pass an excise tax on the production of whiskey, snuff, and loaf sugar. These were all the products of flourishing industries in the United States, and government leaders thought successful businesses should help support the government. There were protests from people involved in producing all three products, but the strongest cries came from whiskey producers in the west.

Many farmers west of the Appalachian Mountains grew grain and then converted it to whiskey because that was easier and cheaper to transport over the mountains. They feared that Hamilton's excise would increase their costs and drive them out of the whiskey business. Western farmers protested through their representatives, but felt that no one listened. Finally, in the summer of 1794, farmers in the four western counties of Pennsylvania held public protests, seeking to prevent the collection of the excise. They terrorized the excise officers and stopped the delivery of the mail. On August 12, 1794, a group met in Braddock's Field (a place intended to recall previous attacks against tyrannical governments) and threatened to attack Pittsburgh (an event averted by the decision of the townspeople to join the protesters).

President George Washington issued a proclamation on August 7, 1794, ordering the protesters to disperse. When that did not happen, he called up the militia, which marched west to face the insurgents. No battle ensued because the real rabble-rousers (few in number) fled across the Ohio River. Still, 20 men were arrested and tried for treason. Two were convicted, but Washington pardoned them.

Many people, both then and ever since, debated just how serious an "insurrection" the Whiskey Rebellion really was. Some said the government authorities overreacted and that the issues could have been settled through negotiations. Others said that the government did the right thing in standing up to the mob. The newspapers of the day reflected these various opinions in the pieces they published.

The selections that support the Whiskey Rebellion emphasize the presence of real concerns and issues on the part of the rebels. The first piece urges caution on the part of the government in order to prevent the situation from becoming worse than it already is. The second piece states that any fighting that takes place should be done by those who like the revenue laws as they are—the wealthy merchants and lawyers. In the third and fourth documents, Benjamin Franklin Bache, editor of the *General Advertiser* in Philadelphia, accuses the Federalists of using the rebellion as an excuse to attack the Republicans.

The documents that oppose the Whiskey Rebellion emphasize that the rebels were breaking the law. The first selection states that they do not want any government at all. The second and third pieces both emphasize that the majority of Americans oppose the activities of the rebels in western Pennsylvania. The final document, written anonymously by Secretary of the Treasury Alexander Hamilton, states that the government is working well and that the rebels only want to undermine and destroy it for their own personal benefit.

Support for the Whiskey Rebellion

Anonymous: "Men Whose Minds Are in State of Inflammation"

This author urges the government to use caution in responding to the western insurrection. Harsh measures would only make the situation worse. According to this author, violence is not a good response to any problem by anyone, and the government should not add to the problem.

General Advertiser (Philadelphia), 16 August 1794

A Correspondent hopes that Government will not resort to extremity against the citizens of the western country; for little doubt can be entertained if violent means are resorted to, the result will be such as every humane heart must deprecate. Lenient measures with men whose minds are in state of inflamation, and who may believe they have just cause for their conduct, will be more prudent, and certainly comport more with the principles of our compact, than the sword or the bayonet; for an immediate reference to them will show a spirit equally hostile with that of the men against whom they are directed, and will prove that the argument of power and not of reason is more in unison with the feelings of government. Few men will be found who will advocate the conduct of violent resistance to our laws; but, it is to be hoped, that as few will be found who will sanction an immediate violence, that may probably end in all the horrors of a civil war. Republicans may be convinced by reason but their spirits will not bend to force, and if force is to be the logic which is first to be employed, the humane heart will, it is feared, find cause to bewail the destruction of the richest harvest ever exhibited to mankind.

Anonymous: "The Western Insurgents"

This author makes it clear that those who benefit from the revenue laws should be the ones to fight the rebels. Many feared that the Whiskey Rebellion was a class war of sorts between the eastern merchants with money and the poorer farmers of the west. Many Americans also hesitated to take up arms against their own countrymen.

General Advertiser (Philadelphia), 20 August 1794

As violent means appear the desire of high toned government men, it is to be hoped that those who derive the most benefit from our revenue laws will be the foremost to march against the western insurgents. Let stock-holders, bank directors, speculators, and revenue officers arrange them-selves immediately under the banners of the treasury, and try their prowess in arms as they have done in calculation. The prompt recourse to hostilities which two certain great characters are so anxious for, will, no doubt, operate upon the knights of our country to appear in military array, and then the poor but industrious citizen will not be obliged to spill the blood of his fel-low citizen before conciliatory means are tried, to gratify certain resent-ments, and expose himself to the loss of life or of limb to support a funding order. The man who has most to expect from government ought to be the first to defend it, and no one will deny that the knights of the funding sys-tem are of this description; it is to be presumed, therefore, that they will equip themselves against the first of September, and not permit those who have less interest in excise laws to be in advance; for as they have already re-ceived most of the emoluments of the revolution, they must expect to re-ceive all the benefits of an *immediate* crusade against our own citizens.

Benjamin Franklin Bache: "The Late Unfortunate Disturbances"

Benjamin Franklin Bache assumes that the Federalists are using the Whiskey Rebellion as an excuse to attack their political opponents, partic-ularly the local democratic societies that had appeared to organize the op-position to government policies. Although he does not mention him by name, he attacks Alexander Hamilton as the leader of the Federalists for at-tempting to put in place in the United States a false aristocracy based on money.

General Advertiser (Philadelphia), 28 August 1794

The late unfortunate disturbances in the western parts of this state are made a tool of by the party among us that has been ever since the establish-ment of government active, by every means, in infusing into the system aris-tocracy in every shape. These disturbances give them an opportunity, tho' a lame one to be sure, of directing their batteries afresh against Democratic societies. The great champion of the party is supposed, indeed, to have come forward on this occasion to lead the van in the attack; but whatever has the reputation of being the production of his pen carries its antidote along with it: The doctrines of a man whose talents since the establishment of our present constitution have been industriously exercised in inventing every trick and scheme to give a bias to the government contrary to the spirit of that instrument, who has been the parent of the dangerous principles engrafted upon it, and the promoter of systems tending to level the natural inequalities among men, arising from a different degree of merit or virtue, for the purpose of erecting on its ruins an artificial aristocracy, subservient to the views of the most dangerous enemies of the liberty of the people,—the doctrines of such a man can never make an impression upon an enlightened nation of freemen, tho' conveyed in the garb of the most insidious eloquence.—Nothing that the champion can advance, will persuade the people, that they have not a right to assemble peacefully, discuss and give their opinion of public men and measures. His efforts toward proving this position will only be an evidence of the earnestness with which he & his party are bent on keeping from the public view their dark transactions, and a strong presumptive proof at least, that their deeds will not bear the light.

Benjamin Franklin Bache: "Returning Order in the Western Counties"

Benjamin Franklin Bache praises the government for restoring peace without having to resort to bloodshed. He also rejoices that the rebellion was not used as an excuse to strengthen the national government, as some had wished to do.

General Advertiser (Philadelphia), 6 September 1794

We most heartily congratulate our fellow citizens on the prospect of returning order in the western counties of this state. The manly and calm decision of our governments has brought to their senses, without bloodshed, those whom probably a designing few had misled, and the hopes of the enemies of republicanism, that the riots would give a pretext for engrafting more *energy* upon the government, are happily blasted.

OPPOSITION TO THE WHISKEY REBELLION

Conservator: "A Cruel and Unprovoked Outrage"

In this essay, Conservator accuses the rebels of wanting no government at all. He states that they are overrepresented in Congress and that they refuse to listen to Congress even when laws are passed. The result is anarchy. Many Americans feared that if the rebels were not brought under control, the Whiskey Rebellion would be the beginning of a period of little or no government in the United States.

General Advertiser (Philadelphia), 12 August 1794

It must yield a painful reflection to all real admirers of a representative government that the only fair experiment of its superior advantages should be disgraced by a cruel and unprovoked outrage on private property and a public opposition to the legitimate voice of the country. It need hardly be mentioned that I refer to the late riotous conduct of the citizens of the western counties, a people, singularly favoured by government, indulged with a surplus share of representation in both houses of Congress, requiring and obtaining a more extensive protection than half the union beside; joined to all this a people loud and clamorous in favour of democratic forms, when they themselves are the first to outrage and destroy their very essence, plainly evincing that by democratic or republican governments (for they are both the same in America) they mean no government at all. Where is the use of their delegates spending 6 or 8 months in congress and carrying home perhaps more money for their attendance than they ever possessed at once before, if they are afterwards to govern the United States themselves in their individual capacities. This cannot be answered no more than their rebellion can be justified, but without a shadow of excuse, without a single plea of palliation, they stand amenable to the vengeance of a country grievously insulted, and to the justice of a government grown almost indignant from long forbearance.

John Fenno: "Bringing the Western People to Their Senses"

Editor John Fenno rejoices that peace has been restored in the west. He thinks that the rebels dispersed because they realized that most Americans were opposed to them and would unite to defeat them if armed conflict ever occurred.

Gazette of the United States (Philadelphia), 18 August 1794

We are informed that intelligence was received on Friday evening from the westward, which wear a more agreeable aspect than has lately reached us from that quarter—it is said reason and consideration are taking place of turbulence and faction—and that the prospect is flattering that affairs there will speedily resume a tranquil appearance.

Reflection says a correspondent must do wonders in bringing the western people to their senses—especially as there appears but one opinion from north to south respecting their late proceedings—and that opinion is against them—for however divided respecting the utility of an excise—all unite in reprobating measures which strike at the existence of Society—and lay the ax to the root of all the blessings of 'peace, liberty and safety.'

Anonymous: "Anarchy and Insurrection"

This author also states that most Americans will not support the rebels. The American economy is in good shape and the government under the Constitution is working well, so this writer does not understand why the farmers in the west are upset.

Gazette of the United States (Philadelphia), 22 August 1794

We understand, with great concern, that the western disturbances have risen to so great a height, that the ordinary powers of government are altogether inadequate to the suppression of them; but we perceive with pleasure that the President of the United States, as well as the Governor of the state, are disposed to pursue a line of conduct that evinces the energy and the moderation of government.

As no Republican Constitution can subsist, where the *minority* (and a very small minority too) attempt to give law to the *majority,* and to oppose, by violence, the general will of the whole nation, it is evident, that laws opposed by force must be executed by force. Congress and the Legislature of Pennsylvania have armed their several executives with powers for such great emergencies; and it appears that measures are preparing to call out the strength, not only of Pennsylvania, but the whole union, if it should be necessary. But, in the mean, before recourse is had to this last resort, Government appears disposed to adopt every measure which may allay the discontents and restore obedience to the laws. For this purpose the honourable Judge Yeates and the honourable William Bradford, Attorney General of the United States, on Sunday, and yesterday morning the Hon. Thomas McKean, Chief Justice of the State, and Gen. William Irvine passed through this place, on their way to the western counties; the two first named gentlemen together with the Hon. James Ross of Washington, are appointed commissioners on behalf of the United States, and the Chief Justice and Gen. Irvine, on the part of the State, vested, it is said, with considerable powers; and we sincerely hope, that a love of order and republican government, will finally prevail over the anarchy and insurrection which at present are predominant in that part of the state.

If the insurgents expect any countenance from their fellow-citizens, they will be miserably disappointed, and there is no doubt but that all good citizens will be ready to vindicate the authority of a free government, when ever they shall be called upon for that purpose. The citizens of the United States in general, (and the people in the disaffected counties in common with their fellow-citizens), have flourished under the present government; every man who is not blind, sees this, and every man who is not infatuated must feel it, every man who is capable of contrasting our former distresses with our present prosperity, must be anxious to support that government under which he sees his neighbours, and feels himself, flourishing, secure and happy.

Tully: "To the People of the United States"

Writing under the pseudonym of Tully, Alexander Hamilton urged Americans to see the threat posed by the Whiskey Rebellion. He reflects the ideas of many who believed that the rebels wanted to undermine the government in such a way that would weaken it and probably ruin it. Hamilton urges Americans not to be fooled by the rebels into believing that the government was not working.

American Daily Advertiser (Philadelphia), 23 August 1794

It has, from the first establishment of YOUR present Constitution, been predicted, that every occasion of serious embarrassment which should occur in the affairs of the government, every misfortune which it should experience, whether produced from its own faults or mistakes, or from other causes, would be the signal of an attempt to overthrow it, or to lay the foundation of its overthrow, by defeating the exercise of constitutional and necessary authorities. The disturbances which have recently broken out in the western counties of Pennsylvania, furnish an occasion of this sort. It remains to see whether the prediction which has been quoted proceeded from an unfounded jealousy, excited by partial differences of opinion, or was a just inference from causes inherent in the structure of our political institutions. Every virtuous man, every good citizen, and especially EVERY TRUE REPUBLICAN, must fervently pray, that the issue may confound and not confirm so ill-omened a prediction.

Your firm attachment to the government YOU have established, cannot be doubted.

If a proof of this were wanting to animate the confidence of your public agents, it would be sufficient to remark that as often as any attempt to counteract its measures appear, it is carefully prepared by strong professions of friendship to the government and disavowals of any intention to injure it. This can only result from a conviction that the government carries with it YOUR affections;—and that an attack upon it, to be successful, must veil the stroke under the appearances of good will.

It is therefore very important that You should clearly discern, in the present instance, the shape in which a design of turning the existing insurrection to the prejudice of the government would naturally assume. Thus guarded, you will more readily discover and more easily shun the artful snares which may be laid to entangle your feelings and your judgment, and will be the less apt to be misled from the path by which alone you can give security and permanency to the blessings you enjoy, and can avoid the incalculable mischiefs incident to a subversion of the just and necessary authority of the laws.

The design alluded to, if it shall be entertained, would not appear in an open justification of the principles or conduct of the insurgents, or in a direct dissuasion from the support of the government. These methods would produce general indignation and defeat the object. It is too absurd and shocking a position to be directly maintained, that forcible resistance by a sixtieth part of the community to the representative will of the WHOLE, and to constitutional laws expressed by that will, and acquiesced in by the people at large, is justifiable or even excusable. It is a position too untenable and disgusting to be directly advocated—that the government ought not to be supported in exertions to establish the authority of the laws against a resistance so incapable of justification or excuse.

The adversaries of good order in every country have too great a share of cunning, too exact a knowledge of the human heart, to pursue so unpromising a cause. Those among us would take upon the present occasion one far more artful, and consequently far more dangerous.

They would unite with good citizens, and perhaps be among the loudest in condemning the disorderly conduct of the insurgents. They would agree that it is utterly unjustifiable, contrary to the vital principle of republican government, and of the most dangerous tendency—But they would, at the same time, slily add, that excise laws are pernicious things, very hostile to liberty (or perhaps they might more smoothly lament that the government had been imprudent enough to pass laws so contrary to the genius of a free people), and they would still more cautiously hint that it is enough for those who disapprove of such laws to submit to them—too much to expect their aid in forcing them upon others. They would be apt to intimate further, that there is reason to believe that the Executive has been to blame, sometimes by too much forbearance, encouraging the hope that the laws would not be enforced, at other times in provoking violence by severe and irritating measures; and they would generally remark, with an affectation of moderation and prudence, that the case is to be lamented, but difficult to be remedied; that a trial of force would be delicate and dangerous; that there is no foreseeing how or where it would end; that it is perhaps better to temporize, and by mild means to allay the ferment, and afterwards to remove the cause by repealing the exceptionable laws. They would probably also propose, by anticipation of and in concert with the views of the insurgents, plans of procrastination. They would say, if force must finally be resorted to, let it not be till after Congress has been consulted, who, if they think fit to persist in continuing the laws, can make additional provision for enforcing their execution. This, too, they would argue, will afford an opportunity for the public sense to be better known, which (if ascertained to be in favor of the laws) will give the government greater assurance of success in measures of coercion.

By these means, artfully calculated to divert YOUR attention from the true question to be decided; to combat, by prejudices against a particular system, a just sense of the criminality and danger of violent resistance to the laws; to oppose the suggestion of misconduct on the part of government to the fact of misconduct on the part of the insurgents; to foster the spirit of indolence and procrastination natural to the human mind, as an obstacle to the vigor and exertion which so alarming an attack upon the fundamental principles of public and private security demands; to distract YOUR opinion on the course proper to be pursued, and consequently on the propriety of the measures which may be pursued. They would expect (I say) by these and similar means equally insidious and pernicious, to abate YOUR just indignation at the daring affront which has been offered to YOUR authority and your zeal for the maintenance and support of the laws; to prevent a competent force, if force is finally called forth, from complying with the call—and thus to leave the government of the Union in the prostrate condition of seeing the laws trampled under foot by an unprincipled combination of a small portion of the community, habitually disobedient to laws, and itself destitute of the necessary aid for vindicating their authority.

Virtuous and enlightened citizens of a new and happy country! Ye could not be the dupes of artifices so detestable, of a scheme so fatal; ye cannot be insensible to the destructive consequences with which it would be pregnant; ye cannot but remember that the government is YOUR own work—that those who administer it are but your temporary agents; that you are called upon not to support their power, BUT YOUR OWN POWER. And you will not fail to do what your rights, your best interests, your character as a people, your security as members of society, conspire to demand of you.

Questions

1. Why are the first two writers so concerned about the potential use of armed force to end the Whiskey Rebellion? Of what other events are they thinking?
2. Why is Benjamin Franklin Bache so critical of the efforts aimed against the rebels? What does he think is really going on?
3. Why do the authors opposed to the Whiskey Rebellion, such as Conservator and John Fenno, fear its results? Of what other events are they thinking?
4. Why is Alexander Hamilton so concerned about the Whiskey Rebellion?

CHAPTER 18

Jay's Treaty, 1795–1796

In 1793, France and Great Britain went to war again. Although officially a reaction to the French Revolution, the war also constituted a continuation of the conflict that had been going on since the late 1600s. A new piece of the puzzle this time, however, was the existence of the United States. Both countries sought to hurt their opponent by cutting off American trade.

Great Britain, in particular, sought to use its navy to enforce trade restrictions that dated from the colonial era. In November 1793, it invoked the "rule of '56," which prohibited trade between the United States and the French West Indies by stating that commerce that was illegal in time of peace was also illegal in time of war. Thomas Jefferson, as the secretary of State, protested, but to no avail. In the winter of 1793–1794, the Royal Navy seized more than 200 American ships and impounded the cargoes.

Many Americans protested, declaring that Great Britain was still treating the United States as colonies. Besides the seizures, the British also refused to evacuate the forts in the Ohio Valley until Americans paid debts left over from before the American Revolution. Tensions increased, and it seemed that the United States was facing another war with Great Britain. In an effort to avoid war, President George Washington sent John Jay, the chief justice of the Supreme Court, to London in June 1794 to negotiate a treaty.

Jay stayed in Britain for five months. While there, he thought the negotiations went fairly well. In the treaty that he negotiated, he secured a promise from the British that they would evacuate the forts in the Northwest Territory. But he could not convince them to fully respect the trading rights of the United States as a neutral nation. He gained access for American merchants to British colonial ports in the Caribbean, but Great Britain continued to insist that restricting American trade with the French was necessary for its war effort. The end result was a treaty that avoided war with Great Britain, but did very little else.

When Jay presented the treaty upon his return to the United States, both George Washington and the Senate knew that the document was far from perfect and would not make many Americans happy. But they considered a flawed treaty better than no treaty at all because it would prevent a war with the British. They decided to keep the details of the treaty secret until it was ratified and then present it to the American people as a done deal.

The desire for secrecy proved elusive. A member of the Senate, Stevens T. Mason of Virginia, leaked the contents of the treaty to Benjamin Franklin Bache, editor of the *General Advertiser* in Philadelphia, before the government released the officially approved version. This constituted the first such leak of a government secret in American history. Bache, a vocal opponent of the Washington administration, printed the contents of the treaty and then strongly attacked it as a betrayal of American interests. The result was a firestorm of debate and discussion in the American press that continued long after the treaty was ratified by the United States Senate on June 24, 1795.

The documents that support the treaty concentrate much of their discussion on why the Republicans opposed it. The first two selections both attack the Republicans for their opposition. The third piece takes a swipe at Southern slavery in discussing the treaty's provisions concerning private property.

The selections that oppose the treaty all appeared after it was ratified by the Senate. They all see the treaty as a big mistake for the United States. The first piece describes the treaty as a disaster. The next three selections all use humor to attack the treaty and to show the dangerous results that will occur because the treaty was ratified. The last piece states that Jay's Treaty has returned the United States to the control of Great Britain.

SUPPORT FOR JAY'S TREATY

Anonymous: "The Treaty under Discussion"

This author discusses what Jay's Treaty would accomplish if ratified by the United States Senate by pointing out why, in his opinion, the Republicans are opposed to it. Jay's Treaty very quickly became a major political issue.

Gazette of the United States (Philadelphia), 9 July 1795

Mr. Fenno,

IF the two *impartial propositions* said to have been offered whilst the Treaty was under discussion in the Senate, as substitutes to the Resolution of Ratification, were to be rendered into plain English, they would read thus:

That the President of the United States be informed, that the Senate will not consent to the ratification of the Treaty, for the reasons following—

1. Because the said Treaty does not provide for the return of the Black Citizens, who, unmindful of the many whippings, brandings, and other blessings resulting from *their share* of the unalienable rights of man, went off with their good friends the British.

2. Because the doctrine of emancipation without a valuable consideration therefor, is hostile to the true interest of some of the most supereminent democrats in the United States; as well as repugnant to the usage which has always obtained and does now obtain with the piratical states of Barbary.

3. Because the 10th article has a direct tendency to discountenance public as well as private ROBBERY.

4. Because the righteous principles of exempting real estates from the payment of just debts, may be endangered by the operation of the 9th article.

5. Because the most effectual mode of terminating national disputes has been neglected, viz. That of insisting upon concessions, which it was morally certain would never be granted.

6. Because altho' this Treaty is in many respects favorable to the United States, and stipulates for the surrender of the Western Posts, an object of the first magnitude, yet, nevertheless, if the advantages to be derived from said Treaty were still more obvious, it would be a bad one, because negociated by John Jay.

7. Because if this Treaty should be ratified, it will blast the fair prospects of a war for the present; by which means *those* who are idle and have no money will miss the opportunity of acquiring some in the general scramble; and ALL who looked forward to a rupture with Great-Britain as tending to overthrow the Federal Government, will have to resort to their old trade of fomenting internal insurrections.

Anonymous: "Justice for the Sufferers"

This author also attacks the Republicans for opposing Jay's Treaty. He uses terms such as Jacobin and Robespierrist to connect the Republicans to the radicals in control of France during the Reign of Terror. Many Federalists feared that the Republicans wanted to lead the United States in more radical directions politically.

Gazette of the United States (Philadelphia), 9 July 1795

A correspondent asks, whether, if the Treaty had been rejected in toto, as some persons wished, we should in that case have the sooner obtained possession of the Western Posts? Whether its rejection would have facilitated a general peace with the Indians? or been a mean of preventing the spoliation of our commerce, or of sooner obtaining satisfaction for our vessels which have been illegally taken from us by the British cruisers? As the Treaty is little more than the arrangement of a plan for adjusting differences, and procuring compensation to our merchants for their losses, that patriotism may well be suspected, which, after clamouring against 'British piracies,' opposes every method of obtaining justice for the sufferers.

While the Jacobins are felicitating themselves on a fancied occasion to abuse the administrators of the government, let not the real friends of their country be inadvertently betrayed into a dereliction of first principles, or a precipitant abandonment of men, whose virtues have rose superior to all the powers of earth and hell, in the darkest moments this country ever saw.

Pray what is Republicanism? Answer, The majority. Are twenty more than ten? The Robespierrists say no.

What is a Constitution? Answer, A political Rule; but as that is a bad rule which will not work both ways, so a majority in favor of a measure is just as if that majority was against it, even if it amounts to two thirds of the whole.

Anonymous: "The Virtuous Ten"

This author discusses the failure of the treaty to deal with private property issues, particularly the return of runaway slaves to their owners. The issue of slavery would slowly grow more divisive in the United States with the passage of time.

Gazette of the United States (Philadelphia), 21 July 1795

Says a Correspondent.

Much abuse is thrown on Mr. Jay, for not obtaining a compensation for the negroes taken from New-York by the British.—That *Citizen Democrat* should feel an interest in having that species of property returned, or even paid for, is a new feature in the *Eastern* politician: But, when we are informed, that the VIRTUOUS TEN[1] prevent any negociation being renewed on the subject of the negroes, and other property taken from America by the British, it is presumed that we shall hear no more complaints on that head. The conduct of some of our *warm* politicians, has a striking likeness to that of a very mischievous boy, who kept this city, for several weeks in the winter of ninety-one, in continual alarm:—This wicked wretch concealed in his pocket a pot of coals, for the purpose of setting fire to some neighbouring buildings, and as soon as he had completed his evening amusement, *He* was the first to cry 'Fire.'—It is the way of most men, who are bankrupts in property and politics to leave a brand in every man's house who permits them to enter.

OPPOSITION TO JAY'S TREATY

Anonymous: "This Imp of Darkness"

Following the ratification of Jay's Treaty, this author mourned that it had been approved. He believed that the treaty would result in the ruin of the United States by destroying its economy.

Aurora (Philadelphia), 26 June 1795

The Treaty of Amity and Commerce (as it is called) between the *court* of Great Britain and the executive of the United States was ratified on Wednesday last. This imp of darkness, illegitimately begotten, commanded but the bare constitutional number required for ratification. Of its hostility to our commerce, to the interests of republicanism, and to the great interests of our country, the people will be fully able to judge, when the ratifications shall have been exchanged and it becomes the supreme law of the land, and not an hour sooner.

Anonymous: "Mrs. Liberty"

This author uses humor to attack the treaty. Through the use of a fake obituary, the author discusses the death of Mrs. Liberty through the ratification of Jay's Treaty. Such humorous pieces were common in eighteenth-century newspapers.

Independent Gazetteer (Philadelphia), 4 July 1795

Died—the 24th day of June last, of a hectic complaint, which she bore with Christian fortitude and resignation, in the nineteenth year of her existence, Mrs. LIBERTY, the ci-devant consort of America. Her tragical exit is generally imputed to a consumptive habit of body, and many are of the opinion that quack Murray's[2] empiricism accelerated her death.

Though some may doubt the authenticity of this intelligence, yet she has certainly relapsed into a state of non-entity. In the extremity of her paroxysms, she detached J—n J. esq. to the court of Great Britain, to supplicate his most gracious majesty to alleviate her misery, and his gracious majesty, it is thought, has administered a dose of subtile poison to quiet this turbulent jade, that has so often thwarted his ambition.

She is to be publicly interred this day. As a mark of heart-felt gratulation to the friends of Aristocracy, a FEU DE JOIE[3] is to be fired over her grave, and a general intoxication is to ensue. IF there is a spark of patriotism left, the bells will be muffled, and the true patriot will bathe her tomb in tears of regret;—will implore heaven for the art of passive submission to a demon's sceptre, and for fortitude to endure the complicated horrors of virtual slavery.

At this fatal, this awful interment, subjects of America, mourn. Our Independence is not even nominal, and it is easy to presage our return to our former station in the scale of political depression. We have incurred the vengeance of France and the bitterness of vassalage seems not our ultimate curse; bloodshed may perhaps render our chains more horrible. Our political fears are not visionary, and our only hope is now in heaven. Our sun which rose with awful splendor has sunk in pristine darkness. Farewell thou radiant goddess that once inspired our souls! may we weep on thy tomb till our abject forms are changed to marble!

Anonymous: "The Political Creed of a Western American"

This author also uses humor to attack the treaty through the form of a political pledge. By calling this piece "the political creed of a western American," he emphasizes the opposition to Jay's Treaty outside the commercial centers of the East Coast. He, too, believes that the treaty will result in the ruin of the United States.

Kentucky Gazette (Lexington), 26 September 1795

I believe that the treaty formed by Jay and the British king, is the offspring of a vile aristocratic few who have too long governed in America, and who are enemies to the equality of men, friends to no government but that whose funds they can convert to their private emolument.

I do not believe that Hamilton, Jay or King and their minions, are devils incarnate: but I do believe them so filled with pride, and so fattened on the spoils of America, that they abhor every thing that partakes of Democracy, and that they most ardently desire the swinish multitude humbled in dust and ashes.

I believe the period is at hand when the inhabitants of America will cease to admire or approve the conduct of the Federal executive, because they esteem the man who fills the chair of state. I believe that the tempestuous sea on which our administration has embarked, will require the strong nerved arm of vigorous age to conduct us from the abyss into which we are descending.

I believe that the political dotage of our good old American chief, has arrived, and that while we record his virtues in letters of gold, we should consign his person to the tender offices due to virtuous age, and transfer him from the chair of state to the chair of domestic ease. I do sincerely believe (from a knowledge of the man) that the Senator from Kentucky who voted in favour of the treaty, was actuated by motives the most dishonorable—that he is a stranger to virtue, either private or public, and that he would his country for a price easily to be told.

I do also believe that Kentucky has as little reason to complain on this important occasion, as any of her sister states; as she had a perfect knowledge of the man she delegated to represent her, knew that he possessed a soul incapable of good, and sentiments opposed to every real friend to her interest.

I do further believe that the period has arrived, when independent Americans ought to mark with infamy, the man who dares trample on the rights of his fellow citizens; that it is in vain to reprobate measures and suffer their authors to pass with impunity.

Anonymous: "The British Treaty"

This author also attacks the treaty through the use of humor. In this case, the tool of choice is sarcasm. Specifically, this author refers to the threat on the part of the House of Representatives not to provide the necessary funds to implement Jay's Treaty. Once it was ratified, many thought that cutting off the funding might be the only way to prevent the bad results expected from the treaty. Eventually, the House did not follow through on the threat.

Vermont Gazette (Bennington), 4 May 1796

Can you believe it, Mr. Printer? The house of representatives are determined to exercise the right delegated to them by the Constitution, in not providing for the British treaty. What but war, civil and foreign, must be the consequence of such obstinacy; We shall be ruined by these unprincipled men! The underwriters, in hopes of higher premiums, will shut their officers; debtors, to obtain a longer time, will refuse payment; Great-Britain, to fill her coffers, will take every vessel we have; not an Albany sloop will escape—Spain will attack us on the south-England on the north—the Indians on the west, and the fleet of our enemies will deprive us of the miserable consolation of drowning ourselves, with our wives and families in the Atlantic.–our speculators will be ruined, land will fall, stocks will go to the devil–Public and private credit will be at an end–For heaven's sake, Mr. Printer, what is to be done?–Let us import half a dozen guillotines, and decapitate, without loss of time, every refractory member of the majority in congress. If this will not do let the President call out the militia, surround the house of representatives, and force them to a compliance with his will.

Benjamin Franklin Bache: "Our Independence Is No More?"

In celebrating the Fourth of July, editor Benjamin Franklin Bache comments that Jay's Treaty has undermined American independence. He worries that the treaty once more puts the United States under the control of Great Britain.

Aurora (Philadelphia), 4 July 1796

This day leads in the 21st year since the country was declared independent of Britain. The wisdom and patriotism which dictated the declaration were well backed by the courage and fortitude that maintained it, and which after a glorious contest, finally effected a peace that had for its basis the independence of the United States.

How far the lapse of a few years since that glorious period has brought us back towards the point whence we started in our career as a nation, let existing facts decide. Since the late treaty has become the law of the land it may be a doubt whether our independence be more than nominal; the British before the revolution insisted on taxing us; they now, under the slightest pretexts, capture and condemn our property on the high seas, and we cannot retaliate, our hands being tied by the treaty.

QUESTIONS

1. Why do the first two authors attack the Republicans for opposing Jay's Treaty? Why would the Republicans not like the idea of the United States signing a treaty with Great Britain?
2. Why does the third author bring the issue of slavery into the debate? What difference could it make?
3. How do three of the authors use humor to attack Jay's Treaty? Historically, humor and sarcasm have often been used to make a political point.

Why does it work so well? Do we still use humor in a similar manner today?

4. Why does Benjamin Franklin Bache believe that Jay's Treaty returns the United States to the control of Great Britain? Do you agree with his assessment of the situation?

NOTES

1. The "virtuous ten" refers to the ten Republican Senators who voted against the ratification of Jay's Treaty—Aaron Burr of New York, John Langdon of New Hampshire, Moses Robinson of Vermont, Henry Tazewell of Virginia, Stevens Thomas Mason of Virginia, John Brown of Kentucky, Humphrey Marshall of Kentucky, Alexander Martin of North Carolina, Timothy Bloodworth of North Carolina, and James Jackson of Georgia.

2. Murray was a British admiral noted for his destructive raids.

3. *Feu de joie* refers to a salute fired by rifles in rapid succession along a line of troops, generally to celebrate a victory.

CHAPTER 19

The Rise of the Party Press, 1797–1800

Throughout George Washington's first term in office, increasing divisions appeared among the officers and legislators involved in the national government. Generally, these divisions fell into two groups—one led by the secretary of the Treasury, Alexander Hamilton, and one led by the secretary of State, Thomas Jefferson. In the aftermath of the debate over Jay's Treaty, these divisions hardened into the first political parties in American history—the Federalists and the Republicans. For the rest of the 1790s, these two parties fought for control of the national government and the loyalty of the American people.

Some American leaders had difficulty accepting the idea of political parties. In an enlightened government, such divisions should not exist because everyone should reach the same logical conclusion once all the evidence was gathered. As a result, the 1790s were a traumatic time for Americans. If political divisions existed, then a conspiracy to commit tyrannical acts must also exist on the part of one group or the other. The Federalists and the Republicans hurled numerous accusations at each other, assuming, of course, that they were right and their opponents were the conspirators.

Newspapers constituted a major mechanism for publicizing these accusations. Both groups had already turned to the press to communicate their ideas. In 1789, Alexander Hamilton encouraged John Fenno to found and publish the *Gazette of the United States* in order to communicate the thoughts and policies of the national government to the American people. In 1791, Thomas Jefferson induced Philip Freneau to move to Philadelphia and publish the *National Gazette* as an antidote to Fenno's paper. These two publications constituted the first party press in United States history. Other party papers founded later in the 1790s included Benjamin Franklin Bache's *General Advertiser* (Republican—later renamed the *Aurora*) and William Cob-

253

Philadelphia, *Nov.* 16.

Congress of the United States

The Market Street Scoundrel.

From Claypoole's Paper.

New-York Nonsense.

'Port of Philadelphia.

ARRIVED.

PRICES OF STOCKS.

MADEIRA WINE.

A quantity for Sale, by
Mordecai L—

This day is published,
By THOMAS DOBSON,

A Journey over Land to India

William Poyntell,

The Party Press. *This page from* Porcupine's Gazette *contains a vicious attack by printer William Cobbett on his Republican opponent, Benjamin Franklin Bache. Note the piece headed* "The Market Street Scoundrel" *in the left-hand column.*

bett's *Porcupine's Gazette* (Federalist). In fact, these two editors were the most vocal of the party editors publishing newspapers in the 1790s.

The editors of these papers took their support of a particular political party very seriously. Their party could do no wrong and the opposing party could do no right. Hence, the party papers praised their supporters with fulsome and overwhelming compliments while attacking their opponents with strong and scathing criticisms that often went far beyond political issues to the personal level. Many of these attacks often seemed to border on libel, but they helped establish the principle of press criticism and questioning of the actions of American political leaders.

The first set of documents favors the Federalist party led by Alexander Hamilton and John Adams. The first selection attacks the Republican newspapers for lying to the American people. The second piece is by William Cobbett, a strongly Federalist printer who believed that one should state one's opinions clearly and attack one's opponents strongly. The third and fourth selections are attacks by Cobbett on his Republican editorial opponent, Benjamin Franklin Bache. The final selection states that the Republicans have a network of newspapers under their control scattered all over the country.

The second set of documents favors the Republican party led by Thomas Jefferson and James Madison. The first piece, by Philip Freneau, discusses the partisan role that newspapers should play in a republic. The second selection is a poem attacking Hamilton because of his admission that he had had an affair with a married woman. The third and fourth documents attack the idea that newspapers could, or should, be impartial in their coverage of politics.

THE PRO-FEDERALIST PRESS

William Cobbett: "These Abominable Publications"

In this proposal for a new newspaper, William Cobbett attacks the Republican papers because, he says, they spread lies about the government. He believes that something must be done to prevent the potential damage that they could cause to the United States.

Washington Gazette (D.C.), 4 February 1797

Porcupine's Gazette

Proposals by WILLIAM COBBETT, opposite Christ Church, Philadelphia, for publishing a news-paper, to be entitled *Porcupine's Gazette, and Daily Advertiser.*

Methinks I hear the reader exclaim: What! have we not Gazettes enough already? Yes, and far too many; but those that we have, are, in general, conducted in such a manner that their great number, instead of rendering mine unnecessary, is the only cause that calls for its establishment.

The gazettes in this country have done it more real injury than all its enemies ever did or can do. They mislead the people at home and misrepresent them abroad. It was these vehicles of sedition and discord that encouraged the counties in the West to rebel; it was they that gave rise to the depredations of Britain, by exiting the people to such acts of violence against that nation, as left no room to doubt that we were determined on war; and it was they, when an accommodation had been happily effected, that stirred up an opposition to it such as has seldom been witnessed, and which was overcome by mere chance. These gazettes it was, that, by misrepresenting the dispositions of the people, encouraged the French to proceed from one degree of insolence to another, 'till at last their Minister braves the President in his chair, and a bullying commander comes and tells us that his only business is to seize our vessels, in violation of a treaty, in virtue of which alone he claims a right to enter our ports: and it is these gazettes that no have the impudence to defend what their falsehood and malice have produced.

I shall be told that the people are not obliged to read these abominable publications. But they do read them, and thousands who read them, read nothing else. To suppress them is impossible; they will vomit forth their poison; it is a privilege of their natures, that no law can abridge; and therefore the only mode left is, to counteract its effects.

This must be done, too, in their own way, Books, or periodical publications in the form of books, may be of some service, but are by no means a match for their flying folios. A falsehood that remains uncontradicted for a month, begins to be looked upon as a truth, and when the detection at last makes it appearance, it is often as useless as that of the doctor who finds his patient expired. The only method of opposition, then, is to meet them on their own ground; to set foot to foot; dispute every inch and every hair's breath; fight them at their own weapons, and return them two blows for one.

A gazette of this stamp is what I have long wished to see, but I have wished and expected it in vain. Indignation at the supineness of others has at last got the better of all diffidence in my own capacity, and has determined to me to encounter the task. People have heard one side long enough; they shall now hear the other.

William Cobbett: "Professions of Impartiality"

In this essay, William Cobbett makes it very clear that he does not believe that an editor can be impartial and fair. In fact, a good editor uses his own judgment to decide what side of a political debate is right and then does everything in his power to make sure that the right side wins.

Porcupine's Gazette (Philadelphia), 4 March 1797

Professions of impartiality I shall make none. They are always useless, and are besides perfect nonsense, when used by a news-monger; for, he that does not relate news as he finds it, is something worse than partial; and as to other articles that help to compose a paper, he that does not exercise his own judgment, either in admitting or rejecting what is sent him, is a poor passive fool, and not an editor. For my part, I feel the strongest partiality for the cause of order and good government, such as we live under, and against every thing that is opposed to it. To profess impartiality here, would be as absurd as to profess it in a war between Virtue and Vice, Good and Evil, Happiness and Misery. There may be editors who look on such a conflict with perfect indifference, and whose only anxiety is to discover which is the strongest side. I am not one of these, nor shall a paper under my direction ever be made an instrument of destruction to the cause I espouse.

William Cobbett: "The Market Street Scoundrel"

William Cobbett lashes out at his primary editorial opponent, Benjamin Franklin Bache, who published the Aurora. *Besides attacking his politics and his friends, Cobbett gets personal by calling Bache ugly and a disgrace to his family.*

Porcupine's Gazette (Philadelphia), 16 November 1797

The Market Street Scoundrel

Has, as usual, published a heathenish republican Calendar for the year 1788. At the head of one of the months he has placed the following:

'*Reign of blood before the Revolution.*

In 1788, Louis XVI had *eight thousand persons murdered,* of both sexes and all ages, at Paris, in the Street Mele'e and the Point Neuf.'

Now, who ever heard of this before? Who ever heard of a massacre at Paris, while poor Louis retained his power as king? never in his life did he authorize the shedding of a drop of human blood. Every one of any information knows that, had it not been for his unconquerable aversion to shedding the blood of his radical subjects, he would this day have been alive, and king of France. And yet, the impudent scoundrel *Franklin* dares not only to accuse him of murder, but to name the number of his victims on a particular occasion, and the spot where they fell; without having even hearsay for a foundation to his charge.

This atrocious wretch (worthy descendent of *old Ben*) knows that all men of any understanding set him down as an abandoned liar, as a tool and a hireling, and he is content that they should do so. He does not want to be thought any thing else. He knows very well, that the story about the *eight thousand murdered people* will be believed by nobody, except by those ignorant creatures, who can scarcely comprehend what they read; but these are the very creatures the information is intended for. These are they whom his masters want to secure on their side.

As this Gazette is honoured with many readers in foreign countries, it may not be improper to give them some little account of this miscreant.

If they have read the old hypocrite Franklin's WILL, they must have observed that part of his library, with some other things, are left to a certain *grandson;* this is the very identicle Market street scoundrel.—He spent several years in hunting offices under the Federal Government, and being constantly rejected, he at last became its most bitter foe. Hence his abuse of general Washington, whom, at the time he was soliciting a place, he panegyrized up to the third heaven.

He was born for a hireling, and therefore when he found he could not obtain employ in one quarter, he sought it in another. The first effect of his paw being greased, appeared soon after Genet's arrival, and he has from that time to this been as faithful to the cut-throats of Paris, as ever dog was to his master.

He is an ill-looking devil. His eyes never get above your knees. He is of a sallow complexion, hollow-cheeked, dead-eyed, and has a *toute ensemble,* just like that of a fellow who has been about a week or ten days in a gibbet.

William Cobbett: "A Fallen Wretch"

In this piece, Cobbett attacks his primary newspaper opponent, Benjamin Franklin Bache, again. In doing so, he calls him a liar and compares him to the worst beings on earth.

Porcupine's Gazette (Philadelphia), 17 March 1798

For me to attempt to dictate to Mr. Fenno would be impertinent, but, I really think he does this stinking carcass too much honour, in thus giving a serious refutation to his falshoods. Nobody, or, at least, nobody worthy notice ever believe; and to contradict him seems to imply that he is sometimes a credible person which is admitting what never ought, even for argument's sake, to be admitted. He knows that all the world knows and says he is a liar; a fallen wretch, a vessel formed for reprobation; and, therefore, we should always treat him as we would a TURK, a JEW, a JACOBIN, or a DOG.

Anonymous: "The Great Speaking Trumpet of the Devil"

This author assumes that the Republican newspaper editors are all being paid by the national party and that they are being guided and directed by William Duane, editor of the Aurora *in Philadelphia.*

United States Oracle (Portsmouth, New Hampshire), 22 March 1800

In all the states new presses are established from Portsmouth in New-Hampshire to Savannah in Georgia; through which the orders of the Generals of the faction are transmitted with professional punctuality; which presses serve as sounding boards to the notes that issue through the great '*speaking trumpet of the devil*,' the *Philadelphia Aurora.*—The Conductors of these Presses, have their rations issued to them, and are prompted in proportion to their abuse and defamation of the President, Congress, and the Northern States; and to the number of lies, innuendoes and suggestions they may produce from day to day.

THE PRO-REPUBLICAN PRESS

Philip Freneau: "The Invaders of the Rights of Man"

Although Philip Freneau did not agree with William Cobbett on political issues, he did agree with him concerning the role of a newspaper editor. Here he discusses what newspapers should contain if they are going to do the best job possible and serve their readers in the best possible way.

Time Piece (New York), 13 September 1797

It is an easy matter to fill the columns of a Gazette, as the world now goes, with the history of military marches, details of battles and sieges, storms, shipwrecks, murders, and that endless variety of events that are continually rising and floating on the surface of human things; but all these do little more than gratify curiosity and leave the mind benighted as to the interests of humanity and bettering the condition of human nature. These casual events undoubtedly should not be forgotten in any publication that

makes pretences to record the history of its own times, but should not occupy so great a space as to operate to an almost total rejection of those ideas
and observations, those hints and sketches of information, those lights and
disquisitions, at the view of which tyrants tremble, and every description of
the invaders of the rights of man shrink back into annihilation and signif-
icance.

Anonymous: "This Noble Goat"

In attacking the political opposition, the party press often went beyond pol-
itics to the personal level. In 1797, Alexander Hamilton confessed to having
an affair with Mrs. Maria Reynolds in order to avoid being blackmailed
by her husband. The Republican newspapers had great fun attacking
Hamilton because of this personal failure. This poet joins in that activity
with this poem.

Independent Chronicle (Boston), 16 October 1797

A SK—who lies here beneath this monument?
L o!—'tis a self created MONSTER, who
E mbraced all vice. His arrogance was like
X erxes, who flogg'd the disobedient sea,
A dultery his smallest crime; when he
N obility affected. This privilege
D ecreed by Monarchs, was to that annext.
E nticing and entic'd to ev'ry *fraud,*
R enounced virtue, liberty and God.
H aunted by whores—he haunted them in turn
A ristocratic was this noble Goat
M onster of monsters, in pollution skill'd
I mmers'd in mischief, brothels, funds & banks
L ewd slave to lust,—afforded consolation;
T o mourning whores, and tory-lamentation.
O utdid all fools, tainted with royal name;
N one but fools, their wickedness proclaim.

Citizen Brutus: "To Be Lukewarm Is to Acquiesce in Slavery"

Citizen Brutus, like Cobbett and Freneau, believes that people should be
passionate about their political beliefs. Americans had fought and died for
freedom and their descendants should have the same fervor even though not
involved in an actual war.

New London Bee (Connecticut), 18 July 1798

The man who can sit a silent spectator on the wreck of a dear bought liberty, a liberty purchased at the expence of thousands of lives and millions of money; who can behold without emotion in the great political drama the descendants of freedom, of those patriots who were lavish of their blood to secure to them their independence, now stupidly surrendering those same privileges which were made indefeasible by their ancestors; he is necessarily a madman, an idiot, or a fiend. Thanks to God there is not worse alternative. To be lukewarm in such a cause is to acquiesce in slavery.

Alexander Martin: "Pretended Impartiality of Printers"

This printer also attacks the attempt by newspaper producers to be impartial. It is impossible, he says, for such to be the case. To be impartial is to surrender to the control of the government.

American and Daily Advertiser (Baltimore, Maryland), 16 May 1799

The American people have long enough been imposed upon by pretended impartiality of printers; it is all delusion; every party will have its *printer,* as well as every sect its *preacher;* and it is as incongruous for a publication to be alternately breathing the spirit of *Republicanism* and *Aristocracy* as for a clergyman to preach to his audience *Christianity* in the morning, and *Paganism* in the evening; it is as inconsistent as for a *chief magistrate* to name an Ambassador to settle a dispute with a foreign nation; and immediately to violate the laws of civility, and make mockery of religion, by heaping upon the same nation and its representatives, the vilest phillippics, scurrility and abuse, in a proclamation for a day of fasting and prayer.—Every editor who is capable of soaring above the flattery of villainy, and the adulation of power has too much at stake, in the contest of liberty against slavery, virtue against vice, and truth against sophistry, to admit of more than a limited *impartiality.*

In supporting the principles of *Republicanism,* the Editor is aware that he shall lay himself open to all the hatred, malice slander and persecution, which form the leading policy of the advocates of *toryism* and *royalty;* but he pledges himself not to allow them a single inch, even should they oppose to him their whole phalanx, from Mr. Pitt's hirelings in Philadelphia and New York, down to their PIGMY IMITATOR *nearer home.*—They can support their opinions only by *scurrility*—he can defend *his* by the most *damning truths.*

QUESTIONS

1. Why do Cobbett, Freneau, and others of these writers believe that newspapers should get actively involved in politics? How is that different from how the news media are involved in politics today?
2. What kinds of personal attacks are included in these documents? Are these attacks justified? Are these attacks just part of being involved in politics? What do you think about the poem attacking Hamilton?
3. The modern media aim for impartiality in their coverage of the news. Is that possible? Is that the way it should be done?

CHAPTER 20

The French Revolution Gone Crazy, 1793–1798

On January 21, 1793, the people of France executed Louis Capet, their former king, for treason. Ten months later, on October 16, 1793, they executed his wife, Marie Antoinette. Between September 1793 and July 1794, more than 200,000 people were arrested and thousands (mostly members of the aristocracy) were executed by order of the French government. This Reign of Terror marked the end of one chapter and the beginning of a new one in the French Revolution. Beginning with the Reign of Terror, the Revolution became more bloody and then more repressive.

In the United States, the French situation became problematic because of the efforts of the new French ambassador, Edmond Genet. He had arrived in the United States on April 22, 1793, the very day that George Washington issued the Neutrality Proclamation declaring that the United States would not get involved in the war between France and Great Britain. Genet had arrived in Charleston, South Carolina, and he quickly ignored the Neutrality Proclamation by issuing letters of marque to American ship captains to enable them legally to raid British trading vessels. He then went on a triumphal trip north to Philadelphia. Both George Washington and Thomas Jefferson made it clear that the United States intended to remain neutral, but Genet continued to plan to use Americans as privateers. When told to stop in no uncertain terms by the president, he threatened to go over Washington's head directly to the American people. Thomas Jefferson then requested his recall and replacement as French minister to the United States. Because of his failure to gain American military and financial support for the French Revolution, Genet was now considered an enemy of France. He sought, and was granted, political asylum in the United States, where he remained until his death in 1834.

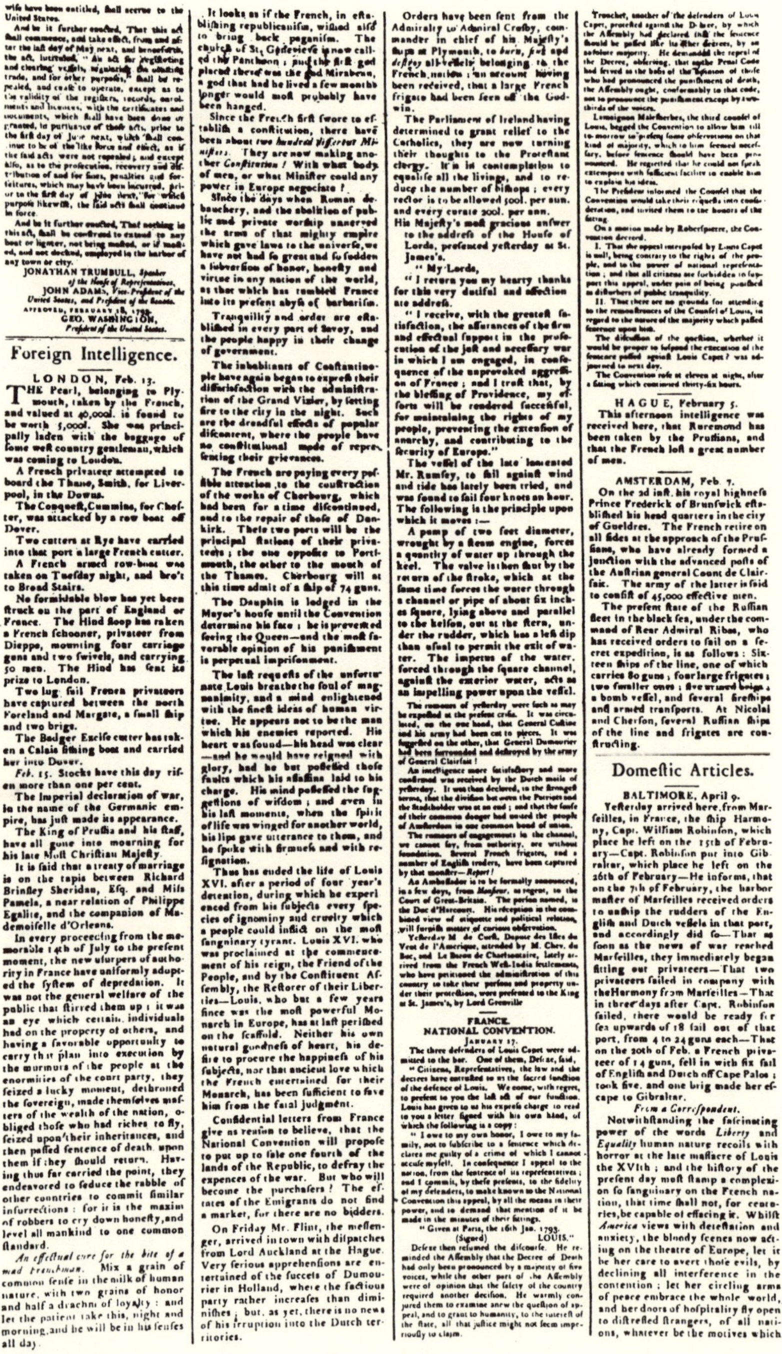

wife have been entitled, shall accrue to the United States.

And be it further enacted, That this act shall commence, and take effect, from and after the last day of May next, and henceforth, the act, intituled, "An act for registering and clearing vessels, regulating the coasting trade, and for other purposes," shall be repealed, and cease to operate, except as to the validity of the registers, records, enrolments and licenses, with the certificates and documents, which shall have been done or granted, in pursuance of those acts, prior to the first day of June next, which shall continue to be of the like force and effect, as if the said acts were not repealed; and except also, as to the prosecution, recovery and distribution of and for fines, penalties and forfeitures, which may have been incurred, prior to the first day of June next, for which purpose likewise, the said acts shall continue in force.

And be it further enacted, That nothing in this act, shall be construed to extend to any boat or lighter, not being masted, or if masted, and not decked, employed in the harbor of any town or city.

JONATHAN TRUMBULL, *Speaker of the House of Representatives,*
JOHN ADAMS, *Vice-President of the United States, and President of the Senate.*
APPROVED, FEBRUARY 18, 1793.
GEO. WASHINGTON,
President of the United States.

Foreign Intelligence.

LONDON, Feb. 13.

THE Pearl, belonging to Plymouth, taken by the French, and valued at 40,000l. is found to be worth 5,000l. She was principally laden with the baggage of some west country gentleman, which was coming to London.

A French privateer attempted to board the Thame, Smith, for Liverpool, in the Downs.

The Conquest, Cummins, for Chester, was attacked by a row boat off Dover.

Two cutters at Rye have carried into that port a large French cutter.

A French armed row-boat was taken on Tuesday night, and bro't to Broad Stairs.

No formidable blow has yet been struck on the part of England or France. The Hind sloop has taken a French schooner, privateer from Dieppe, mounting four carriage guns and two swivels, and carrying 50 men. The Hind has sent its prize to London.

Two lug sail French privateers have captured between the north Foreland and Margate, a small ship and two brigs.

The Badger Excise cutter has taken a Calais fishing boat and carried her into Dover.

Feb. 15. Stocks have this day risen more than one per cent.

The Imperial declaration of war, in the name of the Germanic empire, has just made its appearance.

The King of Prussia and his staff, have all gone into mourning for his late Most Christian Majesty.

It is said that a treaty of marriage is on the tapis between Richard Brinsley Sheridan, Esq. and Miss Pamela, a near relation of Philippe Egalite, and the companion of Mademoiselle d'Orleans.

In every proceeding from the memorable 14th of July to the present moment, the new usurpers of authority in France have uniformly adopted the system of depredation. It was not the general welfare of the public that stirred them up; it was an eye which certain individuals had on the property of others, and having a favorable opportunity to carry their plan into execution by the murmurs of the people at the enormities of the court party, they seized a lucky moment, dethroned the sovereign, made themselves masters of the wealth of the nation, obliged those who had riches to fly, seized upon their inheritances, and then passed sentence of death upon them if they should return. Having thus far carried the point, they endeavored to seduce the rabble of other countries to commit similar insurrections: for it is the maxim of robbers to cry down honesty, and level all mankind to one common standard.

An effectual cure for the bite of a mad Frenchman. Mix a grain of common sense in the milk of human nature, with two grains of honor and half a drachm of loyalty: and let the patient take this, night and morning, and he will be in his senses all day.

It looks as if the French, in establishing republicanism, wished also to bring back paganism. The church of St. Genevieve is now called the Pantheon; and the first god placed there was the god Mirabeau, a god that had he lived a few months longer would most probably have been hanged.

Since the French first swore to establish a constitution, there have been about *two hundred different Ministers.* They are now making another *Constitution!* With what body of men, or what Minister could any power in Europe negociate?

Since the days when Roman debauchery, and the abolition of public and private worship unnerved the arms of that mighty empire which gave laws to the universe, we have not had so great and so sudden a subversion of honor, honesty and virtue in any nation of the world, as that which has tumbled France into its present abyss of barbarism.

Tranquillity and order are established in every part of Savoy, and the people happy in their change of government.

The inhabitants of Constantinople have again began to express their dissatisfaction with the administration of the Grand Vizier, by setting fire to the city in the night. Such are the dreadful effects of popular discontent, where the people have no constitutional mode of representing their grievances.

The French are paying every possible attention to the construction of the works of Cherbourg, which had been for a time discontinued, and to the repair of those of Dunkirk. These two ports will be the principal stations of their privateers; the one opposite to Portsmouth, the other to the mouth of the Thames. Cherbourg will at this time admit of a ship of 74 guns.

The Dauphin is lodged in the Mayor's house until the Convention determine his fate; he is prevented seeing the Queen—and the most favorable opinion of his punishment is perpetual imprisonment.

The last requests of the unfortunate Louis breathe the soul of magnanimity, and a mind enlightened with the finest ideas of human virtue. He appears not to be the man which his enemies reported. His heart was sound—his head was clear—and he would have reigned with glory, had he but possessed those faults which his assassins laid to his charge. His mind possessed the suggestions of wisdom; and even in his last moments, when the spirit of life was winged for another world, his lips gave utterance to them, and he spoke with firmness and with resignation.

Thus has ended the life of Louis XVI. after a period of four year's detention, during which he experienced from his subjects every species of ignominy and cruelty which a people could inflict on the most sanguinary tyrant. Louis XVI. who was proclaimed at the commencement of his reign, the Friend of the People, and by the Constituent Assembly, the Restorer of their Liberties—Louis, who but a few years since was the most powerful Monarch in Europe, has at last perished on the scaffold. Neither his own natural goodness of heart, his desire to procure the happiness of his subjects, nor that ancient love which the French entertained for their Monarch, has been sufficient to save him from the fatal judgment.

Confidential letters from France give us reason to believe, that the National Convention will propose to put up to sale one fourth of the lands of the Republic, to defray the expences of the war. But who will become the purchasers? The estates of the Emigrants do not find a market, for there are no bidders.

On Friday Mr. Flint, the messenger, arrived in town with dispatches from Lord Auckland at the Hague. Very serious apprehensions are entertained of the success of Dumourier in Holland, where the factious party rather increases than diminishes; but, as yet, there is no news of his irruption into the Dutch territories.

Orders have been sent from the Admiralty to Admiral Crosby, commander in chief of his Majesty's ships at Plymouth, to *burn, sink* and *destroy* all vessels belonging to the French nation; an account having been received, that a large French frigate had been seen off the Godwin.

The Parliament of Ireland having determined to grant relief to the Catholics, they are now turning their thoughts to the Protestant clergy. It is in contemplation to equalise all the livings, and to reduce the number of bishops; every rector is to be allowed 500l. per ann. and every curate 200l. per ann.

His Majesty's most gracious answer to the address of the House of Lords, presented yesterday at St. James's.

"My Lords,

"I return you my hearty thanks for this very dutiful and affectionate address.

"I receive, with the greatest satisfaction, the assurances of the firm and effectual support in the prosecution of the just and necessary war in which I am engaged, in consequence of the unprovoked aggression of France; and I trust that, by the blessing of Providence, my efforts will be rendered successful, for maintaining the rights of my people, preventing the extension of anarchy, and contributing to the security of Europe."

The vessel of the late lamented Mr. Rumsey, to sail against wind and tide has lately been tried, and was found to sail four knots an hour. The following is the principle upon which it moves:—

A pump of two feet diameter, wrought by a steam engine, forces a quantity of water up through the keel. The valve is then shut by the return of the stroke, which at the same time forces the water through a channel or pipe of about six inches square, lying above and parallel to the kelson, out at the stern, under the rudder, which has a less dip than usual to permit the exit of water. The impetus of the water, forced through the square channel, against the exterior water, acts as an impelling power upon the vessel.

The rumours of yesterday were such as may be expected at the present crisis. It was circulated, on the one hand, that General Custine and his army had been cut to pieces. It was suggested on the other, that General Dumourier had been surrounded and destroyed by the army of General Clairfait!

An intelligence more satisfactory and more confirmed was received by the Dutch mails of yesterday. It was then declared, in the strongest terms, that the division between the Patriots and the Stadtholder was at an end; and that the sense of their common danger had united the people of Amsterdam in one common bond of union.

The rumours of engagements in the channel, we cannot say, from authority, are without foundation. Several French frigates, and a number of English traders, have been captured by that monster—*Report!*

An Ambassador is to be formally announced, in a few days, from *Monsieur*, as regent, to the Court of Great-Britain. The person named, is the Duc d'Harcourt. His reception in the combined view of etiquette and political relation, will furnish matter of curious observation.

Yesterday M de Curt, Depute des Isles du Vent de l'Amerique, attended by M. Chev. du Bac, and Le Baron de Charlsontaire, lately arrived from the French West-India settlements, who have petitioned the administration of this country to take their persons and property under their protection, were presented to the King at St. James's, by Lord Grenville

FRANCE.
NATIONAL CONVENTION.
JANUARY 17.

The three defenders of Louis Capet were admitted to the bar. One of them, Deseze, said,

"Citizens, Representatives, the law and the decrees have entrusted to us the sacred function of the defence of Louis. We come, with regret, to present to you the last act of our function. Louis has given to us his express charge to read to you a letter signed with his own hand, of which the following is a copy:

"I owe to my own honor, I owe to my family, not to subscribe to a sentence which declares me guilty of a crime of which I cannot accuse myself. In consequence I appeal to the nation, from the sentence of its representatives; and I commit, by these presents, to the fidelity of my defenders, to make known to the National Convention this appeal, by all the means in their power, and to demand that mention of it be made in the minutes of their sittings.

"Given at Paris, the 16th Jan. 1793.
(Signed) LOUIS."

Deseze then resumed the discourse. He reminded the Assembly that the Decree of Death had only been pronounced by a majority of five voices, while the other part of the Assembly were of opinion that the safety of the country required another decision. He warmly conjured them to examine anew the question of appeal, and to grant to humanity, to the interest of the state, all that justice might not seem imperiously to claim.

Tronchet, another of the defenders of Louis Capet, protested against the Decree, by which the Assembly had declared that the sentence should be passed like its other decrees, by an absolute majority. He demanded the repeal of the Decree, observing, that as the Penal Code had served as the basis of the opinion of those who had pronounced the punishment of death, the Assembly ought, conformably to that code, not to pronounce the punishment except by two-thirds of the voices.

Lamoignon Malesherbes, the third counsel of Louis, begged the Convention to allow him till to-morrow to present some observations on that kind of majority, which to him seemed necessary, before sentence should have been pronounced. He regretted that he could not speak extempore with sufficient facility to enable him to explain his ideas.

The President informed the Counsel that the Convention would take their requests into consideration, and invited them to the honors of the sitting.

On a motion made by Robespierre, the Convention decreed,

I. That the appeal interposed by Louis Capet is null, being contrary to the rights of the people, and to the power of national representation; and that all citizens are forbidden to support this appeal, under pain of being punished as disturbers of public tranquility.

II. That there are no grounds for attending to the remonstrances of the Counsel of Louis, in regard to the nature of the majority which passed sentence upon him.

The discussion of the question, whether it would be proper to suspend the execution of the sentence passed against Louis Capet? was adjourned to next day.

The Convention rose at eleven at night, after a sitting which continued thirty-six hours.

HAGUE, February 5.

This afternoon intelligence was received here, that Ruremond has been taken by the Prussians, and that the French lost a great number of men.

AMSTERDAM, Feb. 7.

On the 2d inst. his royal highness Prince Frederick of Brunswick established his head quarters in the city of Gueldres. The French retire on all sides at the approach of the Prussians, who have already formed a junction with the advanced posts of the Austrian general Count de Clairfait. The army of the latter is said to consist of 45,000 effective men.

The present state of the Russian fleet in the black sea, under the command of Rear Admiral Ribas, who has received orders to sail on a secret expedition, is as follows: Sixteen ships of the line, one of which carries 80 guns; four large frigates; two smaller ones; five armed brigs; a bomb vessel, and several fireships and armed transports. At Nicolai and Cherson, several Russian ships of the line and frigates are constructing.

Domestic Articles.

BALTIMORE, April 9.

Yesterday arrived here, from Marseilles, in France, the ship Harmony, Capt. William Robinson, which place he left on the 15th of February—Capt. Robinson put into Gibraltar, which place he left on the 26th of February—He informs, that on the 7th of February, the harbor master of Marseilles received orders to unship the rudders of the English and Dutch vessels in that port, and accordingly did so—That as soon as the news of war reached Marseilles, they immediately began fitting out privateers—That two privateers sailed in company with the Harmony from Marseilles—That in three days after Capt. Robinson sailed, there would be ready for sea upwards of 18 sail out of that port, from 4 to 24 guns each—That on the 20th of Feb. a French privateer of 14 guns, fell in with six sail of English and Dutch off Cape Paloe; took five, and one brig made her escape to Gibraltar.

From a Correspondent.

Notwithstanding the fascinating power of the words *Liberty* and *Equality* human nature recoils with horror at the late massacre of Louis the XVIth; and the history of the present day must stamp a complexion so sanguinary on the French nation, that time shall not, for centuries, be capable of effacing it. Whilst *America* views with detestation and anxiety, the bloody scenes now acting on the theatre of Europe, let it be her care to avert those evils, by declining all interference in the contention; let her circling arms of peace embrace the whole world, and her doors of hospitality fly open to distressed strangers, of all nations, whatever be the motives which

The Trial of Louis XVI. *Buried amidst all the foreign news contained on this page is the report of the trial of Louis XVI (the bottom of the third column). News was generally always presented in a similar format and the reader just had to search for the materials he was interested in reading.*

As the French Revolution seemed to descend into insanity, Americans did not know what to think or do. Their cries of joy over French attempts to copy the success of the American Revolution became gasps of horror as more and more people were guillotined. The French Revolution increasingly did not seem to be protecting the rights of its citizens, and Americans increasingly did not understand how a people's fight for freedom could go so wrong. Discussions in the newspapers clearly reflected this confusion.

The first group of documents supports the French Revolution and sees it as a good event. The first selection discusses the execution of Louis XVI. The second and third pieces discuss the activities of the French ambassador, Edmond Genet. The next two selections seek to remind Americans how hard it is to win the fight for freedom. The next two documents by Benjamin Franklin Bache attack Americans for being ungrateful for French aid during the American Revolution. The final piece accuses the national government of being opposed to France in the war against Great Britain.

The second group of documents opposes the French Revolution and sees it as an insane event. The first two selections talk about how radical the revolt in France has become. The third piece attacks both the French for interfering with American trade and the Republican party for supporting France. The final piece worries that France will never recover from the series of political upheavals that she has suffered.

Support for the French Revolution

Anonymous: "Reflect If Louis Merits Our Tears of Compassion"

This author wonders why Americans mourn the king of France. He points out that Louis XVI was an enemy to the people of France and deserved his fate. This author goes on to worry that the concern over Louis's fate indicates there is still a strong attachment to the idea of a monarchy in the United States.

National Gazette (Philadelphia), 20 March 1793

The general concern that seems to agitate the citizens of the United States at the accounts of the traitorous and perjured Louis XVIth, the inveterate enemy of the people, having lost his head, is a convincing proof of a strong remaining attachment to royalty in this country. But is it possible that prejudice can so far mislead the sympathy of republicans, who in the time of their own struggle for liberty were perhaps less inclined to pardon crimes of treason than the French, especially in the instances of Major Andre, Carlisle, and Roberts.—Let any man recollect the conduct of Louis Capet, his many heinous sins, his flight after having taken an oath to be faithful to the nation, the impediments he constantly threw in the way of the revolution and the aid he afforded to the enemies of France, and lastly, his treason and reiterated instances of hypocrisy—I say when a man considers these things, let him reflect if Louis merits our tears or compassion. On the other hand let him revolve in mind the fate of those victims sacrificed in the Champs de Mars by royalty and Lafayette; also the fate of those patriots who fell on the 10th of August and the 1200 defenders of liberty maimed and massacred at Frankfort—these, and not the momentary fate of a perjured king, should be causes for exciting the sign of sympathy from the breasts of real republicans.

Anonymous: "Citizen Genet"

This writer reports the public reception for the French ambassador, Edmond Genet. Genet later caused problems for the United States, but he was warmly received when he first arrived in the United States.

National Gazette (Philadelphia), 18 May 1793

On Thursday last, at one o'clock, P.M. arrived in this city, Citizen GENET, Ambassador from the Republic of France, to the United States of America. We are authorized to say that Citizen Genet cannot sufficiently express his gratitude for the kind hospitality of the inhabitants of the several states through which he has passed, since his departure from Charleston, to his arrival in Philadelphia. He has every where observed among the Americans, a grateful attachment to those who, like themselves at a former period, are now struggling in the cause of liberty; and has every where received the most flattering marks of attention. On his way hither, both farmers and merchants readily offered him their flour, and other articles of provision, at a lower price than they would dispose of them to the agents of any other nation. The article of flour only, that has been offered him, amounts to more than six hundred thousand barrels.

The crowds of citizens that flocked from every avenue of this city to meet the republican ambassador of an allied nation, at Gray's ferry, were a proof to him that the Pennsylvanians are not behind their fellow citizens of other states in the spirit of republican patriotism. We have no doubt but the popular character and engaging affability of Citizen Genet, will gain him the esteem of the inhabitants of this city and country; and awaken in them sentiments of gratitude for our generous allies the defenders of the rights of man and real friends to America in the dark days of war and desolation.

Philip Freneau: "This Outcry Against the Minister of France"

In this piece, Philip Freneau defends Genet's efforts to help his country. Freneau criticizes those who have attacked the French ambassador for saying he would appeal to the American people. For Freneau, the people were the government, so Genet was going to the source of power if he appealed directly to them. Others did not agree.

National Gazette (Philadelphia), 21 August 1793

Why all this outcry against the minister of France for saying he would appeal to the people? Is the President a consecrated character that an appeal from him must be considered criminal, or are the people in a state of monarchical degradation, that to talk of consulting them must be considered as great an offence as if we were under a dominion equal to that of the old monarchy of France? What is the legislature of the Union but *THE PEOPLE in Congress assembled;* and is it already an offence to them in case of a conceived wrong by the President? Should opinions of this sort obtain already in our infant government, dreary indeed has become our prospect of liberty.

A Republican: "To the Friends of Liberty"

This author calls on Americans to remember what the fight for freedom is all about and also to remember how hard it is to win. He is writing after the beginning of the Reign of Terror in France and seeks to convince Americans to keep supporting the French in their revolution, even though it seems to be going crazy.

New York Journal and Patriotic Register, 16 October 1793

Be not discouraged at the late misfortunes of our noble and brave allies, nor think that the fate of France depends on Conde, Mentz, Valenclennos, or Lisle[1]; though the combined ruffians should penetrate into the heart of the country, and carry fire and sword wherever they go, yet Liberty will still flourish, and inspire her sons with redoubled vigor and energy. Look back on the scenes we have passed; recollect the thousands of our veterans murdered in the infernal Jersey prison-ship by British assassins; remember the many anxious days and tedious nights numbers of us have spent, far exiled from our native homes, destitute of the comforts, and often of the necessaries of life; call to mind the sufferings of a magnanimous army, without cloathing, food, or money; follow them, by the blood covering the ice and snow, through New-Jersey, Pennsylvania, &c. and forget not the cruelties exercised on your countrymen in sugar-houses and goals in this city during a seven year struggle for Independence. If we call to mind these circumstances of distress, we must rationally suppose, that the French nation will also bear up under their present difficulties, and finally establish their Liberty on a permanent basis.

The accounts we receive from Europe, come generally through the London ministerial papers, where defeats are transformed into victories, and repulses appear like conquests. Be not deceived my countrymen by these artifices; the English are remarkable for bragging and boasting, and will never give a true account of an unfortunate engagement on their side.

Look at the *Royal Gazette* printed in this place during the late war, there you will find pages filled with victories gained over the poor, deluded *rebels;* armies captured by an handful of his *majesty's loyal subjects;* a thousand 'yankies' put to flight by half a dozen royal grenadiers, and swarms of vessels taken by the king's privateers.

Yet for all this, America maintained her ground, and became free and independent in spite of tyrannic power. And shall France fall! the nation who stept forward to save us from impending ruin? When their was no one to espouse our cause (save heaven) she nobly came forward, expended her treasure in defence of the United States, and the blood of her heroes moistened the soil on which we now tread. Must this gallant friend, now be subdued by a banditti of crowned villains, who are plotting the destruction of republicanism through the world? Forbid it gracious providence! rather let every true American arise, enlist under the banners of France, &, with her, live *free, or die.* If liberty is extinguished in France, America falls next.

Tyrants know no bounds, and are not to be circumscribed by reason. The moment the French are conquered, the armies of despotism will be wasted across the atlantic to complete their diabolical plan. Excuses will not be wanting, while there is a disposition to excite animosities. We have foes within; and if there are enemies without, who can tell how soon our dear bought liberties may be sacrificed at the altar of tyranny.

American Citizens be watchful! this is an important time, your all is at stake, you are surrounded by adversaries in different shapes; some approach you under the mask of friendship, and would fain palm themselves upon the credulous, as good whigs and supporters of government, while their former actions and present behaviour fully testify that they are inveterate tories. Others talk much of federalism and obedience to the laws, when it is well known they side with the champions of slavery, and are continually villifying our most respectable republican characters.

Freemen of the United States! guard with a jealous eye the sacred temple of liberty; transmit the gem unimpaired to your children, and let it be handed down to the latest posterity.

Look upon the French, as your best friends, nor suffer the charge of ingratitude to stain the American character; remember they fought and bled for that freedom you now possess, and that without their assistance, most probably we had never attained it. Teach your infants to love that brave nation, and impress on their tender minds the importance of vigilance and perseverance in the cause of liberty.

Let us not be shackled with the fopperies of a debauched profligate nation, formerly our foes, nor imitate their vices by following their fashionable manners. Republicans should be more independent than to be led away by the gewgaws of a bankrupt people; and their customs ought to partake more of simplicity and plainness.

Anonymous: "The French Would Maintain Their Republic"

This author emphasizes that the French Revolution is on track and that France is quiet again. The reason for this is that the rights of man are eternal and must win in the end, no matter what problems occur along the way.

Kentucky Gazette (Lexington), 7 April 1795

In France, all is quiet—the nation becomes more moderate, as its enemies are reduced in power. The Marquis La Fayette, we are happy to hear, has made his escape from his long confinement. It is said he intends coming to America. We always predicted that the French would maintain their Republic; and they have maintained it. We always predicted that the fundamental principles of equality would be preserved. They vary their measure with the occasion which presents—but occasion is fugitive—whereas the Rights of man are eternal.

Benjamin Franklin Bache: "Generous, Grateful and Honourable People"

Benjamin Franklin Bache was a strong supporter of France and the French Revolution. His love for France had begun during his childhood when he accompanied his grandfather, Benjamin Franklin, to Europe. He studied in France and Geneva from 1778 to 1785. As a newspaper editor, he pushed for the United States to forget about Great Britain and to ally it-self closely with France. In this piece, he attacks Americans for their ingrat-itude for refusing to help the French when asked to do so. France had helped the United States when it was called for, and Bache believes that Americans can do no less now. The debate over whether to help the French against Great Britain was a major political issue during the 1790s.

General Advertiser (Philadelphia), 13 June 1794

What a generous, grateful and honourable people are the Americans! How nobly have they rewarded the French nation for their services, and how zealous have they discovered themselves in the cause of liberty! A conduct so worthy as they have manifested towards an ally that has fought, and is at this moment fighting their battles, proves how well they deserve freedom, and how much they are entitled to the affection of a generous, magnanimous and gallant nation! During the American struggle we wanted money and France generously gave it; during her struggle, she, thro' her minister requested only a reimbursement of *a part of the sum lent,* and WE have REFUSED it. Yes, that *virtuous* and *patriotic* body, the SEN-ATE OF THE UNITED STATES, have REJECTED a bill, passed in the House of Representatives by a large majority, for granting the minister the sum requested. What have not the people of the United States to expect from the virtue and patriotism of *such* a Senate! Liberty must flourish under its auspices, and the rights of man may slumber in security under such guardianship. Tyrants may well tremble when they see such union and energy in republicans; they will feel their thrones a void when they perceive the fraternity between the sister republics of America and France, when they behold the exertions that freemen make to rescue their brethren from the iron hand of despotism. Let *the Senate of the United States* be held up as an example to the world and to future ages of national gratitude and justice, of love for liberty, and of vigour in defence of op-pressed humanity!!

A Correspondent: "The Ingratitude of Republics"

This author also attacks Americans for their ingratitude. He uses letters from General Washington to point out the problem of the ingratitude of re-publics and then accuses President Washington of leading Americans not to help France as they had helped us. For this author, there is no question about whether the United States should aid France or not.

Aurora (Philadelphia), 22 December 1796

In a letter which Washington wrote to General Putnam he complains of the ingratitude of Republics, and well he might, for he has given as striking an example of ingratitude as ever was exhibited. Without the aid of France it is confessed we should not have established our independence. It was France that supplied us with arms and ammunition. It was France that lent us money, aided us with troops, and sent a fleet upon our coast to capture Cornwallis. Without the assistance of France, Washington would have made a wretched figure, and yet when our blood is scarcely cool'd from the revolution, Washington seems to pant for a war with France. Is not this the basest ingratitude? How is he to expect gratitude from for the services which he rendered, when he is unwilling that such a sentiment should be spent upon France? He has said, that nations are governed by their interest, and so are individuals of whom nations can be and only are composed, and if France was governed by her interest in assisting us, pray what motive actuated him, interest or ambition? A nation is the aggregate of individuals, and if there is no such thing as national disinterestedness, we must not expect to meet with disinterestedness in an individual, not even in Washington.

Anonymous: "Ill Offices toward France"

This author accuses the government of being opposed to the French ever since the beginning of the war with Great Britain. This piece appeared in the midst of the Quasi-War with France (see Chapter 23).

Aurora (Philadelphia), 6 March 1798

From the beginning of the present war down to this time, the conduct of our executive has been a series of ill offices toward France. It was not sufficient to reject her advances for a closer union. The declining of such a scheme was proper, perhaps or otherwise. But for the bare proposal, France and her ambassadors have been loaded with as many reproachful paragraphs, essays and letters as would fill Johnson's folio dictionary. To these, the virulent letter from Pickering to Charles Pinckney and the inflammatory correspondence of Pinckney himself, printed by Congress last summer, we may, in a great measure, ascribe the marked contempt, in which the American envoys have been held at Paris.

OPPOSITION TO THE FRENCH REVOLUTION

Anonymous: "This Scene of Infernal Assassination"

This author notes the execution of Louis XVI. He calls it an assassination, indicating how horrified he is over the event. Most Americans reacted the same way.

Kentucky Gazette (Lexington), 27 April 1793

Conformably to the arrangements made by the Executive Council, Louis was yesterday put to death at the Place de la Revolution, heretofore Place de Louis XV. . . .

The city remained quiet, in gloomy silence, through the whole of the day; in the morning the shops were shut, and no woman allowed to be in the streets till the procession had returned with the body of Louis.

This scene of infernal assassination, which a base and cowardly faction have now degraded human nature by executing calls for a marked execration which it is not in the power of language to convey. Human punishment we would be even totally inadequate to such dire atrocities. Almighty vengeance must be the portion of those who have thus, step by step, arrived at this damnable crisis. In a word, considering that he was pronounced inviolable by the constitution, and that no punishment could be inflicted upon him, but forfeiture of his crown; considering that he was not tried according the determined forms of the criminal code; considering that a part of the adduced evidence, such as it was, was withheld; considering that the offices of judge and jury cannot be united; and that the appeal to the people, whose sovereignty was pronounced the sole authority by which monarchy had been abolished, and the monarch brought to judgment, was set aside; we cannot but conclusively consider that Louis XVI has dyed a martyr.

Anonymous, "The Principles of the Jacobins"

This author points out that the French Revolution has taken a radical turn that is no longer acceptable. They have replaced one evil with another one. Following the Reign of Terror, most Americans agreed with this assessment.

Connecticut Journal (New Haven), 27 May 1795

All men admired the principles of the first Revolutionaries. They were the ornament of the age; and the glory of France. But the principles of the Jacobins, who drove all moderation, and most of the wisdom of France, into exile or retirement, have not only prostrated despotism but have replaced it, with the seeds of faction which will continue to distract the councils and waste the blood of the best citizens of France, for a long time to come. And this party spirit or rather *party rage,* which originated in trifling differences of opinion, seems to suffer no abatement, it rather increases—and it will, on every fair occasion break out with violence and destruction.

William Cobbett: "Their Last Nefarious Measures"

In this piece, Federalist editor William Cobbett attacks the French for their efforts against American commerce. He also attacks his editorial opponent, Benjamin Franklin Bache. Combining these two attacks together shows how impossible it was for these editors to separate news and politics. For Cobbett and the rest of the partisan editors of the 1790s, attacking one's editorial opponent was to undermine your political opponents and thus to boost your own party and its stance on the issues.

Porcupine's Gazette (Philadelphia), 8 March 1798

In this morning's *Aurora*, Young Lightening-Rod has justified the conduct of his friends even in their last nefarious measures against the commerce of this country. I am willing to allow, that he may have done no more than *his* duty; but, when he goes on to assert, that these last rapacious measures will have a *good* effect towards this country, I look upon the fellow as a sort of bedlamite, or I must insist that he looks upon himself as talking to nobody but fools and idiots.

The principal object, is, to impress on the minds of his readers, that, the want of the British manufactures may be supplied by others, made at home, or bought in other European countries; and that, therefore, nothing will suffer but the trade of Britain.

BACHE is not fool enough to believe this; for, he well knows, that we cannot fabricate here, and that we can get what we want no where else. He knows, that all the countries of Europe (*France not excepted*), are at this moment dependent on the manufactories of Great Britain. He knows, that the French army itself is clothed in British cloth, and that those of them, who have any shirts wear Irish linen. The British are at war with those who were their greatest customers, before that war, yet, it is well known, that their trade and manufactories have been on the increase from the beginning of the war to the present day.

No; Britain will not export a bale of goods the less for this plundering decree. America, and every other country, that now wants, will want, and will have those goods. The French will get more of them *for nothing* than they did before; the Americans will pay much dearer for what they get; and, unless some vigorous measures are taken to defend the American commerce, it will be carried on by the armed merchantmen of Great Britain. The vessels will be sold by dozens out of the American ports, or they will lie there and rot; and the sailors will, in less than six months, be three fourths of them on board of British vessels.

If the French had been hired by PITT, they could not have taken a step more consonant to the interests of his country. When Britain is at war, it is her interest, that all actual vessels, with enemies property, should be lawful prizes. See how tenacious she has ever remained on the head of enemies property on board of neutral vessels; and the further the right of seizure is extended, the better she will like it. She being always (and particularly at this moment) able to give ample protection to her own merchantmen, must certainly rejoice at any measure of the enemy that compels the neutral powers to make use of those merchantmen instead of their own; because, it not only enriches herself, but prevents commercial neutral powers from getting the start of her while she is at war. The peculiar situation and genius of Great Britain, is, as Voltaire has well observed, to carry commerce in one hand and the sword in the other; and this she was never so well able to do as at this time.

The French are aware of this; they know it well; but they stand in need of *an intermediate supply,* and any excuse serves to make a sweep on the commerce of nations, whom they are pretty sure will resent nothing that they do.

Charles Snowden: "The Most Violent Commotions in France"

This New York editor points out how France continues to be wracked by revolution and suffering. He cannot understand how anyone can call the problems in France freedom.

New York Daily Advertiser, 8 December 1798

There are letters in town to French Gentlemen of distinction, that induce us to announce with certainty, the approach of the most violent commotions in France during the ensuing year—unhappy country! destined to eternal convulsions and sufferings—One revolution takes place after another—but it is to you only a change of masters, not of condition. It is still slavery, that you are doomed to—Yet there are Americans to be found, who admire and envy French *freedom*—Is this ignorance, or the basest hypocrisy?

QUESTIONS

1. Several documents discuss the execution of Louis XVI. Why was that such a pivotal event? Why were so many Americans upset about it? What did it represent to most people?

2. Several authors remind Americans of the similarities between the American and French revolutions. Why is that becoming more difficult for many Americans to see?
3. Why does Benjamin Franklin Bache accuse Americans of ingratitude? Is he correct in his accusations?
4. Why were Americans, such as William Cobbett and Charles Snowden, increasingly concerned over the direction in which the French Revolution was going? Were they worried that something similar might happen in the United States?

NOTE

1. These all refer to places in France where revolutionary conflicts (battles, riots, etc.) had taken place.

CHAPTER 21

American Neutrality, 1793

The European war that broke out in 1793 created many problems for Americans, as debates occurred over whether to support France or Great Britain. Many people, including Thomas Jefferson, James Madison, and most Republicans, believed that the United States should support France because of the similarities between the American and French revolutions and because of commitments made under the alliance signed in 1778. Other Americans, led by Alexander Hamilton and the Federalists, believed that Americans should support the British because the French Revolution had gone too far, as shown by the Reign of Terror, and because Americans had much more in common with the former mother country than with the new European republic.

President George Washington hesitated over what to do. He had been happy over the early success of the revolution in France, but reacted with horror when the Reign of Terror began. He came to agree with Hamilton that the United States had more in common with Great Britain. But, ultimately, he believed the United States could not afford to get involved in the war at all. He thought that the United States was too young as a nation to get involved in an international war. He discussed the issue with his Cabinet in detail. Then, on April 22, 1793, Washington declared the United States neutral in the war between Great Britain and France.

The Republicans criticized Washington's action, stating that he had overstepped his authority. Alexander Hamilton, in an effort to defend Washington's action, wrote a series of seven essays under the pseudonym Pacificus. They appeared in the *Gazette of the United States* from June 29 to July 27, 1793.

Thomas Jefferson worried that Americans would accept Hamilton's emphasis on broad executive powers without question. He urged James Madison to respond to Pacificus: "Nobody answers him, and his doctrine will therefore be taken for confessed. For god's sake, my dear Sir, take up your pen, select the most striking heresies, and cut him to pieces in the face of the public. There is nobody else who can and will enter the lists with him."[1]

James Madison finally agreed and responded with his own series of essays. Under the pseudonym of Helvidius, he wrote five essays that appeared in the *Gazette of the United States* from August 24 to September 18, 1793. In these pieces, Madison argued that Congress had oversight over foreign relations rather than the president.

The documents included are the first essays in each series. In them, Hamilton and Madison argue and debate over the Constitutional issues regarding who should have power and control over foreign affairs. These essays reflect a debate that continues today between Congress and the president, and both sides quote from these essays to support their side of the debate.

Power to the Executive

Pacificus: "Treaties Are the Law of the Land"

In the first of the Pacificus essays, Alexander Hamilton discusses the role of the president in foreign policy. He believes that diplomacy is solely an executive function and that Congress cannot be involved unless called to do so by the president.

Gazette of the United States (Philadelphia), 29 June 1793

As attempts are making very dangerous to the peace, and, it is to be feared, not very friendly to the Constitution, of the United States—it becomes the duty of those who wish well to both, to endeavor to prevent their success.

The objections of which have been raised against the proclamation of neutrality, lately issued by the President, have been urged in a spirit of acrimony and invective, which demonstrates that more was in view than merely a free discussion of an important public measure. They exhibit evident indications of a design to weaken the confidence of the people in the author of the measure, in order to remove or lessen the powerful obstacle to the success of an opposition to the government, which, however it may change its form according to circumstances, seems still to be persisted in with more untiring industry.

This reflection adds to the motives connected with the measure itself, to recommend endeavors by proper explanations, to place it in a just light.

Such explanations, at least, cannot but be satisfactory to those who may not themselves have leisure or opportunity for pursuing an investigation of the subject, and who may wish to perceive that the policy of the government is not inconsistent with its obligations or its honor.

The objections in question fall under four heads:

1. That the proclamation was without authority.
2. That it was contrary to our treaties with France.
3. That it was contrary to the gratitude which is due from this to that country, for the succors afforded to us in our own revolution.
4. That it was out of time and unnecessary.

In order to judge of the solidity of the first of these objections, it is necessary to examine what is the nature and design of a proclamation of neutrality.

The true nature and design of such an act is—to *make known* to the powers at war, and to the citizens of the country whose government does the act, that such country is in the condition of a nation at peace with the belligerent parties, and under no obligations of treaty to become an *associate in the war* with either, and that this being its situation, its intention is to observe a corresponding conduct by performing towards each the duties of neutrality and as a consequence of this state of things, to give warning to all within its jurisdiction to abstain from acts that shall contravene those duties, under the penalties which the laws of the land (of which the law of nations is a part) annexes to acts of contravention.

This, and no more, is conceived to be the true import of a proclamation of neutrality.

It does not imply that the nation which makes the declaration will forbear to perform to either of the warring Powers any stipulations in treaties which can be executed without become a *party* in the war. It therefore does not imply in our case that the United States will not make those distinctions between the present belligerent Powers which are stipulated in the 7th and 22nd articles of our treaty with France, because they are not incompatible with the state of neutrality and will in no shape render the United States an *associate or party* in the war. This must be evident when it is considered, that even to furnish *determinate* succours of a certain number of ships or troops, to a power at war, in consequence of *antecedent treaties having no particular reference to the existing quarrel,* is not inconsistent with neutrality; a position equally well established by the doctrines of writers and the practice of nations.

But no special aids, succours, or favors, having relation to war, not positively and precisely stipulated by some treaty of the above description, can be afforded to either party without a breach of neutrality.

In stating that the proclamation of neutrality does not imply the non-performance of any stipulations of treaties, which are not of a nature to make the nation an associate in the war, it is conceded, that an execution of the clause of guarantee, contained in the eleventh article of our treaty of alliance with France would be contrary to the sense and spirit of the proclamation; because it would engage us with our whole force as an associate, or auxiliary in the war; it would be much more than the case of a definite limited succour, previously ascertained.

It follows, that the proclamation is virtually a manifestation of the sense of government, that the United States are, *under the circumstances of the case, not bound* to execute the clause of guarantee.

If this be a just view of the force and import of the proclamation, it will remain to see, whether the President in issuing it acted within his proper sphere, or stepped beyond the bounds of his constitutional authority and duty.

It will not be disputed that the management of the affairs of this country with foreign nations, is confided to the Government of the United States.

It can as little be disputed, that a proclamation of neutrality, when a nation is at liberty to decline or avoid a war in which other nations are engaged, and means so to do, is a *usual* and a *proper* measure. *Its main object and effect are to prevent the nation being immediately responsible for acts done by its citizens, without the privity or connivance of the government, in contravention of the principles of neutrality.*

An object this of the greatest moment to a country, whose true interest lies in the preservation of peace.

The inquiry then is, What department of the government of the United States is the proper one to make a declaration of neutrality in the cases in which the engagements of the nation permit, and its interests require such a declaration.

A correct and well informed mind will discern at once, that it can belong neither to the legislative, nor judicial department, and of course must belong to the executive.

The legislative department is not the *organ* of intercourse between the United States and foreign nations. It is charged neither with *making*, nor *interpreting* treaties. It is therefore not naturally that member of the government, which is to pronounce the existing condition of the nation, with regard to foreign powers, or to admonish the citizens of their obligations and duties as founded upon that condition of things; still less is it charged with enforcing the execution and observance of those obligations and those duties.

It is equally obvious, that the act in question is foreign to the judiciary department. The province of that department is to decide the litigation in particular cases. It is indeed charged with the interpretations of treaties, but it exercises this function only where contending parties bring before it a specific controversy. It has no concern with pronouncing upon the external political relations of treaties between government and government. This position is too plain to need being insisted upon.

It must, then, of necessity belong to the executive department to exercise the function in question, when a proper case for it occurs.

It appears to be connected with that department in various capacities:— As the *organ* of intercourse between the nation and foreign nations—as the *interpreter* of the national treaties, in those cases in which the judiciary is not competent—that is, in the cases between government and government—as that *power* which is charged with the execution of the laws, of which treaties form a part—as that which is charged with the command and disposition of the public force.

This view of the subject is so natural and obvious, so analogous to general theory and practice, that no doubt can be entertained of its justness, unless to be deduced from particular provisions of the Constitution of the United States.

Let us see, then, if cause for such doubt is to be found there.

The second article of the Constitution of the United States, section first, establishes this general proposition, that "the EXECUTIVE POWER shall be vested in a President of the United States of America."

The same article, in a succeeding section, proceeds to delineate particular cases of executive power. It declares, among other things, that the President shall be commander—in-chief of the army and navy of the United States, and of the militia of the several States, when called into the actual service of the United States; that he shall have power, by and with the advice and consent of the Senate, to make treaties; that it shall be his duty to receive ambassadors and other public ministers, *and to take care that the laws be faithfully executed.*

It would not consist with the rules of sound construction, to consider this enumeration of particular authorities as derogating form the more comprehensive grant in the general clause, further than as it may be coupled with express restrictions or limitations; as in regard to the co-operation of the Senate in the appointment of officers and the making of treaties; which are plainly qualifications of the general executive powers of appointing officers and making treaties. The difficulty of a complete enumeration of all the cases of executive authority would naturally dictate the use of general terms, and would render it improbable that a specification of certain particulars was designed as a substitue for those terms, when antecedently used. The different mode of expression employed in the Constitution, in regard to the two powers, the legislative and the executive, serves to confirm this interference. In the article which gives the legislative powers of the government, the expressions are: "All legislative powers herein granted shall be vested in a Congress of the United States." In that which grants the executive power, the expressions are: "*The executive power* shall be vested in a President of the United States."

The enumeration ought rather therefore to be considered as intended merely to specify the principal articles implied in the definition of executive power; leaving the rest to flow from the general grant of that power, interpreted in conformity with other parts of the Constitution, and with the principles of free government.

The general doctrine of our Constitution, then, is, that the *executive power* of the nation is vested in the President; subject only to the *exceptions* and *qualifications* which are expressed in the instrument.

Two of these have been already noticed: the participation of the Senate in the appointment of officers, and in the making of treaties. A third remains to be mentioned: the right of the Legislature "to declare war, and grant letters of marque and reprisal."

With these exceptions, the *executive power* of the United States is completely lodged in the President. This mode of construing the Constitution has indeed been recognized by Congress in formal acts, upon full consideration and debate; of which the power of removal from office is an important instance. It will follow, that if a proclamation of neutrality is merely an executive act, as, it is believed, has been shown, the step which has been taken by the President is liable to no just exception on the score of authority.

It may be observed, that this inference would be just, if the power of declaring war had not been vested in the Legislature; but that this power naturally includes the right of judging, whether the nation is under obligations to make war or not.

The answer to this is, that however true it may be that the right of the legislature to declare war, includes the right of judging whether the nation be under obligations to make war or not, it will not follow, that the executive is in any case excluded from a similar right of judgment, in the execution of its own functions.

If the legislature have a right to make war on the one hand, it is on the other, the duty of the executive to preserve peace till war is declared; and in fulfilling that duty, it must necessarily possess a right of judging what is the nature of the obligations which the treaties of the country impose on the government; and when in pursuance of this right it has concluded, that there is nothing in them inconsistent with a state of neutrality, it becomes both its province and its duty to enforce the laws incident to that state of the nation. The executive is charged with the execution of all laws, the law of nations as well as the municipal law which recognizes and adopts those laws. It is consequently bound, by faithfully executing the laws of neutrality, when that is the state of the nation, to avoid giving a cause of war to foreign powers.

This is the direct and proper end of the proclamation of neutrality—It declares to the United States their situation with regard to the powers at war, and makes known to the community, that the laws incident to that situation will be enforced. In doing this, it conforms to an established usage of nations, the operation of which, as before remarked, is to obviate a responsibility on the part of the whole society, for secret and unknown violations of the rights of any of the warring parties by its citizens.

Those who object to the proclamation will readily admit, that it is the right and duty of the executive to judge of, or to interpret those articles of our treaties which give to France particular privileges, in order to the enforcement of those privileges: But the necessary consequence of this is, that the executive must judge what are the proper bounds of those privileges— what rights are given to other nations by our treaties with them—what rights the law of nature and nations gives and our treaties permit, in respect to those nations with whom we have no treaties; in fine, what are the reciprocal rights and obligations of the United States, and of all and each of the powers at war.

The right of the executive to receive ambassadors and other public ministers, may serve to illustrate the relative duties of the executive and legislative departments. This right includes that of judging, in the case of a revolution of government in a foreign country, whether the new rulers are competent organs of the national will, and ought to be recognized or not; and where a treaty antecedently exists between the United States and such nation, that right involves the power of giving operation, or not, in such treaty. For until the new government is *acknowledged,* the treaties between the nations, as far at least as regards *public* rights, are of course suspended.

This power of determining virtually in the case supposed upon the operation of national treaties, as a consequence of the power to receive ambassadors and other public ministers, is an important instance of the right of the executive to decide the obligations of the nation with regard to foreign nations. To apply it to the case of France, if there had been a treaty of alliance *offensive* and defensive between the United States and that country, the unqualified acknowledgment of the new government would have put the United States in a condition to become an associate in the war in which France was engaged—and would have laid the legislature under an obligation if required, and there was otherwise no valid excuse, of exercising its power of declaring war.

This serves as an example of the right of the executive, in certain cases, to determine the condition of the nation, though it may consequently affect the proper or improper exercise of the power of the legislature to declare war. The executive indeed cannot controul the exercise of that power further than by it exercise of its general right of objecting to all acts of the legislature; liable to be overruled by two thirds of both hours of Congress. The legislature is free to perform its own duties according to its own sense of them; though the executive in the exercise of its constitutional powers, may establish an antecedent state of things, which ought to weigh in the legislative decisions.

From the division of the executive power, there results, in reference to it, a *concurrent* authority in the distributed cases.

Hence in the case stated, though treaties can only be made by the President and Senate, their activity may be continued or suspended by the President alone.

No objection has been made to the President's having acknowledged the Republic of France, by the reception of its minister, without having consulted the Senate; though that body is connected with him in the making of treaties, and though the consequence of his act of reception is to give operation to the treaties heretofore made with that country. But he is censured for having declared the United States to be in a state of peace and neutrality with regard to the powers at war; because the right of *changing* that state and *declaring war* belongs to the legislature.

It deserves to be remarked, that as the participation of the Senate in the making of treaties, and the power of the legislature to declare war, are exceptions out of the general "executive power" vested in the President, they are to be construed strictly, and ought to be extended no further than is essential to their execution.

While therefore the legislature can alone declare war, can alone actually transfer the nation from a state of peace to a state of war—it belongs to the "executive power" to do whatever else the law of nations, co-operating with the treaties of the country, enjoin in the intercourse of the United States with foreign Powers.

In this distribution of powers, the wisdom of our constitution is manifested. It is the province and duty of the executive to preserve to the nation the blessings of peace. The legislature alone can interrupt those blessings, by placing the nation in a state of war.

But though it has been thought advisable to vindicate the authority of the executive on this broad and comprehensive ground, it was not absolutely necessary to do so. That clause of the constitution which makes it his duty to "take care that the laws be faithfully executed," might alone have been relied upon, and this simple process of argument pursued:

The President is the constitutional EXECUTOR of the laws. Our treaties, and the laws of nations form a part of the law of the land. He who is to execute the laws must first judge for himself of their meaning. In order to the observance of that conduct which the laws of nations, combined with our treaties, precribed to this country, in reference to the present war in Europe, it was necessary for the President to judge for himself, whether there was any thing in our treaties incompatible with an adherence to neutrality. Having judged that there was not, he had a right, and if in his opinion the interests of the nation required it, it was his duty as executor of the laws, to proclaim the neutrality of the nation, to exhort all persons to observe it, and to warn them of the penalties which would attend its non-observance.

The proclamation has been represented as enacting some new law. This is a view of it entirely erroneous. It only proclaims a *fact* with regard to the *existing state* of the nation informs the citizens of what the laws previously established require of them in that state, and warns them that these laws will be put in execution against the infractors of them.

POWER TO THE LEGISLATURE

Helvidius: "The Power to Make Treaties"

In the first of his Helvidius essays, James Madison responds to Hamilton's statement that only the president can engage in foreign policy. He reminds his readers that the Constitution provides for shared powers between the president and the Congress.

Gazette of the United States (Philadelphia), 24 and 28 August 1793

Several pieces with the signature of Pacificus were lately published, which have been read with singular pleasure and applause, by the foreigners and degenerate citizens among us, who hate our republican government, and the French revolution; whilst the publication seems to have been too little regarded, or too much despised by the steady friends to both.

Had the doctrines inculcated by the writer, with the natural consequences from them, been nakedly presented to the public, this treatment might have been proper. Their true character would then have struck every eye, and been rejected by the feelings of every heart. But they offer themselves to the reader in the dress of an elaborate dissertation; they are mingled with a few truths that may serve them as a passport to credulity; and they are introduced with professions of anxiety for the preservation of peace, for the welfare of the government, and for the respect due to the present head of the executive, that may prove a snare to patriotism.

In these disguises they have appeared to claim the attention I propose to bestow on them; with a view to shew, from the publication itself, that under colour of vindicating an important public act, of a chief magistrate, who enjoys the confidence and love of his country, principles are advanced which strike at the vitals of its constitution, as well as at its honor and true interest.

As it is not improbable that attempts may be made to apply insinuations which are seldom spared when particular purposes are to be answered, to the author of the ensuing observations, it may not be improper to premise, that he is a friend to the constitution, that he wishes for the preservation of peace, and that the present chief magistrate has not a fellow-citizen, who is penetrated with deeper respect for his merits, or feels a purer solicitude for his glory.

This declaration is made with no view of courting a more favourable ear to what may be said than it deserves. The sole purpose of it is, to obviate imputations which might weaken the impressions of truth; and which are the more likely to be resorted to, in proportion as solid and fair arguments may be wanting.

The substance of the first piece, sifted from its inconsistencies and its vague expressions, may be thrown into the following propositions:

That the powers of declaring war and making treaties are, in their nature, executive powers:

That being particularly vested by the constitution in other departments, they are to be considered as exceptions out of the general grant to the executive department:

That being, as exceptions, to be construed strictly, the powers not strictly within them, remain with the executive:

That the executive consequently, as the organ of intercourse with foreign nations, and the interpreter and executor of treaties, and the law of nations, is authorized, to expound all articles of treaties, those involving questions of war and peace, as well as others;—to judge of the obligations of the United States to make war or not, under any casus federis[2] or eventual operation of the contract, relating to war—and to pronounce the state of things resulting from the obligations of the United States, as understood by the executive:

That in particular the executive had authority to judge whether in the case of the mutual guaranty between the United States and France, the former were bound by it to engage in the war:

That the executive has, in pursuance of that authority, decided that the United States are not bound:—And,

That its proclamation of the 22nd of April last, is to be taken as the effect and expression of that decision.

The basis of the reasoning is, we perceive, the extraordinary doctrine, that the powers of making war and treaties, are in their nature executive;

and therefore comprehended in the general grant of executive power, where not specially and strictly excepted out of the grant.

Let us examine this doctrine: and that we may avoid the possibility of mistating the writer, it shall be laid down in his own words; a precaution the more necessary, as scarce any thing else could outweigh the improbability, that so extravagant a tenet should be hazarded, at so early a day, in the face of the public.

His words are—"Two of these[3] have been already noticed—the participation of the senate in the *appointment of officers,* and the *making of treaties.* A *third* remains to be mentioned—the right of the legislature to *declare war, and grant letters of marque and reprisal.*"

Again—"It deserves to be remarked, that as the participation of the Senate in the *making treaties,* and the power of the legislature to *declare war,* are *exceptions* out of the general *executive power,* vested in the President, they are to be construed *strictly,* and ought to be extended no farther than is *essential* to their execution."

If there be any countenance to these positions, it must be found either, 1st, in the writers, of authority, on public law; or 2d, in the quality and operation of the powers to make war and treaties; or 3d, in the constitution of the United States.

It would be of little use to enter far into the first source of information, not only because our own reason and our own constitution, are the best guides; but because a just analysis and discrimination of the powers of government, according to their executive, legislative and judiciary qualities are not to be expected in the works of the most received jurists, who wrote before a critical attention was paid to those objects, and with their eyes too much on monarchical governments, where all powers are confounded in the sovereignty of the prince. It will be found however, I believe, that all of them, particularly Wolsius, Burlemaqui, and Vattel, speak of the powers to declare war, to conclude peace, and to form alliances, as among the highest acts of the sovereignty; of which the legislative power must at least be an integral and preeminent part.

Writers, such as Locke and Montesquieu, who have discussed more particularly the principles of liberty and the structure of government, lie under the same disadvantage, of having written before these subjects were illuminated by the events and discussions which distinguish a very recent period. Both of them too are evidently warped by a regard to the particular government of England, to which one of them owed allegiance;[*] and the other professed an admiration bordering on idolatry. Montesquieu, however, has

---

[*] The chapter on prerogative shows how much the reason of the philosopher was clouded by the royalism of the Englishman.

rather distinguished himself by enforcing the reasons and the importance of avoiding a confusion of the several powers of government, than by enumerating and defining the powers which belong to each particular class. And Locke, notwithstanding the early date of his work on civil government, and the example of his own government before his eyes, admits that the particular powers in question, which, after some of the writers on public law he calls *federative*, are really *distinct* from the *executive*, though almost always united with it, and *hardly to be separated into distinct hands*. Had he not lived under a monarchy, in which these powers were united; or had he written by the lamp which truth now presents to lawgivers, the last observation would probably never have dropt from his pen. But let us quit a field of research which is more likely to perplex than to decide, and bring the question to other tests of which it will be more easy to judge.

2. If we consult for a moment, the nature and operation of the two powers to declare war and make treaties, it will be impossible not to see that they can never fall within a proper definition of executive powers. The natural province of the executive magistrate is to execute laws, as that of the legislature is to make laws. All his acts therefore, properly executive, must pre-suppose the existence of the laws to be executed. A treaty is not an execution of laws: it does not presuppose the existence of laws. It is, on the contrary, to have itself the force of a *law*, and to be carried into *execution*, like all *other laws*, by the *executive magistrate*. To say then that the power of making treaties which are confessedly laws, belongs naturally to the department which is to execute laws, is to say, that the executive department naturally includes a legislative power. In theory, this is an absurdity—in practice a tyranny.

The power to declare war is subject to similar reasoning. A declaration that there shall be war, is not an execution of laws: it does not suppose pre-existing laws to be executed: it is not in any respect, an act merely executive. It is, on the contrary, one of the most deliberative acts that can be performed; and when performed, has the effect of *repealing* all the *laws* operating in a state of peace, so far as they are inconsistent with a state of war; and of *enacting* as a *rule for the executive*, a *new code* adapted to the relation between the society and its foreign enemy. In like manner, a conclusion of peace *annuls* all the *laws* peculiar to a state of war, and *revives* the general *laws* incident to a state of peace.

These remarks will be strengthened by adding that treaties, particularly treaties of peace, have sometimes the effect of changing not only the external laws of the society, but operate also on the internal code, which is purely municipal, and to which the legislative authority of the country is of itself competent and complete.

From this view of the subject it must be evident, that although the executive may be a convenient organ of preliminary communications with foreign governments, on the subjects of treaty or war; and the proper agent for carrying into execution the final determinations of the competent authority; yet it can have no pretensions, from the nature of the powers in question compared with the nature of the executive trust, to that essential agency which gives validity to such determinations.

It must be further evident that, if these powers be not in their nature purely legislative, they partake so much more of that, than of any other quality, that under a constitution leaving them to result to their most natural department, the legislature would be without a rival in its claim.

Another important inference to be noted is, that the powers of making war and treaty being substantially of a legislative, not an executive nature, the rule of interpreting exceptions strictly, must narrow instead of enlarging executive pretensions on those subjects.

3. It remains to be enquired, whether there be any thing in the constitution itself which shows that the powers of making war and peace are considered as of an executive nature, and as comprehended within a general grant of executive power.

It will not be pretended, that this appears from any *direct* position to be found in the instrument.

If it were *deducible* from any particular expressions it may be presumed that the publication would have saved us the trouble of the research.

Does the doctrine then result from the actual distribution of powers among the several branches of the government? Or from any fair analogy between the powers of war and treaty and the enumerated powers vested in the executive alone?

Let us examine.

In the general distribution of powers, we find that of declaring war expressly vested in the Congress, where every other legislative power is declared to be vested, and without any other qualification than what is common to every other legislative act. The constitutional idea of this power would seem then clearly to be, that it is of a legislative and not an executive nature.

This conclusion becomes irresistible, when it is recollected, that the constitution cannot be supposed to have placed either any power legislative in its nature, entirely among executive powers, or any power executive in its nature, entirely among legislative powers, without charging the constitution, with that kind of intermixture and consolidation of different powers, which would violate a fundamental principle in the organization of free governments. If it were not unnecessary to enlarge on this topic here, it could be shewn, that the constitution was originally vindicated, and has been constantly expounded, with a disavowal of any such intermixture.

The power of treaties is vested jointly in the President and in the Senate, which is a branch of the legislature. From this arrangement merely, there can be no inference that would necessarily exclude the power from the executive class: since the senate is joined with the President in another power, that of appointing to offices, which as far as relate to executive offices at least, is considered as of an executive nature. Yet on the other hand, there are sufficient indications that the power of treaties is regarded by the constitution as materially different from mere executive power, and as having more affinity to the legislative than to the executive character.

One circumstance indicating this, is the constitutional regulation under which the senate give their consent in the case of treaties. In all other cases the consent of the body is expressed by a majority of voices. In this particular case, a concurrence of two-thirds at least is made necessary, as a substitute or compensation for the other branch of the legislature, which on certain occasions, could not be conveniently a party to the transaction.

But the conclusive circumstance is, that treaties when formed according to the constitutional mode, are confessedly to have the force and operation of *laws,* and are to be a rule for the courts in controversies between man and man, as much as any *other laws.* They are even emphatically declared by the constitution to be "the supreme law of the land."

So far the argument from the constitution is precisely in opposition to the doctrine. As little will be gained in its favour from a comparison of the two powers, with those particularly vested in the President alone.

As there are but few it will be most satisfactory to review them one by one. "The President shall be commander in chief of the army and navy of the United States, and of the militia when called into the actual service of the United States."

There can be no relation worth examining between this power and the general power of making treaties. And instead of being analogous to the power of declaring war, it affords a striking illustration of the incompatibility of the two powers in the same hands. Those who are to *conduct a war* cannot in the nature of things, be proper or safe judges, whether *a war ought* to be *commenced, continued,* or *concluded.* They are barred from the latter functions by a great principle in free government, analogous to that which separates the sword from the purse, or the power of executing from the power of enacting laws.

"He may require the opinion in writing of the principal officers in each of the executive departments upon any subject relating to the duties of their respective offices; and he shall have power to grant reprieves and pardons for offences against the United States, except in case of impeachment." These powers can have nothing to do with the subject.

"The President shall have power to fill up vacancies that may happen during the recess of the senate, by granting commissions which shall expire at the end of the next session." The same remark is applicable to this power, as also to that of "receiving ambassadors, other public ministers, and consuls." The particular use attempted to be made of this last power will be considered in another place.

"He shall take care that the laws shall be faithfully executed and shall commission all officers of the United States." To see the laws faithfully executed constitutes the essence of the executive authority. But what relation has it to the power of making treaties and war, that is, of determining what the *laws shall be* with regard to other nations? No other certainly than what subsists between the powers of executing and enacting laws; no other, consequently, than what forbids a coalition of the powers in the same department.

I pass over the few other specified functions assigned to the President, such as that of convening the legislature, &c., &c., which cannot be drawn into the present question.

It may be proper however to take notice of the power of removal from office, which appears to have been adjudged to the President by the laws establishing the executive departments; and which the writer has endeavoured to press into his service. To justify any favourable inference from this case, it must be shewn, that the powers of war and treaties are of a kindred nature to the power of removal, or at least are equally within a grant of executive power. Nothing of this sort has been attempted, nor probably will be attempted. Nothing can in truth be clearer, than that no analogy, or shade of analogy, can be traced between a power in the supreme officer responsible for the faithful execution of the laws, to displace a subaltern officer employed in the execution of the laws; and a power to make treaties, and to declare war, such as these have been found to be in their nature, their operation, and their consequences.

Thus it appears that by whatever standard we try this doctrine, it must be condemned as no less vicious in theory than it would be dangerous in practice. It is countenanced neither by the writers on law; nor by the nature of the powers themselves; nor by any general arrangements, or particular expressions, or plausible analogies, to be found in the constitution.

Whence then can the writer have borrowed it?

There is but one answer to this question.

The power of making treaties and the power of declaring war, are *royal prerogatives* in the *British government,* and are accordingly treated as *executive prerogatives* by *British commentators.*

We shall be the more confirmed in the necessity of this solution of the problem, by looking back to the aera of the constitution, and satisfying ourselves that the writer could not have been misled by the doctrines maintained by our own commentators on our own government. That I may not ramble beyond prescribed limits, I shall content myself with an extract from a work which entered into a systematic explanation and defence of the constitution; and to which there has frequently been ascribed some influence in conciliating the public assent to the government in the form proposed. Three circumstances conspire in giving weight to this contemporary exposition. It was made at a time when no application to *persons or measures* could bias: The opinion given was not transiently mentioned, but formally and critically elucidated: It related to a point in the constitution which must consequently have been viewed as of importance in the public mind. The passage relates to the power of making treaties; that of declaring war, being arranged with such obvious propriety among the legislative powers, as to be passed over without particular discussion.

"Tho' several writers on the subject of government place that power [*of making treaties*] in the class of *Executive authorities*, yet this is *evidently* an *arbitrary disposition*. For if we attend *carefully*, to its operation, it will be found to partake *more* of the *legislative* than of the *executive* character, though it does not seem strictly to fall within the definition of either of them. The essence of the legislative authority, is to enact laws; or in other words, to prescribe rules for the regulation of the society. While the execution of the laws and the employment of the common strength, either for this purpose, or for the common defence, seem to comprise *all* the functions of the *Executive magistrate*. The power of making treaties is *plainly* neither the one nor the other. It relates neither to the execution of the subsisting laws, nor to the enaction of new ones, and still less to an exertion of the common strength. Its objects are contracts with foreign nations, which have the *force of law*, but derive it from the obligations of good faith. They are not rules prescribed by the sovereign to the subject, but agreements between sovereign and sovereign. The power in question seems therefore to form a distinct department, and to belong properly neither to the legislative nor to the executive. The qualities elsewhere detailed as indispensable in the management of foreign *negociations*, point out the executive as the most fit agent in those transactions; whilst the vast importance of the trust, and the operation of treaties *as laws*, plead strongly for the participation of the whole or a part of the *legislative bod*, in the office of making them."–Federalist. Vol. 2. p. 273.

It will not fail to be remarked on this commentary, that whatever doubts may be started as to the correctness of its reasoning against the legislative nature of the power to make treaties: it is *clear, consistent* and *confident* in deciding that the power is *plainly* and *evidently* not an *executive power*.

QUESTIONS

1. What sparked the debate between Alexander Hamilton and James Madison? What difference does it make who is involved in making foreign policy decisions?
2. What were the main arguments used by each writer to support his rationale for power in foreign policy?

NOTES

1. Thomas Jefferson to James Madison, 7 July 1793. James Morton Smith, ed., *The Republic of Letters: The Correspondence Between Thomas Jefferson and James Madison, 1776–1826*, 3 vols. (New York: W.W. Norton & Company, 1995), 2:792.

2. A case or event covered by the provisions or stipulations of a treaty or compact.

3. Exceptions and qualifications to the executive powers.

Chapter 22

The Election of 1796, September–November 1796

In 1792, George Washington seriously considered not running for re-election. However, James Madison convinced him that his country still needed him. By 1796, however, Washington had determined that he was going home to Mount Vernon and nothing was going to stop him. In September, he issued his Farewell Address, in which he stated that he would not run for a third term. This set the stage for the first truly contested presidential election in American history.

By the time Washington decided not to run again, two political parties had developed in the United States—the Federalists, led by Alexander Hamilton and John Adams, and the Republicans, led by Thomas Jefferson and James Madison. The race for president very quickly narrowed down to two candidates, John Adams and Thomas Jefferson. Both were well-known leaders from the Revolutionary era and, in fact, both had been mentioned as potential presidential candidates even before Washington announced his plans. No real campaigning could take place until Washington pulled out for fear of alienating people who wanted Washington to run again. Once he was no longer a factor, the party newspapers began actively pushing their favorite nominee and explaining why the people had only one real choice—to vote for their respective candidate.

When it was all over, John Adams was elected president and Thomas Jefferson was elected vice president. Electing a president and vice president from different political parties happened because the electoral college had been originally set up to give the presidency to the man with the most votes, and the vice presidency to the runner-up. This plan would work fine as long as political parties did not develop. Once the Federalists and Republicans came on the scene, with very different political platforms, choosing national leaders became more complicated. Eventually, the Twelfth Amendment

The Farewell Address. *In September 1796, George Washington announced he would not run for reelection. He had his Farewell Address published in the* American Daily Advertiser, *indicating that he believed that newspapers constituted the most effective means of communication with the American people at that time.*

would be adopted in order to allow for separate votes in the electoral college for president and vice president. With each elector casting one vote for president and one vote for vice president in separate processes, the chances of electing a president and vice president from different political parties disappeared.

The first document is a portion of President George Washington's Farewell Address, which he originally published in the *American Daily Advertiser,* a Philadelphia newspaper. It is followed by several pieces in favor of Jefferson and Adams for president. Because of the shortness of the campaign, the comments about the candidates were limited. The two documents in favor of Thomas Jefferson for president both emphasize his support for the rights of the people. The two selections in support of John Adams for president both emphasize the stability of the government and how it will be maintained if Vice President John Adams is chosen to succeed George Washington.

THE BEGINNINGS

George Washington: "The Farewell Address"

In this portion of his Farewell Address, George Washington explains why he has chosen to retire. This decision set off the campaigning for the presidency in the fall of 1796.

American Daily Advertiser (Philadelphia), 19 September 1796

Friends, & Fellow-Citizens.

The period for a new election of a Citizen, to Administer the Executive government of the United States, being not far distant, and the time actually arrived, when your thoughts must be employed in designating the person, who is to be cloathed with that important trust, it appears to me proper, especially as it may conduce to a more distinct expression of the public voice, that I should now apprise you of the resolution I have formed, to decline being considered among the number of those, out of whom a choice is to be made.

I beg you, at the same time, to do me the justice to be assured, that this resolution has not been taken, without a strict regard to all the considerations appertaining to the relation, which binds a dutiful citizen to his country; and that, in withdrawing the tender of service which silence in my Situation might imply. I am influenced by no diminution of zeal for your future interest, no deficiency of grateful respect for your past kindness; but am supported by a full conviction that the step is compatible with both.

The acceptance of, & continuance hitherto in, the Office to which your Suffrages have twice called me, have been a uniform sacrifice of inclination to the opinion of duty, and to a deference for what appeared to be your desire. I constantly hoped, that it would have been much earlier in my power, consistently with motives, which I was not at liberty to disregard, to return to that retirement, from which I had been reluctantly drawn. The strength of my inclination to do this, previous to the last Election, had even led to the preparation of an address to declare it to you; but mature reflection on the then perplexed & critical posture of our Affairs with foreign nations, and the unanimous advice of persons entitled to my confidence, impelled me to abandon the idea.

I rejoice, that the state of your concerns, external as well as internal, no longer renders the pursuit of inclination incompatible with the sentiment of duty, or propriety; & am persuaded whatever partiality may be retained for my services, that in the present circumstances of our country, you will not disapprove my determination to retire. . . .

SUPPORT FOR THOMAS JEFFERSON FOR PRESIDENT

Anonymous: "A Steadfast Friend to the Rights of the People"

This author believes the American people have no real choice in choosing the next president. Thomas Jefferson is the only candidate who can be depended on to protect the rights of the people.

Aurora (Philadelphia), 13 September 1796

It requires no talent at divination to decide who will be candidates for the chair. THOMAS JEFFERSON & JOHN ADAMS will be the men, & whether we shall have at the head of our executive a steadfast friend to the Rights of the People, or an advocate for hereditary power and distinctions, the people of the United States are soon to decide.

One of the People: "An Alarm"

This author also believes that Thomas Jefferson is the only viable candidate. He reminds his readers that John Adams had favored a more hereditary-based government at the time the United States was formed.

Aurora (Philadelphia), 29 October 1796

TO THE CITIZENS OF PENNSYLVANIA.

JOHN ADAMS, the advocate of a kingly government and of a titled no-bility to form an upper house and to keep down the swinish multitude, as one of his brethren calls you—JOHN ADAMS, who would deprive you of a voice in chusing your president and senate, and make both hereditary—this champion for kings, ranks and titles is to be your president unless you will turn out on Friday the fourth day of November, & by your votes call forth Thomas Jefferson, the friend of the people, a republican in principle and manners, whose talents will bear a comparison with those of any man of the United States.

SUPPORT FOR JOHN ADAMS FOR PRESIDENT

John Fenno: "He Alone Is Best Able to Fill the Office"

In this piece, editor John Fenno states that John Adams, if elected, will keep the same people in federal office that are there now and thus help maintain stability. This proved true, because John Adams did not feel that he could replace George Washington's Cabinet.

Gazette of the United States (Philadelphia), 26 October 1796

If Mr. Jefferson is elected President of the United States, all the present officers of government will be put out of office. Perhaps Burr will fill the place of Pickering, as secretary of state, and the 18 virtuous Virginians will canvas for the other vacant offices. Pinckney will be recalled from France, and Mason (that treaty hero) will be substituted. In 15 months we will be involved in a ruinous war, which will terminate in the fall of the present fab-ric of government, and a disunion of the states. In the mean time, every

Frenchmen in America will become a pensioner. On the other hand, if Mr. Adams is elected to that important office, which he alone is best able to fill, the citizens of America will walk forth to their fields in peace, there will be no revolution among the present officers of government; wholesome laws will be administered to us; the fame of the republic, from Georgia to New Hampshire, will be clothed with abundance and peace; the people will be united; our rivers will swell with commerce; our villages in a few years will grow to cities; and our United Eagle will float the most respectable of flags, in all the ports, rivers and bays in the universe.

Phocion: "Mr. Jefferson and His Pretensions"

Phocion criticizes Thomas Jefferson as a philosopher, stating that he only pretends to be one. He further declares that Jefferson will prostrate the United States at the feet of France if he is elected president.

Gazette of the United States (Philadelphia), 24 November 1796

We shall now take leave of Mr. Jefferson and his pretensions, as a philosopher and politician.—The candid and unprejudiced, who have read with attention the foregoing comments on his philosophical and political works, and on his public conduct, must now be convinced, however they may have hitherto been deceived by a plausible appearance, and specious talents, or misled by designing partizans, that the reputation he has acquired, has not been bottomed on solid merit; that his abilities have been more directed to the acquirement of literary fame, than to the substantial good of his country; that his philosophical opinions have been wavering and capricious, often warped by the most frivolous circumstances; that in his political conduct he has been timid, inconsistent and unsteady, favouring measures of a factious and disorganizing tendency; always leaning on those which would establish his popularity, however destructive of our peace and tranquility; that his political principles are sometimes whimsical and visionary, at others, subversive of all regular and stable government; that his writings have betrayed a *disrespect* for *religion,* and his partiality for the *impious Paine,* an enemy to *christianity;* that his advice, respecting the Dutch company, and his open countenance of an incendiary printer, and of the views of a faction, manifest a want of due regard for *national faith* and *public credit;* that his *abhorrence* of *one* foreign nation, and *enthusiastic devotion* to *another,* have extinguished in him every germ of real *national character;* and, in short, that his elevation to the Presidency, must eventuate either in the *debasement* of the American name, by a whimsical, inconsistent and feeble administration, or in the *prostration* of the United States at the *feet of France*, the *subversion* of our excellent *constitution*, and the consequent *destruction* of our present *prosperity*.

QUESTIONS

1. Why could no one actively run for President until George Washington announced he would not run? Why do you think he waited so long to announce his decision not to run for reelection?
2. Why do the two supporters of Thomas Jefferson want him to be elected? What is their major concern which they believe he will address?
3. Why do the two supporters of John Adams want him to be elected? What is their major concern which they believe he will address?
4. Are the concerns of these writers unique to this period? Why or why not?

CHAPTER 23

The Quasi-War with France, 1797–1798

When the United States and France signed their alliance in 1778, they both committed to defend each other when attacked. But, when France and Great Britain went to war in 1793, President George Washington issued the Neutrality Proclamation because he believed the United States was not strong enough to get involved in a war. Then, in 1795, the United States negotiated and signed Jay's Treaty with the British. France felt betrayed. Partially because of what they perceived as betrayal, and partially because of military setbacks in the war with Great Britain, France began to threaten American shipping. The result was the "quasi-war" between France and the United States.

Between March and June 1797, France seized 316 American ships and threatened to continue doing so unless the United States stopped supporting and favoring Great Britain. Instead of apologizing, the Federalist-controlled Congress prepared for war. The XYZ Affair (see Chapter 24) only made matters worse. Following the president's report about the XYZ Affair in the spring of 1798, Congress voted to triple the size of the army and authorized American privateers to attack French vessels. During the summer of 1798, Congress came within a few votes of declaring war on France, even though President John Adams had not requested such a declaration.

But President Adams knew that the United States was not ready for a war with France, Although he signed the Alien and Sedition Acts (see Chapter 25), he balked at doing anything else. In fact, he worked to defuse the situation. In 1799, he sent new American representatives to France: William Vans Murray, William R. Davie, and Oliver Ellsworth. Murray, also the ambassador to the Netherlands, was able to negotiate the Convention of Mortefontaine in September 1800. This agreement terminated the alliance of 1778 and finally ended the Quasi-War. The restoration of good relations with France set the stage for the Louisiana Purchase in 1803.

Throughout these troubles, pieces in the newspapers discussed and debated the controversy. They continued to argue over whether France was an honorable country or not. As war clouds loomed on the horizon, writers debated whether going to war with France was a good idea or a bad idea.

The documents in favor of going to war with France tended to appear in Federalist newspapers. Increasingly, writers in the newspapers expressed concerns over what the French planned to do in regards to the United States. The first selection declares that other nations were justified in their attack on France. The second document states that France plans to undermine the American government. The third and fourth pieces state that Congress should go ahead and declare war because we are already at war because France has attacked our shipping on several occasions.

The documents opposed to a war with France appeared primarily in Republican newspapers. The first selection worries that the Americans in favor of a war have no idea of its consequences. The next two pieces complain because national leaders are seriously contemplating war with France and not with Great Britain, who also has raided American trading vessels. The fourth selection reminds Americans that they owe their independence to the help given by France during the American Revolution. The fifth piece worries about the economic impact of all the war talk. The final selection jokes about the great naval victory of the United States navy over a lone French schooner.

SUPPORT FOR WAR WITH FRANCE

William Cobbett: "Inexpressible Injuries and Indignities"

Editor William Cobbett criticizes France for all its complaints against the United States. He implies that the French deserve what is happening to them because of the barbarity of their revolution. He also criticizes all American political leaders who support the French.

Porcupine's Gazette **(Philadelphia), 11 September 1797**

There never was a nation on earth so unjustly and so contemptuously treated by another, as America has been by France. Nations have been invaded, laid under contribution, conquered, and enslaved; but this has been effected by force or by treachery; it has been the fortune of war, or the result of conspiracy. Never did we before hear of a nation at peace with all the world, and pretending to be in the full enjoyment of independence, suffering a millionth part of what we suffered from the French (even before a whimper of complaint escaped from our lips) without declaring war or making reprisals.

This tameness following so close upon the heels of that Revolution which in its origins, its progress, and its conclusion was so strongly marked with irascibility and stubbornness, will naturally excite astonishment in all those who shall read the American history. When they are told of the innumerable and inexpressible injuries and indignities we have received from the French; that this despicable race of beings lorded it over our bays and rivers; and, not content with plundering and chastising our mariners, made them put the seal to their degradation by exacting from them payment for the shot fired at them; when we are told this, and that we bore it all without even talking of revenge, will they not wonder what was become of the men of 1776 who, with the scroll of their imaginary rights in one hand, and the sword in the other, swore to preserve the full enjoyment of the former, or to perish by the latter? And what will be their astonishment when they are told that the greater part of those very men were still living, and were still the rulers of the land?

Were the bold, the undaunted, the haughty language of the first Congress, in their public remonstrances and addresses, compared with the faltering, the timid, the tame, the humble, the whining tone of the answer to the President's firm and manly speech, what a contrast, great God! would it present!

Mr. Adams's speech seems to be the last gleam of the spirit of the Old Whigs. It was his protest against the degradation of his country—as if he had said to the House of Representatives: 'I see that you are resolved to blast your reputation and that of America, but you shall not blast mine.

Anonymous: "An Attempt to Reduce Us to Disgrace and Ruin"

By the summer of 1798, many Americans feared the French and their plans. This author warns that France intends to engage the United States in military activity, if not in an out-and-out war. He believes that they intend to try and overthrow the American government and that war is almost inevitable.

Gazette of the United States (Philadelphia), 9 June 1798

We have authentic information from Europe, and have authority to state, that unless we unite as a band of brothers in defence of our independence, we shall be called to witness, and that soon, an open attempt to reduce us to the same disgrace and ruin, as the Swiss, Dutch and other free nations have experienced under the domination of the French in consequence of their attachment to foreign nations and internal divisions.

The Directory have undoubtedly settled their plan respecting America, and this plan is not consistent with a reception of our Envoys and an accommodation of differences. They have been informed by their own agents who have been in this country, and by our own citizens, that we are a divided people; that our government does not possess the hearts of our citizens; that the great body of people are displeased with their rulers, and passionately attached to France; and that they could make a fourth of Sept. at Philadelphia with as much ease as at Paris. (Our readers will recollect this was the arrest and banishment of Barthelemy and Pichegru[1]—The declaration, when uttered in plain language, is that, with the help of their friends and agents here, they could seize President Adams, the heads of departments and all the supporters of administration, send them into banishment, and put Jefferson, Madison, Monroe and Burr in their places.)

A Frenchman by the name of Bayard, who lately returned from America, has published his travels through the United States, which book has been printed in Paris, in which he says, 'That France wants only a footing upon the Continent to regulate the destinies of the United States.'

If any man can read these facts, without a glow of indignation, he must be a traitor to his country, and fitted to be the vile slave of a foreign despotism.

Our time, though delayed by the great projects of France in Europe, which occupy her forces, will certainly come, when we are to be invaded by a body of their troops, who are expected to be joined by their friends among us, our Jacobins, and when our 'destinies are to be regulated by the French Directory.' Our elections are to be annulled by an edict of some French commissary at the head of a few thousand foreign troops, and a great body of domestic traitors. These men will take possession of our forts and arsenals, as they have done in Switzerland, and we must receive a constitution of government from Paris, as the Dutch and Swedes have been compelled to do—This project is unquestionably settled in the French councils, and delayed only by the invasion of England and other revolutionary schemes. On these points we have to make up our minds and that very soon—We must soon be called upon to draw a line of distinction between patriots & traitors—to separate the wheat from the chaff.

William Cobbett: "The Language of History"

William Cobbett reports what he believes is the first blow in the war with France. An American naval vessel had recently captured a French man-of-

war and brought it to the Philadelphia harbor. Cobbett, and many other Americans, believed that such events would become more common in the near future.

Porcupine's Gazette (Philadelphia), 9 July 1798

The Historian, who is to record the events of the present times, after relating the long suffering of America; the injuries and insults and cruelties she has received at hands of the perfidious French; after painting her humiliation, her degradation, in their true colours, and raising on the cheek of his reader a blush for his country, will then say: 'But, the native spirit of the nation was at last roused by the demand of a TRIBUTE. The government annuled the treaties with France, fitted out vessels to scour the coast of her barbarian corsairs, and, on the 7th of July, 1798, the *first blow* of that conflict, *which preserved the independence of America and finally brought France to her feet,* was struck by Captain STEPHEN DECATUR, who, in the sloop of War DELAWARE, attacked and brought into the Port of Philadelphia, a French privateer of 12 guns and 70 men."–This, I hope, will be the language of History.

Anonymous: "A Moral Obligation"

This author believes that the United States has no choice but to declare war on France because of all that country has done to insult America. France has already attacked the United States on several occasions, so the country has actually been at war for some time—what remains is to formalize reality.

Gazette of the United States (New York), 19 December 1798

Our government is under a moral obligation to DECLARE WAR against France—or the principles upon which their late measures respecting her have been founded, must be abandoned as false. It is true those measures would have been sufficient to have roused any nation, possessing one spark of national honor or self-respect, or feeling any energy in her resources, either to propose an honorable accommodation, or to declare an open and honorable war. But the last act is left for our government. It is true this formality will not much alter our relations to France, but it will very materially affect our internal situation; for until that is done, France will not abandon her hopes here; and divisions will be constantly excited and fomented by them. But that act would take us at once out of our present *amphibious* situation, and crush the *French* party in this country, at the same time it would not create an enemy, but only put us in a situation to act with more energy against the enemy that has already attacked us.—Every measure yet taken by government against France, has been opposed by men who have afterwards been convinced that it ought to have been taken before; and this will undoubtedly share the fate of the rest.

Opposition to War with France

Anonymous: "To Prevent the Flames of War"

This author worries that those in favor of a war with France have no idea what they are asking. He encourages those in Congress who fight against the idea of war.

Time Piece (New York), 9 June 1797

Much is due to that description of men in Congress who have endeavored to prevent the flames of war from being kindled in these States; and it is be hoped that their virtuous efforts will in the end defeat the hostile projects of the secret enemies of the peace of the United States, and the friends of the orders, checks, and balances of what is called the British Constitution. It is to be suspected that providing for friends in an American army and navy contributes in some degree to the thirst of certain persons for a war with France. Have all these people known what war is?—or do they suppose it a frolic, that may be ended at pleasure?—have they ever witnessed the consequences of a battle either at sea or land, and the whole diabolical scene of broken bones, cleft skulls, and mangled carcasses—scenes which can only be justified in cases of resistance to oppression or invasion, and not from lighter considerations? If selfishness be the motive of some for warfare, let it be remembered that a whole nation is never selfish in this respect. It is for the interest of the few that men are turned into bulldogs and butchers—the selfishness of the many is their enjoyment of peace and quiet.

Cetera Desunt: "Madness Itself Is the Order of the Day"

This essayist cannot understand why government leaders favor Great Britain over France. Both have acted against the United States, yet the government is urging war only against the French. This author believes this is madness. He still fears Britain more.

Aurora (Philadelphia), 23 March 1798

Every act of our government has shewn their partiality for Britain in preference to France; and tho' the latter has claims on our gratitude and was engaged in a contest for the liberty of mankind, yet even in such a cause, every unfair advantage was taken of her situation, and, as far as it was possible without actual hostility, we assisted her Enemy.

If such has been the conduct of the American government, what other consequences could with reason be expected to follow—Unhappily all the arguments of a virtuous Minority have been fruitless; Vain hath been the appeal to reason; Remonstrances have only served to confirm the obstinacy of the ruling party; and our Country is left to mourn over their mistakes, if candour itself can use so mild a name for actions which in their result threaten our very existence.

Would the Executive explain the whole mystery perhaps some other remedy than war, might yet be found; But,

Quos Deus vult perdere, prius dementat.[2]

Madness itself is the order of the day; Yes, we are advised, Good God, we are advised to go to war with France. Realize this, ye Lovers of Liberty. Ye Rulers of our Country consider seriously before, you determine. Say, what can be gained even if Victory should declare in our favour. Alas, would England respect our rights; would they value our liberty, after we had basely assisted to enslave another Nation, and a Nation too to whom we owed our own independence. No, she would in that event either compleat her former plans of domination over us; Or perhaps condescend to give us a Prince of her own—But as in all human probability, the battle should be to the strong, what then must be our condition: I tremble for my Country, when I consider the mighty odds we shall contend against; when I review the powerful Nations who have already submitted to the arms of France, and even proud England in dread lest the present conflict may terminate in the total destruction of her government—When I say, I reflect on these things I cannot but look with contempt on the proud Heroes of the Day, who in spite of all the suggestions of common sense, would venture thus desperately—Let them however remember, that to their Country they are accountable, and consider what may be their situation when in their turn they must sue for mercy.

Centinel: "That Awful Situation"

Centinel questions why the president is considering war against France and not against Great Britain. He is suspicious of some sort of conspiracy.

Such fears of conspiracy were widespread in the 1790s because Americans had not yet developed an awareness that political opposition could exist safely in a republic.

Aurora (Philadelphia), 24 March 1798

Awakened to the sense of that awful situation in which the late message of the President to Congress has placed you—let me ask for what cause does the President desire war with France? Is it to support the British treaty, which, if left to itself will certainly produce your ruin, without the mad quixotism of engaging in war for it, under all the concomitant horrors which war produces. Is it to protect British trade and commerce with the United States, and the annual exportation of her manufactures, which impoverishes our country and throws an annual balance of trade of upwards of six millions of dollars of hard cash, in favour of Britain and against the United States? Or is it to produce an alliance offensive and defensive between Great Britain and the United States, the more effectually to defeat and destroy republicanism in France and reestablish monarchy and thereby maintain that favorite government which Mr. Adams wrote his book to support, and which he has declared 'is the most stupendous fabric of human invention'? If it be for any of these purposes, the object is not legitimate nor just, but results from baseness, wickedness and depravity, and demands to be opposed and forbidden by 'You the people.'

Columbus: "The Alliance of France Saved Us from Perdition"

Columbus reminds Americans that they owe their very political existence to France because of its help during the American Revolution. How can the United States possibly consider going to war with France when we owe such a huge debt?

Aurora (Philadelphia), 4 April 1798

The reasons insisted on by the advocates for a war with France, are, that our national honor hath been insulted, our commerce violated; and our peaceful citizens engaged therein imprisoned, and other wise maltreated. If they have any *others*, they have hitherto disguised them, though conjecture has not been wanting in her endeavours to *unmask* them. I shall confine my observations to such as are avowed, believing that they are most likely to operate upon the people at large, how convincing soever *secret* reasons may be to a *few* individuals. . . .

Those who speak in so lofty a tone on the subject of national honor seem to forget that the existence of the United States as a nation is but of yesterday. That neither our situation nor the genius of the people, nor that of their government can be supposed to lead us to engage in frequent wars. If peace be the proper system of republican policy, much more so is it that of an agricultural people, dispersed over an immense territory, unused to arms, and unequal to the cultivation of the tenth part of the soil they occupy. Never was there a military republic formed of such materials. It is not till our country is filled with populous cities, or till our government has put off its republican form, that we are to expect it to assume the dignified attitude of a warlike nation. Our late contest with Great Britain might have made us remember our imbecility and inaptitude for war. Defenceless on every side, the enemy changed the point of attack at every moment, and everywhere found us vulnerable and weak. The alliance of France, whatever *diplomatic ingenuity* may suggest to the contrary, saved us from perdition. Have we forgot the portentous year when one half the United States was overrun by our enemy, when we were almost without an army, and that army without money to subsist it? Have we forgotten the mission of the younger Lawrence to France, the object of the mission the deplorable and just picture he was enjoined to present of our distresses, the relief we obtained, and its consequences? If we have not, must we not be astonished that there are men among us who would hurry us into war with that very power whose succour alone saved us from perdition? And for what is such a state of danger to be hazarded? Truly, to compel France to receive our ambassadors!!

Anonymous: "Popular Clamour against the French"

This author bemoans the creation of fears among merchants and seamen because of all the calls for war against France. He fears the end result will be a downturn in the economy.

New York Argus, 5 June 1798

They serve to increase the popular clamour against the French; and did they stop here it would be well enough; but a more cruel and serious mischief is produced. They depress the spirit of commerce and discourage seamen from entering into the merchant's service, and create a thousand unnecessary fears and anxieties for the safety of our friends at sea.

Benjamin Franklin Bache: "The Taking of a French Schooner"

Benjamin Franklin Bache demeans the rejoicing over the capture of a French schooner. He downplays the victory as a joke because it really was not a battle at all.

Aurora (Philadelphia), 10 July 1798

Yesterday morning was ushered in with the ringing of bells and other demonstrations of joy; great numbers of the opulent mercantile interest of this flourishing city assembled at the Coffee house to reciprocate their congratulations on the occasion—the *taking of a French schooner* after a desperate action of *one gun*.

It is the custom of nations to demonstrate their joy on the gaining of signal victories, by ringing of bells, &c. and surely the taking of a schooner is a victory!

The captured schooner, it appears, mistook the Delaware for a British ship of war and, being an inferior force, took refuge in *Egg-Harbor*, that same harbor where British *magnanimity* and *valour* were displayed during the revolution.

The French schooner, it appears did not fire on the Delaware; her orders being, no doubt, not to commit hostilities in a neutral territory.

QUESTIONS

1. Why do some of the pro-war authors, such as William Cobbett, believe that war with France is a good idea and is probably inevitable?
2. The fourth author in support of the war on France states that the United States has a "moral obligation" to declare war on France. Do you agree with that statement? Are wars ever morally unavoidable?
3. Why do some of the anti-war authors, particularly Centinel, suspect a conspiracy on the part of the national government? Do you agree that the government was treating Great Britain and France differently? Why or why not?
4. Columbus thinks that war with France is unthinkable because of the debt we owed them from the American Revolution. Do you agree? Why or why not?

NOTES

1. Both men were accused of conspiring to restore the French monarchy in 1797.

2. Common proverb by an unknown author: "Those whom God wills to destroy, he first deprives of their senses."

CHAPTER 24

The XYZ Affair, 1798

In seeking to defuse the conflict with France, President John Adams originally sent three special representatives to try and negotiate a settlement. Elbridge Gerry, John Marshall, and Charles Pinckney arrived in France in the fall of 1797. They hoped to negotiate an end to the treaties of 1778 and get French-American relations back on an even keel.

Shortly after their arrival, the three Americans were approached by three representatives of the French Foreign Minister, Charles Maurice de Talleyrand-Périgord. The three men told the Americans that negotiations would begin after France was given a loan of $12 million and Talleyrand was given a bribe of $250,000. Such financial exchanges were a fairly normal part of European diplomacy, but the Americans reacted in horror. Seeing these demands as a form of extortion and bribery, Marshall and Pinckney sailed for home. Gerry remained, hoping to salvage some sort of agreement from the negotiations, but he met with little success.

When word of this incident reached the United States, many Americans reacted with anger. John Adams, in reporting to Congress, used the letters X, Y, and Z instead of the real names of the French representatives. Hence, the incident became known as the XYZ Affair. The XYZ Affair brought the United States very close to a real war with France. The Federalists in Congress called for some sort of retribution because of the insult to American honor. Attempts were made to silence supporters of France through the adoption of the Sedition Act (see Chapter 25). The Federalists also voted money to increase the size of the army and navy so that the United States would be better prepared for any military activity that occurred. The partisan press became very involved in the debates over the XYZ Affair. The Federalist newspapers called for war to defend American honor, while the Republican news sheets called for an investigation into how the negotiations could have been bungled so badly.

The documents supporting the French all appeared in Republican newspapers. They all assert that the French have been wronged or misunderstood in the midst of this debacle. In the first piece, Benjamin Franklin Bache calls on the administration to be patient until all the facts are in. The second document reports on the events of the negotiations and blames the problems on the Federalist leadership of the American government. The third selection also urges caution, particularly when it comes to talking about war. The final piece attacks the delegates (John Marshall and Charles Pinckney) who came home from France rather than complete their assignment.

The documents opposing the French all appeared in Federalist newspapers. The first piece points out how pivotal an event the XYZ Affair was in relations between France and the United States. The second selection informs the Republicans that they can no longer, in good conscience, support France. The final piece discusses the national humiliation because of the attempted bribery scheme.

The French Are Allies

Benjamin Franklin Bache: "The Attempted Negociation with France"

In this piece, Benjamin Franklin Bache again shows his support for France and the political changes that have occurred there. He reports that the negotiations with France have apparently failed. He urges the government not to overreact to the stories coming out of France about how the American delegates were treated. France is still an ally worth having. He blames most of the trouble on American leadership.

Aurora (Philadelphia), 22 January 1798

The issue of the attempted negociation with France can no longer be doubted. Tho' we want direct, official and circumstantial information, yet the indirect accounts received are so concurrent, that a doubt can scarcely be entertained, that Messrs. Pinckney, Gerry and Marshal (with their present instructions at least) will be unable to adjust our differences. It is true neither says they have been actually dismissed, but all express an expectation that they will not be received. Being on the spot they are best able to judge of the temper of the French government, and know *whether their instructions give latitude enough for accommodation.*

What is to be done. Will the administration possess magnanimity enough to make reparation where they have injured, and sacrifice their private feelings and their private views to the good of the public; or will they either suffer the present state of affairs so ruinous to our commerce to continue, or brave the storm they have raised by taking such measures as will make an open rupture with the French republic inavoidable? They have brought their country to a critical situation; from which, we fear they have neither the wisdom nor prudence to extricate it. The only step still in their power to heal the mischief they have done, is to retire & leave to more skillful and fortunate pilots to save the vessel of state.

Benjamin Franklin Bache: "A Correct Outline of Their Content"

Benjamin Franklin Bache presents a summary of what he has heard about events in France. He states that it has been a big misunderstanding and that blame lies with the Federalist leadership of the United States. He believes that the negotiations can still be salvaged.

Aurora (Philadelphia), 7 April 1798

Dispatches from the Envoys.

Until we are able to publish them in detail, we offer the following as a correct outline of their content, and think we can safely pledge ourselves for its general accuracy.

The Envoys had no regular intercourse with the French government, but in delivering their letters of credence and receiving cards of hospitality.— Some short time after these ceremonies had passed, a merchant of respectability introduced a Mr. X. as a person to be relied on, who had something of consequence to communicate. Mr. X. said he came at the instance of Mr. Y. the confidential friend of Mr. Talleyrand, to inform the Envoys, that Mr. Talleyrand felt great interest in the accommodation between France and the United States; but that he feared the resentment of the directory at the speech of the President of the United States to Congress in May last would prevent unless some means could be found to soften them. On inquiry by the Envoys as to the means in their power, they were told that it would be necessary to engage a powerful person in their interest and deposit in his hands the sum of £50,000 sterling, for such uses as he should chuse. He mentioned Mr. Talleyrand as the person, and intimated that the money would go to some members of the directory. He said it would be further necessary for the Envoys to offer a loan of money to the French government.

Mr. X. afterwards introduced Mr. Y. to the Envoys and the same overtures were made by him and renewed by them both on a variety of occasions; but were always rejected by the envoys. The loan to the government was positively declared to be out of their power, and the douceur [A conciliatory gift] was countenanced by them, only on the supposition, that they could be assured of the completion of their business. These agents of Mr. Talleyrand urged on the envoys, the power of France and mentioned the fate of the European powers who had offended, and the pending fate of others; and also suggested, that they would fail of support from what it called the French party in this country, if they refused the offered terms. The irritation occasioned by the President's speech was repeated and the parts objected to were pointed out. These projects were renewed, in a variety of forms and once by a lady, in the confidence of Mr. Talleyrand, to Gen. Pinckney. The envoys had declared they would receive no more unauthorized proposals, but could not prevent the renewal of the same kind of proposals, at times when they met the private persons before spoken of. Mr. Gerry, being personally acquainted with Mr. Talleyrand had visited him and received an invitation to dinner. About the time of the last dispatches, he waited on Mr. Talleyrand, to ask him to fix a day to dine with him, and mentioned that he intended to invite his colleagues, to have an opportunity of introducing them to Mr. Talleyrand. Mr. Talleyrand fixed a distant day; which had not arrived when the dispatches came away. In this interview Mr. Gerry mentioned, that he had received some overtures from Mr. Y. in Mr. Talleyrand's name. Mr. T. said Mr. Y. was always entitled to credit. Mr. Talleyrand himself wrote some proposals, the principal of which was, that the United States should lend a sum of money to France of only half the amount of that asked by his agent. He said nothing of the 50,000. After shewing his proposals he burned them.

Remarks on the above.

We think it will appear from the above statement of facts that the negociation ought not be considered as at an end. The anxiety of the negociators of this disgraceful business; the variety of forms in which it was presented and the abatement made in the overture of Talleyrand himself, shew that the proposals were by no means ultimata. There was a prospect too of drawing Talleyrand into a personal intercourse; which does not admit of the pursuit of infamous views so well as one conducted by intermediaries. It is not meant to say, that the negociation can be certainly counted on; but there is surely ground to think it not so desperate as the president seems to have thought it.

The papers are given to the public by the Senate; the house of representatives we understand, very generally, deemed the publication improper. Such a disclosure hazarding the safety of the commissioners; being calculated to defeat any pending negociation and perhaps to bring on a declaration of war against the United States, must have had objects of a domestic nature, extremely flattering to the views of Messrs. Goodhue, Hillhouse, Sedgwick & Co. who we understand were the principal supporters of the measure, to induce them to hazard it. From the political views of these gentlemen, heretofore, and the nature of the facts in the dispatches it will not be difficult to conjecture their present objects.

These are, to depreciate the character of republicanism; to lessen the aversion of the people of the United States to war with France, which they falsely suppose is founded in affection to that country; and to destroy the credit of the opposers of their measures and views, by representing them as acting in concert with France.

To repel the first attempt we shall only say, that no man can be found silly enough to believe that the ministers of a republic cannot be corrupt, that if there was proof of the directory being concerned in the swindling of our commissioners (of which there is none) that it must leave opinion where it was;—That Mr. Talleyrand is notoriously anti-republican; that he was the intimate friend of Mr. Hamilton, Mr. King and other great federalists, and that it is probably owing to the determined hostility which he discovered in them towards France that the Government of that country consider us only as objects of plunder.

An Old and Uniform Whig: "Any Possible Advantage?"

This writer fears that American leaders are preparing for war because of the French attacks on American ships and, more important, because of the perceived insult to the American delegates to France. He does not see how going to war with the French will help the American situation any at all, particularly when the British are also raiding our commerce.

Aurora (Philadelphia), 13 April 1798

If any person can suggest a possible, not to say probable, advantage from it, I will confess it has not occurred to me.

Oh yes, it will gratify our resentment—Our trade has been despoiled—Our neutral rights invaded, and our sovereignty insulted in the refusal to receive and treat with our ambassadors. I feel sensibly both the injury and the insults; and though I think it probable that both proceeded from our having abandoned our neutral station by the British Treaty; yet it might be justifiable to support our rights by reprisals, if such as would be effectual, were in our power; if not, we may shew a spirit indeed; but increase the injury upon ourselves. Let it be remembered that success in war is not to be attained by high sounding words in Congress—nor fleets and armies raised by figures representing sums of money, not quite so easy to be got at. Let it also be re-membered that national councils ought to be influenced by no passions, but pursue the real interest of the Society, which, in our case I am sure is op-posed to a war with any European nation, especially France, who, whatever else may be said of her, is a powerful one. I believe at the same time it is our true interest to have no intimate connection with any of them.

To arm our merchant ships for defence would undoubtedly be proper if we could secure against their acting offensively and bringing on a war which it is supposed they would do. But there is another difficulty. To per-mit the arming against France, when Britain is also daily taking our vessels would be strange, and yet, is it intended to arm against Great Britain, or can it be done consistent with the treaty, permitting her to board and search our vessels, &c.

John Barber: "How Cheaply Is Popularity Gained"

Editor John Barber comments on the return of John Marshall and Charles Pinckney to the United States. He clearly believes that they should not be honored in such a public manner for having failed in their assignment in France.

Albany Register (New York), 29 June 1798

How cheaply is popularity gained at the present day! The Americans send a man on a foreign errand; they allow him *nine thousand dollars* to fit himself for the mission, and an additional *nine thousand* per annum during the time he is employed in it; not content with paying him thus liberally for his services, they discover a propensity to *deify* him when he returns home. No country or party ought to indulge this *idolizing* spirit; it is the offspring of blind confidence in the many, and of *design* in the few: it has already been carried to too great lengths in this country by all parties, and should it con-tinue to be indulged, must eventually prove the bane of liberty and of pub-lic virtue.

THE FRENCH ARE ENEMIES

Anonymous: "A Very Conspicuous Figure"

This author uses Shakespeare to emphasize the tragedy of the XYZ Affair. Many Americans loved the plays of Shakespeare and read them often, as can be seen by how many times he is quoted or referred to in writings from the eighteenth century.

Gazette and General Advertiser (Charleston, South Carolina), 9 November 1798

Shakespeare calls Z an unnecessary letter. Our immortal Bard surely would have retracted this contemptuous epithet, had he lived to see this identical letter make a very conspicious figure in an important negociation.

William Cobbett: "Now There Can Be No Delusion"

William Cobbett calls on the Democratic Republicans to realize that they have been deluded by the French. No one can possibly favor France after the way it has treated America's ambassadors.

Porcupine's Gazette (Philadelphia), 24 April 1798

Now is the time for them to distinguish, and to set a mark upon the enemies of their country.—Hitherto there may have been, and there certainly have been, amongst the democrats, some honest deluded men; but now there can be no *delusion*. The sun, at long meridian height, is not more clear to the view of all men, than is the execrable intentions of the despots of Paris. He, therefore, who still perseveres in his attachment to them, and in his justification of their abominable measures, ought to be branded as a hired villain, or a natural seeker of pillage and blood. Let, therefore, a mark be set upon the miscreant; let all men stand aloof from him; let him be banished from the converse of honesty and virtue; let him associate with BACHE, the Printer, and his patricide crew, and with them let him sink through the vault of poverty into oblivion with the curse of the country on his head.

William Cobbett: "The Dispatches"

William Cobbett, in discussing the diplomatic dispatches relating to the XYZ Affair, attacks the French for their efforts to solicit a bribe from the Americans. He states that the United States has been humiliated. Most Americans agreed. Attitudes towards France became pretty hostile in the wake of the XYZ Affair.

Porcupine's Gazette (Philadelphia), 7 June 1798

THE DISPATCHES,

From our envoys at Paris, which are published at length in this day's paper, present us nothing new. They only place all the propositions of X. Y, Z to the account of the minister of Foreign Affairs. Infamous BACHE can therefore no longer impute the insolent demands to *'unauthorized agents.'* Talleyrand, the old hopping Bishop, is no *unauthorized* agent; he is the authorized agent of the Directory, just as lord Grenville was the authorized agent of his Britanic Majesty, so that, there is no longer any room for excuse; there is no hole to creep out at. A *tribute* has been demanded by the tyrants of France, and all that the people have to do, is to determine whether they will be their *vassals* or not.

The Dispatches are extremely humiliating to this country. Observe, the *tribute* (or the *loan,* call it by what name you will) was refused, not because it was an insolent demand; not because it was debasing to America; not because it was treating her free men like vassals; but because it would be a *breach of neutrality!* Was this a reason to be given by the ambassadors of America? The tyrants say: 'Your two Presidents have *misbehaved;* to attone for which you must pay us a tribute, before we will condescend to treat with you at all.'—To this the Embassadors reply: 'We cannot do this, *because it would endanger our neutrality.*' Which is as much as to say, if this danger did not exist, we would do it!—Oh, God! is this Independence? Is this the *republican spirit,* with which one can have been so incessantly and so unmercifully assailed?

However, I must confess, that this humiliating language in the embassadors in a great measure, to be attributed to the people themselves. When the former went away, the pulse of the nation bent very low. There were such a desire for *peace on any terms;* such a whining after *reconciliation;* such callousness to injuries and insults of the most mortifying and degrading nature, that the embassadors might with reason fear to assume any thing like a becoming tone.

QUESTIONS

1. Why did newspaper writers such as Benjamin Franklin Bache and William Cobbett react so strongly to the request for money from the French? Do the newspaper articles reflect this reaction?
2. Clearly, some of these authors believe the XYZ Affair is grounds for war, while others do not. What are the reasons for going to war with France, according to William Cobbett and the other writers? What are the reasons for not going to war with France, according to An Old and Uniform Whig? With which set of reasons do you agree? In other words, do you think the United States should have gone to war with France because of the XYZ Affair?

3. Benjamin Franklin Bache and William Cobbett both make references to attempts by the Federalists and the Republicans to take advantage of the situation to advance their own political agenda. Do you think that was happening? Why or why not?

CHAPTER 25

The Sedition Act, 1798–1800

When the leadership of the Federalist party in Congress heard about the XYZ Affair, it decided the time had come to get the political opposition under control. Some believed that the Republicans truly presented a threat to the stability of the United States, while others saw a golden opportunity to destroy their political opponents. The result was the passage of the Alien and Sedition Acts.

The Alien and Sedition Acts consisted of four separate laws. The first three dealt directly with immigrants in one way or another. The last one, the Sedition Act, defined any criticism of the national government (whether based on fact or not) as seditious libel. British law had recognized seditious libel as dangerous to the stability of the government. However, the spread of newspapers in the eighteenth century had weakened this concept in Great Britain. The attempt to put the concept of seditious libel into American law through the Sedition Act created a furor and sparked the first widespread debate over freedom of expression in American history. In many ways, this debate has continued ever since.

The Republicans charged that the Sedition Act infringed on people's rights by violating the First Amendment. The Federalists responded that no one really believed that the concepts of freedom of speech and liberty of the press were intended to protect vicious criticism of the government. This debate continued for more than a year in the party newspapers. As it continued, American politicians slowly developed a broad definition of freedom of expression which allowed, and even expected, criticism of the government as a normal part of a successful republic.

But, before the debate subsided and the Sedition Act was allowed to expire on March 3, 1801, 14 people were indicted for seditious libel. Numbers of other people were arrested, but not charged, under the Sedition Act. Almost everyone arrested or charged was a Republican newspaper editor, and

The Matthew Lyon Cartoon. *This cartoon shows a fight between two congressmen on the floor of the House of Representatives. Matthew Lyon was a Republican congressman from Vermont. He verbally goaded a congressman from Connecticut, Roger Griswold, until Griswold attacked him with a cane. Lyon responded with a pair of fire tongs. This fight took place in February 1798. Lyon also edited a Republican newspaper in Vermont. He was indicted and convicted under the Sedition Act in 1798. He then ran for reelection to Congress from his jail cell and easily won the election.*

the Republicans quickly claimed that the Federalists were using the Sedition Act to destroy political opposition.

Protests against the Sedition Act expanded beyond the partisan press. In November 1798, the state legislature of Kentucky adopted a series of resolutions (secretly written by Vice President Thomas Jefferson) protesting the Sedition Act. In December 1798, the Virginia legislature also adopted a series of protest resolutions (secretly written by Congressman James Madison). The Kentucky resolves not only protested the Sedition Act, but talked generally about states having the right not to obey a federal law that they thought was illegal. In the 1820s, this idea would be further developed by John C. Calhoun of South Carolina into the doctrine of nullification. The Virginia and Kentucky Resolutions also sparked debate, as Federalists and Republicans discussed whether it was legitimate for states to protest the actions of the federal government.

The documents opposing the Sedition Act all appeared in Republican newspapers. The first selection identifies the Sedition Act as despotism. The second document urges Americans to arm themselves to fight for their freedom. The third and fourth pieces are by editors who have been arrested who swear they will never back down in the face of official threats. The next two documents state that persecution only increases editorial comments about the government. The seventh document compares the results of the Sedition Act to efforts by the British to control their newspaper printers in the 1760s. The last piece praises the Virginia legislature for taking a stand against the Sedition Act.

The documents in support of the Sedition Act all appeared in Federalist newspapers. The first four pieces praise the government for efforts to silence its detractors who have gone too far and are encouraging sedition. The fifth selection describes a public demonstration against the Sedition Act and urges officials to prevent other such illegal activities. The final piece criticizes the Virginia legislature for acting out of line by criticizing federal law.

OPPOSITION TO THE SEDITION ACT

Benjamin Franklin Bache: "An Unconstitutional Exercise of Power"

Benjamin Franklin Bache insists that the Sedition Act constitutes a form of despotism. Americans who opposed the legislation perceived it as being reminiscent of British attempts to control American actions.

Aurora (Philadelphia), 16 July 1798

The people as well as the government have certain rights prescribed by the constitution, and it is as much the sworn duty of the administration to protect the one as the other. If the government is instituted for the benefit of the people, no law ought to be made to their injury. One of the first rights of a freeman is to speak or to publish his sentiments; if any government founded upon the will of the people passes any ordinance to abridge this right, it is as much a crime as if the people were, in an unconstitutional way, to curtail the government of one of the powers delegated to it. Were the people to do this, would it not be called anarchy? What name shall then be given to an unconstitutional exercise of power over the people? In Turkey the voice of the government is the law, and there it is called despotism. Here the voice of the government is likewise the law and here it is called liberty.

Anonymous: "To Arms!"

This author urges Americans who value their freedom to arm themselves to protect their liberties. For this writer, failure to fight for freedom is disastrous.

Aurora (Philadelphia), 30 August 1798

It behooves every republican who values the liberties of his country, his own security and that of his family to provide himself with arms and to habituate himself to the constant use of them—for the *tenets* preached up by the wretches who follow in the train of our administration are calculated to convert the people of these free states into two classes—*Janisaries*[1] *and Mutes!*

Thomas Adams: "We Will Never Sit Quiet"

Following his arrest under the Sedition Act, Thomas Adams, editor of the Independent Chronicle, *promises that he will not let that event intimidate him. He reflects the ideas of several editors who were arrested and became even stronger in their criticism of the government following their arrest.*

Independent Chronicle (Boston), 16 July 1798

At a time when *external alarms* are improved for the purposes of *internal oppression,* and dangers from abroad are called in to further the work of injustice at home, it would ill become a faithful centinel upon the Walls of Freedom, to decline the dangers of his post, or to blow the trumpet of alarm with a feeble or equivocal sound. Such is not the spirit which actuates *this paper,* nor are such the reproaches by which it shall be silenced. The hand of power may *suppress,* but never shall *disgrace* it, and tho' it may be crushed by the lawless *acts* of violence, it shall never be intimidated by its *threats.* For defeat is preferable to desertion, and to be forcibly overpowered is better than tamely to submit.—This is not the language of vaunting;—It is that which is suggested by the urgency of the times;—to hold a different one, would be resigning the spirit of a man, and the independent rights of a freeman.

There was a time Citizens, when under the protecting influence of a Constitution ("which we once fondly hoped would be immortal,") we flattered ourselves, that *the Liberty of the press* was a right too dear to Americans to be resigned with tameness, and too firmly secured to be violated with impunity. We will not say that that time is past;—but we will say that under the influence of an exaggerated & mischievous system of alarm, and the insidious pretexts of order and submission to the Laws, we have seen a system maturing openly hostile to the spirit of freedom, and measures carried *in the face of our Constitution;*—for what?—to screen from scrutiny the conduct of your own Government, & to silence by an agreement of force the remonstrances of reason; to wrest from your hands the weapon which conducted you to freedom, "a right inestimable to freemen, and formidable to tyrants only." To the laws of our own country we owe that profound submission, which a Republican will never withhold. But *to the Constitution* upon which alone those laws must be founded, and *to the people* for whose security it was established, we owe duties, still more sacred, & these we will never violate; fully confident that to no laws "abridging the freedom of speech or of the press," can submission ever be lawfully required,—and that the man who falls a victim to these will but seal the Constitution with his blood.

Such are our sentiments with respect to the present unwarrantable system of *legalized* terror with which we are menaced. But this is not all?—personal violence is threatened, and insolent suggestions held up to deter!—with whatever design these are thrown out, *they will be ineffectual;*—from whatever quarter they may come, *they will come in vain.* We fear those threats, as little as we deserve the imputations upon which they are founded. Small indeed would be any pretensions to that confidence we claim, were we to be deterred from the path of our duty by the efforts of misguided zeal, or the menaces of intemperate partizans;—and poor and debased would be the spirit of the people could they behold *such threats* executed with impunity. It would be but encouraging the commencement of a storm, which must e'er long burst upon their own heads, or recoil upon that of its fomenters. To that people we again pledge ourselves, "*that we will never sit quiet while their Liberties are invaded, or look in silence upon public oppression. We will use our exertions at whatever hazard to repel the invader and drag the criminal to justice, whoever may protect him in his transgression or partake of his crime.*" Our motto and principles are, *an attachment to the* CONSTITUTION, and we will pursue every legal measure to support it.

Benjamin Franklin Bache: "The Cause of Truth and Republicanism"

Benjamin Franklin Bache was also arrested and, like Adams, he promised not to abandon the cause for which he was fighting.

Aurora (Philadelphia), 27 June 1798

The editor thanks his numerous friends for the solicitude they have shewn on this occasion, and pledges himself that prosecution no more than persecution, shall cause him to abandon what he considers the cause of truth and republicanism; which he will support, to the best of his abilities, while life remains.

Nathan Sleek: "No Good Comes from Those Trials for Sedition"

Nathan Sleek points out the mistake that has been made by arresting newspaper printers. They come out of jail feeling persecuted and thus become martyrs to the cause of freedom.

Bee (New London, Connecticut), 3 September 1800

Oh, no good comes from those trials for sedition; punishment only hardens printers, and pleases the fellows, for they come out of jail holding their heads higher than if they had never been persecuted. Finally, they assume the appearance of innocent men who have suffered wrongfully.

William Duane: "The Number of Free Presses Increase"

William Duane, who became editor of the Aurora *following the death of Benjamin Franklin Bache in the yellow fever epidemic of 1798, states that the attempts to silence the opposition press have backfired. In fact, more newspapers are appearing to protest the attempts to infringe the liberty of the press in the United States.*

Aurora (Philadelphia), 9 April 1800

It is pleasing to perceive that in proportion to the violence and daring with which the freedom secured to the press, by the constitution, is attacked by odious laws, and more odious usurpation under the name of privilege, the spirit of the country and the number of free presses increase. We witness these things with peculiar satisfaction, because it shews that the spirit of the country instead of being subdued or terrified, rises with an electricity commensurate with the pressure of the danger & determined to repel it. In the southern states, to their credit, the press retains its manly and free prerogatives of discussion—it is observable, however, that while the frankness, and the openness congenial with truth and liberty, and the wit, talents, and lustrous character of the southern writings are confined with few and rare exceptions to the republican prints; the prints retained by the administration, are as distinguishable like their compeers here, for the nearly total absence of genius, as for their scurrility and disingenuity.

Among the papers newly established which we have not noticed on a former occasion, we find the "MIRROR, or *Scourge of Aristocracy,* published by Messrs. Lion and Field, at Martinsburg, Virginia, ably and elegantly conducted; in Maryland, at Easton, on the eastern shore, "*The* STAR, *or Eastern Luminary,*" conducted by *Thomas P. Smith,* obtains a rapid and merited circulation; at Wilmington, Delaware, a paper has been established a few months by Mr. James Wilson, called "The MIRROR," in which we have discovered more ingenuity and original effort than in any other country paper on the continent, this paper holds a very high claim to general patronage; and we doubt not will continue to obtain it in a state so long hoodwinked, but at length open to past deception. In our own state "*The Intelligence,*" published by Messrs. Dixon at Lancaster; this paper is distinguished for elegance and accuracy of printing, and for fidelity and good sense in its public news, and political information. *Some* other papers have lately appeared to the eastward, of which we cannot yet determine the merits.

William Duane: "A Parallel"

William Duane compares the impact of the Sedition Act to actions of the British in England in the 1760s. For Duane, both groups of events reflected tyranny on the part of governments. The Republicans continually attacked the Sedition Act as an act designed to undermine the rights of Americans.

Aurora (Philadelphia), 13 May 1800

PARALLEL.

Dr. Johnson defines the substantive "Parallel," to be a "resemblance or conformity continued through many particulars"—and the sons of *Sirach*[2]— 'By their works shall you know them.'

IN GREAT-BRITAIN.

From Dec. 1764 to July 65—in the 5th year of the reign of George III, the following prosecutions for libels were tried.

1. Mr. Wilkes for republishing No. 45 of the North Britain.
2. Mr. Wilkes for printing a Poem.
3. Mr. Corbet for an advertisement in the White-Hall Evening Post.
4. The celebrated D'Eon, for publishing a book in French, entitled Letters, &c.
5. Mr. Wilkes again for the original publication of No. 45 of the North Britain.
6. Mr. Williams for publishing the same in a book.
7. Mr. Kearsey for publishing the same in a book.

IN AMERICA.

In the third year of the Presidency of John Adams, under the *Sedition Law*—alias the indemnity law.

1. Abijah Adams, printer of a republican paper at Boston for an alleged libel, under the English Common Law.
2. Matthew Lyon, a member of Congress from Vermont under the sedition law, for a letter written before the law was made, and publishing an extract of a letter written by Joel Barlow, on the public affairs of the nation.
3. Anthony Haswell, a printer in Vermont, for publishing an extract of a letter written by James M'Henry, Secretary at war, to General Drake in Virginia, recommending tories for officers in the standing army.
4. Charles Holt, printer at New-London, Connecticut, for publishing moral arguments against the vices and abuses of military establishments, and an army confessedly useless, and subsequently abolished.
5. Thomas Frothingham, a journeyman printer at New York, for republishing an article from a news paper, stating that Alexander Hamilton had endeavored to destroy the Aurora, where the English common law was asserted, and the accused not permitted to bring evidence to prove the truth.
6. Luther Baldwin of N. Jersey for wishing the wadding of a cannon fired on a day of rejoicing were lodged in the president's posterior.
7. Benjamin Franklin Bache, Grandson of Benjamin Franklin, for publishing an article declaring that a bribe had been taken in the Secretary of State's office, although the fact was acknowledged and the clerk who had taken the bribe was dismissed for the fact.
8. Thomas Cooper of Northumberland for publishing a number of truths about public men and measures. . . .
9. William Duane of Philadelphia for asserting that Mr. Adams had asserted the writing, and that William Duane possessed the letter so asserting that British influence had been used under the federal Government with effect. Indicted for asserting that the British Government was a corrupt one.

(N.B. These two indictments have been withdrawn, but they shall be published.) Indicted for publishing *Liston's* Letters found on Sweezy, in which it was declared that the American Government was provoking France to a war.

Two or three other suits which he does not know what they relate to.

The balance of this account is immensely in favour of the United States, and the facts are seriously recommended to the commissioners under the British treaty.

Anonymous: "Contravening the Constitution"

This author discusses the Virginia Resolutions protesting the Sedition Act. These resolutions, along with those passed by the legislature of Kentucky, had created quite a stir because they protested a law of the national government. This author states that state officials are bound to refuse to enforce any laws that are unconstitutional or violate their oath as state officers. The implication is that the Sedition Act is such a piece of legislation which should not be enforced.

The Observatory (Richmond, Virginia), 9 August 1799

Is not every officer of a state government sworn to support the constitution of the U. States? If the federal government passes laws contravening the constitution, is it not a breach of oath in a state officer to carry such laws into effect? Are not the states as well as the federal government to judge of the Constitution? Is not the Constitution a contract between the different states? Are not they to judge whether this contract be broken or violated? If congress can annul a contract with a foreign nation because of its violation, will not the same justice operate to modifying or annulling a contract between States, which is no longer regarded?

SUPPORT FOR THE SEDITION ACT

Anonymous: "Sedition Is Criminal"

This writer has no problem with the government punishing seditious attacks on the government. To fail to do so is to endanger the nation's future.

Guardian: Or New Brunswick Advertiser (New Jersey), 13 November 1798

Sedition, by all the laws of God and man, is, and ever has been criminal; and when it is not, the laws will be crimes and magistrates will swing. Behold France! Government after government has been laid down, till the sword cut off the tip of Sedition's tongue.

Anonymous: "A Libel on the Government"

This author believes that Thomas Adams and others arrested under the Sedition Act deserve what has happened because of their attacks on the fed-

eral government. He even blames the Independent Chronicle *for Shays's Rebellion back in 1787.*

Albany Centinel (New York), 2 November 1798

By the Boston papers it appears that *Tom Adams,* the publisher of the *Independent Chronicle,* has been arrested, to take his trial before the Federal Circuit Court, in session at Boston, (the honorable Judge Patterson, presiding) on a charge of publishing libellous and seditious productions, tending to defame the government of the United States. The contents of the *Independent Chronicle* have been for a long time a libel on government, on truth, and decency; and the lenient laws of our country have too long withheld the lash of Justice from its conductors. Poor Adams is not otherwise in fault respecting the infamous contents of the *Chronicle,* than by consenting to their being admitted into a paper published in his name: the author of a great proportion of the scandalous, false, inflammatory, and seditious stuff, which appears in the *Chronicle,* is a lank, lantern'd-jaw'd proprietor of a rope manufactory, whose writings in the same paper some years since, were supposed to have no inconsiderable effect in producing the insurrection, which took place in the western part of Massachusetts.

Barzillai Hudson and George Goodwin: "Their Complete Popularity"

These two Connecticut editors blame all the trouble on foreigners. They have no problem with the national government passing and enforcing legislation such as the Sedition Act in order to get such people under control.

Connecticut Courant (Hartford), 29 July 1799

The only thing that is wanting to establish their complete popularity is a prompt and faithful execution of them. If several hundred intriguing, mischief-making foreigners, had been sent out of the country twelve months ago, and a few more Matthew Lyons had been shut up in prison for their seditious libels, we should not have had so many *Duanes, Burkes, Bees,* and a host of other villains, filling the country with falsehoods, slanders, and factions.

Noah Webster: "Purge Your Country"

Noah Webster (of dictionary fame) also believes that uncontrolled criticism of the government can lead to trouble. He believes that the nation could be destroyed from within if critics of the government are not silenced and removed from office.

Commercial Advertiser (New York), 4 June 1799

WHAT a lesson is this to all the government, which by the protection of providence do yet exist!–Can any thing prove more strongly the necessity to scrutinize every department of Office, civil and military, but especially the latter?–to bring every man, as far as possible, to the ordeal, and where there is the smallest reason to suspect a collusion with the enemy, or a strong disposition to favor him, instantly to cashier the guilty person. No connection, no friendship, no consideration whatever, should screen the man, to whom the smallest suspicion is attached. But what shall we think, when there are many notorious characters fattening in public offices, at this awful crisis, who are unworthy of the smallest public trust even in times of profound peace.

Hear then, ye guardians of the public welfare!–Ye watchmen on the walls of our Zion!–and thou, great and much respected *Chief!* hear the voice of wisdom, speaking from the tombs of martyred monarchies and republics: 'PURGE YOUR COUNTRY, but especially all its Public Offices, BEFORE IT IS TOO LATE, OF DOMESTIC TRAITORS'.

Loring Andrews: "Punish These Jacobins"

Editor Loring Andrews reports on a public demonstration against the Sedition Act. The demonstration included a "sedition pole," reminiscent of the "liberty poles" from the 1760s. Andrews does not see the connection and urges authorities to get the situation under control before it is too late.

Albany Centinel (New York), 14 December 1798

An eastern correspondent informs us, that a gang of insurgents have erected a Sedition-Pole, at Vassalboro and burnt the Alien and Sedition Laws. Among the ringleaders were, *Charles Webber, George Goodwin,* and *Benjamin Brown.* The arm of government ought to punish these Jacobins immediately, to prevent the baneful consequences of civil commotion. The erection of these poles, and the burning of the laws, is an open insult to the government and the people; and if the former is relax, the latter will perhaps be driven, on the principle of the *lex talionis,* to erect, and to rally round Federal Poles;–and to take measures to prevent a continuation of the insult.

Anonymous: "Support Our Government"

This author attacks the Virginia Resolutions. He is shocked that the state legislature would challenge the authority of the national government by criticizing the Sedition Act. He urges the voters to turn those who had voted for these resolutions out of office at the next election.

Columbian Mirror (Alexandria, Virginia), 18 April 1799

My God! can it be possible! that a body, supposed to be collected from the wisdom and virtue of the State, convened to deliberate for its honor and advantage, and to cooperate with the General Government in maintaining the independence, union, and constitution thereof, against foreign influence and intrigue, should so far lose sight of that object as to attempt to foment divisions, create alarms, paralize the measures of defense, and, in short, render abortive every prudent and wise exertion? Had an angel predicted this some years ago, it would not have gained belief—yet it is too evident now to need testimony. Attempts have been made to separate us from our government; they are daily making; and I am sorry to say, with too much success. Again I say, my fellow-citizens, support our government, do not support in your elections anyone who is not friendly thereto.

QUESTIONS

1. What are the major criticisms voiced by Benjamin Franklin Bache against the Sedition Act? Do you think he is justified?
2. Thomas Adams, William Duane, and other writers state that putting newspaper editors in jail only makes them more determined to criticize the actions of the government. Does that seem to be true in these cases? Do you think that would be true in all cases?
3. Several anonymous writers support the Sedition Act. What are the major reasons mentioned in support of the Sedition Act? Do you think they are correct?
4. The last document in each section discusses the Virginia and Kentucky Resolutions. Does a state legislature have the right to formally criticize the actions of the national government? In other words, were the legislatures of Virginia and Kentucky correct in the actions they took against the Sedition Act? What about today?

NOTES

1. Janissaries were Turkish slaves who served the Sultan, but the term was often applied to any Turkish soldier because the Janissaries made up the bulk of the Turkish army.

2. The son of Sirach was the author of Ecclesiasticus, included in the Roman Catholic canon of the Old Testament and in the Protestant Apocrypha.

CHAPTER 26

The Election of 1800, February 1800–March 1801

The Quasi-War with France, the XYZ Affair, and the Alien and Sedition Acts were all on people's minds as the year 1800 dawned. And, very soon, people focused their concerns about these issues in the political arena, as the election of 1800 approached.

The year 1800 seemed to be a landmark year for Americans in many ways. Many hoped that the approaching new century would be one of development and growth for the young United States. George Washington's death in December 1799 seemed to mark the end of an era and just added to the sense of the dawn of a new age. As people considered what the future would bring, they worried about the divisions that existed in the United States.

The major candidates in 1800 were the same as in 1796: John Adams for the Federalists and Thomas Jefferson for the Republicans. The electoral college still worked as it had in 1796—the person with the most votes became president and the person with the second highest number of votes became vice president. This time, rather than people from different political parties being chosen, the Republican candidates (Thomas Jefferson for president and Aaron Burr of New York for vice president) came out of the electoral college in a tie. The tie had to be broken by the House of Representatives. The House of Representatives was still controlled by the Federalists, and so, in one of the greatest ironies in American history, the Federalists got to choose which Republican candidate would be the next president of the United States. After several months of debate, Alexander Hamilton threw his support to Thomas Jefferson, who was elected.

By 1800, most Americans had generally accepted the idea of political parties. They no longer assumed that the opposition was evil. Instead, they increasingly discussed and debated what the future would be like, depending on which party won the 1800 election. The newspapers led this discussion, as they pondered and debated the issues and candidates of the campaign.

The documents that support John Adams emphasize the concerns of many if Thomas Jefferson was elected president. The first two pieces express great fears about what will happen to the economy of the United States if Jefferson wins. The third selection states that the United States will not be able to avoid a civil war if Jefferson is elected. The fourth document connects a Jefferson victory to France and fears the United States will follow France into ruin. The fifth piece places the blame for Jefferson's apparent success in the election on men who failed to do their civic duty and go vote.

The documents that support Thomas Jefferson emphasize the freedoms Americans will enjoy if Jefferson wins. The first piece warns of an attempt in the United States Senate to control the outcome of the election. The second document states that Jefferson's election is the only way to avoid a war. The next piece compares the political platforms of the Federalist and Republican parties. The fourth selection celebrates the Republican victory, even though it is not clear who has actually won. The last piece, Jefferson's inaugural address, encourages everyone to work together for the future greatness of the United States.

SUPPORT FOR JOHN ADAMS FOR PRESIDENT

Burleigh: "If Mr. Jefferson Is President"

This Federalist author expresses great concerns over the future if Thomas Jefferson is elected president in 1800. Most Americans believed that the outcome of the election of 1800 would have a major impact on the direction that the United States would take, and this writer reflects those concerns.

Connecticut Courant (Hartford), 11 August 1800

If Mr. Jefferson is President, this navy is to be laid up, the ships are to rot at our wharves, our commerce is to be again plundered, and our country produce to perish on our hands, our farmers are to be impoverished, and our merchants ruined. Will it be said that Mr. Jefferson will keep up the navy, notwithstanding his own dislike of it, and the clamour of his party? If he does, must he not keep up the burthens? and if we must pay a land tax, &c. may we not as well pay it to a Federal, as to a Jacobinical administration?

Anonymous: "Aye, Aye, Vote for Mr. Jefferson"

This writer also worries about the future of the United States if Thomas Jefferson is elected. He believes that the economy will be undermined and that the nation will be defenseless. With the continuing war in Europe, the state of American defenses was a major concern for most Americans.

Virginia Federalist (Richmond), 26 February 1800

Aye, aye, fellow-citizens, vote for Mr. Jefferson—he'll cure all our disorders—he'll relieve us from taxes—he'll make us rich as Croesus—besides he prefers the tempestuous sea of liberty—the furious storm of revolution—aye, aye, vote for Mr. Jefferson—he'll make us happy—he'll turn your army and navy adrift—all the federal officers, all the old patriots—he'll play the devil with the damned banks, the funding system, the bane of democracy—he'll put a stop to commerce—he'll introduce a new order of things—such a one as will make every demo happy, no doubt.

Burleigh: "A Civil War"

This author believes that Jefferson's election would result in a civil war. Because the United States had never really experienced a full-fledged presidential election before, many people were unsure what would happen in the aftermath of the election.

Connecticut Courant (Hartford), 15 September 1800

There is scarcely a possibility that we shall escape a *Civil War*. Is there an evil so great, which ever afflicts nations, as this?. . . .

. . . . Let us bear in mind, that there will be circumstances attending a civil war in this country, which will render it peculiarly calamitous, and terrible. We are now fatally divided into parties; members of each party are dispersed through the country, and tho' in the northern states, the balance is greatly in favour of Federalism, yet there are Jacobins enough, even here, to divide, and distract us, with their arts, their plots, and their wickedness.—When these parties have taken arms, we must expect all the heats, and animosities, which have hitherto been in a degree stilled, and kept under, will break out with tenfold fury. Unrestrained by law, or the fear of punishment, every deadly passion will have full scope, private quarrels will be revenged, and public feuds and rivalships will call forth the bitterest hate and vengeance. Neighbours will become the enemies of neighbours, brothers of brothers, fathers of their sons, and sons of their fathers. Murder, robbery, rape, adultery, and incest will all be openly taught and practiced, the air will be rent with the cries of distress, the soil will be soaked with blood, and the nation black with crimes. Where is the heart which can contemplate such a scene, without shivering with horror?

Jacobins, in all countries, are destitute of morality and religion. Our own are as depraved, and they only wait an opportunity, to be as cruel and abandoned, as those of France. When our government is gone, this opportunity will be found, and we must then prepare for the same miseries, which France has experience. Those miseries consist not only in the loss of personal security, peace, and freedom; they consist primarily in the introduction of general national depravity, and a total overthrow of integrity, justice, benevolence, friendship, and affection; and substituting dishonesty, injustice, cruelty, revenge, and hatred. In such a community, parental ties, filial duty, conjugal tenderness and fidelity, and social intercourse, are contemned, ridiculed, and destroyed. What a dreadful spectacle, to see a great nation like France, in which every thing amiable, and endearing, in which, "whatsoever things are just, pure, lovely, and of good report," are done away—to see 25 millions of frail, dying, accountable beings, openly denying God, reviling his attributes, profaning his holy name; banishing every vestige of his worship, and committing without remorse, time after time national perjury! Let us remember, that HE, who has declared in the thunders of Sinai, that he "will not hold him guiltless, who shall take his name in vain," has also declared, that he will pour out his fury upon a people who "knew him not, who call not upon his name," and who impiously "rush upon the thick bosses of his buckler."

Anonymous: "The Approaching Election for President"

This author connects the Republicans to France and indicates that Thomas Jefferson's election as president would lead the United States down a road similar to that the French had followed in the 1790s. With Napoleon's takeover of the French government, some Americans worried about a similar downfall of freedom happening in the United States.

Farmers Museum (Walpole, New Hampshire), 13 October 1800

The approaching election for President, and the situation of our mission to France are the two most important political subjects on which the public mind is now agitated. In the latter, scarce a point of progress has been made, even from the commencement of the first embassy, and we think it highly probable it will continue in its present state till a sum is expended in fruitless negotiation, which will nearly equal the depredations of that nation on our commerce. France, like almost every other nation, will not deviate from what she deems her interest, and it is not her interest to adjust with us our respective differences. All the effect which, it is probable, this last attempt at conciliation will have, will only be to discover the hollowness of the professions of the tri-consulate.

To effect the election of Mr. Jefferson to the head of the government is the favourite wish of every jacobin from Georgia to New-Hampshire. No stone is left unturned to accomplish the object. Should these exertions be crowned with success, our fears, respecting the effect which a new system of politics, and the gradual change and probable resignation of executive officers, will produce, are great, though we will hope, unfounded. We cannot, however, believe that such men as Giles, Gallatin, and others of the jacobin colossi, to whom Mr. Jefferson will be indebted for his elevation, will remain unnoticed by him.—These it is probable, will be his prime favourites. Places of petty profit will not content such aspiring characters. They must sit in the first places in the synagogue. The real and native patriot who has done his country service for years in public employment, must then yield his place to some favourite foreigner, some graceless Genevan, whose whole merit consists in reviling and vilifying the acts of an administration which has raised this country to its present state of prosperity, opulence, and respectability. These observations are made that our present, pious and able President may still continue to fill the chair of state. It is hardly possible that one material benefit can accrue to America by a change. The affairs of the nation have progressed and prospered as when our beloved Washington was our pilot. Why then should we not continue to support the man who has proved himself in the most difficult situations, the able and active friend of his country, rather than by electing another, 'to rush on evils that we know not of.'

Caleb P. Wayne: "The Man Whom Americans Did Not Desire"

Caleb P. Wayne became publisher of the Gazette of the United States *in May 1800, when he purchased the paper from John W. Fenno. He sold the paper in November 1801. In this piece, he bemoans the apparent outcome of the 1800 election. He blames Thomas Jefferson's election on the failure of some men to go and participate in the electoral college vote. They let other things interfere with this important duty.*

Gazette of the United States (Philadelphia), 16 December 1800

From recent information, it appears highly likely that Mr. Jefferson will be the President of the United States for the four ensuing years, commencing on the fourth day of March next. This circumstance, so much regretted by the Editor of this Gazette and all real Americans, may be attributed to one of two things, *accident* or *design*, on the part of certain Gentlemen whose non-attendance at the post of the duty at the important hour will be remembered, and we trust amply rewarded by their constituents at next election, and it is hoped those *'other causes'* which prevented their attendance, will be revealed and the people made acquainted with the *real cause* of that absence which will place in the Executive Chair, the *man* whom Americans did not desire.

SUPPORT FOR THOMAS JEFFERSON FOR PRESIDENT

William Duane: "The Approaching Presidential Election"

William Duane became editor of the Aurora *following the death of Benjamin Franklin Bache in 1798. Bache had founded the* Aurora *(originally named the* General Advertiser*) in 1790. With the suspension of the* National Gazette *in 1793, the* Aurora *became the leading Republican newspaper in the United States. It retained that position until the founding of the* National Intelligencer *in Washington, D.C., in October 1800. In this piece, Duane discusses an apparent attempt to influence the results of the election. Although political parties had become somewhat acceptable in the United States by 1800, many Americans still feared conspiracies to limit the rights of the people. Duane's concern reflects such fears. The details really did not matter because Duane did not trust the Federalists, no matter what they were doing.*

Aurora (Philadelphia), 19 February 1800

In our piece of the 27th ult. we noticed the introduction of a measure into the Senate of the United States, by Mr. Ross calculated to *influence* and *affect* the approaching presidential election, and to frustrate in a particular manner the wishes and interests of the people of the *Commonwealth of Pennsylvania*.

We this day lay before the public a copy of that bill as it has passed the Senate.

Some curious facts are connected with this measure, and the people of the Union at large are intermediately and the people of this state immediately interested to consider the *movement,* the *mode* of operation, and the *effects.*

We noticed a few days ago the Caucuses (or secret consultations) held in the Senate Chamber—An attempt was made in an evening paper to give a counter-action (for these people are admirable at the system of intrigue) to the developments of the Aurora, and to call these meetings *jacobinical;* we must cordially assent to the *Jacobinism* of these meetings—they were in the perfect spirit of a *jacobinical* conclave.

The plain facts we stated are, however, unquestionable; but we have additional information to give on the subject of those meetings. We stated that intrigues for the presidential election were among the objects. We now state it as a fact that cannot be disputed upon fair ground that the Bill we this day present was discussed at the *Caucus on Wednesday* evening last.

It is worthy to remark how this Bill grew into existence.

The opponents of independence and republican government who supported *Mr. Ross* in the contest against governor *McKean,* are well known by the *indecencies,* the *slander,* and the *falsehood* of the measures they pursued—and it is well known that they are all devoted to the *federal party* which we *dissected* on Monday. *Mr. Ross* proposed this in the federal senate (how confidently with the decency of his friends will be seen), a committee of five was appointed to prepare a bill on the subject, on this committee Mr. *Pinckney* of South Carolina was appointed,—on Thursday morning last (the *Caucus* held the preceding evening) Mr. Ross informed Mr. *Pinckney* that the committee had drawn up a bill on the subject, when in fact Mr. Pinckney had never been consulted on the subject, though a member of the committee! The bill was introduced and passed. . . .

William Duane: "The Friend of Peace"

William Duane states clearly that the issue of war will be settled by the election. Either of the Federalist candidates would take the United States into war, while only Thomas Jefferson would keep the peace.

Aurora (Philadelphia), 4 October 1800

In plain truth, the question is now come to this issue—Whether *Adams* or *Pinckney* were the president, we should have war.—With Jefferson, we shall have peace, therefore, the friend of *peace will vote for Jefferson*—the friends of war will vote for *Adams* or for *Pinckney*.

William Duane: "Federalism vs. Republicanism"

In this piece published on election day, Duane compares the Federalists and the Republicans on a variety of issues. This is one of the first published uses of a party platform in a national campaign.

Aurora (Philadelphia), 14 October 1800

FEDERAL

Things As They Have Been

1. The principles and patriots of the *Revolution* condemned and stigmatized.

2. *Republicanism*, a badge for persecution, and federalism a mask for monarchy.

3. The *Nation* in arms without a foe, and divided without a cause.

4. *Federalists* graduating a scale of "*hatred and animosity*," for the benefit of the people; and aiming "*a few bold strokes*" at political opposition, for the benefit of themselves.

5. The reign of terror created by false alarms, to promote domestic feuds and foreign war.

6. Systems of rapine, fraud, and plunder by public defaulters under countenance of public servants.

7. Priests and Judges incorporated with the Government for political purposes, and equally polluting the holy altars of religion, and the seats of Justice.

REPUBLICAN

Things As They Will Be

1. The Principles of the *Revolution* restored; its Patriots honored and beloved.

2. *Republicanism* proved to mean something, and Federalism found to mean nothing.

3. The *Nation* at peace with the world, and united in itself.

4. *Republicanism* allaying the fever of domestic feuds, and subduing the opposition by the force of reason and rectitude.

5. Unity, peace, and concord produced by republican measures and equal laws.

6. Public plunderers and defaulters called to strict account, and public servants compelled to do their duty.

7. Good government without the aid of priestcraft, or religious politics, and Justice administered without political intolerance.

8. Increase of Public Debt
Additional Taxes
Further Loans
New Excises
Higher Public Salaries, and
Wasteful Expenditure of public
money.

8. Decrease of Public Debt
Reduced Taxes
No Loans
No Excises
Reduced Public Salaries, and a
system of economy and care of
the public money.

9. Quixotish embassies to the
Turks, the Russians, Prussians, and
Portuguese, for Quixotish purposes
of holding the balance of Europe.

9. The republican maxim of our
departed Washington, "Not to in-
termeddle with European politics."

10. A Sedition Law to protect corrupt magistrates and public defaulters.

10. The Liberty of the Press, and
free enquiry into public character,
and our constitutional charter.

11. An established church, a religious test, and an order of Priesthood.

11. Religious liberty, the rights of
conscience, no priesthood, truth
and Jefferson.

William Duane: "A New Declaration of Independence"

*William Duane celebrates over the election of a Republican president. At
the time he wrote this piece, it was unclear whether the new president
would be Thomas Jefferson or Aaron Burr. However, it was clear that the
Federalists had lost and that a new party would be in power in Washington, D.C.*

Aurora (Philadelphia), 24 December 1800

The Fourth of March 1801 will become as celebrated in history as the 4th
of July 1776 for the emancipation of the American states from British influence and tyranny. The election of a Republican President is a new declaration of independence, as important in its consequences as that of '76, and of
much more difficult achievement.

Our former contest with England was merely a matter of strength. The
contest which has just been closed was a war of interest, vice and corruption
against principle, virtue, and patriotism. Our country became filled with foreign spies and domestic traitors who were on the eve of subverting our constitution and liberty—but the irresistible voice of a free people has banished
them forever and declared that the fourth of March 1801 shall become the
birthday of our regenerated independence and liberty.

Thomas Jefferson: "First Inaugural Address"

As Thomas Jefferson was inaugurated as the third president of the United States, he hoped to put the partisan bickering of the 1790s behind him and the nation. Ultimately, that did not happen, but his inaugural address tried to quiet the fears of many as he emphasized that no one wanted to destroy the United States government. Rather, they disagreed over the best way to carry out the various goals of the nation.

Aurora (Philadelphia), 7 March 1801

Friends and fellow citizens: Called upon to undertake the duties of the first executive office of our country, I avail myself of the presence of that portion of my fellow citizens which is here assembled, to express my grateful thanks for the favor with which they have been pleased to look toward me, to declare a sincere consciousness that the task is above my talents, and that I approach it with those anxious and awful presentiments which the greatness of the charge and the weakness of my powers so justly inspire. A rising nation, spread over a wide and fruitful land, traversing all the seas with the rich productions of their industry, engaged in commerce with nations who feel power and forget right, advancing rapidly to destinies beyond the reach of mortal eye—when I contemplate these transcendent objects, and see the honor, the happiness, and the hopes of this beloved country committed to the issue and the auspices of this day, I shrink from the contemplation, and humble myself before the magnitude of the undertaking. Utterly indeed, should I despair, did not the presence of many whom I here see remind me, that in the other high authorities provided by our constitution, I shall find resources of wisdom, of virtue, and of zeal, on which to rely under all difficulties. To you, then, gentlemen, who are charged with the sovereign functions of legislation, and to those associated with you, I look with encouragement for that guidance and support which may enable us to steer with safety the vessel in which we are all embarked amid the conflicting elements of a troubled world.

During the contest of opinion through which we have passed, the animation of discussion and of exertions has sometimes worn an aspect which might impose on strangers unused to think freely and to speak and to write what they think; but this being now decided by the voice of the nation, announced according to the rules of the constitution, all will, of course, arrange themselves under the will of the law, and unite in common efforts for the common good. All, too, will bear in mind this sacred principle, that though the will of the majority is in all cases to prevail, that will, to be rightful, must be reasonable; that the minority possess their equal rights, which equal laws must protect, and to violate which would be oppression. Let us, then, fellow-citizens, unite with one heart and one mind. Let us restore to social intercourse that harmony and affection without which liberty and even life itself are but dreary things. And let us reflect that having banished from our land that religious intolerance under which mankind so long bled and suffered, we have yet gained little if we countenance a political intolerance as despotic, as wicked, and capable of as bitter and bloody persecutions. During the throes and convulsions of the ancient world, during the agonizing spasms of infuriated man, seeking through blood and slaughter his long-lost liberty, it was not wonderful that the agitation of the billows should reach even this distant and peaceful shore; that this should be more felt and feared by some and less by others; that this should divide opinions as to measures of safety. But every difference of opinion is not a difference of principle. We have called by different names brethren of the same principle. We are all republicans—we are all federalists. If there be any among us who would wish to dissolve this Union or to change its republican form, let them stand undisturbed as monuments of the safety with which error of opinion may be tolerated where reason is left free to combat it. I know, indeed, that some honest men fear that a republican government cannot be strong; that this government is not strong enough. But would the honest patriot, in the full tide of successful experiment, abandon a government which has so far kept us free and firm, on the theoretic and visionary fear that this government, the world's best hope, may by possibility want energy to preserve itself? I trust not. I believe this, on the contrary, the strongest government on earth. I believe it is the only one where every man, at the call of the laws, would fly to the standard of the law, and would meet invasions of the public order as his own personal concern. Sometimes it is said that man cannot be trusted with the government of himself. Can he, then, be trusted with the government of others? Or have we found angels in the forms of kings to govern him? Let history answer this question.

QUESTIONS

1. Burleigh and several anonymous authors express great concerns for the future of the United States if Thomas Jefferson wins the election of 1800? Why are they so concerned? What do they think he will do once he gets in office?
2. One writer connects Thomas Jefferson to the revolutionary leaders in France. What is the basis for this connection? Does Jefferson have a lot in common with the revolutionaries in France? Why or why not?

3. In several pieces, William Duane expresses great optimism for the United States with a Republican as President. What does he think will happen once the Republicans take over control of the national government?

4. In his inaugural address in March 1801, Thomas Jefferson tried to calm the partisan fears following his election by stating that "we are all republicans—we are all federalists." What did he mean by that statement? Is he realistic in his outlook concerning political parties and how they operate in the United States? Why or why not?

Selected Bibliography

Adams, John. *A Defence of the Constitutions of Government of the United States, 1787–1788*. In *The Works of John Adams*, 10 vols., edited by Charles Francis Adams, 4:269–588. Boston: Little, Brown, 1850–56.

Alexander, John K. *The Selling of the Constitutional Convention: A History of News Coverage*. Madison, Wis.: Madison House, 1990.

"American Memory." http://memory.loc.gov

"Archiving Early America." http://earlyamerica.com

"Avalon Project at the Yale Law School: 18th Century Documents." http://www.yale.edu/lawweb/avalon/18th.htm

Bailyn, Bernard. *The Ideological Origins of the American Revolution*. Cambridge, Mass.: The Belknap Press of Harvard University Press, 1967.

Bailyn, Bernard, and John B. Hench, eds. *The Press and the American Revolution*. Worcester, Mass.: American Antiquarian Society, 1980.

Brant, Irving. *The Bill of Rights: Its Origin and Meaning*. Indianapolis: Bobbs-Merrill, 1965.

Brigham, Clarence S. *History and Bibliography of American Newspapers, 1690–1820*. 2 vols. Worcester, Mass.: American Antiquarian Society, 1947.

Cunningham, Noble. *The Jeffersonian Republicans: The Formation of Party Organization, 1789–1801*. Chapel Hill: University of North Carolina Press, 1957.

Davidson, Philip. *Propaganda and the American Revolution, 1763–1783*. Chapel Hill: University of North Carolina Press, 1941.

DeConde, Alexander. *The Quasi-War: The Politics and Diplomacy of the Undeclared War with France, 1797–1801*. New York: Charles Scribner's Sons, 1966.

"Documents for the Study of American History." http://www.ukans.edu/carrie/docs/amdocs_index.html

Dowd, Gregory Evans. *A Spirited Resistance: The North American Indian Struggle for Unity, 1745–1815*. Baltimore: Johns Hopkins University Press, 1992.

Evans, Sara M. *Born for Liberty: A History of Women in America*. New York: Free Press, 1989.

Ferguson, Robert A. *The American Enlightenment, 1750–1820*. Cambridge, Mass.: Harvard University Press, 1997.

Fiske, John. *The Critical Period of American History, 1783–1789*. Boston: Houghton Mifflin, 1897.

Gibson, Arrell Morgan. *The American Indian: Prehistory to the Present*. Lexington, Mass.: D.C. Heath, 1980.

Hart, Jim Allee. *The Developing Views on the News: Editorial Syndrome, 1500–1800*. Carbondale: Southern Illinois University Press, 1970.

Higginbotham, Don. *The War of American Independence: Military Attitudes, Policies, and Practice, 1763–1789*. New York: Macmillan Publishing Company, Inc., 1971.

"History Wired: A Few of Our Favorite Things." http://www.historywired.si.edu

Humphrey, Carol Sue. *The Press of the Young Republic, 1783–1833*. Westport, Conn.: Greenwood Press, 1996.

———. *"This Popular Engine": New England Newspapers During the American Revolution, 1775–1789*. Newark: University of Delaware Press, 1992.

Jensen, Merrill. *The New Nation: A History of the United States During the Confederation, 1781–1789*. New York: Alfred A. Knopf, 1950.

Kerber, Linda K. *Women of the Republic: Intellect and Ideology in Revolutionary America*. Published for the Institute of Early American History and Culture, Williamsburg, Virginia. Chapel Hill: University of North Carolina Press, 1980.

Levy, Leonard W. *Emergence of a Free Press*. New York: Oxford University Press, 1985.

Lewis, Jan. "The Republican Wife: Virtue and Seduction in the Early Republic." *William and Mary Quarterly*, 3rd series 44, (1987): 689–721.

Main, Jackson Turner. *The Antifederalists: Critics of the Constitution, 1781–1788*. Published for the Institute of Early American History and Culture, Williamsburg, Virginia. Chapel Hill: University of North Carolina Press, 1961.

Mather, Cotton. *The Angel of Bethesda*. 1724. Reprinted in ed. Jones, G.W. Barre, Mass.: American Antiquarian Society and Barre Publishers, 1972.

May, Henry F. *The Enlightenment in America*. New York: Oxford University Press, 1976.

Middlekauf, Robert. *The Glorious Cause: The American Revolution, 1763–1789*. New York: Oxford University Press, 1982.

Miller, John C. *Crisis in Freedom: The Alien and Sedition Acts*. Boston: Little, Brown and Company, 1951.

———. *The Federalist Era, 1789–1801*. New York: Harper & Brothers, 1960.

Morgan, Edmund S. *American Slavery, American Freedom: The Ordeal of Colonial Virginia*. New York: W.W. Norton, 1975.

Morris, Richard B. *Witnesses at the Creation: Hamilton, Madison, Jay, and the Constitution*. New York: Henry Holt, 1945.

Norton, Mary Beth. *Founding Mothers and Fathers: Gendered Power and the Forming of American Society*. New York: Alfred A. Knopf, 1996.

———. *Liberty's Daughters: The Revolutionary Experience of American Women, 1750–1800*. Boston: Little, Brown and Company, 1980.

Risjord, Norman K. *Forging the American Republic, 1760–1815*. Reading, Mass.: Addison-Wesley, 1973.

Rossiter, Clinton. *1787: The Grand Convention*. New York: Macmillan, 1966; New York: W. W. Norton, 1987.

Royster, Charles. *A Revolutionary People at War: The Continental Army and American Character, 1775–1788*. Published for the Institute of Early American History and Culture, Williamsburg, Virginia. Chapel Hill: University of North Carolina Press, 1979.

Rutland, Robert Allen. *The Birth of the Bill of Rights, 1776–1791*. Published for the Institute of Early American History and Culture, Williamsburg, Virginia. Chapel Hill: University of North Carolina Press, 1955.

———. *The Ordeal of the Constitution: The Antifederalists and the Ratification Struggle of 1787–1788*. Norman: University of Oklahoma Press, 1965.

Silver, Rollo G. *The American Printer, 1787–1825*. Charlottesville: University Press of Virginia, 1967.

Slaughter, Thomas P. *The Whiskey Rebellion: Frontier Epilogue to the American Revolution*. New York: Oxford University Press, 1986.

Sloan, Wm. David, and Julie Hedgepeth Williams. *The Early American Press, 1690–1783*. Westport, Conn.: Greenwood Press, 1994.

Smith, James Morton. *Freedom's Fetters: The Alien and Sedition Laws and American Civil Liberties*. Ithaca, N.Y.: Cornell University Press, 1956.

Smith, James Morton, ed. *The Republic of Letters: The Correspondence Between Thomas Jefferson and James Madison, 1776–1826*. 3 vols. New York: W. W. Norton & Company, 1995.

Smith, Jeffery A. *Printers and Press Freedom: The Ideology of Early American Journalism*. New York: Oxford University Press, 1988.

Stewart, Donald H. *The Opposition Press of the Federalist Period*. Albany: State University of New York Press, 1969.

Szatmary, David P. *Shays' Rebellion: The Making of an Agrarian Insurrection*. Amherst: University of Massachusetts Press, 1980.

"United States National Archives and Records Administration." http://www.archives.gov

Weisberger, Bernard A. *The American Newspaperman*. Chicago: University of Chicago Press, 1961.

Wood, Gordon S. *The Creation of the American Republic, 1776–1787*. Published for the Institute of Early American History and Culture, Williamsburg, Virginia. Chapel Hill: University of North Carolina Press, 1969.

———. *The Radicalism of the American Revolution*. New York: Vintage Books, 1993.

Wright, Esmond. *Fabric of Freedom, 1763–1800*. New York: Hill & Wang, 1961.

Index

Adams, Abijah, 330
Adams, John, xi, xiv, xvii, xxiii, 1, 255,
    295–97, 298–301, 303, 313,
    337–42, 343–44
Adams, Samuel, xv
Adams, Thomas, 125, 165–66, 326–27,
    331–32
Albany (N.Y.) *Centinel,* 332, 333
Albany (N.Y.) *Register,* 318
American and Daily Advertiser (Balti-
    more), 261
American Daily Advertiser (Philadel-
    phia), 240–42, 297–98
American Herald (Boston), 149
American Journal (Providence, R.I.),
    42–43
American Mercury (Hartford, Conn.),
    120–21
American Revolution, 33–66; Battle of
    Camden, xx, 57–60; Battle of Ger-
    mantown, xix, 52–55; Battle of
    Saratoga, xix, 55–57; Battle of Tren-
    ton, xix, 50–52; Battle of Yorktown,
    xx, 61–65; Wartime morale, 33–48
Andrews, Loring, 147, 333
Anti-Federalists, 138, 145, 147–59
Antoinette, Marie, 263
Argus (Boston), 202–3, 204–5
*Argus, or Greenleaf's New Daily Adver-
    tiser* (New York), 218
Arnold, General Benedict, xx, 81–92
Articles of Confederation, xi, xiii,
    xix–xx, 93–104, 105–6, 127
Aurora (Philadelphia), 184, 197, 198,
    217, 218–21, 247, 250, 253, 257–58,
    259, 270–71, 273, 298–99, 309–11,
    312, 314–18, 325–26, 327–28,
    328–30, 342–47,

Babcock, Elisha, 120–21
Bache, Benjamin Franklin, 184,
    185–86, 206, 214, 217, 218–19,
    228, 234, 236–37, 244, 250, 253,
    257–58, 265, 269–70, 273–74,
    311–12, 314–17, 325–26, 327–28,
    330
Bailey, Francis, 205
Baldwin, Luther, 330
Barber, John, 318
Bee (New London, Conn.), 261, 328
Bill of Rights, xxi–xxii, 161–80
Bishop, Abraham, 204–5
Boston Gazette, 84–85
Breckinridge, Hugh Henry, xv
Burgoyne, General John, xix, 55
Burleigh, 338–40

Calhoun, John C., 324
Capet, Louis, 263
Carter, John, 109–10, 146–47
Centinel, 150–58, 309–10
A Citizen of New Haven, 175–77
Claypoole, David C., 97–98
Cobbett, William, 208, 253–59,
    273–74, 304–5, 306–7, 319–20
Columbian Centinel (Boston), 138, 228
Columbian Mirror, (Alexandria, Va.),
    334
Commercial Advertiser (New York), 333
Common Sense, 35–42, 90

Congress, xxi–xxiii, 161, 233, 237–38,
    244, 249–50, 277–94, 303–4, 313,
    323–24, 337
Connecticut Courant (Hartford), 63–64,
    72–73, 121, 131, 132, 230–31, 332,
    338, 339–40
Connecticut Gazette (New Haven), 108,
    139
Connecticut Journal (New Haven), 272
Constitution, xiii, xxi, 127–60; ratifica-
    tion, 137–60
Constitutional Convention, xxi, 120,
    127–36
Continental Army, 5, 49
Continental Congress, xi, xix, 1–5,
    13–18, 93–94
Continental Journal (Boston), 196
Cooper, Thomas, 330
Cornplanter, 183–84, 186–87
Cornwallis, General Charles, xx, 49, 57,
    61, 63, 88
Country Journal (Poughkeepsie, N.Y.),
    166–69
"The Crisis" #1, xi, xix, 34–42

Dana, Eleutheros, 213–14
Decatur, Captain Stephen, 307
Declaration of Independence, ix–xi,
    xix, 1–3, 13, 21–23, 33, 223
Dickinson, John, 93
Dixon, John, 22
Duane, William, 259, 328–30, 342–45,
Duché, John, 3, 5–12, 24
Dunlap, John, 85–87

Edes, Benjamin, xi–xii
Edes, Peter, xiii
Elections: (1796), 295–301; (1800),
    337–48

Farewell Address, xxii, 297–98
Farmers Museum (Walpole, N.H.),
    340–41
Federalist Papers, 137, 140–43, 169–73
Federalists, xiv–xvii, 253–259, 277–78,
    295–97, 313–14, 323–25, 337–38
Fenno, John, xv, xxi, 182–83, 215, 238,
    253–55, 299–301, 342
First Amendment, xiv, xvii, 323–24
Fiske, John, 105

Franklin, Benjamin, 9, 129–30, 147–48
Freeman, Edmund, 147
Freeman's Journal (Philadelphia),
    61–63, 99–101, 133–35, 203–4,
    205, 206–7
Freeman's Oracle (Philadelphia), 108–9
French Revolution, xiv; American neu-
    trality, xxiii, 211, 277–94, 303; early
    years (1789–1793), xxi, 223–32;
    later period (1793–1798), 263–76
Freneau, Philip, xv, xxii, 184–85,
    207–8, 217–18, 253–55, 259–60,
    267
Frothingham, Thomas, 330

Gaine, Hugh, 43–44, 52, 59–60
Gallatin, Albert, xv
Gates, Horatio, xix–xx, 55–60
Gazette and General Advertiser
    (Charleston, S.C.), 319
Gazette of the United States (New York),
    xv, xxi, 177–78, 182–83, 209, 215,
    224–25, 226, 230, 238–40, 244–47,
    253, 277–94, 299–301, 305–6,
    307–8, 342
General Advertiser (Philadelphia),
    183–84, 185–87, 206, 214–15, 226,
    228, 234, 235–38, 244, 253, 270
Genet, Edmond, xvi, 263–65, 266–67
George III, xii, 3, 13, 22
Gerrish, Robert, 143–44
Goodwin, George, 63–64, 72–73, 131,
    132, 332
Green, Timothy, 108, 139
Greene, General Nathaniel, xi, 82–83
Greenleaf, Thomas, 208
Guardian: Or New Brunswick Advertiser
    (New Jersey), 331

Haiti, 201–10
Hall, David, 23–24
Hall, Samuel, 63
Hall, William, 23–24
Hamilton, Alexander, xiv–xvi, xxi–xxii,
    140, 211, 224, 233–34, 240,
    253–55, 260, 277–85, 295–97, 337
Hampshire Gazette (Springfield, Mass.),
    122–23, 124
Hampshire Herald (Springfield, Mass.),
    107–8

Hancock, John, xv, 1, 6–8, 25
Haswell, Anthony, 330
Helvidius, 278, 285–92
Henry, Patrick, 56
Herald of Freedom (Boston), 147
Hispaniola, 201
Holt, Charles, 330
Hudson, Barzillai, 63–64, 72–73, 131, 132, 332
Humphreys, James, Jr., 57
Hunter, William, 22

Independence, 1–32
Independent Chronicle (Boston), 58–59, 72, 106–7, 113–14, 124–26, 144, 165–66, 260, 326–27, 331–32
Independent Gazetteer (Philadelphia), 148, 150–58, 162–64, 247–48
Independent Journal (New York), 140–43, 169–73, 191, 233
Israel, John, xv

Jay, John, xv, xvii, 140, 211, 243–44
Jay's Treaty, xvi–xvii, xxii, 211, 243–51, 253, 303
Jefferson, Thomas, ix–x, xiv–xvii, xxiii, 1, 243, 253–55, 263, 277–78, 295–97, 298–301, 324, 337–47

Kentucky Gazette (Lexington), 227, 248–49, 269, 272
King, Rufus, xv
Kollock, Shepard, 159

Lafayette, Marquis de, xvi, 223–24
Lee, Charles, 69, 73–76
Locke, John, 1
Lord North, 142
Loudon, Samuel, 58
Louis XV, 272
Louis XVI, 263–66, 271–72
Loyalists (Tories), xii, 3–18, 35, 43–46, 49, 52, 53–55, 56–57, 59–60, 64–65, 76–78, 81–82, 91–92, 94, 99
Lyon, Matthew, 324, 330

Madison, James, xiv–xv, 105, 127–28, 140, 161, 255, 277–78, 285–92, 295–97, 324
Martin, Alexander, 19, 261

Martin, J. P., 204–5
Maryland Journal and Baltimore Advertiser, 24–30, 73–76, 81, 94–97
Mason, Stevens T., 244
Massachusetts Centinel (Boston), 130, 131, 143, 145, 193–95, 227
Massachusetts Gazette (Boston), 145
Massachusetts Spy (Worcester), 21
Meigs, Josiah, 213–14
Middlesex Gazette (Middletown, Conn.), 197
Minerva (New York), 216

Napoleon, 340
National Gazette (Philadelphia), xv, xxii, 207–8, 225–26, 253, 265–67
Native Americans, 181–88
New Hampshire Gazette (Portsmouth), 89, 129–30
New Hampshire Mercury (Portsmouth), 144
New Haven Gazette and Connecticut Magazine, 214
New Jersey Journal (Elizabeth Town), 159
New London (Conn.) *Bee*, 261, 328
New York Argus, 311
New York Daily Advertiser, 196, 274
New York Daily Gazette, 229
New York Gazette and Weekly Mercury, 4, 43–44, 52, 59–60
New York Journal, 208, 267–269
New York Packet (Fishkill), 58, 82–83
New York Packet (New York), 175–77
Newport (R.I.) *Herald*, xiii, 144–45
Newport (R.I.) *Mercury*, 35
Norwich (Conn.) *Packet*, 90, 109, 116
Nourse, John, 125, 165–66

Observatory (Richmond, Va.), 331
Oswald, Eleazer, 158

Pacificus, 12, 277–85
Paine, Thomas, xix, 35–42
Parke, John, 24–30
Patriots, 19–30, 35–43, 49–52, 52–53, 55–56, 58–59, 61–64, 69–73, 81–91
Pennsylvania Evening Post, xx, 1, 6–12, 23

Pennsylvania Gazette (Philadelphia), 21, 23–24, 110–13, 190–93, 213

Pennsylvania Herald and General Advertiser (Philadelphia), 164–65, 173–75

Pennsylvania Journal (Philadelphia), 36–42

Pennsylvania Ledger (Philadelphia), 57

Pennsylvania Packet (Lancaster), 102–3

Pennsylvania Packet (Philadelphia), 83–84, 86–88, 89–90, 97–98, 127–28, 193

Porcupine's Gazette (Philadelphia), 195, 198, 208, 253–55, 257–59, 273–74, 304–5, 307, 319–20

Powars, Edward Eveleth, 148–49

Press, Political Party, xiv–xvii, 253–62

Providence (R.I.) *Gazette*, 42, 85, 90–91, 98–99, 109–10, 114–16, 130–31, 146–47, 148, 149–50

Pseudonyms: Algernon Sidney, 149–50; The American, 230–31; An American Loyalist, 12–13; Argus, 108–9, 115; Camillus, 123; Candid, 116; Cassius, 166–69; Centinel, 150–58, 309–10; Cetera Desunt, 308–9; Cincinnatus, 148; A Citizen, 98; Citizen Brutus, 260–61; A Citizen of New Haven, 175–77; Civis, 102–3; Columbus, 310–11; Common Sense, 35–42, 90; Conservator, 237–38; A Correspondent, 270–71; A Countryman, 42; Democritus, 115–16; Federalist, 143; Freethinker, 124; Harrington, 110–13, 130–31; Helvidius, 278, 285–92; Honestus, 125–26; Humanus, 193–95; Independens, 99–101; Observer, 196; An Officer in Camp, 52–53; An Officer of the Late Continental Army, 147–48; An Old and Uniform Whig, 317–18; An Old Whig, 162–64; One of the People, 299; Pacificus, 12, 277–85; Phocion, 300–301; Plain Dealer, 114; Publius, 140–43, 169–73; A Republican, 267–69; T.T.L., 219–21; Tully, 240–42; A Yeoman, 124; Z, 133–35

Publius, 140–43, 169–73

Purdie, Alexander, 55

Quasi-war with France, xxiii, 303–12, 337

Reed, Esther Deberdt, xx, 190–93

Republicans, xiv–xvii, 253–55, 259–62, 277, 295–97, 313–14, 323–25, 337–38

Reynolds, Mrs. Maria, 260

Rivington, James, 35, 45–46, 56–57, 64–65, 69, 76–78, 92

Robertson, James, 44–45, 99

Royal Gazette (New York), 12–13, 45–46, 53–55, 56–57, 64–65, 76–78, 92, 268

Royal Pennsylvania Gazette (Philadelphia), 5, 12, 44–45, 99

Russell, Benjamin, xii, 130, 131, 138, 227

Russell, John, 107–8

Salem Gazette (Mass.), 63

Santo Domingue, 201–10

Sedition Act, xiv, xvii, xxiii, 303, 313, 323–36, 337

Sellers, William, 23–24

"The Sentiments of an American Woman," 190–93

Shakespeare, William, 144–45, 318–19

Shays's Rebellion, xx, 119–26, 332

Sherman, Roger, 175–77

Slave revolt, 201–210

Sleek, Nathan, 328

Snowden, Charles, 274

South Carolina and American General Gazette (Charleston), 91–92

South Carolina Royal Gazette (Charleston), 13–18

Southwick, Solomon, 35

Steuben, Baron von, 42

T.T.L., 219–21

Talleyrand, Charles Maurice, French Foreign Minister, xvii, xxiii, 313, 315–17

Thomas, Isaiah, xii, 21, 121–22, 123–24, 133

Time Piece (New York), 184–85, 259–60, 308

Tories (Loyalists), xii, 3–18, 35, 43–46, 49, 52, 53–55, 56–57, 59–60,

64–65, 76–78, 81–82, 91–92, 94, 99
Tully, 240–42

United States Chronicle (Providence,
   R. I.), 132
United States Oracle (Portsmouth,
   N. H.), 259

Vermont Gazette (Bennington), 88,
   249–50
Virginia and Kentucky Resolutions,
   xxiii, 324, 331, 334
Virginia Federalist (Richmond), 339
Virginia Gazette (Williamsburg),
   19–21, 22, 50–52, 53, 55–56, 69–72

Washington (D.C.) *Gazette*, 255–56
Washington, George, xi, xvi–xvii,
   xix–xxiii, 3, 5, 20, 24, 42, 49–52,
   61–63, 81, 84, 120, 129–30,

138–39, 147–48, 161, 201, 233–34,
   243–44, 253, 263, 270–71, 277,
   295–98, 303, 337; public opinion
   while he was general of the Conti-
   nental Army, 67–80; public opinion
   while he was president, 211–22
Wayne, Caleb P., 209, 341–42
Webster, Noah, x, 332–33
Wells, John, 91–92
Wheeler, Bennett, 42–43, 132
Whiskey Rebellion, xxii, 233–242
Whitehill, Robert, 164–65
Willis, Nathaniel, 58–59, 106–7
Wilson, James, 173–75, 329
Women, 189–99
Worcester Magazine (Mass.), 122–24,
   133

XYZ Affair, xvii, xxiii, 303, 313–22,
   323, 337, 395

About the Author

CAROL SUE HUMPHREY is Professor of History at Oklahoma Baptist University. She is the author of *This Popular Engine: The Role of New England Newspapers During the American Revolution* and *The Press of the Young Republic, 1783–1833* (Greenwood, 1996).